P9-CFT-017

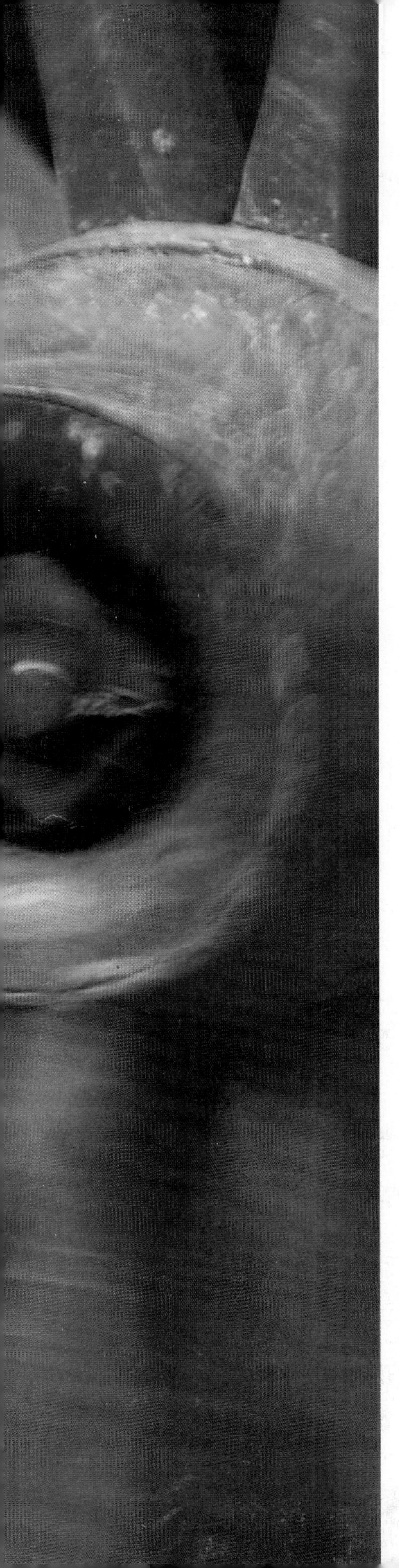

Student Edition

Social Studies Alive!®

America's Past

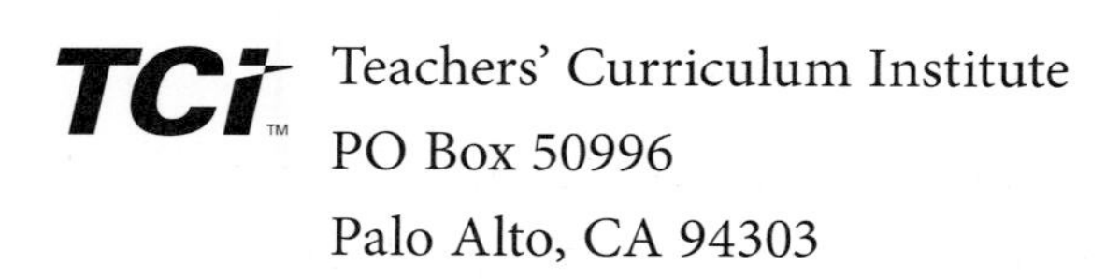

Teachers' Curriculum Institute
PO Box 50996
Palo Alto, CA 94303

Customer Service: 800-497-6138
www.teachtci.com

ISBN 978-1-58371-876-6
3 4 5 6 7 8 9 10 -WC- 15 14 13 12 11 10
Manufactured by Webcrafters, Inc., Madison, WI
United States of America, February 2010, Job# 81403

Program Director
Bert Bower

Consultants
Diane Hart, Social Studies Specialist, Assessment Consultant, Menlo Park, California

Kate Kinsella, Ed.D., Reading and TESOL Specialist, Department of Secondary Education, College of Education, San Francisco State University, San Francisco, California

Student Edition Writers
Joyce Bartky
Vern Cleary
Terry Coburn
Peter Lacey
Anne Maloney
Kelly Shafsky

Teacher Consultants
Lynn Casey, Teacher, Husmann Elementary School, Crystal Lake, Illinois

Ann Dawson, Educational Consultant, Intermediate Curriculum Specialist, Gahanna, Ohio

Nancy Einstein, Teacher, Cynwyd Elementary School, Bala Cynwyd, Pennsylvania

Leslie Frizzell, Teacher, Oakland Elementary, Bloomington, Illinois

Cathy Bonneville Hix, Teacher, Swanson Middle School, Arlington, Virginia

Shirley Jacobs, Library Media Specialist, Irving Elementary School, Bloomington, Illinois

Eleanor C. Jones, Teacher, Otice Parker Intermediate, Houston, Texas

Joan Kinder, Teacher, Ortona Elementary, Daytona Beach, Florida

Sharon Ratto, Teacher, Colonial Heights Elementary, Stockton, California

Becky Suthers, Retired Teacher, Stephen F. Austin Elementary, Weatherford, Texas

Literature Consultant
Regina M. Rees, Ph.D., Assistant Professor, Beeghly College of Education, Youngstown State University, Youngstown, Ohio

Maps
Mapping Specialists, Ltd. Madison, Wisconsin

Contents

Maps

This image shows how Earth might look from a space shuttle.

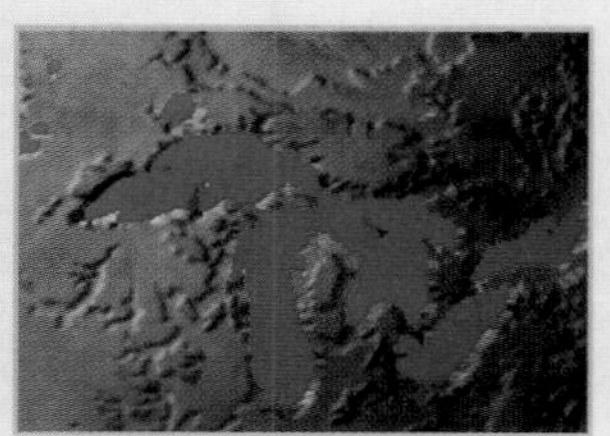

Can you name the two countries that border these lakes?

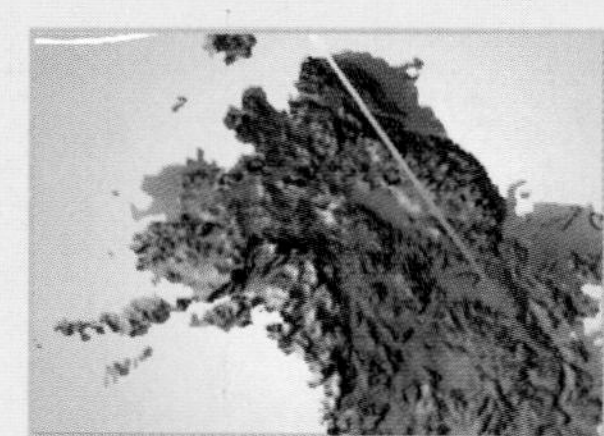

Can you name this state?

Geography of the United States

What can geography teach us about the United States?

1.1 Introduction

Before you study the history of the United States, you need to know about our country's **geography**. The word *geography* comes from two Greek words—*geo,* meaning "Earth," and *graph,* meaning "describing." Geography is the study of our physical world and how we interact with it. Geographers help us locate places. They describe plants, bodies of water, landmasses, and **climate**. Climate refers to aspects of weather, such as temperature, rainfall, and wind, that are measured over time in an area.

Geographers also study how our physical surroundings affect us. For example, they look at the reasons why mountains make it hard for people to move from place to place. Learning about the geography of the United States will help you understand our country's history.

In this chapter, you will learn some geography skills for reading maps. You will first learn how to read a **globe**. A globe is a model of Earth. It is the most accurate way to represent Earth. You will then learn how to use **latitude** and **longitude**. These lines form a grid that helps us find any place on Earth. Next, you will learn some key **geographic terms**. These terms describe bodies of water, such as bays, and landmasses, such as islands. Finally, you will learn about major **physical features** of the United States. Physical features include landmasses, like the Great Plains, and bodies of water, like the Mississippi River.

Look at the picture of the globe on this page. What do you think a globe can teach you about the United States?

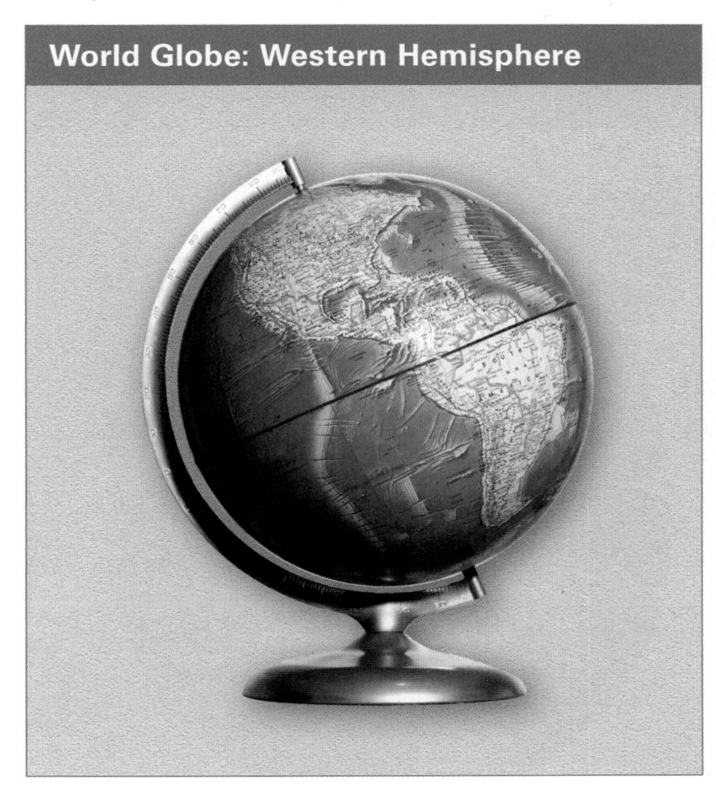

World Globe: Western Hemisphere

compass a tool or instrument for finding directions by first locating north

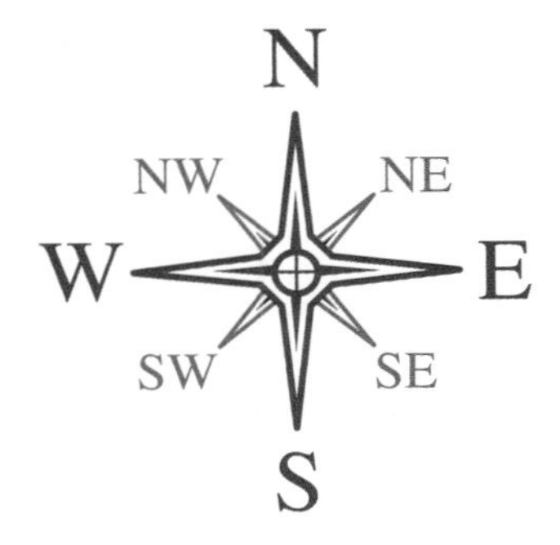

This compass rose shows the cardinal directions. They are the four main points in blue. Points in between them (in red) are intermediate directions.

1.2 Understanding the Globe

Earth is a huge sphere. A sphere is something that is shaped like a ball. A globe is also a sphere. Most maps that show Earth's surface are flat. Because a globe is shaped like Earth, it provides a more accurate picture of our planet.

The most northern point on Earth is the North Pole. The most southern point is the South Pole. No matter where you are on Earth, north is always in the direction of the North Pole. South is always in the direction of the South Pole. When you face north, east is to your right, and west is to your left. These four directions are the main points on a **compass**. They are called cardinal directions.

Points in between the cardinal points are called intermediate directions. These points include northeast, northwest, southeast, and southwest. Many maps have a symbol that shows all or some of these directions. This symbol is called a compass rose.

An imaginary line circles Earth halfway between the North Pole and the South Pole. This line is called the equator. The equator divides Earth into two half-spheres called hemispheres. The half of Earth north of the equator is the Northern Hemisphere. The southern half is the Southern Hemisphere.

The Hemispheres

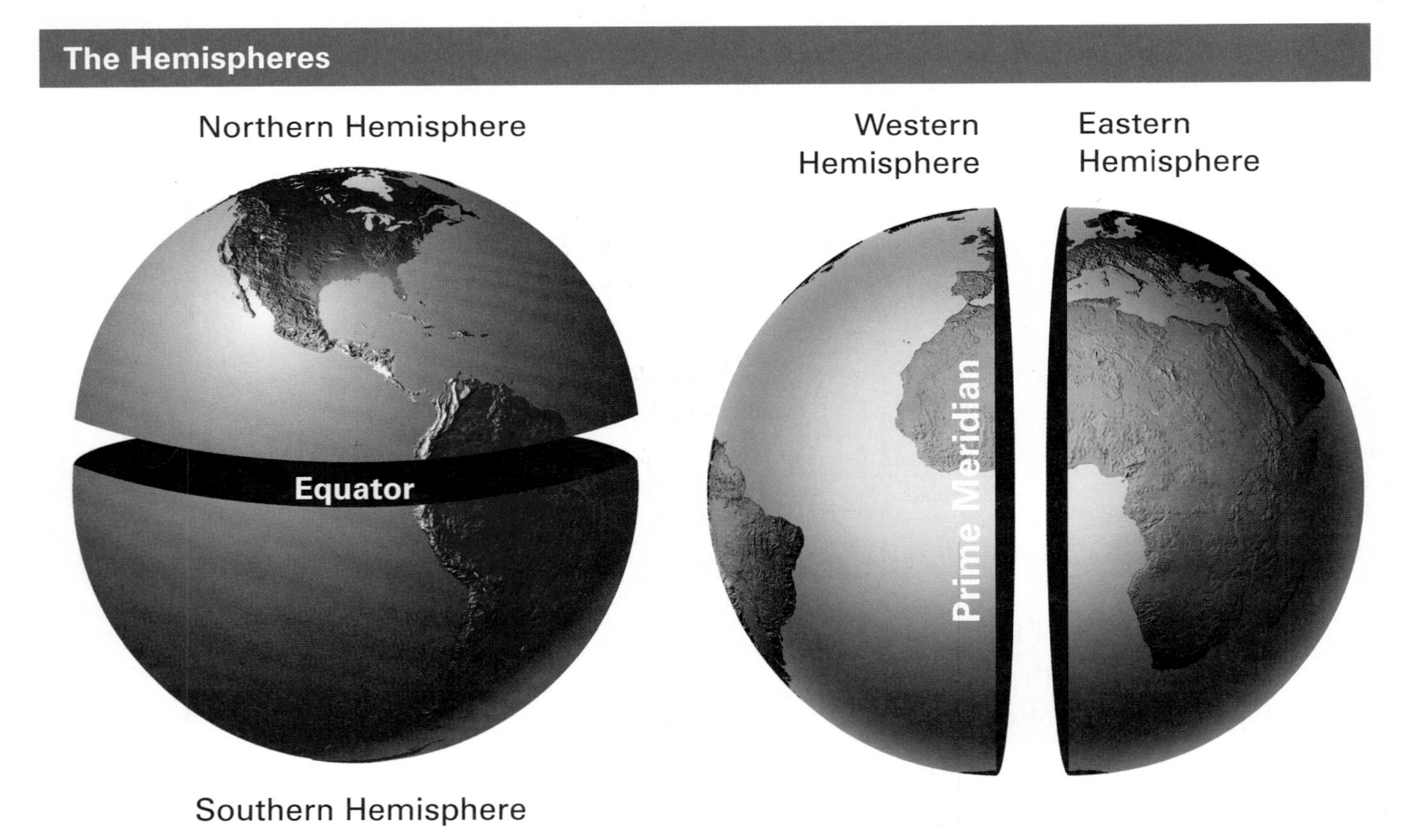

World Map: Continents and Oceans

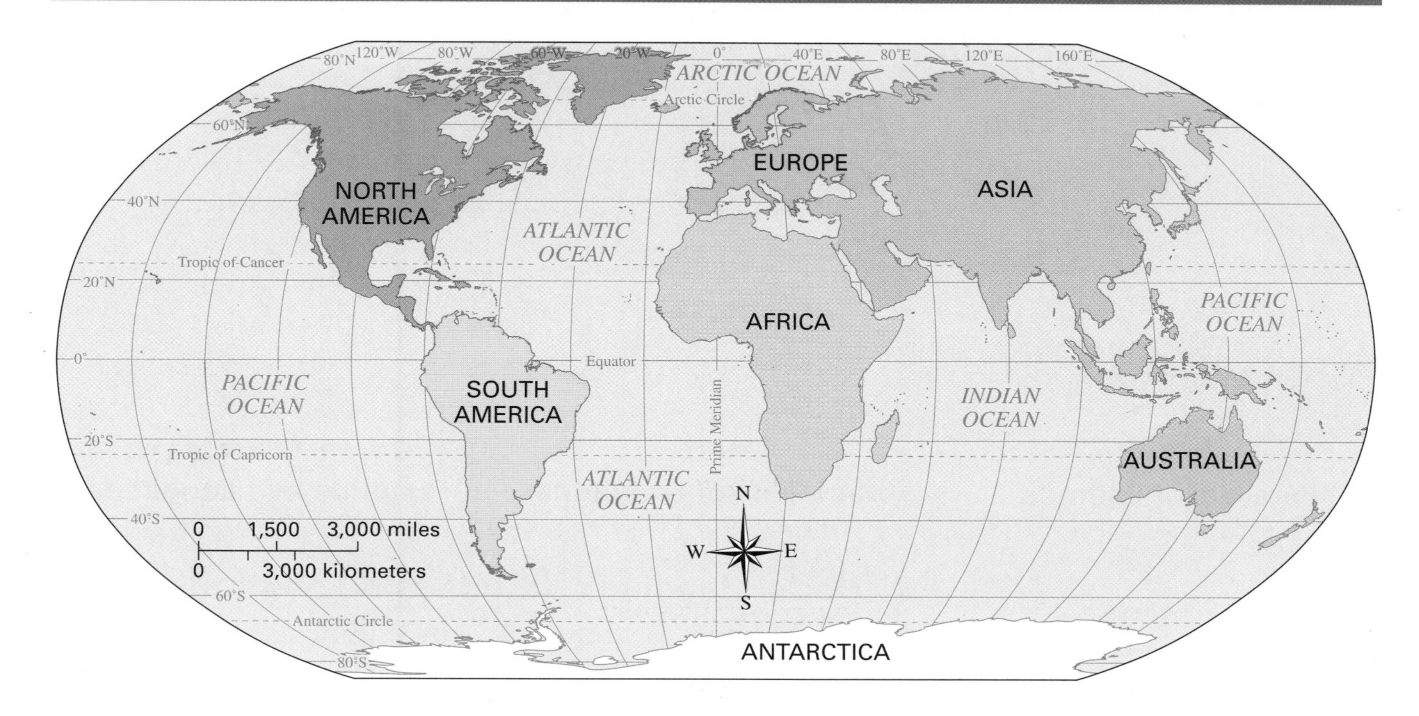

Another special line runs from the North Pole to the South Pole. It forms half of a circle that divides Earth into two equal parts. This line is called the prime meridian. The half of Earth to the east of the prime meridian is the Eastern Hemisphere. The half to the west is the Western Hemisphere.

A globe shows that we live on a watery planet. In fact, water covers almost three-fourths of Earth's surface. This is mainly the salt water of oceans. Oceans are the largest bodies of water on Earth. There are four oceans. From largest to smallest, they are the Pacific Ocean, the Atlantic Ocean, the Indian Ocean, and the Arctic Ocean.

Oceans surround large masses of land called continents. There are seven continents on Earth. In order from largest to smallest, they are Asia, Africa, North America, South America, Antarctica, Europe, and Australia.

The Global Grid

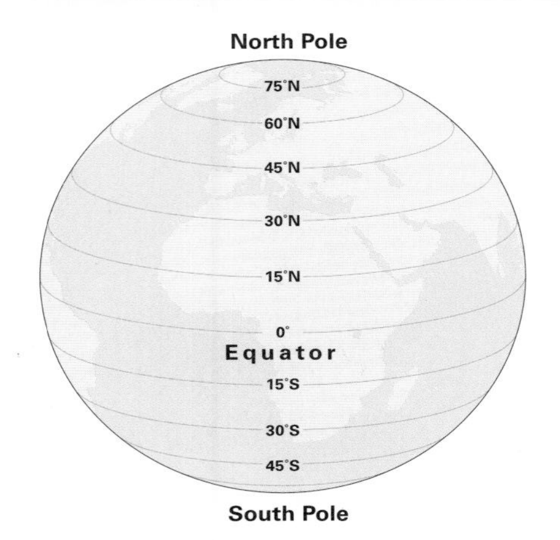

Parallels of Latitude

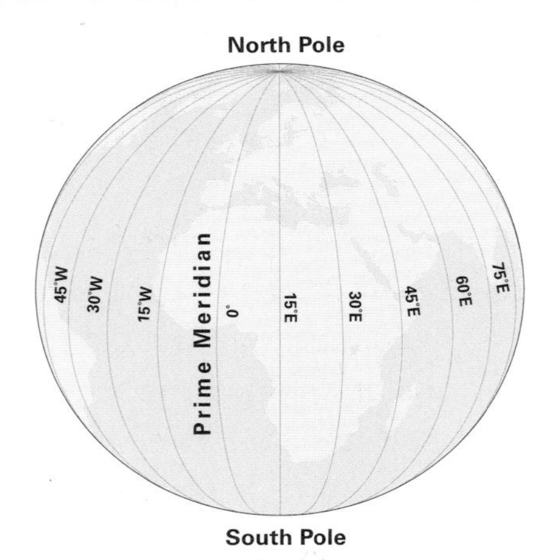

Meridians of Longitude

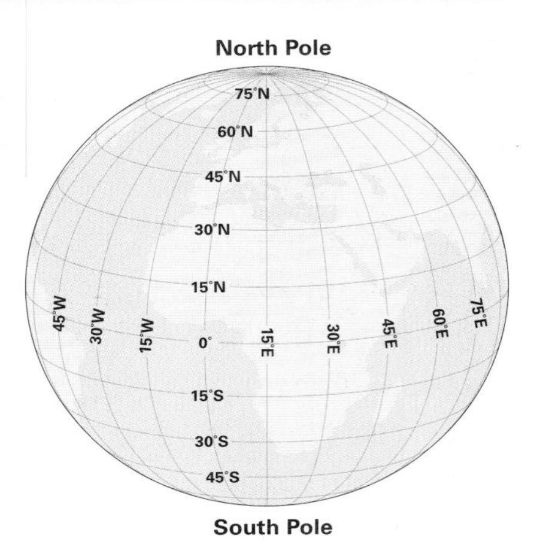

Latitude and Longitude

1.3 Understanding Latitude and Longitude

Geographers begin to study a place by finding its absolute location, or exact "address" on Earth. To do so, they use two types of measurements, called lines of latitude and longitude. With these lines, they can pinpoint any place on Earth. Distances between these lines are measured in degrees (°).

The lines that circle Earth from west to east are called parallels of latitude. They show how far north or south a place is. The distance between parallel lines is always the same.

The starting point for measuring parallels of latitude is the equator. The equator is halfway between the North Pole and the South Pole. It is at 0° latitude. All places north of the equator are north latitude. Places south of the equator are south latitude. The places farthest from the equator are the poles. The North Pole is at 90° north latitude. The South Pole is at 90° south latitude.

Other parallels of latitude have special names. The Arctic Circle is located at 66.5° north latitude, also written as 66.5° N. The Tropic of Cancer is at 23.5° N. The Antarctic Circle is at 66.5° S. The Tropic of Capricorn is at 23.5° S. Find these special lines on the map on page 7. These lines mark areas of Earth that receive different amounts of sunlight throughout the year.

You can find any spot on the globe by using latitude and longitude. This boat is in Earth's largest ocean at 40° S, 100° W. Read the next page to find this place on the world map.

The lines that run from the North Pole to the South Pole are called meridians of longitude. They show how far east or west a place is. These lines are half-circles. They are not parallels because they are not always the same distance apart. They are farthest apart where they cross the equator. All meridians of longitude meet at the two poles.

The starting place for measuring longitude is the prime meridian, or first meridian. It is numbered 0°. All lines to the east of this line are east longitude. Lines to the west of this line are west longitude. There is one line that is the same distance east and west of the prime meridian. This line, at 180° longitude, is exactly halfway around the world from the prime meridian. Together, these two lines—180° longitude and the prime meridian—form a circle that divides Earth into the Eastern and Western hemispheres.

To note the location of a place on Earth, first name its latitude, including north or south. Then name its longitude, including east or west. For example, one location on Earth's surface is at 30° N, 90° W. Find this place on the map below.

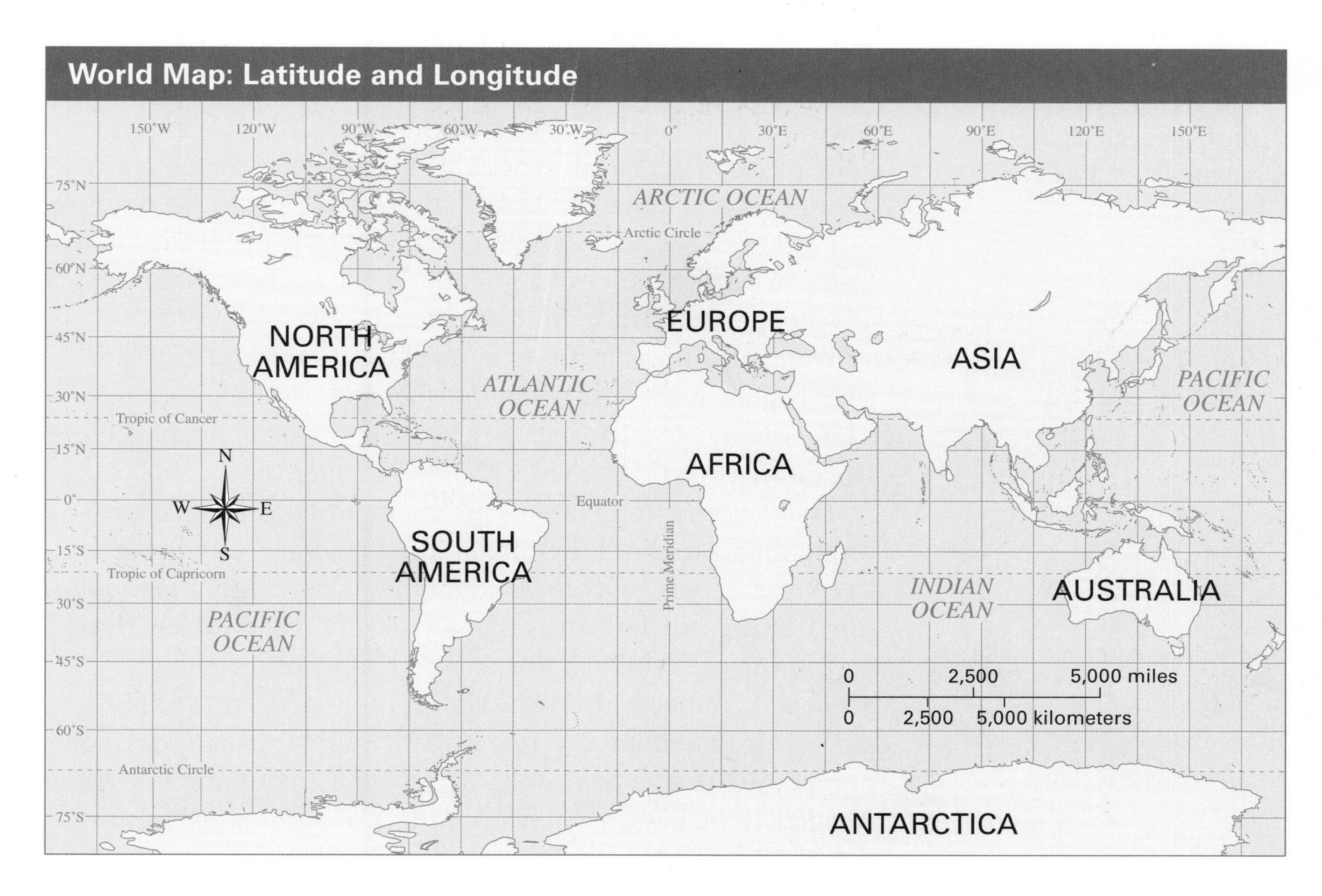

Geographic Terms

landform a physical feature on Earth's surface such as a mountain or a plain

1.4 Geographic Terms for Water and Landforms

Geographic terms help us describe **landforms** and bodies of water. Most of Earth's water is in the four oceans. A smaller body of salt water is called a *sea*. Sometimes part of a sea or an ocean cuts into a mass of land. This is called a *gulf*. An example is the Gulf of Mexico, along the southeastern part of the United States. A *bay* is similar to a gulf, but it is usually smaller. A body of water surrounded by land is called a *lake*.

Water also flows in *rivers*. A river has a *source*, where the river begins. It also has a *mouth*, where the river empties into a larger body of water, such as an ocean or a lake. A smaller stream that runs into a river is called a *tributary*.

The major types of landforms are mountains and plains. Mountains rise above the surrounding land and usually have steep sides. A row of connected mountains is called a *mountain range*. *Plains* are land areas that are mostly flat, with few trees.

You can see other landforms in the illustration above. A *peninsula* is surrounded by water on three sides. A *cape* is a piece of land that juts out into the water and is usually smaller or narrower than a peninsula. An *island* is surrounded by water. A *valley* is the low area between ranges of mountains or hills. A *delta* is formed when soil is deposited at the mouth of a river. It is usually shaped like a triangle.

1.5 Physical Features of the United States

The United States is on the continent of North America. In land, it is the world's third largest country. (Russia is the largest. Canada is the second largest.) Our country is bordered by three large bodies of water. The Pacific Ocean is to the west. This is Earth's largest ocean. The Atlantic Ocean is to the east. This is Earth's second largest ocean. The Gulf of Mexico lies to the southeast.

From a space shuttle, you would see mountain ranges that run from north to south in North America. In the west, the Rocky Mountains stretch about 3,000 miles from Alaska, through Canada, to New Mexico. The Rockies are the largest mountain range in the west. The Appalachian Mountains are the largest range in the east. They extend more than 1,500 miles, from Quebec Province in Canada to Alabama. The Sierra Nevada range in the far west is about 400 miles long. It includes Mount Whitney, the tallest peak in the continental United States, or the 48 states not including Alaska and Hawaii.

Physical Features of the Continental United States

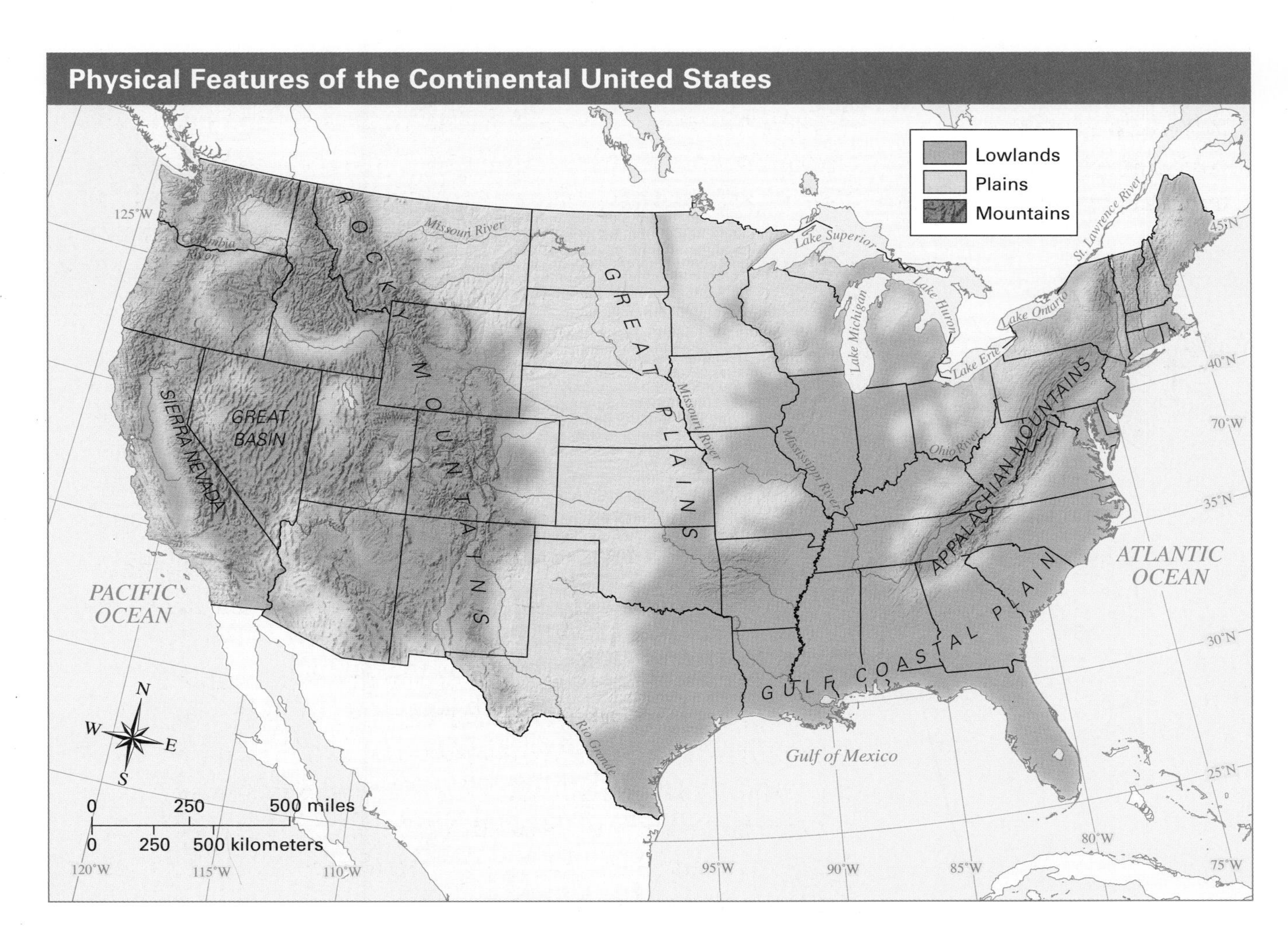

Glacier National Park is in northern Montana. The Rocky Mountains run through the park. They are the largest mountain range in the western United States.

While viewing North America from space, you would also see large areas covered by plains. The biggest of these areas is the Great Plains. They reach from Canada to Texas. At one time, they were huge natural grasslands where buffalo roamed. Today, American farmers in the Great Plains grow much of the world's wheat.

The other large area of flat land is the Gulf Coastal Plain in the southeast. These are lowlands that sometimes experience flooding. The floods bring rich soil down from the mountains, making the land ideal for farming.

One of the most striking features of the United States is its system of mighty rivers and lakes. These waterways have provided routes for ships and power for industry. In this way, they have helped the United States become a wealthy nation.

The largest river in the nation is the Mississippi River. The Mississippi has its source in Minnesota and runs 2,350 miles before emptying into the Gulf of Mexico. Two of its largest tributaries are the Ohio River and the Missouri River.

The St. Lawrence River is a key river in the northeastern United States. It flows from one of the Great Lakes, Lake Ontario, into the Atlantic Ocean. The St. Lawrence forms part of the border between the United States and Canada.

In the south, the Rio Grande forms much of the U.S. border with Mexico. The Columbia River is a major river in the west. It forms part of the border between the states of Oregon and Washington. The Columbia River runs into the Pacific Ocean. Turn to the physical world map at the back of this book to see a detailed view of the physical features you have read about.

Summary

In this chapter, you learned that geography is vital to the study of history. Geography explains how our physical surroundings affect our lives. You used globes and maps to learn about U.S. geography.

Geographers use special tools to study Earth. A globe has the same shape as Earth. It displays physical features such as oceans and continents. A compass shows directions. Lines of latitude and longitude help us to locate places on Earth.

Geographic terms such as *mountain* and *ocean* describe Earth's landforms and bodies of water. In this chapter, you used these terms to study geographic features of our country. In this book, you will learn how these features, including mountains, plains, and rivers, played a key role in the history of the United States.

This is a photograph taken from a satellite. Picture yourself in a spaceship, looking down at this view of Earth. What do you see?

Reading Further 1

Where Geography Meets History

In the mid-1800s, thousands of people rushed to California, hoping to get rich by mining gold. Most were from the eastern United States. Many went west across the continent. What did people learn about the geography of the United States on their journey?

Luzena Stanley Wilson was sure of one thing. If her husband was setting off for California, so was she. The Wilsons' two children would also make the difficult trip.

Wilson was used to hardship. After all, she and her family lived in a log cabin in Missouri. For the past two years, they had struggled to carve a farm and a home out of their land on the plains. It had been backbreaking work. Now the Wilsons were going to leave it all behind.

Why would they give up what they had worked so hard to build? What made them willing to undertake the grueling, dangerous journey to the West Coast? In 1848, a man named James Marshall had found treasure in a California stream. It was gold! The yellow metal had formed in the mountains long ago. Over the centuries, wind and rain wore away the mountain rock—and the gold. Streams then washed the gold away. It collected in the streambeds.

Overland Route to California, 1849

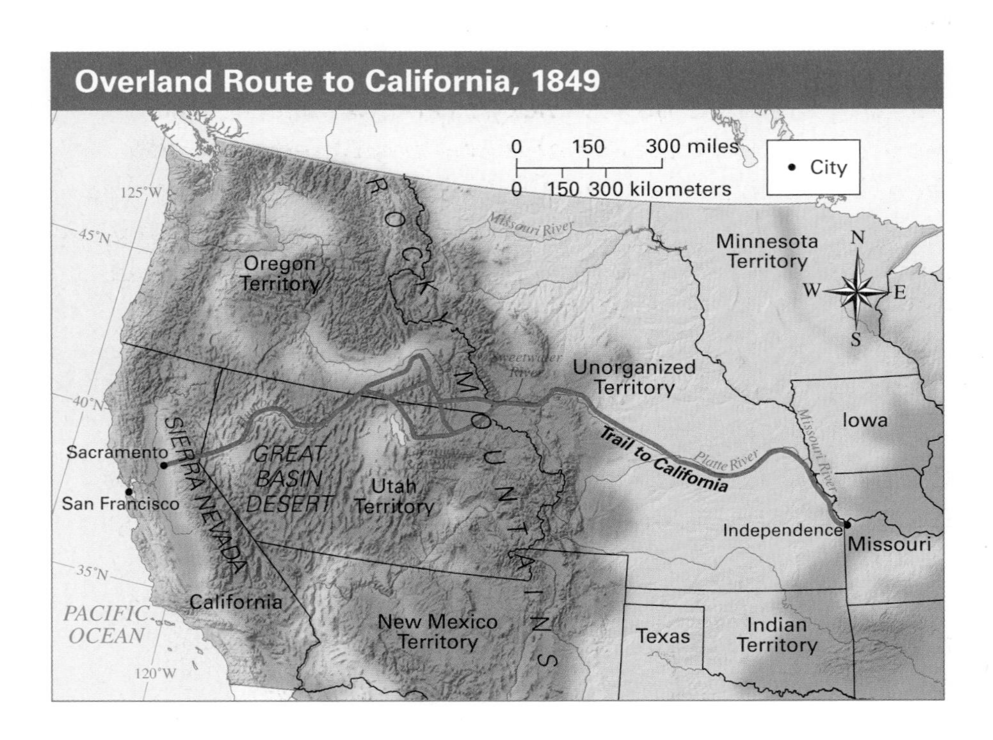

Marshall's discovery touched off a frenzy. Around the United States—and around the world—people began dreaming of striking it rich in the California goldfields.

Luzena Stanley Wilson and her husband shared that dream. But first, they had to travel across many kinds of land to get to California. It would be no easy task.

Wilson was closer to California than many gold-seekers. Missouri was then one of the westernmost states. Many people heading to the West Coast in 1849 faced a long trip just to reach Missouri.

People with money could reach Missouri in some comfort in a matter of days. Railroads linked many eastern cities. Canals and steamboats provided water transportation. Then the real trip began.

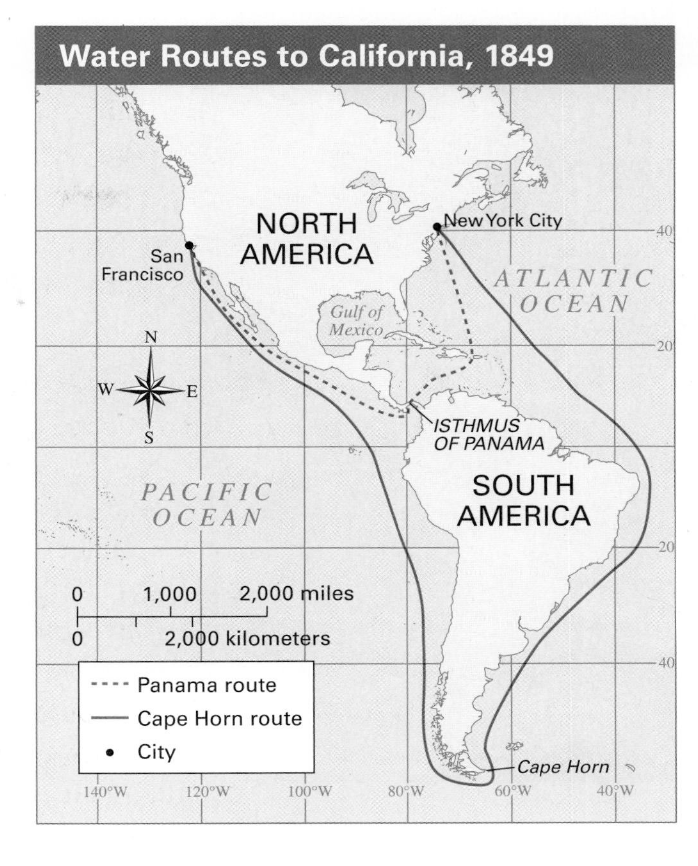

From Missouri, the trip west got much more difficult. Between Missouri and the goldfields stretched a twisting trail of some 2,000 miles. Wilson and others who took this route had to start in the spring. They clattered along dusty, bumpy trails in wagons drawn by oxen. Usually, they had to walk beside their wagon. They crossed rivers, mountains, and deserts. On a good day, they might cover 15 miles.

But many days were far from good. Animals got hurt, and wagons broke down. Tricky river crossings slowed progress. Weary travelers needed a day of rest now and then. The journey took months to complete. "Day after day, week after week, we went through the same routine," Wilson later recalled. Each day meant "breaking camp at daybreak, yoking the oxen, cooking our meager rations on a fire of sage-brush and scrub-oak, packing up again."

Some gold-seekers traveled by water. They took a ship around Cape Horn, on the southern tip of South America. Others sailed to the Isthmus of Panama. After crossing the **isthmus** (IS-mus) overland, they finished their trip by ship.

isthmus a narrow strip of land connecting two larger land areas

Sailing to California, like the trip by wagon, was a long and difficult journey. Going around South America could take six months or more. The trip across Panama was shorter. Both routes, though, were challenging.

The trip along the overland trail was very hard. Many died during the journey.

Luzena Stanley Wilson spent her first days on the overland trail on plains much like her Missouri farmland. Still, there were unexpected dangers. One was river crossings. There were no bridges or ferries. At Wilson's first crossing, she and her family made it safely to the other side. But the wagon behind her got stuck in the river. The oxen pulling the wagon sank into the sands of the riverbed. The poor beasts disappeared under the water, taking the loaded wagon with them.

The Wilsons would face more river crossings. They would also pass amazing sights. But they could not enjoy them. "There was not time to note the great natural wonders that lay along the route," Wilson later recounted. "Some one would speak of a remarkable valley, a group of cathedral-like rocks, some mineral springs, a salt basin, but we never deviated [strayed] from the direct route to see them."

After three months, the Wilsons had managed to cross the plains. Next, they made the grueling climb over the Rocky Mountains. Then, they entered the most dangerous region yet—the desert.

In the desert, the trail was littered with abandoned wagons. Wilson saw animal and even some human bones. She must have feared that her family would meet the same fate. The heat was terrible. A fine, dry dust covered them. Thirst tormented them. Their oxen seemed ready to collapse at any time. Still, the Wilsons kept going.

Finally, the ragged family reached a river. Their oxen drank eagerly. Wilson rejoiced. She and her family had survived. Their exhausting trip would soon be over. Once they crossed the high Sierra Nevada, they would reach the goldfields of California!

Life in California differed from the life Wilson had known in Missouri. On her first night there, a miner paid her $10 for some bread. This was a great amount of money at the time. Wilson could see that she might get rich—but not in the goldfields.

Thousands of people sailed to California during the gold rush. The San Francisco harbor was filled with ships.

"In my dreams that night," she wrote, "I saw crowds of bearded miners striking gold from the earth with every blow of the pick, each one seeming to leave a share for me." She could earn her fortune by cooking for hungry miners.

Why was the miner willing to pay so much? It was a matter of supply and demand. There were tens of thousands of miners. Most were men who could not cook. What Wilson offered—home-cooked meals—was in short supply. The men were willing to pay huge sums for her meals. Wilson spent her gold-rush years running a hotel and restaurant.

People kept coming. Cities sprang up quickly. Before the gold rush, San Francisco had fewer than 1,000 people. Soon, it had tens of thousands of residents. Many came from foreign countries, such as China. The Chinese people have been an important part of California's population ever since.

Most of the gold-seekers did not strike it rich. Some went home, but many, like the Wilsons, stayed on in their new land. In fact, because so many newcomers stayed, California joined the United States in 1850.

Two decades later, a railroad linked California to the eastern part of the country. No longer would travelers to the West Coast have to endure a long, dangerous journey like that of Luzena Stanley Wilson and her family. Passengers could now watch the geographic wonders of the United States—broad plains, majestic mountains, deep rivers—rush by their train windows. California—and the rest of the country—had been transformed.

What might these objects have been used for, and how do you think they were made?
What might this dog be carrying?
What type of animal skin might this clothing be made from?

American Indians and Their Land

2

How did American Indians adapt to different environments in North America?

2.1 Introduction

In this chapter, you will read about the first people to live in North America. You will find out where they came from and settled.

The descendants of these first Americans are the American Indians. Most American Indians tell **origin stories,** or tales that explain where their ancestors came from. In this chapter, you will read an origin story.

Many scientists believe that these early people first **migrated,** or moved from one region to another, thousands of years ago. They came from the continent of Asia to North and South America. They traveled into many parts of the American continents over hundreds of years.

These early people settled in different natural **environments**. A natural environment is everything that surrounds us. It includes such things as sunlight, air, water, land, animals, insects, and plants. You will read about different environments in which American Indians lived and see why they had different ways of life.

Have you looked through the zoom lens of a camera? A zoom lens lets you look closely at the parts of a scene. The drawing below shows how this chapter is like a zoom lens. You will begin with a view of the routes the first Americans took to get here. Then you will zoom in on four environments on this continent. Finally, you will take a close look at the way of life of the Inuits (IN-oo-its) in the ice fields of the Arctic. You will discover how this group learned to **adapt,** or adjust, to that environment.

Environments of American Indians

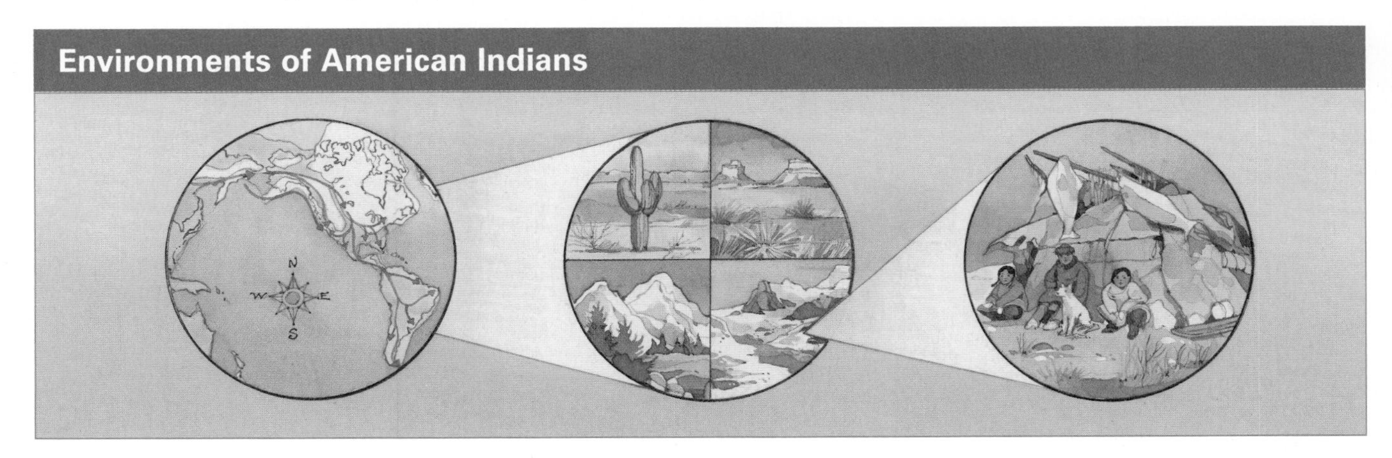

kiva a circular area, sometimes underground, where tribe members talk, work, or perform religious ceremonies

2.2 American Indian Origin Stories

Storytelling has always been important to American Indians. In some tribes, members would meet in a **kiva** and share stories or reenact them during spiritual ceremonies. They told stories to entertain one another and to teach about their beliefs and ways of life. They used stories to explain and record their experiences for future generations.

One kind of tale American Indians passed down through the years was the origin story. This type of story tells how Earth and its people came to be. The Hopis (HO-pees) are an American Indian group who live in the Southwest, in what is now the state of Arizona. The following is a Hopi origin story.

This is a kiva recreated in an Arizona museum. The Hopis told origin stories in kivas. Hopi artists Michael Kabotie and Delbridge Honanie painted the mural on the walls.

Hopi Origin Story

In the beginning, Earth was damp and dark. There were no animals or birds. At first, the people lived happily inside Earth. After a while, however, their caves became too crowded. People began to argue with one another. The worried chief agreed that his people needed to leave Earth's dark inside.

The chief's advisors made a mockingbird that found a hole at the top of Earth and flew around the world. When the bird came back, he reported that life above them was very different.

The chief's advisors grew sturdy plants that reached like a ladder to a hole in Earth's crust. The chief guided his people up the plants to Earth's surface.

Once there, the people did not know where they should settle, so they set out in different directions. They traveled east, west, north, and south until they found good land upon which they could grow crops and build villages. This is how it all began for the Hopis.

2.3 Migration Routes of the First Americans

Today, most scientists agree that the first people in North America came from Asia. They arrived at least 12,500 years ago. This **migration** took place during the last ice age. An ice age is a long period of time during which much of Earth's surface is covered with ice.

migration movement of people from one country or area of the world to a new home in another country or area

The last ice age began about 1.6 million years ago. It ended about 10,000 years ago. During the last part of the ice age, about 25,000 years ago, the Bering Sea did not separate Asia and North America, as it does today. Instead, a bridge of land almost 1,000 miles long connected them.

Most scientists believe that the first Americans came from Siberia. This is a region in northeastern Asia. They hunted big game. These were animals such as mammoths (large, elephant-like animals), bison (also called buffalo), and caribou (reindeer).

Scientists believe that these large animals ate the grass on the land bridge. As years passed, they moved across the bridge. Small groups of Siberian hunters followed the animals. They got to North America after a long, long time. Other Siberians may have moved along the southern coast of the land bridge in small boats. They may have continued along the Pacific coast of Alaska and Canada and then turned south.

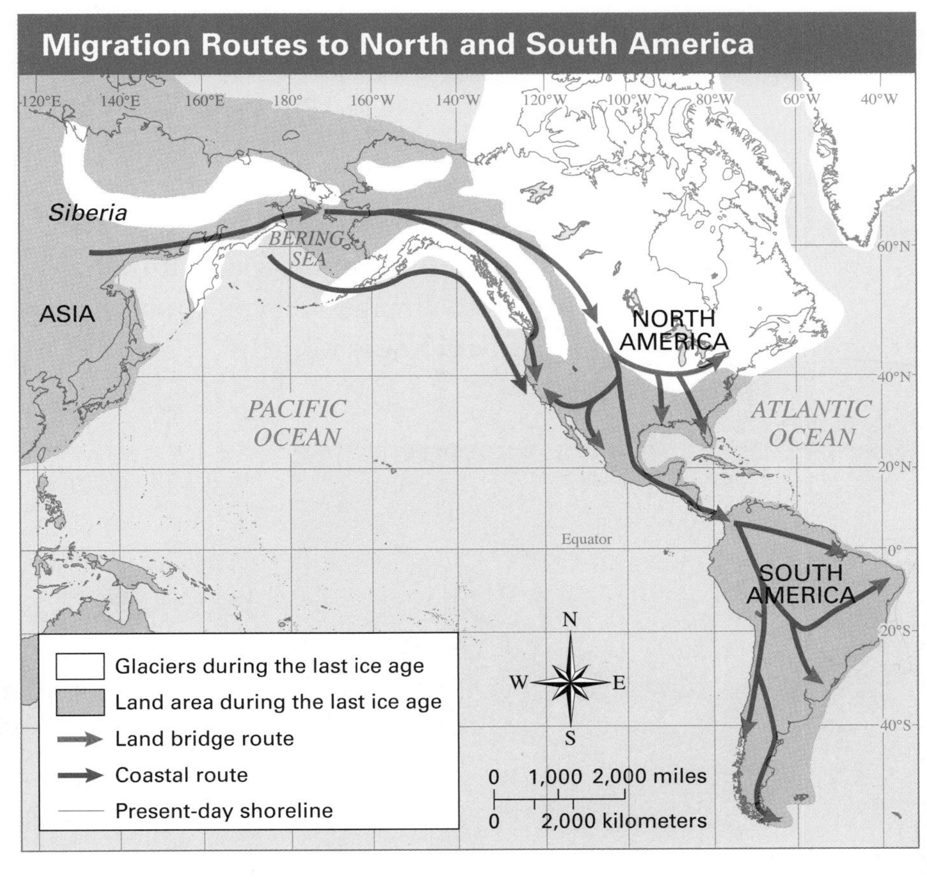

Scientists think that the first Americans used these migration routes. They came from Asia to North and South America at least 12,500 years ago.

For hundreds of years, early Americans hunted big game. The animals led the hunters south through North and South America. Some groups of people settled in areas along the way. Others kept moving until they reached the southern tip of South America. The paths they took to reach their new homes are called migration routes.

2.4 American Indians and the Environment

After the last ice age, there were changes in the climate. This affected the plants and animals found in each area. A variety of natural environments appeared across North America. Over time, early American Indians settled in areas that differed greatly from one another.

natural resource something from nature that is useful to people, such as soil, water, and minerals

One feature of an environment is its climate. The climate supports certain kinds of vegetation, or plant life. Animals that are able to live in the climate and eat the plants thrive. An environment also has **natural resources**. These include soil, water, timber from trees, and minerals such as copper. Things that people and animals eat are natural resources, too.

The early American Indian tribes migrated across North America. They settled in many types of environments. In each place, people survived by adapting their ways of life. They used what was around them in nature to build homes, make clothes, and find food. Their homes and clothing fit their climate.

Look at the four natural environments shown here. What do the images tell you about the climate, vegetation, and natural resources of each?

One environment American Indians lived in was grasslands. Some grasslands in North America get only enough rain to support different types of grasses. Most trees and bushes need more water to survive.

A second type of environment American Indians settled in was the desert. Deserts get very little rain. People living in desert areas must often dig wells and ditches to get enough water for drinking and for raising crops.

Some American Indians lived in mountain regions. The mountains of North America get lots of rain and snow. The tops of mountains have little or no plant life. Forests of pine, fir, and spruce often grow below the highest points.

Other groups settled in the Arctic ice fields. Earth's Arctic region is near the North Pole. Here, huge sheets of ice cover the land for most of the year.

Most American Indians chose areas that were rich in natural resources. These environments had mild climates and plenty of food and water. A few groups stayed in regions where resources were scarce. Life was hard in places such as the desert of the Southwest and the icy Arctic region.

Here are four types of environments. American Indians settled in areas like these and many others.

An Inuit family sits in front of a camp at Plover Bay near northern Alaska. Inflated sealskins hang from the wooden poles on the tent frame.

2.5 American Indians Adapt to the Environment

American Indians adapted their way of life to what they found in the area around them. Each group found ways to use nearby natural resources wisely. This helped the people survive in their environment. In areas with few resources, life was difficult.

One group that lived in a harsh environment was the Inuits, who are also known as Eskimos. They built their culture in present-day northwestern Alaska, northern Canada, and Greenland. These places are part of Earth's Arctic region. The Arctic ice fields have long, cold winters and land that is frozen most of the time.

The Inuits had to make **adaptations** to their harsh environment. They hunted animals such as whales, walruses, seals, caribou, polar bears, Arctic foxes, squirrels, and birds. They fished for salmon.

adaptation a change or adjustment in a way of life that allows people to survive in a particular environment

The Inuits did not waste any part of the animals that they caught. They ate the meat. They sewed animal skins together to make clothing, blankets, and tents. They burned animal fat for fuel. They used bones to make dogsleds and to support tent frames. They also carved bones into tools such as knives and harpoons, or long spears.

The Inuits even learned to fill sealskins with air so that they would float. The Inuits attached the skins to the harpoons they used to hunt walruses and whales. These floats helped to tire out the animals when they tried to escape by diving underwater.

To build shelters, the Inuits used the materials that they found around them. In the summer, they made tents by stretching the skins of caribou or seals over driftwood. Sometimes they used whale bones to support the roof. They placed heavy stones at the bottom of a tent to keep it in place. In the winter, they built houses, called igloos, out of snow and ice.

To keep warm, the Inuits dressed in animal skins and furs. To protect their eyes from the bright glare of the sun shining on snow and ice, they wore snow goggles. Snow goggles were made from bone or wood and had narrow openings to look through.

This young Inuit man wears traditional snow goggles made from driftwood.

Summary

In this chapter, you found out about the first people who came to North America. You used the idea of a zoom lens to look at American Indians and their surroundings. You learned that they passed down stories about their history and way of life.

Scientists think that the first Americans were from Asia. They came to our continent during the last ice age. Over hundreds of years, they migrated across North and South America. Groups settled in many different places. American Indians are the descendants of these first Americans.

Where early American Indians settled, they adapted to the environment. You "zoomed in" on four environments. You learned about the climate, vegetation, and natural resources of each environment.

The Inuit people settled in the Arctic environment. They found natural resources around them. They used these to survive in the harsh land.

For thousands of years, groups of American Indians were the only people in North America. How did they adapt to different environments? What did they see and do? Next, you will learn how one group used materials nearby to record important events. Their records have helped us learn about their lives.

Reading Further 2

Recording Sioux History

For a long time, American Indians did not write. They told stories about their history. And sometimes they kept records. American Indians called the Sioux (soo) lived on the Great Plains. What do their drawings tell about their history and how their surroundings affected their lives?

pictograph a picture that represents an important event or idea

A group of Sioux families watched the night sky. They thought the world was coming to an end. Streaks of bright light darted above the Great Plains. Quickly, the lights fell away into the blackness. Then new streaks flashed and fell across the sky—so many that one could not count them.

What was this grand display of fire in the heavens? Historians now know what the Sioux observed. It was the Leonid meteor shower of November 12, 1833. Scientists say that hundreds of thousands of shooting stars fell toward Earth on that cold, clear night.

The Sioux who watched this amazing natural event would never forget it. They wanted to be sure that their children and grandchildren would know about it, too. So they made a record of the meteor shower for future generations.

Lone Dog, a Sioux man, painted the meteor shower. He made the falling stars red and the moon black.

To do this, the Sioux would add a **pictograph**—such as a star—to an animal skin, or hide. The hide would already have other pictographs painted on it. These represented memorable events from earlier years. One pictograph might show a buffalo hunt. Another might show a war dance. The new image would show the meteor shower. It would also stand for the year 1833. The Sioux began calling this year the Year the Stars Fell.

Nature was important to the Sioux. They used the first snowfall of winter to mark the start of each year. They called the records they made with pictographs "winter counts." Each pictograph on a winter count stood for a different year. The pictograph showed a key event from that year.

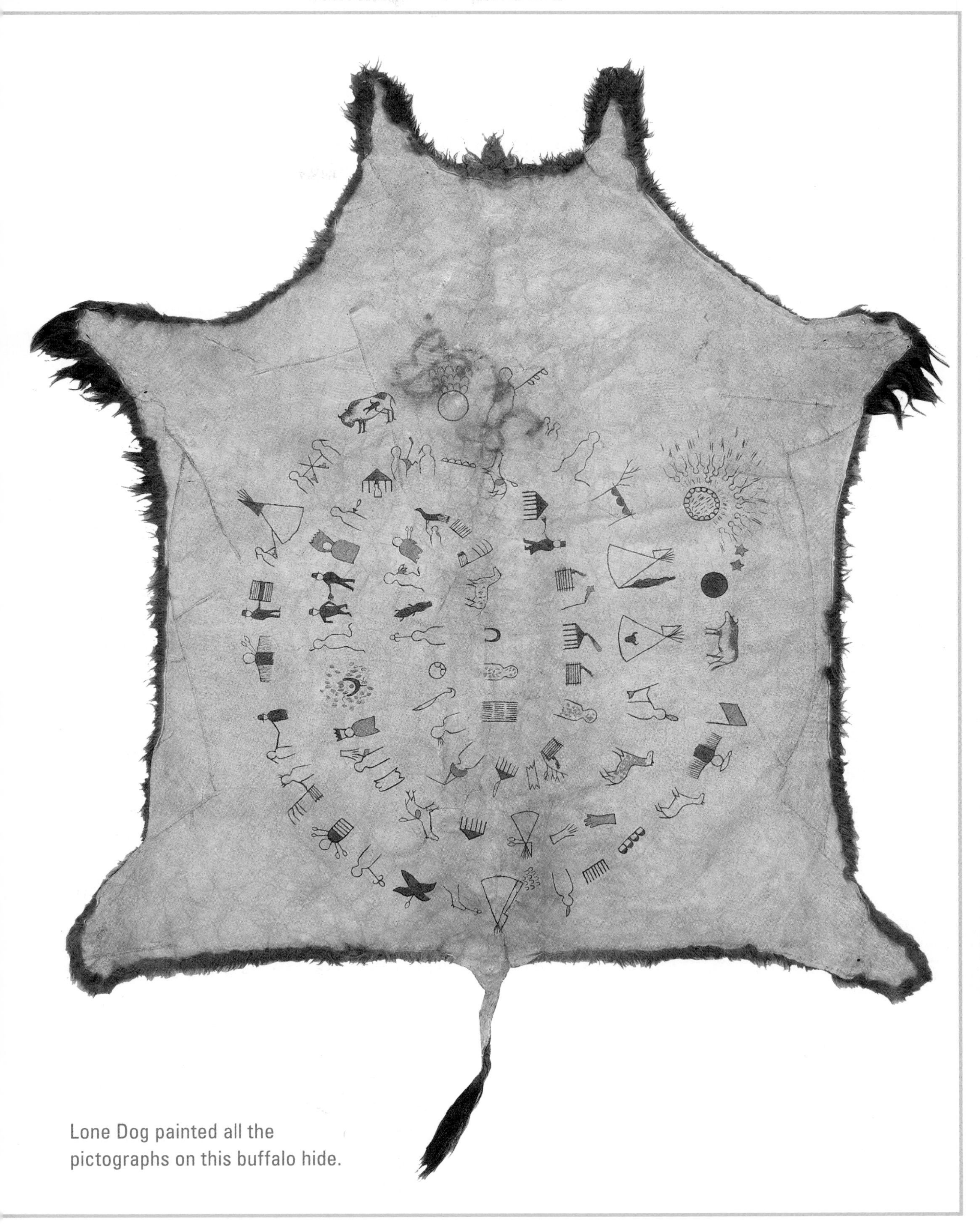

Lone Dog painted all the pictographs on this buffalo hide.

The winter count below records 105 years, starting in 1798. The pictographs form a spiral. They begin at the top left. The first pictograph represents the time when a pipe was given to a Sioux man as he became a chief. The pictographs continue to the right, wrapping around in a clockwise direction. The last year counted is in the center. This final picture stands for the death of a man named Gray Bear in 1902.

The geography of the Great Plains played a key role in the lives of the Sioux. Many of the pictographs show how the climate and natural resources of the Sioux's environment affected their lives. Some pictographs tell of heavy snowfalls or long periods without rain. Some show hunts for animals that roamed the plains. Others represent visits to nearby hills, forests, and waterholes to gather wood and water.

A primary source is a record of an event created by someone who was there. The winter count below is a primary source. Each image was added by a member of the tribe called the keeper. Long Soldier, a Sioux from North Dakota, explained these pictographs.

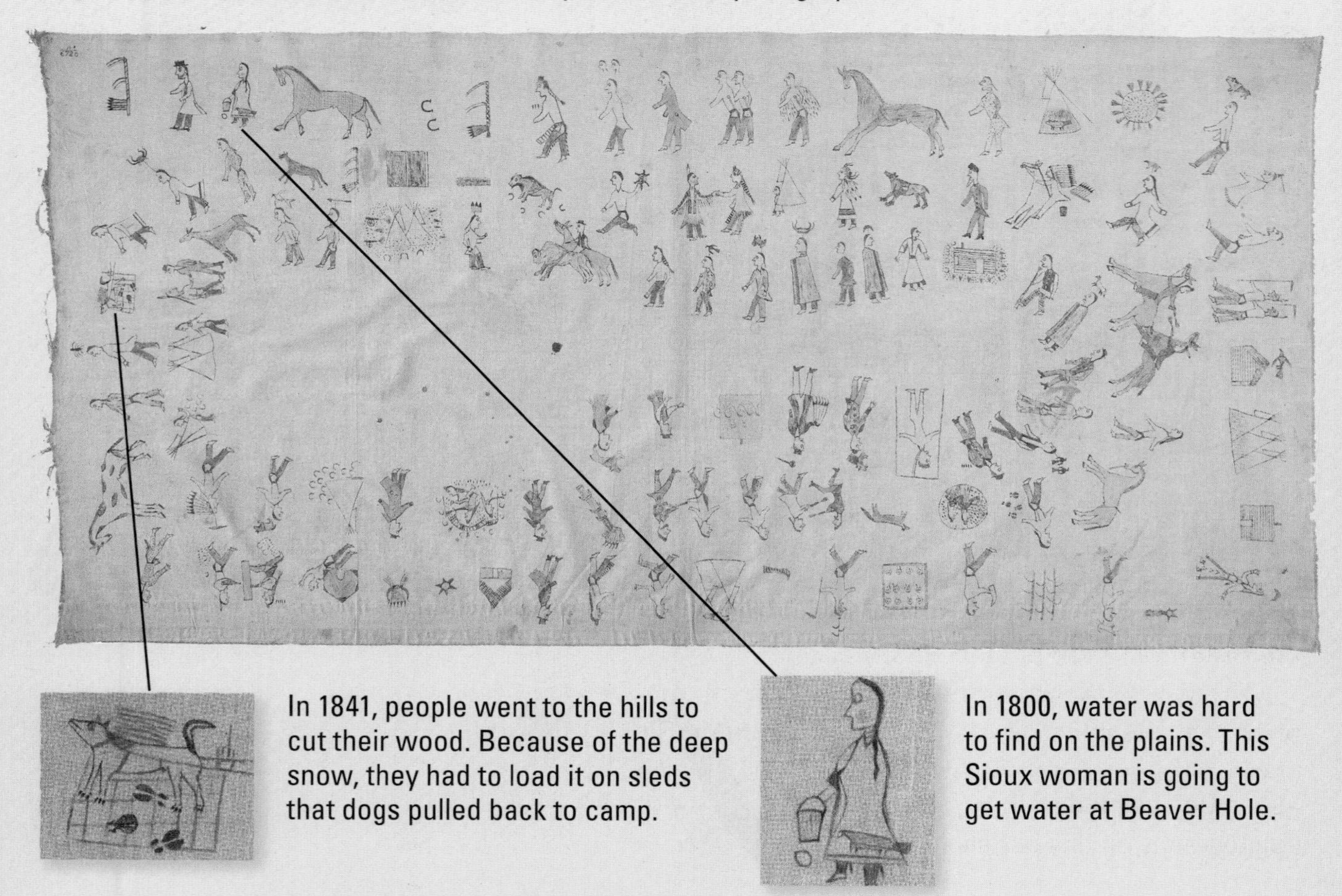

In 1841, people went to the hills to cut their wood. Because of the deep snow, they had to load it on sleds that dogs pulled back to camp.

In 1800, water was hard to find on the plains. This Sioux woman is going to get water at Beaver Hole.

Here, a Sioux man paints a new pictograph on a winter count on an animal hide.

In each band of Sioux, one person had the honor of painting the pictographs on the winter count. This person was called the keeper. For a long time, only a man could be the keeper. By the 1900s, the role sometimes passed to a woman.

In the picture above, a keeper paints a new symbol on an animal hide. The Sioux painted many winter counts on hides. They hunted buffalo and other animals on the plains. They used all the parts of the animal to meet food, clothing, shelter, and other needs.

Over time, the hides wore out. Then the keeper repainted the winter counts onto other hides. He might use cloth or paper if it was available. The Sioux winter count shown on the previous page is painted on cloth.

The Sioux made winter counts for many generations. But once they began to write in the 1800s, many Sioux stopped using pictographs to keep records. Today, some Sioux use new forms of communication—like video and the Internet—to keep the spirit of the winter count alive.

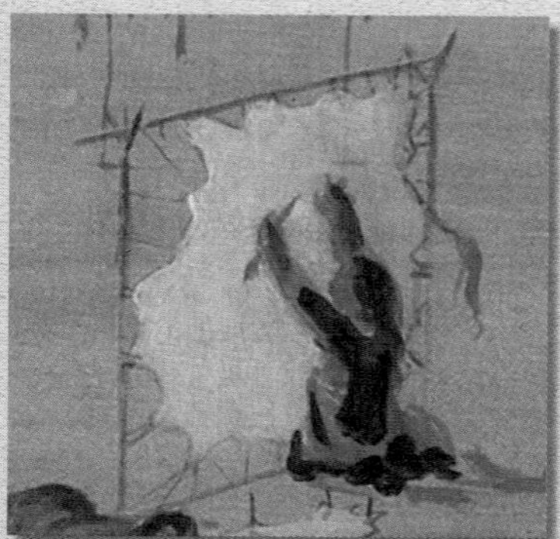

How do you think the environment affected the clothes these people wore?

How do you think the environment affected the homes these people lived in?

How do you think the environment affected the food these people ate?

American Indian Cultural Regions

3

How and why did American Indian cultural regions differ?

3.1 Introduction

In Chapter 2, you read about the first people to settle the American continents. You also learned how the Inuits adapted to their environment. In this chapter, you will see how other American Indian groups adapted to their surroundings.

By the 1400s, American Indians had a variety of **cultures,** or ways of living. Many groups lived in villages. Other groups were **nomadic.** This means they moved from place to place as changes in seasons made food available in different areas. Historians call the areas where similar cultures developed **cultural regions.** There are different ways of describing them, but one way is to divide them into seven regions. They are the Northwest Coast, California-Intermountain, Southwest, Plateau, Great Plains, Eastern Woodlands, and Southeast regions.

Historians determined these regions by looking at the **artifacts** they found. Artifacts are human-made objects that help us understand how the people who made them lived. Each American Indian group made clothes, tools, and other things they needed. They used nearby natural resources. For example, American Indians living near the forests of the Northwest Coast made wooden boxes for food storage. Hopis, in the Southwest where there are few trees, kept food in pots made of local clay.

This map shows the seven major American Indian cultural regions. As you read, use the map to help you note facts about how each group lived. What was the environment like in each region? How did these environments affect American Indian cultures?

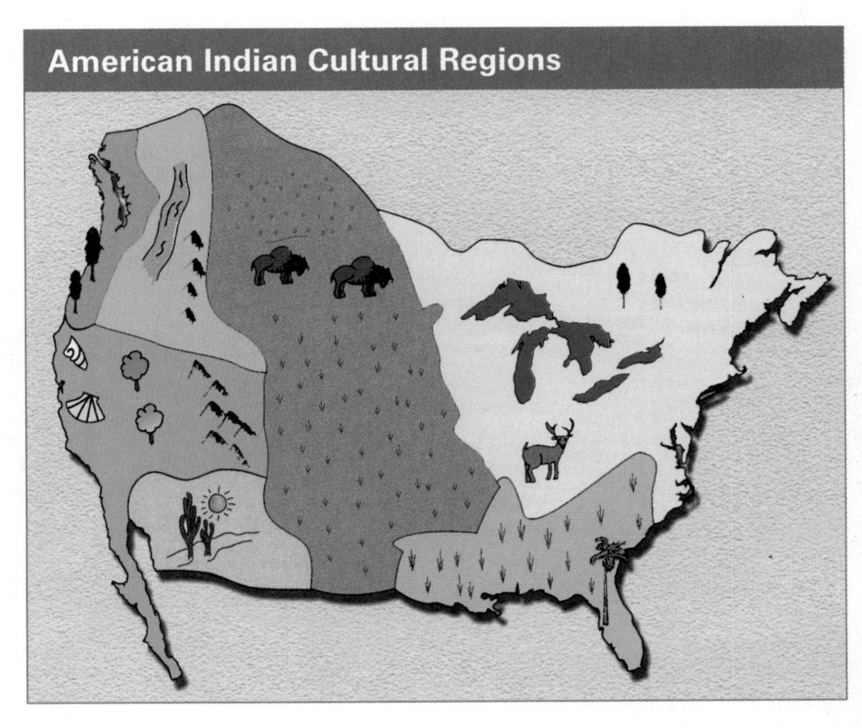

3.2 American Indians of the Northwest Coast

The Northwest Coast American Indians lived on a narrow strip of land along the Pacific Coast. This region was south of the Inuits' ice fields. It stretched from present-day Alaska to California. Dense fir, pine, and cedar forests grew right to the ocean's shore. This forced many people to settle on the few flat, rocky beaches. The climate here is mild, but the area receives heavy rainfall most of the year. Many tribes, including the Tlingits, Chinooks, and Kwakiutls (kwah-kee-YOO-tels), adapted to life here.

There was plentiful wildlife in the area. Fish, especially salmon, filled the streams. Migrating whales swam up and down the coast. Deer, elk, mountain goats, bears, and wolves lived in the forests.

The Kwakiutls used wood from the forest for housing. They built huge wooden structures that served as homes for several families. Outside each home they placed totem poles. On these cedar poles, the Kwakiutls carved figures of animals, humans, and spirits. These carvings told about important events in the family's history and indicated the family's social position.

Clothes made from cedar bark protected Kwakiutls from the wet climate. Women wove the bark's soft inner core into warm, waterproof coats and hats.

Kwakiutls also used cedar bark to make rope. They used this rope for fishing nets and to hold together fish traps made from willow trees. They shaped each trap like a cone. Salmon swam into the cone and could not escape.

In the Northwest Coast cultural region, American Indians settled on rocky beaches bordered by thick forests.

The ocean provided many resources for American Indians living in the California-Intermountain region.

3.3 American Indians of the California-Intermountain Region

The California-Intermountain cultural region ran inland from the Pacific coast of California. It contains the Sierra Nevada, a high mountain range, and reaches into the Great Basin. This region has many kinds of environments. For example, the Great Basin is a desert. It has extreme heat and cold and limited rainfall, so few plants and animals live there. American Indians in this area were nomadic, moving on after using up available food, such as rabbits, ants, and berries. Many tribes, including the Shoshones and the Paiutes, made this region their home.

Unlike the Great Basin, California has different landscapes and a milder climate that provides rich resources. In the 1400s, huge redwood trees covered the coastal mountains. Oak trees, grasses, and berries grew inland. There were many deer, rabbits, and birds. Streams were filled with fish. Clams and other shellfish were found along the seashore. Among the tribes who lived here were the Miwoks and the Pomos (PO-mos).

The California Pomos lived along the California coast and also a short way inland. Coastal Pomos used nearby trees, such as redwoods, to build their homes. They piled thick pieces of bark against a center pole. These homes looked like upside-down ice-cream cones.

The Pomos made beads from the sea's resources. They used them as money. Artisans made the beads from clamshells. They broke the shells into pieces that they shaped into beads. They strung the beads on cords that looked like necklaces.

Pomos used natural materials to make useful and artistic things. For example, to hold food, they wove beautiful baskets from roots, grasses, reeds, bark, and small willow branches. They decorated the baskets with shells, beads, and feathers.

mesa a flat-topped hill with steep sides

3.4 American Indians of the Southwest

The driest cultural region was the Southwest. It stretched from the southwestern United States to northern Mexico. In this region, there are mountains, **mesas,** canyons, and deserts. These places receive little rainfall, and they often have extreme temperatures. Days are hot. Nights are cold. There are long, hot summers and short, mild winters. This climate supports few trees or plants.

Some of the American Indians who lived here, like the Apaches, were nomadic. Others, like the Hopis, lived in villages and learned to farm with little water. They raised crops like corn, beans, squash, and cotton.

The geography affected how people lived. The Anasazis, believed to be ancestors of the Hopis, lived in this region more than 2,000 years ago. At first, they made houses of stone and adobe, a type of clay that hardens like cement. Later, they built similar homes against and inside cliff walls. These were called cliff dwellings. Because there were few trees, their descendants, the Hopis, also made homes of stone and adobe. They built apartment buildings called *pueblos.* These pueblos were up to four or five levels high. People moved from one story to another by ladder.

The Anasazis built cliff dwellings against and inside cliff walls. These are remains of such homes in Mesa Verde National Park in Colorado.

Hopi women wore cotton cloth to stay cool in the summer heat. They used plants to make dyes in colors such as orange, yellow, red, green, and black. The men wove the cloth for blankets and clothing. The Hopis also embroidered designs on their clothes.

The Hopis created clay pots in which they cooked, served, and stored their food. They decorated these pots with black geometric designs and images of living creatures.

Large rivers provided water and salmon for American Indians in the Plateau region.

3.5 American Indians of the Plateau

The Plateau cultural region lay between the Cascade and the Rocky mountains. This region included parts of what is now the northwestern states and British Columbia. It has flatlands, rolling hills, and **gorges**. Summers are hot and winters are very cold. As in the Southwest, rainfall is light. However, the Plateau region gets water from the large Columbia and Fraser rivers. These rivers are fed by rainfall in the mountains. Many tribes, such as the Nez Percés (NEHZ-pers-es), Spokanes, and Yakimas, now called Yakamas (YA-kuh-muhs), lived here.

gorge a narrow, deep valley with steep sides

Various types of plants and animals survived on the plateau. Forests grew near the mountains. Other areas had only thick grasses, berries, or camas, a type of lily. The camas root was an important food source for people on the Plateau because few animals lived there. Some deer and bear roamed the forests. Jackrabbits lived in drier sections. The rivers held fish.

Yakima artifacts show the culture that developed as people adapted to the harsh climate and available resources. For instance, the Yakimas built their winter homes partly underground to escape from the cold. Each home was a three-foot-deep, circular hole with a grass-mat roof. To help keep heat inside, the Yakimas covered the mat with earth.

The Yakima women wove local grasses into clothing, such as basket hats. These hats were cone-shaped but flat on top. The women decorated them with designs.

To harvest foods such as camas and other roots, the Yakimas developed a digging stick. They used a hardwood stick that was curved and pointed at one end. They attached a short handle of animal horn to the other end. The women pushed a digging stick under a root and then lifted it out of the ground.

In the 1500s, the Sioux began to use horses to move their camps and to hunt buffalo.

3.6 American Indians of the Great Plains

East of the Plateau lay the Great Plains. This region extended from the Rocky Mountains to the Mississippi River Valley. From north to south, it stretched from Canada to Texas. Among the many tribes who lived here were the Cheyennes (shy-ANS), Pawnees, Comanches (koh-MAN-chees), and Sioux (soo).

The Great Plains region has cold winters and hot summers. In the 1400s, it was mostly treeless grassland. Many animals lived there, including pronghorn antelope, deer, and bear. To American Indians, the most important creature on the plains was the buffalo.

The Western Sioux considered the buffalo sacred because it was so valuable to them. They used parts of this animal to make many things they needed to survive. For example, the Sioux made their homes, called tepees, from buffalo hides, or skins. To build a tepee, women sewed the hides together. Then they constructed a cone out of long poles and covered the cone with the hides. On the outside of the tepee, men painted scenes from daily life.

In addition, the Sioux used buffalo hides to make warm blankets to wear in winter. They decorated the flesh side of the hides and placed the fur side next to their skin. In Chapter 2, you learned how they also recorded important events by painting winter counts on hides.

Warriors even made shields from buffalo hides. Men painted their shields with scenes from their dreams. They believed these images came from heaven and protected them from harm. They also decorated their shields with fur and feathers.

3.7 American Indians of the Eastern Woodlands

The Eastern Woodlands stretched east from the Mississippi River to the Atlantic Ocean. It ran south from the Great Lakes to the Ohio Valley. American Indians settled among its hills and valleys, and along seacoasts. Most tribes spoke either Iroquois (EER-uh-kway) or Algonquian (al-GOHN-kwee-in). Iroquois tribes included the Mohawks and the Senecas. The Mohegans and the Delawares were two Algonquin (al-GOHN-kwin) tribes, or tribes that spoke Algonquian.

The area has four seasons, including cold winters and hot summers. Lots of rain helps fill streams and rivers. In the 1400s, birch, oak, and maple trees grew in woodland forests. These were home to animals such as turkey, deer, and beaver.

The Algonquins used the region's forests to build their homes, called wigwams. Winter wigwams were larger than summer wigwams. They were used for years. For a summer wigwam, the men bent small trees into a dome-shaped frame and tied them together. Then women covered this frame with birch bark or mats made from plants.

The Algonquins used animal skins, such as deer hides, for clothing. Algonquian tribes also wore capes made of wild turkey feathers that kept them warm and dry. They made these by sewing together overlapping feathers.

The Algonquins made fast, light canoes from several types of trees. They first built a cedar frame. Then they covered it with birch tree bark. They sewed the bark together with spruce roots. They used maple wood to hold the boat's sides together. A man could carry this kind of canoe from one stream to another.

In the Eastern Woodlands, dense forests of birch, oak, and maple trees protected deer, beaver, and other wildlife.

Razor-sharp saw grass and palmetto trees grew in the Everglades swamplands of the Southeast.

3.8 American Indians of the Southeast

The Southeast cultural region reached south from the Ohio Valley to the Gulf of Mexico. It ran east from Texas to the Atlantic Ocean. This territory includes river valleys, mountains, coastal plains, and swamps. In both dry and wet areas, weather is usually hot. Many tribes, such as the Creeks and the Choctaws, lived in the Southeast cultural region. In the 1700s, the Seminoles (SEH-meh-nols) came to live in the Everglades swamplands of southern Florida.

These swamps are very hot and steamy. Shallow streams crisscross the land. Tall, razor-sharp saw grass rises from the waters. Giant ferns, cypress, and palmetto trees grow in the humid jungle. Deer roam the forests. Fish, alligators, and snakes lurk in the swampy waters.

Several American Indian groups, mostly Creeks, lived in what are now Georgia and Alabama. Members of these tribes moved south into Florida in the 1700s. This area was under Spanish rule. Over time, people from other tribes arrived. This group became the Seminoles. In the 1800s, escaped slaves from the United States also joined this tribe.

The Seminoles had a culture suited to swamplands. They built their homes, called chickees, on wooden platforms three feet above the ground. This protected the houses from the swampy ground. Wooden posts supported a slanted roof made of palm tree leaves. To allow breezes to blow through, the chickee had no walls. This was a good design for the hot climate.

The swamp environment sometimes forced Seminoles to wear clothing that was unusual for a warm climate. For example, to protect their legs from sharp saw grass and mosquitoes, Seminoles wore leggings. They made the leggings out of deer hides.

To move along the shallow streams, the Seminoles made flat-bottomed dugout canoes. They built each canoe from a tree log. They hollowed it out with stone and bone scrapers.

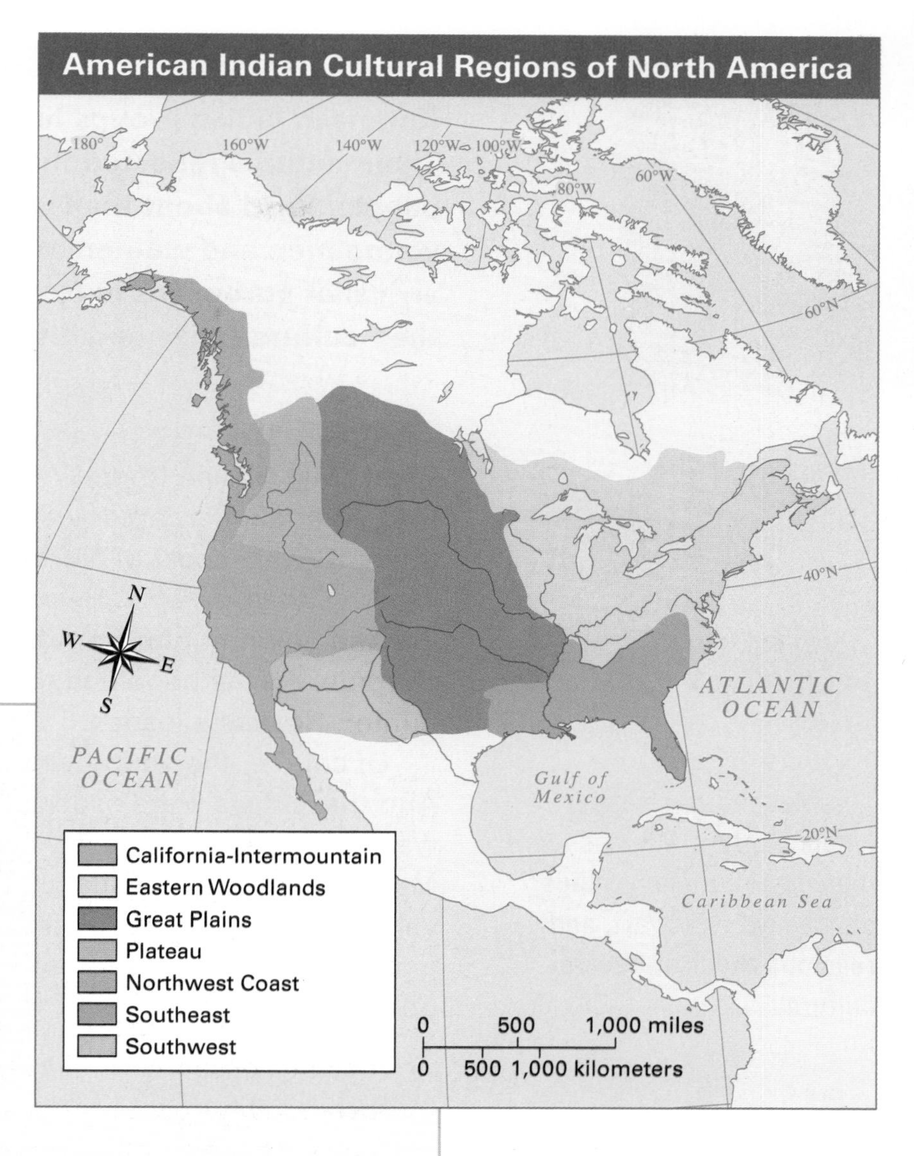

Summary

In this chapter, you read about how many American Indians lived. You used a map to find the seven American Indian cultural regions. You learned how the environment of each region affected the cultures that developed there.

American Indians in each area used nearby natural resources. With these, they made their homes, clothing, tools, and art. In the forested Northwest, the Kwakiutls built wooden homes. In the dry Southwest, the Hopis made homes of clay.

Each group adapted to its environment. In the cold Plateau winters, the Yakimas built their homes partly underground. In the hot and humid Southeast, the Seminoles built houses without walls.

You will now meet four young American Indians. Each one lives in a different cultural region. And each one belongs to a tribe with its own way of life. Find out how these young people spend their time.

Reading Further 3

Four Young American Indians

American Indian groups had different ways of living. Their cultures reflected the land and the history of their people. Read about the lives and thoughts of these four young men and women of the late 1400s, before the arrival of Europeans in North America. In what ways were their cultures alike and different?

The Makahs

The young Makah (mah-KAH) girl was fortunate. She knew that. After all, her father was a headman in her village on the northwest coast of North America. This meant he was wealthy and powerful. He was a whale hunter. This job was handed down to him from his father. It required skill and courage. All the people in the village looked up to the whale hunter. He was a leader.

Of course, the young woman had her own work to do. And these days were especially busy. For soon, her father was hosting a potlatch. This was a special ceremony for the Makah people. At a potlatch, the host gave many of his most valuable possessions to others. The upcoming potlatch was a chance for the girl's father to demonstrate his wealth and power in the village.

The Makahs were expert whale hunters. Whales were the subject of many songs, dances, works of art, and religious rituals in Makah culture.

New Bedford Whaling Museum, New Bedford, Massachusetts

The girl's family had been preparing for the potlatch for many months. After all, they had to collect fancy gifts for each guest. Such gifts might include baskets, woven blankets, or decorated pieces of copper. The Makahs made a variety of useful and beautiful things from the parts of whales and other animals they caught.

Another Makah talent was wood carving. They made their whale-hunting canoes by hollowing out long trees. They also made totem poles and other carvings. Some potlatch guests might receive a skillfully carved object as a gift.

The Makahs made beautiful carvings. The carvings often told a story from Makah folklore. These stories were passed down within families.

There was more to a potlatch than giving gifts. The event also featured a great feast. Most of the food for the potlatch had already been prepared. And there was a lot of food. The girl's Makah village was located between a river and an ocean in the area that we now call the Northwest Coast. There were always plenty of good things to eat. The men hunted not only for whales but also for seals. They caught fish. Sometimes, they hunted in the woods for deer and bear.

The Makah women also gathered food. This morning, for example, the girl was going out with some other women to collect shellfish and good plants to eat.

They had to work quickly. For later, the seal hunters were supposed to return from a hunting trip. Then the girl would help the other women cut up the men's catch and bring it back to the village. This would take a long time and would also make quite a mess. The Makahs did not let anything go to waste. All parts of the seal were used for meat, tools, and clothing. For example, the Makahs made inflatable floats out of seal skins. They used these floats during the whale hunt.

"Well," the girl said to herself with a sigh, "I had better start my chores. Today will be a long day."

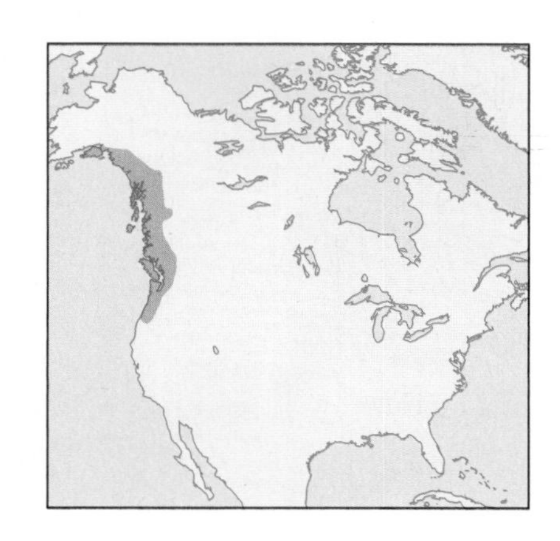

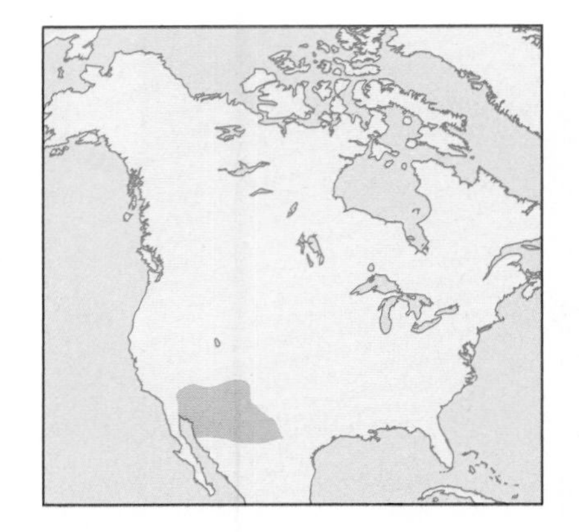

The Taos

The Taos boy was excited. After months of training, he was ready. Soon, he would be made a full member of his people's religion. His father had told him this important step usually took place as a boy neared age 10. He would reach this age next month.

The Taos lived in a mountainous area of what is today New Mexico. They practiced their religion in special meeting rooms called kivas. These were built near the multi-level pueblos in which the people lived. The Taos gathered in a kiva to take part in secret religious ceremonies.

To become a full member of the Taos religion was a great honor. Only members could hope to sit on the council that governed the tribe. But this honor was given only to boys. And not every boy was chosen.

The boy was impatient to begin the upcoming ceremony. This would take place at a sacred lake high in the mountains. The Taos believed that their people were created from these waters. So, it was forbidden to take fish from this lake.

However, the men could fish in other waters near the Taos pueblo. Fish, such as trout, were part of the Taos diet. The men hunted wild animals and the women gathered food. This was a major activity. The Taos also farmed. But unlike many other American Indian people of the Southwest, they did not grow cotton near their pueblo. And they did not keep sheep. They relied on neighboring groups in the Southwest to provide them with woven blankets of cotton and wool.

The Taos were skilled at making leather from animal hides. They used the leather to make clothing, drums, and other items. They also kept birds, including eagles. Feathers from these and other birds were highly prized.

Hunting, farming, or making leather would likely be this boy's job when he got older. For now, though, all he could think of was the upcoming religious ceremony. Then he would take his place as an adult—and, perhaps, a future leader of his people.

The Taos lived in multi-level pueblos like these. They used ladders to get from one level to the other.

The Iowas

This Iowa man has traditional ornaments and tattoos.

Finally, it was warm again. The young Iowa woman loved this time of year best.

She had spent the long winter traveling over the plains that stretched thousands of miles across the middle part of North America. In the cold weather, plants did not grow. So her people followed the roaming buffalo herds. The Iowas relied on the buffalo for food and other necessary materials. Buffalo provided leather for clothing, bones and horns for tools, and hair for ropes.

But now the season for planting had begun. The Iowa woman had returned to her people's camp near a river in what is today the state of Iowa. For a few months, she and her family would put away their tepees. These were the portable homes they used when they followed the buffalo. Here, in camp, the Iowas lived in large dome-shaped lodges. These would be their homes until the fall. Then they would break camp once again.

Life in the camp brought a welcome change. For one thing, the women had different jobs. In the winter, they spent much of their time breaking or setting up camp. In the growing season, they worked at planting and tending crops.

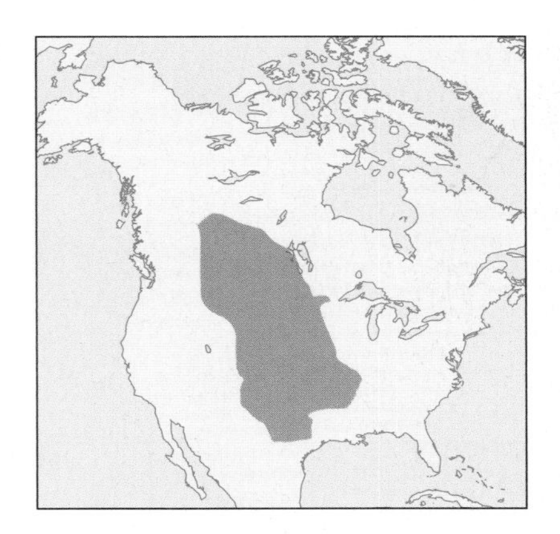

Also, camp life meant more friends and neighbors. All the Iowa families gathered in camp during the warm months. The men formed large hunting parties. It took many men working together to safely hunt the huge herds of buffalo that gathered in the warm weather. When the weather turned cool, the herds scattered. It was then that the tribe separated into smaller groups. These groups headed in different directions, following the animals.

The Iowa women also had to work as a team in camp. The big hunts meant large numbers of buffalo to butcher and process. Women performed this task.

Camp life was not perfect. This year, the Iowas had a new tribal leader. The most powerful men among the Iowas took turns filling this role. The young woman had heard some grumbling about their new leader.

For now, though, she did not care. She was happy to be back in camp. She was looking forward to the summer.

The Senecas, like other Iroquois tribes, lived in longhouses. Each house could hold several families. They built these homes out of small trees. Then they covered the houses with bark. The Iroquois called themselves "people of the longhouse."

The Senecas

These were anxious but exciting days for the young Seneca man of the Eastern Woodlands. He and the rest of his people lived in what is today New York state. He was the son of a great and beloved man among his people. His father's acts of strength and courage had won him fame as a warrior. These achievements had earned his father the title of war chief in his village. He had brought great honor to his family.

But now it was time for the young man to build his own reputation. He had heard that the Senecas might soon be going to war. Like other Seneca boys, he had been training for this moment since he was very young. He had learned how to use a war club and a bow and arrow. He knew how to behave on the battlefield. He had survived months of living nearly alone in the forest—part of his training to become a man. This war could be the chance that he had been preparing for.

The young man understood what was at stake. His father's position as war chief would not be automatically passed down to him. He would have to earn it. The Senecas did have chiefs who inherited their power. These men were called sachems. But they inherited their positions from their mothers. His mother had not passed such power on to him.

Indeed, the Seneca women held great power. They named the sachems. They ruled village life. It was the women who grew the crops that helped feed the village of several hundred people.

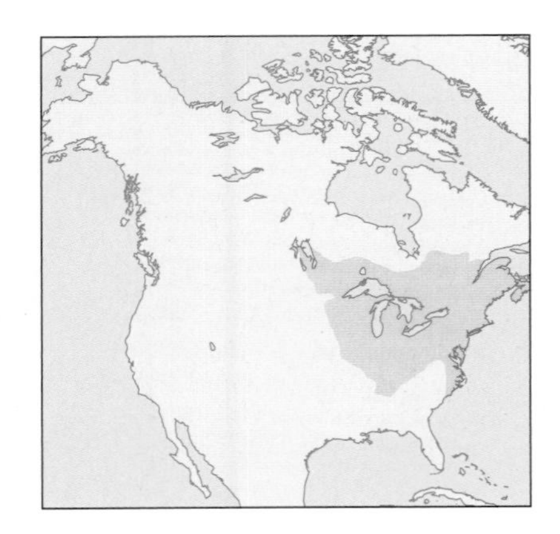

The Seneca men ruled in other ways. They were expert hunters. They spent many months of the year away from the village on hunting trips. And Seneca men were fierce warriors. They took pride in their fighting skills. People throughout the Eastern Woodlands feared them.

In the recent past, the Senecas had often fought with their neighbors. There had been terrible bloodshed, and many had died. Then, five of the tribes had gathered to end the wars. In addition to the Senecas, these tribes were the Mohawks, the Cayugas (KAY-yoo-guhs), the Onandagas, and the Oneidas. Together, they formed a **government** called the League of the Iroquois. An Iroquois legend tells of the forming of this great league by two men named Hiawatha and Dekanahwida.

government the organization that makes the laws in a country, state, or community and has the power to enforce them

The Iroquois were proud of their government. Each tribe had representatives at the great council and its own special role. All the members of the league had to agree on major decisions. And, best of all, members agreed not to fight among themselves. For this reason, the people called the league the Great Peace. They also called it the Long House. This referred to the type of large houses in which families live together.

But today, peace was not on the mind of the young Seneca man. Today, he was thinking of glory on the battlefield. He was thinking of the chance to gain power and honor among his people.

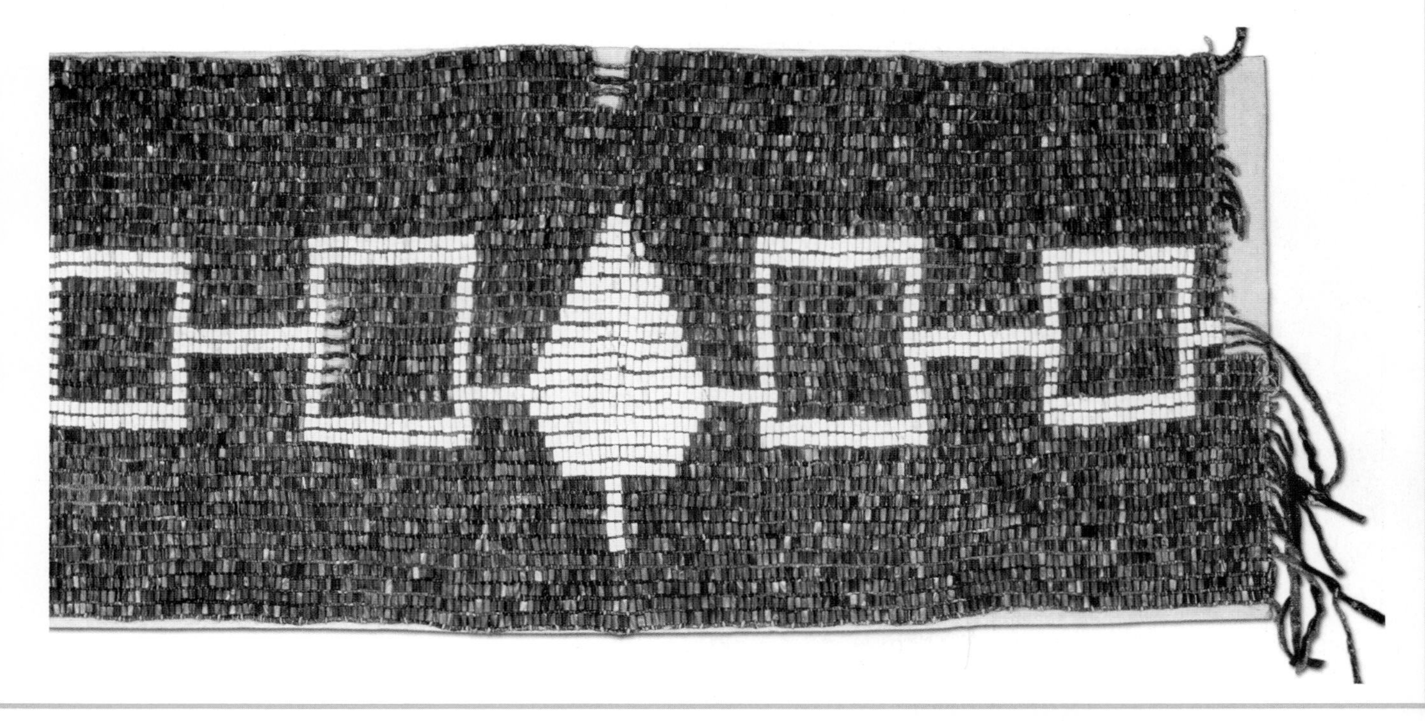

The Iroquois wove designs into wampum belts as public records. They made the belts with beads of polished shells called wampum. This belt design represents the five tribes of the League of the Iroquois.

Underwater archaeologists investigate the remains of a 17th-century ship.

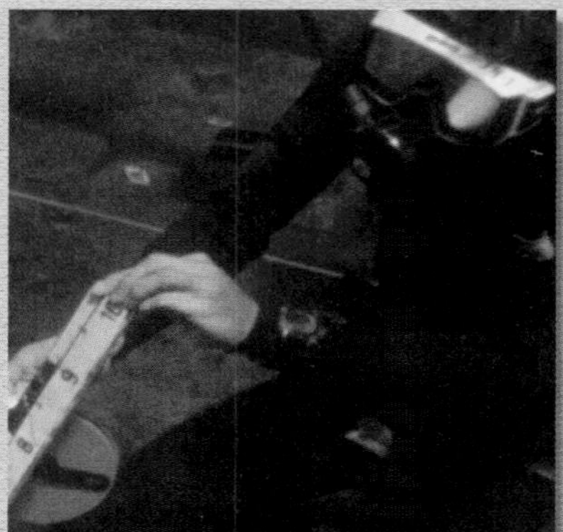

Why do you think divers might use measurements?

What do you think these tools help divers to do?

What might this diver be writing?

How and Why Europeans Came to the New World

4

What did explorers take to and from the New World during the Age of Exploration?

4.1 Introduction

In Chapter 3, you read about American Indian cultural regions. In this chapter, you will learn how and why Europeans set out for the lands across the Atlantic, which they called the **New World**. Of course, to American Indians this was not a new world. Their tribes had lived here for thousands of years.

The European **Age of Exploration** began in the late 1400s. The earliest **explorers** did not set out to find new continents. They sailed unknown seas, looking for routes to Asia. Europeans wanted spices and silks from Asia. Merchants from Italy and the eastern Mediterranean controlled this trade. To share in this business, other countries sought their own trade routes. Thus, the Age of Exploration was born.

Few people in the 1400s had traveled far from Europe. Then, in 1492, Christopher Columbus sailed to North America. Other explorers followed. They used special navigation tools to help them cross the ocean. They brought back things of value.

Sometimes, ships were lost at sea. Today, scientists search for these sunken ships. They study artifacts that remain at the wrecks. These objects tell us about the explorers' expeditions.

As you read this chapter, picture yourself as a diver examining a sunken ship like this one. What objects might you find? What clues would these objects give you about how and why Europeans came to North America?

Examining a Sunken Ship

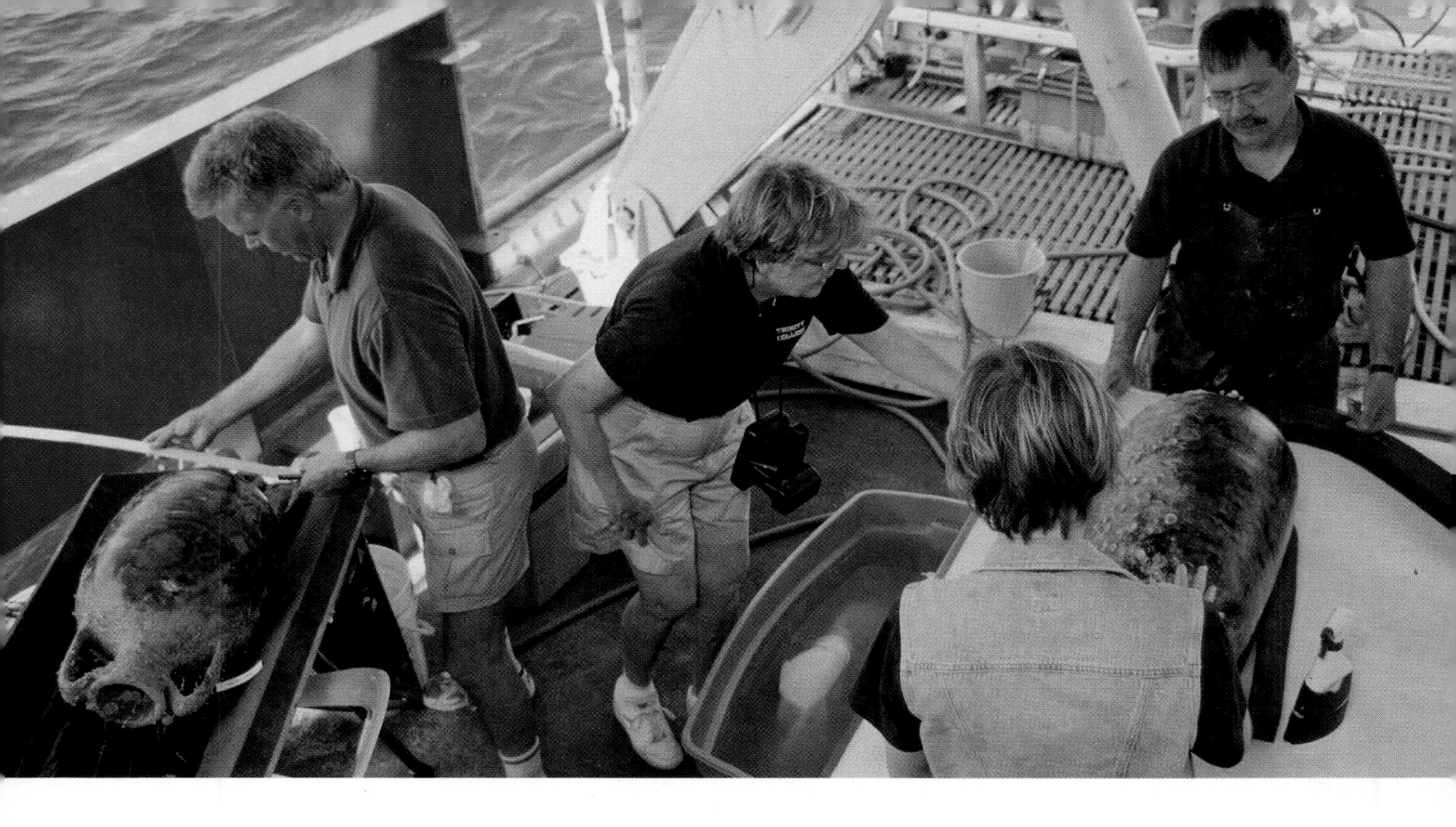

This is a team of scientists called archaeologists. They record and measure pottery that divers have brought to the surface.

4.2 Underwater Archaeology

Underwater **archaeologists** study sunken ships. Some study the ships that explorers used to come to the Americas. How do these scientists find a sunken ship? They look at old ship records kept by European merchants. They read tales told by shipwreck survivors. They use new machines and methods to locate a ship's anchors or cannons. For example, sonar uses sound waves to detect sunken objects.

archaeologist a scientist who studies artifacts to learn about past cultures

Archaeologists want to know the position of each artifact found on the ship. Divers use cables to mark off the site in squares. The divers use this grid to note exact location. This helps archaeologists learn who used the objects and how.

Divers photograph and tag each artifact. Then they bring it out of the water. Next, someone records and measures it. Finally, the artifact goes to a laboratory where it is studied. Everyone takes care in handling the artifacts. Metal artifacts are usually the most intact. Objects made of plant or animal products are more fragile. After studying hundreds of artifacts, archaeologists may learn the name of the ship, where it was going, and why. They might also figure out who was on board.

It can take years to find a sunken ship. Bringing up the remains can take weeks. Understanding what the objects mean is another long process. Read on to learn how artifacts give clues about how and why Europeans sailed to the New World.

4.3 Ocean Crossing

When sailors cross the ocean, they need a way to stay on course. They have no landmarks to guide them in the open sea. Explorers in the late 1400s and in the 1500s used astrolabes to find their position.

An **astrolabe** is a circular piece of metal with marks around its edges. A bar attached to it can be rotated about the center as a pointer. A sailor would hold the astrolabe by a loop at the top. He would then tilt the bar so it lined up against the sun, the North Star, or another known star. He would measure the latitude of his ship by measuring the angle of the star above the horizon (where Earth and sky meet). The angle would tell him how far north or south the ship was from the equator. Astrolabes enabled explorers to sail accurately by day or night.

astrolabe an early scientific tool used to observe and calculate the position of the sun and other stars

4.4 Directions

European explorers used another tool for figuring out direction—a compass. We still use this tool today. The compass has a magnetic needle balanced on a small metal post. The needle is allowed to spin freely. The needle's point is attracted by the powerful magnetic field that lines up close to the North Pole. So the compass needle always points north.

If a ship's navigator knew which direction was north, he could find the other directions. South is the opposite of north. When facing north, east is to the right and west is to the left. A compass did not tell the navigator where he was. But it did show which direction the ship was heading, even when it sailed through fog or in total darkness.

The compass (left) and the astrolabe (right) were used in the 1500s. These tools helped explorers sail across the Atlantic Ocean to the New World.

This world map is a mural that was painted in 1574. It covers an entire wall of an Italian palace. Can you find North America? South America?

4.5 Maps

Maps are drawings of the shapes of bodies of land and water. They also show where key physical features are. Maps use a scale, which shows how the distance on the map relates to the actual distance on Earth. Ocean maps show such features as rocky shores and safe ports. Navigational charts are maps that show where winds blow and ocean currents flow. European explorers carried these maps and maps of the places to which they journeyed.

Mapmakers in Europe got new information from sailors, explorers, and scientists. They added these details to their maps. In the 1400s, mapmakers knew that the world was round. But before Columbus sailed, they didn't know about the New World. No one realized how wide the Atlantic Ocean was. For centuries after Columbus's trip, maps of **the Americas** still had many blank spots. They showed places that remained unknown. Often, maps also had drawings of imaginary sea monsters, such as undersea dragons.

the Americas the land masses of North America, Central America, and South America

4.6 Claimed Lands

During the Age of Exploration, rulers wanted to spread their power to the New World. Sometimes they paid for the explorers' ships and crews. These explorers carried flags or banners to honor their kings and queens. Spanish ships often flew a flag that showed a cross. Their flags also had the letter "F" for King Ferdinand and a "Y" for Queen Ysabel ("Isabella" in English). Once explorers reached a new land, they planted a flag to claim, or take, that land for their country.

Flags have always been symbols of the power of countries and their rulers. And more power was what King Ferdinand and Queen Isabella wanted. Gaining more land and natural resources would strengthen their kingdom of Spain.

4.7 Religious Beliefs

Christianity began in the Middle East. It reached Europe almost 2,000 years ago. This was in the time of the Roman Empire. Later, Europeans spread this religion to other parts of the world.

Christians in Europe belonged either to the Roman Catholic Church or to Protestant churches. Many believed that all people should share their beliefs. Catholic rulers sent priests and armies to other lands. Part of their mission was to convert people to the Catholic Church.

In the 1500s, explorers from Europe were Christians. Many carried a Bible with them. The Bible contains the stories and teachings of the Christian faith. It has two parts. The Old Testament contains writings from the Jewish religion. The New Testament contains writings by the followers of Jesus Christ.

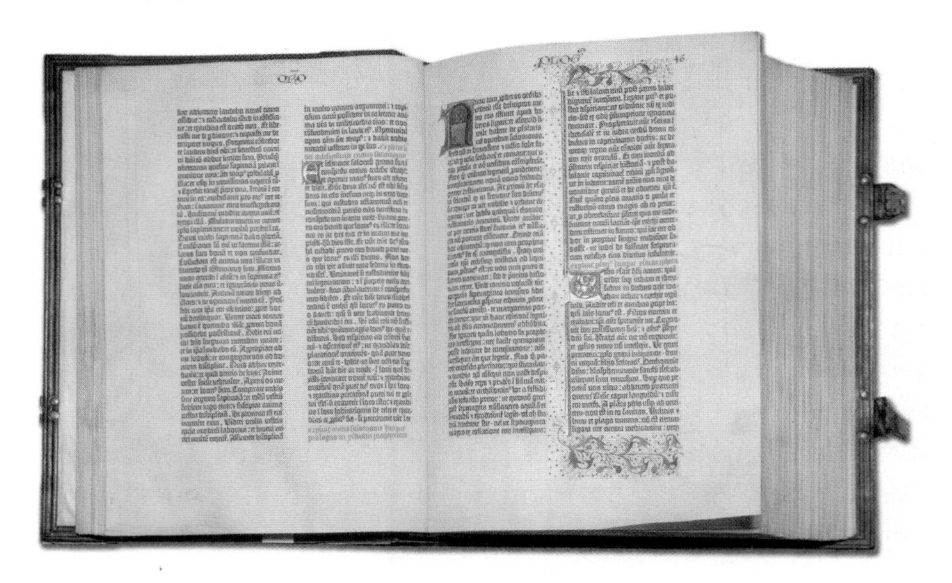

European explorers brought along Bibles. This one was written in Latin and published in 1455.

4.8 Wealth

Europeans counted wealth in gold and silver. They made their most valuable coins from these metals. In the late 1400s, Spain had just fought a costly war. So its king and queen wanted to build up their country's supply of gold and silver. They hoped that the explorers they sent to the New World would bring back these precious metals.

In Mexico and South America, the Spanish found gold and silver. They forced American Indians to work in mines as slaves. The Spanish turned the gold and silver ore from the mines into bars, coins, and other valuable objects. Ships carried these riches back to Spain.

4.9 New Foods

However, some of the most valuable things explorers found and brought back were new foods. These are natural products, not artifacts. Historical records tell us about them. For example, all over the New World, American Indians grew different types of corn. They roasted, boiled, and popped the corn. They ground it into flour. The explorers liked this new food. It was as healthful and had as many uses as wheat, but its seeds were bigger and tastier.

New foods from the Americas changed what people ate around the world. Some vegetables that came from the Americas include potatoes, sweet potatoes, beans, and squash. Fruits such as tomatoes and pineapple were first grown by American Indians, too. As these foods spread, people began to eat a more healthful diet. Populations grew in many places. Do you like chocolate? American Indians were the first to grow cacao, from which chocolate is made. They used it in drinks and in medicines.

American Indians introduced European explorers to corn (below) and to beans in cacao pods (below right).

4.10 Cash Crops

Explorers saw a tall, leafy plant called tobacco. It grew throughout the Americas. American Indians dried the leaves. Some people smoked them in pipes or in cigars. Others chewed tobacco or inhaled it as a powder, which Europeans called snuff. In most tribes, men were addicted to tobacco. They thought it was good for their health. Tobacco was a part of religious and peacemaking ceremonies. Few women used tobacco.

Explorers took tobacco back to Europe. Some thought it was a medicine. Many Europeans became addicted to it. Soon, tobacco was in great demand. It grew well in the New World. American colonists planted large fields of tobacco. They sold the crop to Europeans. Tobacco became a valuable **cash crop**. The money colonists earned from tobacco sales helped them buy goods from Europe.

Tobacco is a New World crop that Europeans soon became addicted to.

cash crop a crop that is grown in large quantities for sale

Summary

In this chapter, you read about artifacts that might have been found on ships that sank during the Age of Exploration. These objects give us clues about how and why Europeans came to the New World.

You learned about navigation tools of that time. These tools helped explorers sail across the Atlantic Ocean. You also found out why some explorers set out for the New World. They wanted to spread Christianity. They also hoped to gain new lands and wealth for their countries.

Finally, you read about the valuable cargo of New World plants that explorers brought back to Europe. People in Europe soon began to eat new foods, such as corn and potatoes. As tobacco became popular, the colonists grew it as a cash crop that they sold to Europeans.

In the next pages, you will read more about why European nations became interested in the Americas.

Reading Further 4

Changes in Europe Spur Exploration

The late 1400s and the early 1500s brought great changes to Europe. One old religious conflict ended. Then a new one began. How did Europe's conflicts help spur the Age of Exploration?

Walking up the hill, King Ferdinand and Queen Isabella smiled. Before them stood the magnificent palaces of Granada. This elegant city had been a stronghold of Muslim Spain for centuries. Christians had tried to regain control of the land many times. At last, in 1492, Ferdinand and Isabella succeeded. Their armies had defeated the Muslims and retaken Spain. Now the city was theirs. Happily, they accepted the keys to their new home. Boabdil, the Muslim ruler of the city, gave them over with a sigh.

Muslims are people who follow the religion of Islam. The Muslim world began in Southwest Asia. But it quickly spread. In the 700s, the Muslims crossed the Mediterranean Sea. They gained control of the land we now call Spain.

This painting shows King Ferdinand and Queen Isabella accepting control of Granada from the leader of the Muslims in 1492.

The Muslims built a great center of culture and learning in Spain. Much of the rest of Europe, however, followed the Christian religion. Many European Christians were troubled by the Muslim presence. They did not want to allow the practice of other religions in the region. Groups of Christians fought to drive the Muslims out of Spain off and on for centuries.

But finally, Isabella and Ferdinand had completed the reconquest of Spain. All the lands of Spain were now under Christian rule.

The Queen Meets Columbus

Not long after taking control, Queen Isabella met a newcomer to her land. He came from Genoa, Italy. His name was Christopher Columbus and he needed her help.

Columbus wanted to sail ships west across the Atlantic Ocean in search of a new trade route to Asia. This would help Spain expand its trade in spices and other goods from China and the islands of the East. Columbus also hoped to find and bring back gold and silver. Both the route and the riches could make Spain more powerful.

But exploration by sea was still a new idea in 1492. Sailors from the country of Portugal had sailed as far as the coast of Africa. Nobody really knew what lay beyond the Atlantic Ocean.

Columbus showed his plans to Queen Isabella and King Ferdinand. The queen gave Columbus ships and funds for his journey. She wanted to spread the Catholic religion and to gain wealth for Spain.

Many people in Spain did not take Columbus's ideas seriously. Queen Isabella rejected his plans twice. But the reconquest of Spain had inspired her. She now ruled over a unified, Christian Spain—a great and powerful **nation-state**. Her victory over the Muslims filled her with deep religious feeling. She was determined to continue to spread her Catholic faith beyond Spain. This was one reason that Columbus's ideas finally caught her attention.

nation-state an independent country whose people mostly share a common identity

Queen Isabella met with Columbus. She finally decided that Columbus's voyage could mean new wealth and a chance to spread Spain's rule and religion to other lands.

Queen Isabella agreed to support Columbus. She and her husband gave him ships and money. Now, Columbus could make the journey to search out new places to claim for Spain. He would seek to bring more people to God—and more power and wealth to Spain. A new age of discovery had begun.

Religious Wars in Europe

Twenty-five years had passed since Christopher Columbus set sail. A man named Martin Luther stood before a Catholic church. In his hands was a document. It included 95 reasons why he questioned the authority of the Catholic Church. Some say that Luther nailed his questions to the church door. Europe—and the world—would never be the same.

In 1517, there was only one type of Christian religion in Europe—the Catholic Church. Luther's questions challenged this Church.

Luther hoped to improve, or reform, the Church. For this reason, he is known as the founder of a movement called the Reformation. Luther's actions started a great conflict. Catholic Church leaders rejected his complaints. But many people agreed with Luther. Some of them left the Catholic Church. They formed new churches and became known as Protestants. The term *Protestant* comes from the word *protest*.

The Reformation divided Europe. At that time, people did not easily accept religious differences. Catholic leaders launched a movement called the Counter Reformation. The word *counter* means "against." Kings and queens waged war with one another over religion. Many people were forced to follow their rulers' beliefs. Europe in the 1500s became a bloody battleground. Thousands died in religious wars.

Wars spread across Europe in the 1500s. Protestants and Catholics fought each other.

The launching of the Spanish Armada showed how powerful Spain had become. But England's navy defeated Spain's ships.

Conflict Between England and Spain

Tensions between England and Spain had been high for many years. One major reason was religion. In the 1530s, England's King Henry VIII had broken with the Catholic Church. As a Protestant country, England found that it had new enemies. Among them were Spain's Catholic rulers, who were deeply religious.

Queen Elizabeth I came to power in England in 1558. She spent much of her reign in disputes with Spain. For a time, Queen Elizabeth helped pirates who preyed on Spanish ships in the English Channel. She also assisted Protestants who fought against Spanish rule. Meanwhile, the Spanish king supported plots against Queen Elizabeth.

The conflict reached a peak in 1588. Spain had assembled a huge fleet of warships. This Spanish Armada was one of the most powerful forces ever gathered. Its 130 ships carried 30 thousand sailors and bristled with guns. When it set sail for England, the future looked dark for Queen Elizabeth and her country. But the English navy fought fiercely against the Spanish. In one of history's greatest naval battles, the English navy defeated the Spanish Armada.

However, Spain's power remained a threat. England had been slower than many other European nations to explore overseas. Queen Elizabeth now chose a new course. England, too, would seek wealth and power across the ocean. The conflicts and rivalries among the nations of Europe would spread to the Americas. These struggles would spur exploration and settlement.

This medal has an anti-Catholic message. It was worn by Dutch pirates who attacked Spanish ships. Queen Elizabeth supported these pirates.

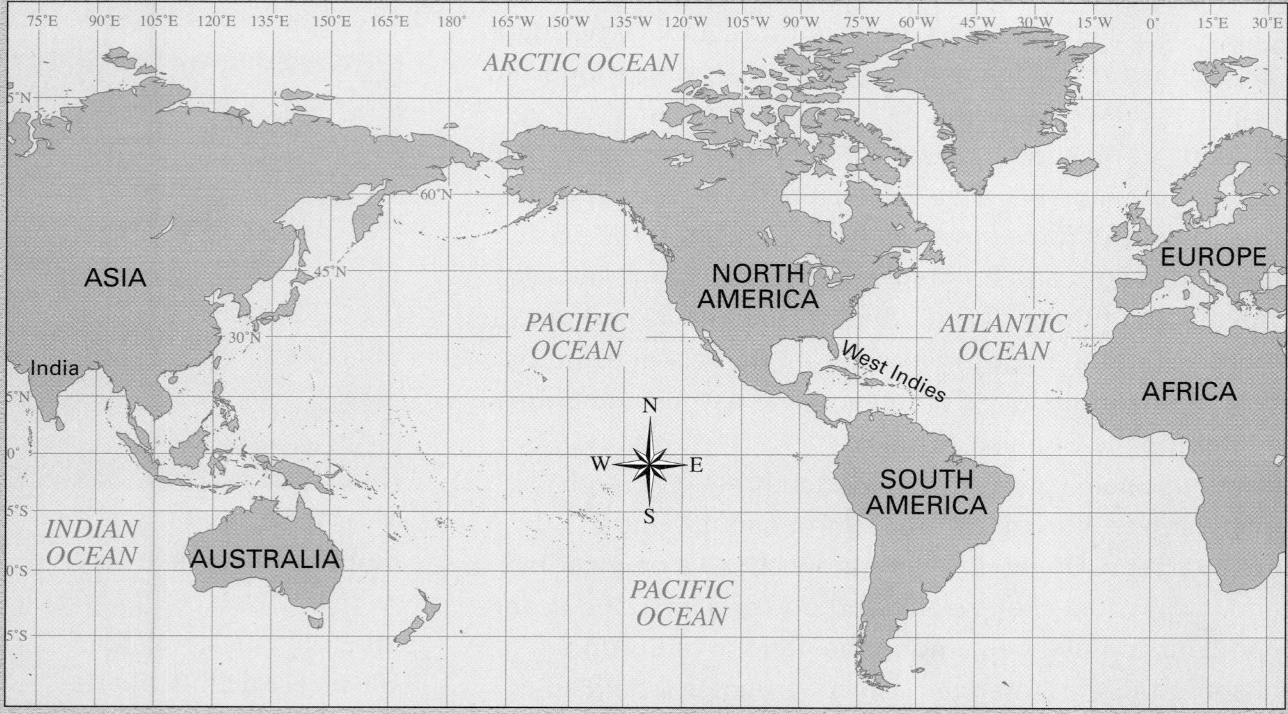

The top map shows the world as people thought it was in 1540. The bottom map shows the world as we know it today. Find three details of the 1540 map that are not accurate.

Routes of Exploration to the New World

5

How did exploration of the Americas lead to settlement?

5.1 Introduction

In Chapter 4, you read about why some Europeans sailed to the Americas. In this chapter, you will learn why eight explorers came to the New World. How did they affect the native peoples there?

In 1492, Christopher Columbus landed on a Caribbean island. He claimed it for Spain. More **conquistadors** (kahn-KEES-tah-dors), or Spanish explorers, followed. They planted Spain's flag on other lands in the Americas.

Explorers from England, France, and Holland came, too. Some looked for a **Northwest Passage,** a faster sea route from Europe to Asia through North America. They never found it. But they did claim North American land for the countries that sent them.

Were these explorers great men? Certainly, they accomplished much. They found new trade routes and helped mapmakers draw better world maps. They opened the way for settlers.

But they also caused harm. They fought with American Indians who opposed them. They enslaved whole tribes and forced them to work in mines and on farms. The Europeans also carried **contagious diseases**. These are sicknesses that spread quickly among people. American Indians had not been exposed to these illnesses before. Many became sick and died.

Look at the matrix on this page. A matrix is a chart with rows and columns. As you read this chapter, you can use a matrix like this one to organize and compare information about the explorers.

Comparing New World Explorers

	Christopher Columbus	John Cabot	Juan Ponce de León	Hernán Cortés
Personal Background				
Sponsor				
Motives				
Dates				
Route of Exploration				
Impact				

5.2 Christopher Columbus

East Indies Southeast Asia, including India, Indonesia, and Malaysia

Christopher Columbus was born in 1451 in Genoa, a busy seaport on the coast of Italy. As a child, he read about the travels of Marco Polo. In the late 1200s, Polo had journeyed to Asia by land and sea. He brought back stories of the riches and customs of China and the **East Indies**. Columbus wanted to see these faraway lands.

When Columbus was about 14, he became a sailor. He traveled south along the coast of Africa and north to Ireland. He may have gone to Iceland. Viking sailors from Norway had already explored Greenland and the eastern Canadian shores. But Columbus and others did not know about these voyages.

Nations in Europe wanted to find better trade routes to obtain the spices and silks of Asia. The Portuguese tried to reach Asia by sailing around the southern tip of Africa. However, in the 1400s, people knew less about the geography of the world than is known today. Columbus believed that Earth was much smaller than it is and that it had only one ocean. He thought he could reach Asia faster by sailing west across the Atlantic.

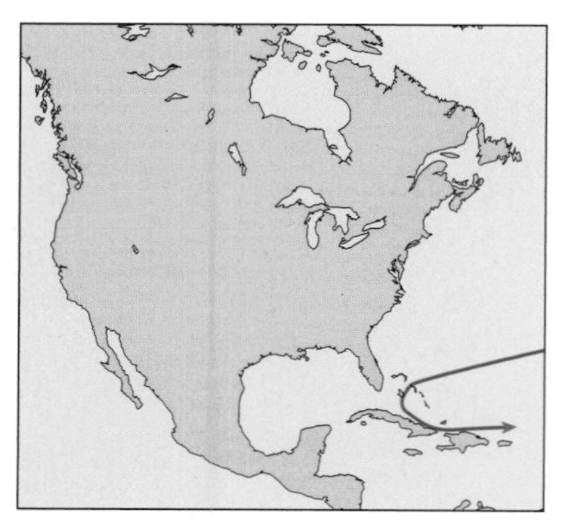

This is the route of Columbus's first voyage in the Caribbean.

Columbus asked the king of Portugal to pay for his trip. The king turned him down. His advisers thought that the route around Africa was shorter. Finally, after almost 13 years, Columbus convinced Queen Isabella and King Ferdinand of Spain to help him. They gave him three small ships and about 90 men. Columbus promised to return with riches for Spain.

On August 3, 1492, Columbus left Spain with his three ships—the *Niña,* the *Pinta,* and the *Santa Maria.* They sailed southwest past the Canary Islands and then west across the Atlantic Ocean. Early on October 12, a sailor saw an island with white beaches and dense green forests.

Columbus named the island San Salvador, which means "Holy Savior" in Spanish. He claimed it for Spain. Friendly people greeted him. These people had lived in the Americas for thousands of years. Columbus called them Indians, because he thought that he had reached the East Indies. Some of them guided him to the island of Cuba. There, he found people wearing gold ornaments and pearls, similar to those worn by the people of San Salvador.

For three months, Columbus searched for gold and spices. In 1493, he sailed back to Spain, with a few gold ornaments and American Indian captives. The queen and king agreed to pay for more voyages. Columbus promised to bring them "as much gold as they need . . . and as many slaves as they ask."

The Granger Collection, New York

Columbus made three more trips. He explored more islands near Cuba and the coasts of Central and South America. But he found little gold. When he died in 1506, he still did not know that he had reached the New World.

However, his trips opened up a trade route that changed the history of the world. Later, Spanish explorers did find gold. They also found the perfect climate for growing crops such as sugarcane. To get enough crops and minerals to trade with Europe, early Spanish settlers forced American Indians to work in fields and mines.

Soon, Europeans had **colonies** in the New World. Trade between Europe and the New World grew. Animals and crops from one side of the Atlantic were introduced to the other side. Sailors also brought ideas from one land to another. Even diseases crossed the ocean. Today, we call this flow of goods and ideas between the Americas and Europe the Columbian Exchange, in honor of Columbus—the man who started it all.

Early on the morning of October 12, 1492, Christopher Columbus landed on an island in the Caribbean Sea. He thought he was in Asia.

colony a settlement ruled by another country, not by its own people

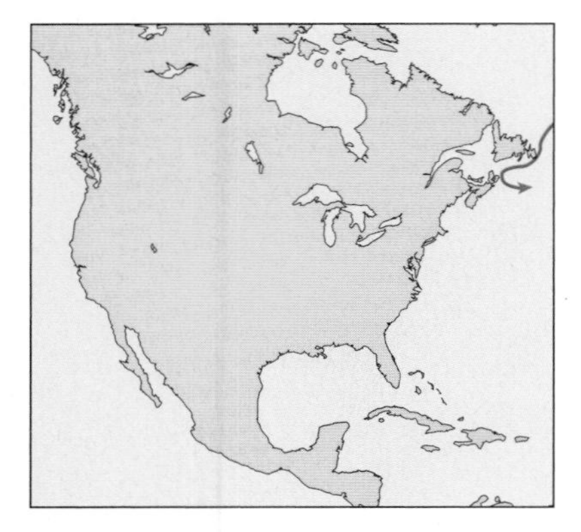

John Cabot traveled along this route during his first voyage in 1497.

5.3 John Cabot

The opportunity for new trade interested many explorers in addition to Columbus. Giovanni Caboto, later called John Cabot, was a young merchant, or shopkeeper, in Venice, Italy. He was also a skilled navigator who wanted to explore the world. He had seen the spices and silks that traders brought from Asia. He wanted to take part in this trade. Like Columbus, he thought the best way to get to Asia was to sail west.

In 1496, some merchants in England agreed to pay for his voyage. King Henry VII gave Cabot permission to explore any "unknown land." Cabot set out to find a faster and safer route to the East Indies. He left Bristol, England, in May 1497. He had only one small ship and 17 men. They traveled around the coast of Ireland and then west across the Atlantic. They sailed north of Columbus's route to avoid land claimed by Spain.

On June 24, Cabot reached the eastern coast of present-day Canada. He claimed the land for England. He saw thick green forests and plenty of fish but no rich Asian cities. Cabot sailed back to England. He told the king that he had reached Asia and would soon find its wealth.

The following year, Cabot sailed back to North America. On this try, he may have explored as far south as Chesapeake Bay, near present-day Maryland. Historians do not know what happened to Cabot; some say he was killed in a shipwreck, others that he returned to England and died soon after arriving.

Like Columbus, Cabot never knew that he had reached a continent unknown to Europeans. But his voyage opened the way for English settlers to North America.

John Cabot stands on his ship's deck as he leaves what is now Labrador, Canada.

5.4 Juan Ponce de León

When Columbus made a second voyage to the Americas in 1493, a young soldier named Juan Ponce de León (wahn pahnss duh lee-OHN) went with him. Once Ponce de León arrived in the New World, he settled on a Caribbean island named Hispaniola (today divided into the countries of Haiti and the Dominican Republic). There he became a military commander under the governor.

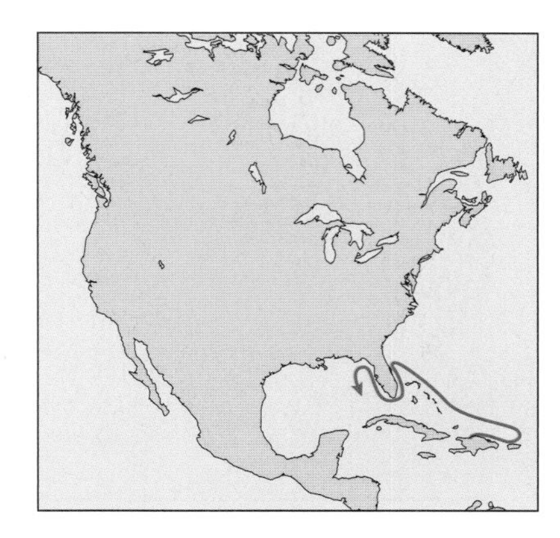

Juan Ponce de León explored along this route.

In 1506, Ponce de León explored an island named Borinquen (soon to be renamed Puerto Rico). There he heard many stories about gold. Hoping to discover this gold, Ponce de León led soldiers to conquer the island. He and his men killed many native people. Later, Spain's King Ferdinand made him governor of the island.

Ponce de León soon heard of a magic fountain on another island. Stories told of a "fountain of youth" whose waters were said to make people young again. Ponce de León asked permission to search for this island. He wanted the glory of finding such a wonderful spot.

Can you find Florida on this map of North America from 1555?

In 1513, Ponce de León set sail. After a month, he reached a coast with palm trees, sweet-smelling flowers, and beautiful birds. He landed on the Catholic feast day called Easter of Flowers, or Pascua Florida in Spanish. Ponce de León named the land Florida and claimed it for Spain. He sailed up and down the coast, but he did not find the fountain of youth. So he went back to Puerto Rico.

In 1521, he returned to Florida to start a settlement. He brought 200 men as well as horses, cattle, and seeds to plant. The American Indians there resented the invasion. They attacked, and an arrow struck Ponce de León. Wounded, he sailed to Cuba and soon died. He never knew that Florida was not an island but part of a vast continent.

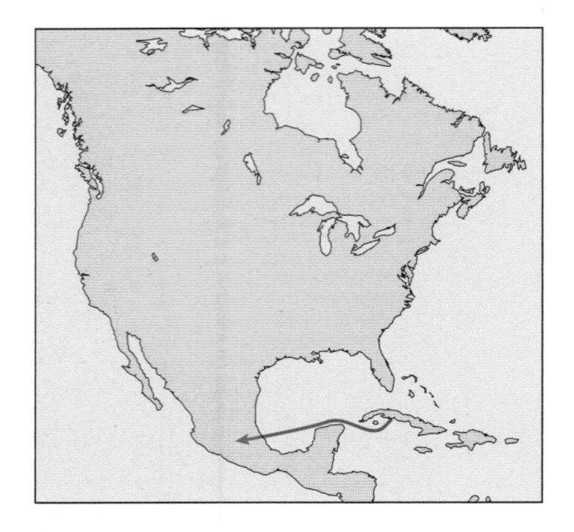

Here is the route Hernán Cortés took from Cuba to Mexico City.

5.5 Hernán Cortés

The Spanish heard stories of a rich Mexican empire ruled by the Aztecs, a powerful American Indian group. In 1519, Hernán Cortés (hehr-NAHN kohr-TEHZ), a Spanish nobleman living in Cuba, sailed to Mexico in search of adventure and wealth.

Cortés arrived at a time when the Aztecs expected one of their gods to return. Stories say that the Aztec emperor, Montezuma II, thought Cortés might be this god and sent him gifts of gold. This made Cortés eager to conquer the Aztecs.

For months, the two men exchanged gifts and messages. Then Cortés and his men marched to the Aztec capital. Many local American Indians joined them, hoping to overthrow the Aztec leaders. The capital was on a series of islands in a lake, in the place where Mexico City is today. Montezuma welcomed Cortés. After a week, Cortés took the emperor prisoner.

For six months, Cortés held Montezuma captive. Then Cortés took a short trip away from the Aztec capital. As he returned, the Aztecs attacked. Fierce warriors surrounded Cortés and his army. The Spanish fled. Before leaving, they stuffed their pockets with gold. Many soldiers were so weighed down that they drowned as they crossed the canals that ran like roads through the city.

Hernán Cortés sits in a chair (on the right). His translator, Malinche, stands at his side. He is meeting with some American Indians he hopes will join him in fighting the Aztecs.

After their defeat, the Spanish surrounded the Aztec capital for nearly a year. The Aztecs could not get supplies. Many of them had already been weakened or killed by smallpox, a contagious disease carried by Europeans. Now, the Aztecs began to starve. Finally, Cortés and his army attacked. Although the Aztecs put up a strong defense, they were defeated in 1521. Cortés claimed their lands for Spain.

The Spanish now ruled Mexico. The Aztec Empire lay in ruins. An Aztec poet wrote a sad poem about his people:

We are crushed to the ground; we lie in ruins.
There is nothing but grief and suffering in Mexico and Tlatelolco,
where once we saw beauty and valor.

Jacques Cartier sails up the St. Lawrence River in 1534.

5.6 Jacques Cartier

In 1521, Spanish explorers reached Asia by sailing around the southern tip of South America. Europeans now knew that the Americas lay between Europe and Asia. But they still thought that China was not far beyond the west coast of North America. King Francis I of France hoped to reach China's riches by sailing across North America. But no one had yet looked for such a water passage.

In 1534, the French king sent an experienced sailor and navigator, Jacques Cartier (zhahk cahr-TYAY), to find the Northwest Passage. Cartier sailed west to Newfoundland, in present-day Canada. He entered a large gulf through a strait, or a narrow waterway between two large land areas. He claimed the surrounding land for France. Just before returning to France, he saw a waterway leading west.

The next year, King Francis sent Cartier back to map the waterway. Cartier reached its mouth on the Catholic feast day of Saint Lawrence. So Cartier named the river the St. Lawrence. With American Indian guides, he sailed as far as present-day Quebec, until his ship could go no farther. He visited an American Indian village and brought some of its chiefs back to France. They told the king of great riches farther west.

In 1541, the king sent Cartier and some settlers on a third voyage, to set up a French empire in North America. Cartier took more than 100 settlers. After enduring a harsh winter, Cartier and the settlers gave up. In 1542, they returned to France. Still, Cartier had staked France's claim in North America. Sixty years later, New France had its first permanent settlers.

Jacques Cartier followed this route along the St. Lawrence River.

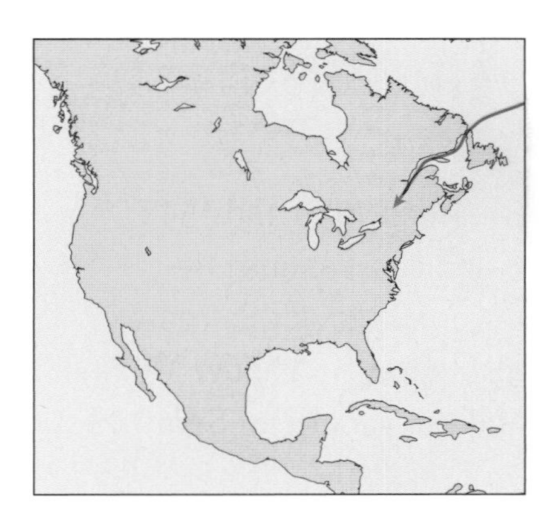

The Granger Collection, New York

Francisco Vásquez de Coronado and his men searched for one of the Seven Cities of Gold in Cibola, which was then in Mexico.

5.7 Francisco Vásquez de Coronado

Spain's rulers gained wealth and power from lands in Mexico and South America. They wanted lands in North America, too. In 1540, hundreds of Spanish conquistadors marched into North America. Their commander was Francisco Vásquez (VAHS-kehz) de Coronado.

Coronado had come to the Americas to seek glory and wealth. He was a nobleman, but his brother had inherited most of the family fortune. Coronado's rich wife, along with the viceroy, or governor, of Mexico, paid for Coronado's expedition.

A priest had told Coronado about one of the Seven Cities of Gold in Cibola (present-day New Mexico). The Seven Cities were said to have as much gold as the Aztec Empire once had. Coronado led his army to Cibola. He found American Indian pueblos but no gold. Scouts looked further. They found the Grand Canyon and the Rio Grande valley but no gold.

Then Coronado listened to the tale told by an American Indian slave. The slave described a land where boats with golden eagles sailed past trees hung with golden bells. To find this land, Coronado marched across the plains to what is now Kansas. Again, he found no gold. Angry, he had the slave killed.

Coronado and his men returned in disgrace to New Spain in 1542. He was later charged with bad leadership and the mistreatment of American Indians. Only the Spanish priests thought his expedition had succeeded. It gave them a chance to spread Christianity to American Indians in the southwestern part of North America.

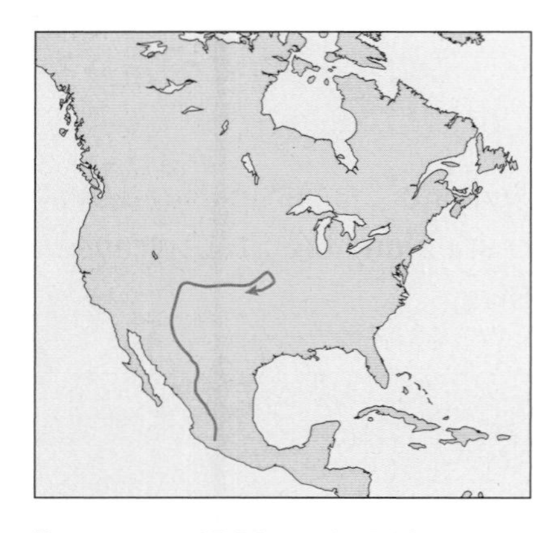

Between 1540 and 1542, Francisco Vásquez de Coronado took this route through what is now Mexico and the American Southwest.

5.8 Henry Hudson

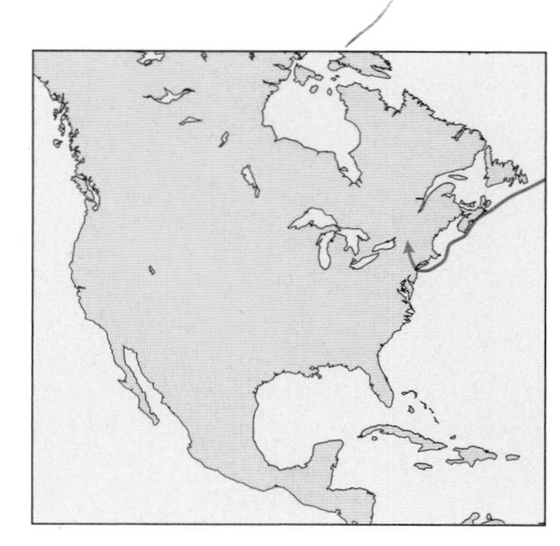

On his first voyage, in 1609, Henry Hudson sailed up a river now named the Hudson River.

England kept searching for a northern sea route to Asia as did the country called Holland or the Netherlands. In 1609, the Dutch East India Company in Holland hired Henry Hudson, an English sea captain. He set out to reach China by sailing around the northern shores of Europe, near the Arctic Circle. But his crew grew tired of ice and cold. They rebelled. Hudson agreed to change course and sail west across the Atlantic instead.

While sailing along the Atlantic coast of North America, Hudson and his men entered a narrow harbor. From there, Hudson saw a large body of water leading north. Believing that this was the Northwest Passage, Hudson sailed up the waterway. When the water became too shallow for his boat, Hudson realized that it was only a river. (Today, this is called the Hudson River.) But his voyage gave Holland a claim in North America. By 1624, the Dutch had settled in the Hudson Valley.

In 1610, English merchants paid Hudson to cross the Atlantic again. Reaching Canada, Hudson sailed farther north. He passed through a long, narrow strait into a large body of water. Hudson was sure that he had reached the Pacific Ocean. But, sailing down the coast, he found no opening. Then the waters froze, trapping the ship for the winter. In fact, Hudson had not reached the Pacific. The large body of water was a bay. It is now called Hudson Bay.

In the spring, the crew rebelled again. They set Hudson, his son, and seven others afloat in a small boat. Hudson was never seen again. But his voyage did give England a claim to eastern Canada.

Henry Hudson's first voyage gave Holland a claim in North America.

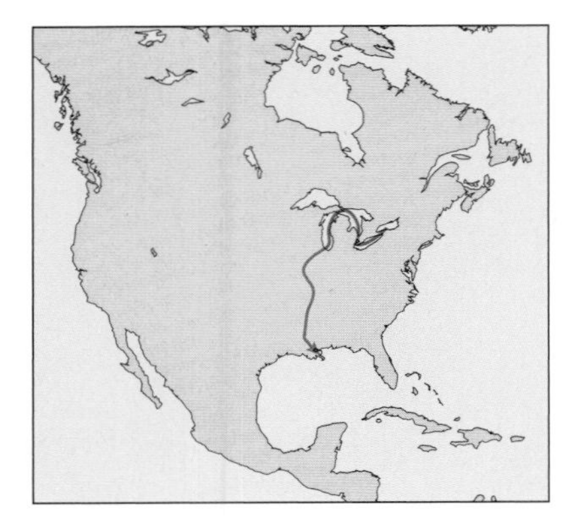

Robert de La Salle explored the Mississippi River.

5.9 Robert de La Salle

In the 1600s, the French began to settle on their land claims. In 1666, Robert Cavelier de La Salle, a French nobleman, sailed to New France. As a fur trader along the St. Lawrence River, La Salle learned American Indian languages and explored the Ohio River. The American Indians told him about a great river that flowed south all the way to the Gulf of Mexico.

La Salle dreamed not only of personal wealth but also of a French empire of trading posts, forts, and settlements. King Louis XIV of France liked La Salle's plan, but the king wanted La Salle to pay for the journey himself. La Salle had to borrow money to finance his expedition. In 1681, La Salle set out in a canoe to travel down the Mississippi River. When he reached the mouth of the Mississippi River, he named the vast region he had crossed Louisiana, for the French king.

La Salle then planned to establish a sea route from France to the Mississippi River. He went to France and received the king's permission. In 1684, La Salle sailed to North America with more than 200 settlers. After spending six months crossing the Atlantic, the ships missed the mouth of the Mississippi and landed 500 miles to the west.

La Salle founded a colony there, on the coast of what is now Texas. Soon, the settlers were starving. La Salle set out for help. Convinced that La Salle was crazy, his own men murdered him. Although most of the colonists died, La Salle had given France a claim to the entire Mississippi Valley.

In 1682, Robert de La Salle claimed the Mississippi River and the lands around it for France.

European Routes to the Americas

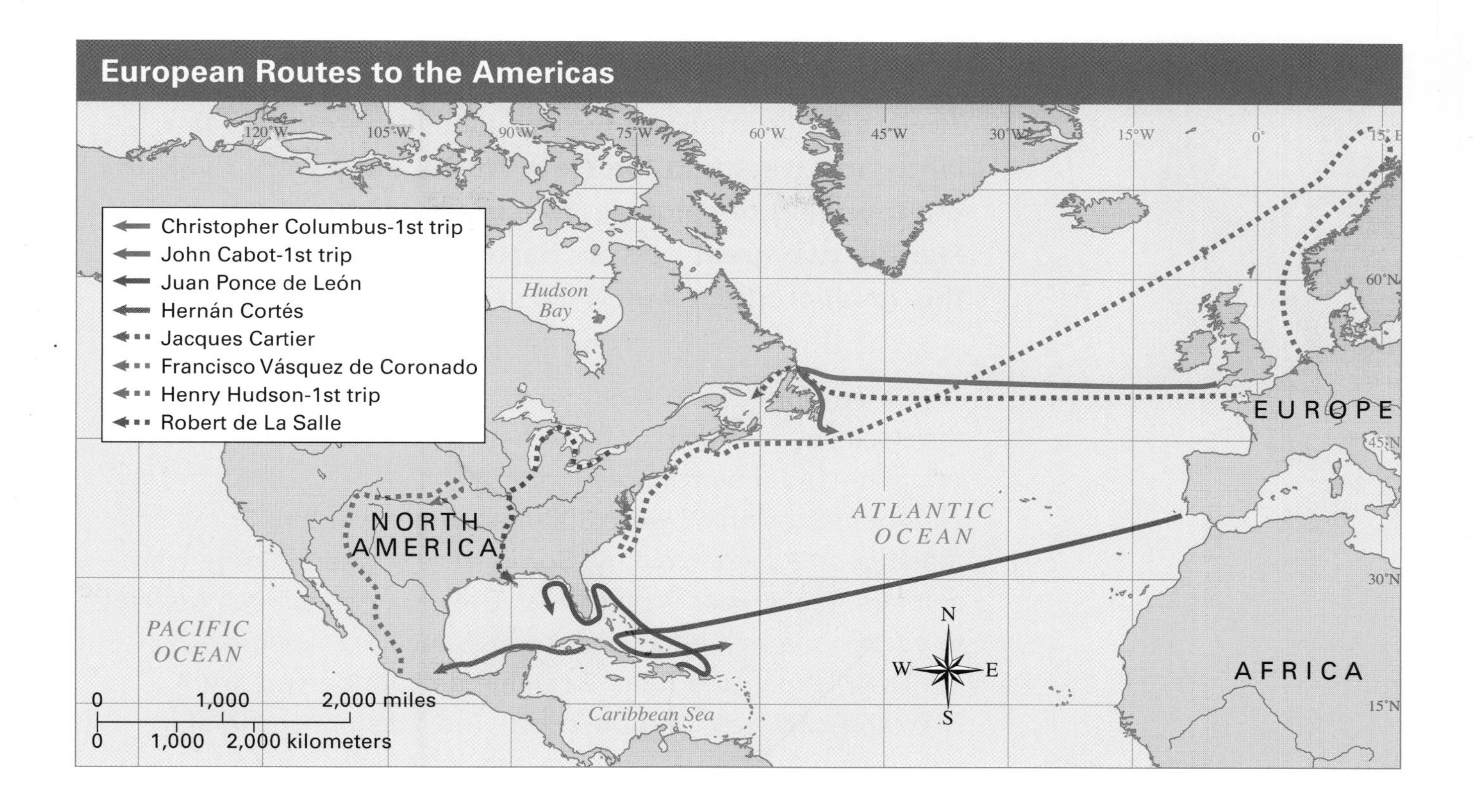

Summary

In this chapter, you learned about eight early European explorers of the Americas. You used a matrix to organize facts about them.

Europeans wanted a trade route that would be a shortcut to Asia's riches. Columbus sailed west and reached land. Others followed. These explorers thought that they had reached Asia. In time, however, they realized that this land was actually a new continent. Some explorers, such as Cartier and Hudson, kept searching for a fast route to Asia. But the real wealth for European countries was the American land they claimed.

American Indians suffered greatly as a result of European exploration. The explorers fought against tribes who opposed them. American Indians were often enslaved. In addition, Europeans brought contagious diseases that killed many American Indians.

In Chapter 4, you learned that Spain and England were enemies. In the next pages, you will learn about the rivalry between Spain and France. How did this conflict affect early settlements in North America? Read on to find out.

Reading Further 5

Who Wins Florida?

The leading nations of Europe all competed to claim lands and wealth in the New World. They were rivals in the founding of colonies, too. In the land we now call Florida, two great powers battled for control. How did this conflict affect American settlement?

On an April day in 1564, three ships slipped silently from the docks of a French harbor. They were bound for the wide Atlantic—and the coast of Florida.

Aboard the ships were 300 men and 4 women. Some of these people were wealthy. Some were workers. Some were soldiers. Most were Protestants. They may have been hoping to escape the religious violence in France at this time.

Their leader was René Goulaine de Laudonniére (ruh-NAY goo-LEN duh loh-don-YEHR). His mission was to start a colony in the New World. He, too, may have hoped to find religious freedom. But the French rulers who sent him wanted something else.

These rulers knew that great quantities of silver and gold filled the Spanish galleons, or ships, that sailed from the New World. The riches came from Spanish conquests in the Caribbean, Mexico, and beyond. Such treasures made Spain strong. Other European nations feared and envied Spain. Their rulers wanted a share of this wealth and power.

Spain had also suffered some failures. It had tried unsuccessfully to claim land in Florida and north of the Rio Grande. These failures offered opportunities for Spain's rivals. France now hoped to succeed where Spain had not.

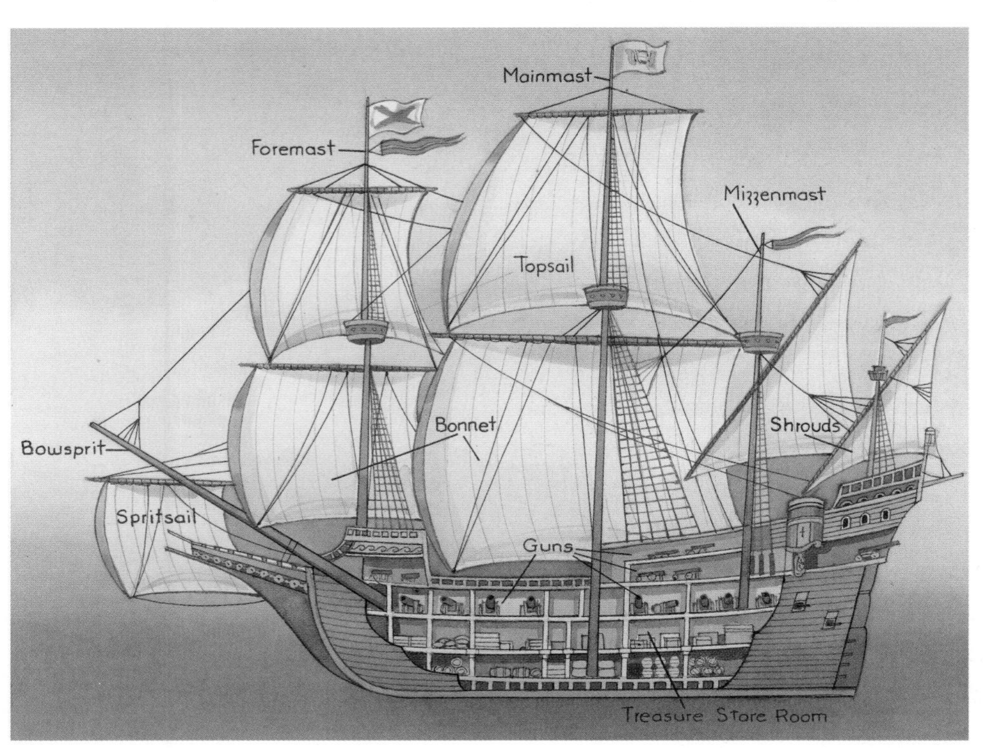

The Spanish built large, well-armed ships for sailing back and forth to the New World. Spanish galleons often carried a valuable cargo of gold and silver. Other nations of Europe used similar ships.

Artist Jacques le Moyne created pictures of the French experience in Florida. Here, he shows the building of Fort Caroline.

The French ships reached Florida in June 1564. Laudonniére quickly put his people to work building their new settlement. They chose a site that they could easily defend. First, they built a fort, which they called Fort Caroline. Then they unloaded their supplies. These included guns, gunpowder, and many other weapons.

The new settlers needed to protect themselves because they knew that the Spanish would try to force them from Florida. After all, the French meant to challenge Spanish control of the region. Fort Caroline was in good position to attack Spanish treasure ships sailing for Europe.

Laudonniére also had to worry about his own people. Many did not want to do the hard work necessary to build a settlement. They wanted quick and easy wealth. As they hunted for gold, supplies dwindled. American Indians living nearby at first willingly gave food to the settlers. Soon, though, they grew tired of feeding the hungry French.

By the summer of 1565, the colony was in trouble. The settlers challenged Laudonniére's leadership. One group stole two ships and sailed off to make their fortunes as pirates. Other settlers decided to abandon Fort Caroline.

Before they could leave, however, supply ships arrived from France. Several hundred new settlers joined the struggling colony. The colony also got a new leader, named Jean Ribault (zhahn ree-BOH). It seemed as if the colony that had nearly collapsed had now been given another chance.

A Turning Point for Spain and France

But in fact, Fort Caroline was in great danger. Long before Ribault's arrival, spies in Europe had told the Spanish about the new French settlement. As the French had predicted, Spain did not plan to allow the colony to survive and grow.

Spain's King Philip II ordered the removal of the French threat in Florida. He put one of his best soldiers in charge of the mission. The soldier's name was Pedro Menéndez de Avilés (meh-NEN-dez day ah-vee-LAYS). Menéndez sailed from Spain in the summer of 1565. His ships reached the coast of Florida at about the same time that Ribault's ships arrived.

Menéndez wasted little time in seeking out Fort Caroline. Finding Ribault's ships there, Menéndez attacked and scattered them. He then wanted to attack the fort, but his large ships could not reach it because of the shallow water. So Menéndez left to find a place on land for his forces to gather. There, he would plan his attack on Fort Caroline.

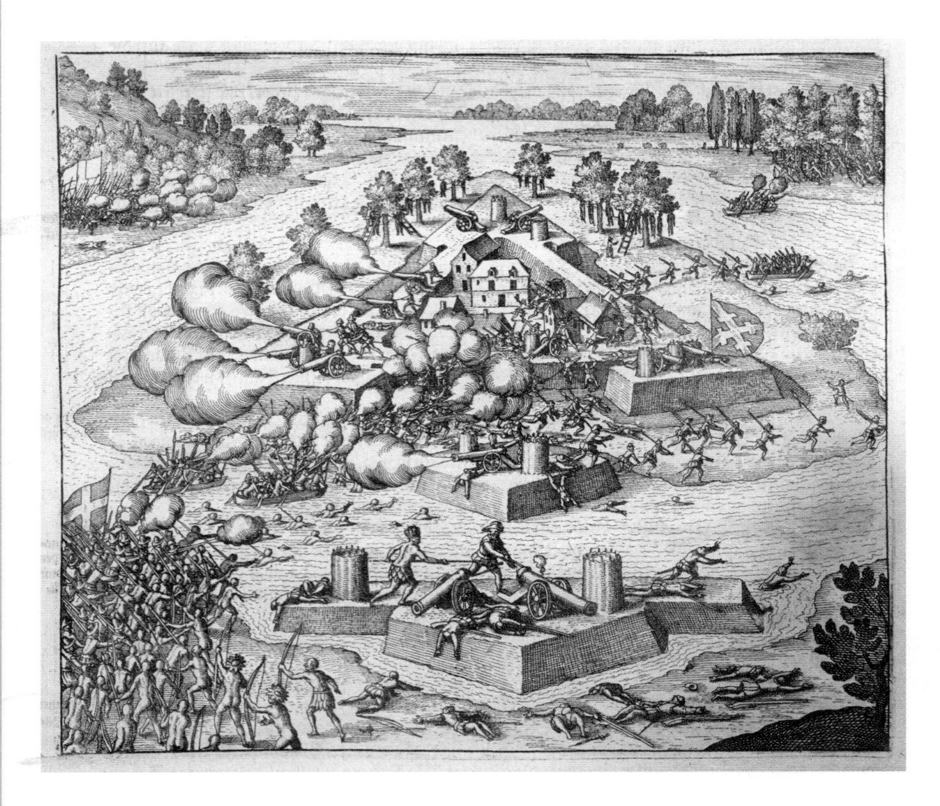

The Spanish soldiers were Catholic. They killed many of the French settlers, who were mostly Protestants.

Menéndez chose a site a few dozen miles from Fort Caroline. He called this place St. Augustine. On September 8, 1565, he led his troops ashore and began to build a new settlement.

Meanwhile, Ribault's scattered ships had returned to Fort Caroline. The French decided to launch their own attack. The plan ended in disaster. Before they could strike at St. Augustine, a sudden and powerful storm arrived. It destroyed the French warships. St. Augustine had been spared.

Now, it was Menéndez's turn to attack again. He led his forces on a march over land and through swamps to reach Fort Caroline. The difficult journey took four days. But the Spanish had achieved surprise. They were easily able to overwhelm the fort's weakened defenses. In a bloody rampage, they killed many of the French settlers.

The year 1565 was a turning point for Spain and France in the Americas. In that year, Spain had its first success in establishing a settlement in Florida. The base that Pedro Menéndez de Avilés built at St. Augustine survived and flourished. It grew into a town. Today, it is celebrated as the first permanent European settlement in the United States.

In 1565, France's plan for a colony in the New World ended—at least for a time. The French did send a force to the area in 1567. But they came only for revenge. French soldiers killed some Spaniards at Fort Caroline. Then the French left.

France did not give up its New World dreams. The French would later build an empire in North America as fur traders. These frontier businesses did not require large settlements of colonists. As a result, the French population in North America was never very large.

Spain had other jealous rivals in Europe. These countries would seek their own share of Spain's American treasure. They would send pirates to raid Spanish ships. They would send settlers to start new colonies.

Spain had won a victory in 1565. But the larger struggle for control of the New World continued.

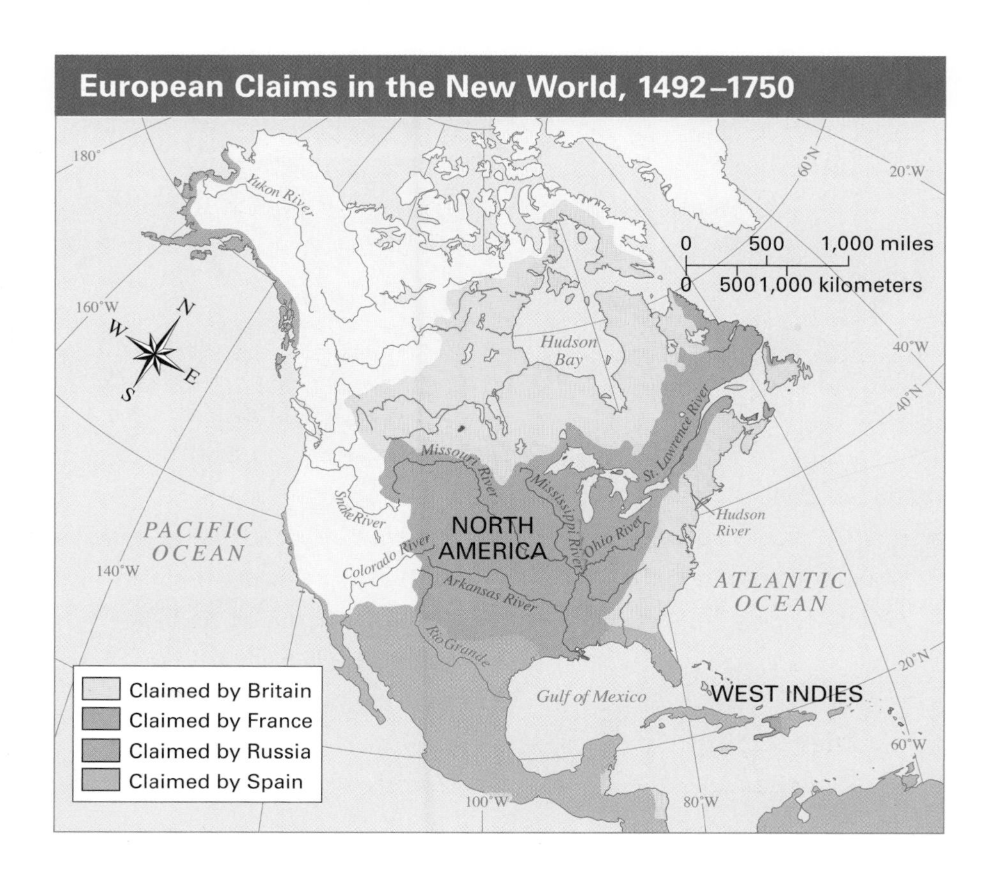

John Gadsby Chapman, *Good Times in the New World (The Hope of Jamestown)*, 1841, Oil on panel, 7 7/8"H x 11 3/8" W, Virginia Museum of Fine Arts, Richmond. The Paul Mellon Collection. © Virginia Museum of Fine Arts.

Why do you think these people have come to the New World?

What is this man doing?

How do you think these American Indians feel about the new visitors to their country?

Early English Settlements

6

What challenges faced the first English colonies?

6.1 Introduction

In Chapter 5, you read about eight European explorers who came to the Americas. In this chapter, you will learn about three groups of English people who came to settle there. They made the hard voyage across the Atlantic Ocean. Then they built small communities, or **settlements**. They faced many challenges.

Roanoke was the first English settlement. Roanoke is an island off the coast of North Carolina. No one knows what happened to the settlers there. Few signs of them remained when ships came to find them. That is why, today, Roanoke is called the "lost colony."

Shortly after the attempt to settle Roanoke, 105 Englishmen arrived in present-day Virginia. They hoped to find gold and other riches. They began a settlement called **Jamestown** in 1607. Despite many hardships, Jamestown became the first successful English colony in North America.

A few years later, 102 English people arrived in present-day New England. They built a settlement called **Plymouth,** in what is now Massachusetts. Most of these people left England to seek religious freedom. They became known as the Pilgrims. Pilgrims are people who go on a religious journey.

As you read this chapter, think about the hardships faced by these three groups of English settlers. Why did some settlements survive, while others did not?

6.2 The Lost Settlement of Roanoke

In the 1500s, Spain was a powerful nation. Its ships sailed to the Spanish colonies in the Americas. They brought back riches to Spain.

Sir Walter Raleigh was a friend of England's Queen Elizabeth. He believed that American colonies could make England more powerful. In 1584, he sent two ships to explore the coast of North America.

The ships landed on an island near present-day North Carolina. The sailors named the island Roanoke, for the American Indians who lived there. The explorers returned to England. They told Raleigh that the island had fish, animals, fruits, vegetables, and friendly people.

The next year, Raleigh sent some men to start a colony. But few of the settlers were farmers. Supplies ran short because the men could not grow food. When fighting broke out between the English and the Roanokes, the settlers gave up and went home.

In 1587, Raleigh sent over 100 new settlers to Roanoke. This time there were farmers and skilled workers. Later that year, Captain John White went back to England for supplies. Because England was fighting a war with Spain, White's ships were not allowed to return to the colony.

Three years later, White finally returned to Roanoke. There was no sign of the settlers. Even their houses were gone. The word CROATOAN was carved on the gatepost of a ruined fort. White thought the settlers might have moved to the island of Croatoan or joined an American Indian group with that name. Before he could find out, however, the weather turned bad, and he could not search the area. No one has ever discovered what happened to the colony.

The only clue about what happened to the settlers at Roanoke was the word CROATOAN carved into a gatepost.

The Granger Collection, New York

To survive, everyone in Jamestown had to work, even those who were used to having servants.

6.3 Jamestown Colony

In 1606, England's King James gave permission to a group of wealthy men to start a colony in North America. The group sent 105 men to settle in Virginia. They hoped the colony would make them richer.

In May 1607, the settlers arrived in Virginia. Most hoped to find gold. They chose a place near a river. The deep water allowed them to anchor their ships close by. The site was upriver from Chesapeake Bay. It was far enough from the river that Spanish ships could not easily attack the settlement. Located on a peninsula, the town would be easy to defend by land. The group built a settlement enclosed by the walls of a fort. In honor of King James, they called their new home Jamestown.

Unfortunately, the settlers built Jamestown on a **marsh**. The water around the town was dirty and salty. The land was not good for farming. And mosquitoes carried a deadly disease, malaria. By the end of 1607, disease and other hardships had killed many of the settlers.

marsh wet, low-lying land that is poorly drained

In late 1607, some American Indians captured a Jamestown settler named Captain John Smith. They took Smith to their chief, Powhatan (pow-uh-TAN). According to the story Smith later told, the chief was about to kill him. But Powhatan's young daughter, Pocahontas, saved his life. Many historians, however, think that Smith's life was never in real danger.

colonist a person who settles in a colony

After this incident, Pocahontas visited Jamestown several times. She and her people brought food to trade to the few surviving **colonists**.

In January 1608, more men arrived from England. Many had come only to seek gold, so there were not enough people growing the food needed to feed the colony. In September, John Smith became the leader of the colony. He knew that the settlement needed everyone's help to survive. He said that any man who would not work to maintain Jamestown would not eat. Smith's leadership helped save the colony.

Pocahontas traveled to England with her husband and their young son. While there, she dressed like an Englishwoman. This portrait is based on a drawing made of her during that visit.

In the summer of 1609, a new group of settlers arrived, including women and children. The next month, Smith returned to England after having been badly burned by an explosion of gunpowder. The colonists had lost a strong leader. To make matters worse, Powhatan stopped trading with them. Local tribes attacked the people they found outside the settlement. The winter of 1609–1610 was known as the Starving Time. Many settlers had to eat horses and dogs. Hundreds of people died. Only about 60 settlers survived in Jamestown.

The Jamestown settlers never found gold. Therefore, they needed another way to support their colony. Colonist John Rolfe learned how to grow a new kind of tobacco. The settlers planted this cash crop. In 1614, they began to trade their tobacco for money and supplies. People in England loved it. Tobacco became Virginia's "gold."

Meanwhile, Powhatan's people worried about so many settlers coming to their land. In 1614, John Rolfe married Pocahontas. For a time, the colonists and the American Indians were at peace. Pocahontas even went to England and met King James. Before she could return home, she became ill. In 1617, she died.

democratic relating to a form of government in which people have the power to rule themselves, often through elected representatives

Meanwhile, Jamestown was growing and changing. In 1619, the men elected representatives to make laws for the colony. This was the first representative government in an American colony. They called this governing body the House of Burgesses. (*Burgess* is an English word for an elected representative.) Only wealthy men could have this job. Even so, Virginia now had a more **democratic** government than England.

When Powhatan died, his brother became chief and the peace between the American Indians and the settlers ended. In 1622, the new chief and his men attacked Jamestown and killed 347 colonists. But Jamestown survived to become the first successful English settlement in North America.

6.4 The Settlement of Plymouth

The third English settlement in North America was started by people who were looking for religious freedom. King James said that everyone in England had to belong to the Church of England. Some people refused. Among them were people called Separatists. This group wanted to have a separate, or independent, church.

The Separatists decided to move to a place where they could be free to practice their own religion. In time, this group came to be known as the Pilgrims.

In September 1620, the Pilgrims sailed from England. They traveled on a ship called the *Mayflower*. After more than two months at sea, they landed on the tip of Cape Cod in what is now Massachusetts. Before going ashore, the Pilgrims drew up a plan of government. They wrote down rules to help them live together peacefully. Most of the men signed this agreement known as the Mayflower Compact. Then they elected a governor.

American artist Edward Percy Moran painted this scene. It is called *The Signing of the Compact in the Cabin of the Mayflower*. In it, William Bradford, later elected governor, signs the compact.

Courtesy of the Pilgrim Society, Plymouth, Massachusetts

The Granger Collection, New York

The Pilgrims landed at Plymouth in winter. Almost half of the new settlers died of disease and starvation during the first months.

After exploring the area, the Pilgrims decided to sail the *Mayflower* across a bay that separated them from the mainland. They landed at a place they named Plymouth. Soon they began to build houses and a meeting hall called the Common House.

The first winter was very hard. The Pilgrims had landed too late in the year to plant crops. The climate was cold and harsh. Nearly half of the 102 Pilgrims died of disease and starvation before spring. Only a few settlers remained healthy enough to care for the others.

In March 1621, a man named Squanto visited the Pilgrims. He was a member of the Pawtuxet tribe but was living with the nearby Wampanoags (wahm-puh-NOH-ags). Some years earlier, Squanto had lived in England and could speak English. Squanto stayed with the Pilgrims and taught them how to plant corn, catch fish, and get sweet syrup from maple trees. The Pilgrims were so grateful that they thought Squanto had been sent by God.

Squanto also told the Pilgrims about the many American Indians who had died from a disease that they had caught from English and French fishermen. While Squanto had been away in England, the members of his Pawtuxet tribe had died from this sickness.

Another American Indian who visited the Pilgrims was Massasoit (MAS-uh-soyt). He was the sachem, or chief, of the Wampanoags. Squanto helped arrange a peace treaty, or agreement, between Massasoit and the Pilgrims. The Wampanoags and the Pilgrims promised not to fight each other. They also agreed to help protect each other against attacks by other American Indians.

The Pilgrims' corn ripened during the summer. In the fall, they decided to celebrate the harvest—the food they had collected from the plants they had grown. They invited Massasoit to a feast of thanksgiving. He and his people brought deer to cook and eat. The Pilgrims had goose, duck, deer, fish, lobster, and wild turkey. The feast lasted three days. Today, people in the United States still observe this harvest celebration. We call it Thanksgiving Day.

In 1621, William Bradford was elected governor of Plymouth. He held this post for more than 30 years.

In the next few years, ships brought more and more settlers to the colony. In time, other groups would join the Pilgrims in the area we now call New England.

Summary

In this chapter, you read about the first English settlements in North America. You found out why people came to live here. You learned why some settlements survived, while others did not.

The early settlers faced many hardships. One settlement, on the island of Roanoke, disappeared. Another settlement, Jamestown, survived after many bad times. Settlers often did not have enough food. They became sick from unhealthy surroundings. At times, local American Indians helped them. At other times, the settlers and the American Indians fought.

Many settlers were searching for riches. But the Pilgrims hoped to find religious freedom. The Wampanoags helped them survive in Plymouth.

These early settlements were the first of what would become 13 English colonies in North America. How did the American Indians react as more and more people arrived? Read on to find out.

Reading Further 6

King Philip Decides on War

American Indians and English settlers had a complex relationship. At times, they worked together. At other times, they fought bitterly. As more English settlers arrived, they took lands on which American Indians lived. In 1675, one chief went to war to stop this. How did the English colonies in New England face this challenge?

King Philip was a proud and powerful leader. He was angered by what he saw as unfair treatment of his people by the English settlers.

In the darkness, the people watched as the shadow of Earth slowly moved over the moon. Soon, the great glowing disk was covered completely. Today, we call such an event a lunar eclipse. But the Wampanoag people living in 1675 saw it as a sign: it was time for war.

The eclipse came at a key moment for Metacomet, the son of Massasoit, and his people. Wampanoag relations with the English settlers were badly strained.

It had not always been so. For many years, the Wampanoags had watched as settlers from England moved into their homeland. They had not only tolerated the newcomers but also assisted them. In fact, the settlement at Plymouth might never have survived without the Wampanoags' help. In 1621, Massasoit had made peace agreements with the leaders of Plymouth Colony. His son, Metacomet, had even taken the English name of Philip. When Philip became the Wampanoag leader, he had hoped to work with the settlers to protect and provide for his people. He also wanted to prevent further English settlement and to organize the local tribes.

But there had been trouble. In 1662, King Philip's brother had died suddenly. King Philip believed that the English had killed him. Although the Wampanoags continued to work with the English, King Philip's trust was shaken.

Just a few weeks before the eclipse, the English had put two Wampanoag men to death after finding them guilty of murder. King Philip thought that the men were innocent. He believed that their trial under English laws had been unfair. An angry group of Wampanoag warriors struck back. They killed nine English settlers in a village called Swansea.

King Philip and his people now faced a choice. They could seek peace with the English. Or they could go to war against them.

As the Wampanoags pondered this decision on the night of June 26, 1675, the moon slipped into Earth's shadow. The Wampanoags saw the sign. They knew that much bloodshed would follow. Even so, they decided to fight the English.

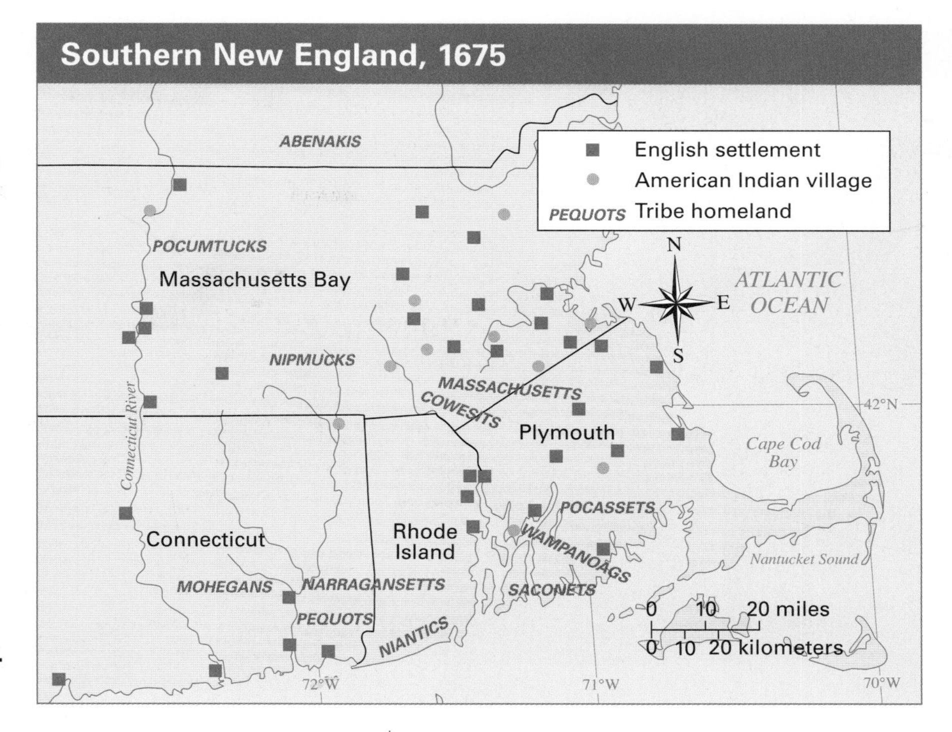

King Philip made a fateful choice. The war he began changed the lives of thousands of people across New England. The battles to come were among the deadliest in American history.

King Philip's War, as it is now known, was a complex struggle. It was not just a war between English settlers and the Wampanoags. New England was home to many other American Indian groups. These included the Nipmucks, the Narragansetts, the Mohegans, and others. Each group faced a hard choice. As one Englishman noted, "Many of the Indians were in a kind of maze, not knowing well what to do." Some would join King Philip. Others would side with the settlers.

Why were American Indians undecided? Many groups shared King Philip's anger at the English. But others had friendly ties with settlers. Some had become Christians.

American Indians had fought side by side with English soldiers before. In the Pequot War of 1637, some tribes had joined the English to defeat the Pequot tribe. This war showed that New England's American Indians were not always friendly with each other. In 1675, deep rivalries still divided many groups. Some would settle old scores by joining the English.

The English settlers were more united than the American Indians. When war broke out, they soon organized to meet King Philip's challenge. Yet, as with the American Indians, old rivalries and conflicts caused trouble. Communities blamed each other for causing the war. They argued over who would lead and supply troops. Some feared that the war would be an excuse for a rival settlement to take disputed land. Such squabbles harmed English defenses.

The Great Swamp Fight of December 1675 was the bloodiest battle of King Philip's War.

ally one person or nation united with another for a common purpose

At first, the American Indians had success. They surprised the English by making hit-and-run raids. They would sneak up on a target, launch a surprise attack, and then disappear. The English had trouble adjusting to this type of warfare. They wanted to fight in the open.

King Philip's forces made great gains. Now that victory seemed possible, new **allies** joined him. Once-friendly tribes turned against the English. This made the English suspect even loyal American Indians. In one town, officials imprisoned a large group of Christian American Indians on an island in Boston Harbor. Elsewhere, officials tried to take weapons away from American Indians. English commanders refused to use American Indian soldiers in battle. Such treatment turned former friends into enemies.

In the fall of 1675, the English were worried. The mighty Narragansett tribe had not yet joined the war. But the English feared that the tribe might join King Philip. To stop them, the English attacked a large Narragansett settlement. The Great Swamp Fight left many hundreds of Narragansett men, women, and children dead. More than 200 English fighters were also killed or wounded.

The Great Swamp Fight was a terrible blow to the Narragansetts. But it did not stop the American Indian onslaught. Warriors still raided terrified English settlements. In the winter of 1676, villages just 10 miles from Boston came under attack.

As spring approached, the English were on the verge of defeat. Many of their villages lay in ashes. But their fortunes were about to change.

The English did not know that King Philip was in trouble, too. After the Narragansetts' defeat in the Great Swamp Fight, Philip needed more help. He took a large force to present-day New York. There, he hoped to win the support of the fierce Mohawk tribe. Instead, the Mohawks attacked him. His forces limped back to New England.

At this time, the English made a key decision. They again made use of friendly American Indian soldiers, such as the Christians who had been held on the island.

And they got results. Within months, combined English and American Indian troops were winning the war. King Philip's forces were on the run.

The end came for King Philip in August 1676. He was shot by an American Indian soldier who had joined with the English. By summer's end, King Philip's War was over.

King Philip's War took little more than a year. Yet its effects were long lasting. A dozen settlements had been destroyed. About 1,000 English settlers in the region, out of a total of about 52,000, had died. The damage to the American Indian population was even worse. Some experts think that as many as 3,000 out of a total of 20,000 American Indians in New England died. Many more were captured and sold as slaves.

When the war was over, New England was in ruins—but completely under English control. American Indians had played a big part in the survival of the first English settlements. Some had helped the English win King Philip's War. But in 1676, American Indians were largely gone from the region. Only a few tribal communities were left.

The English, on the other hand, would recover. Their settlements would once again grow and prosper.

King Philip's War was the most deadly in our history in terms of the percentage of the colonial and American Indian populations that died.

The Granary Burying Ground is one of several cemeteries in Boston that hold the remains of colonists who died during King Philip's War.

What do you think this building is?

What do you think these men are doing?

What do you think this ship is used for?

Comparing the Colonies

7

How were the three colonial regions alike and different?

7.1 Introduction

In Chapter 6, you read about the first English colonies in North America. In this chapter, you will learn about other colonies. These, too, were on the Atlantic coast of what would become the United States.

In 1707, England and Wales joined Scotland under one government. This nation was called Great Britain. Its people were the British. By the mid-1700s, Great Britain had 13 colonies in North America.

There were three regions within the colonies: the New England Colonies, the Middle Colonies, and the Southern Colonies. The regions had distinct geographic features, including landforms, natural resources, and climate. Their **economies** were based on local products and services. An economy is the way in which people use resources to produce, sell, or trade goods and services to meet their needs and wants. Some colonies had governments that were more democratic than others.

The map and matrix below help organize facts about the three colonial regions. Use these tools to remember this information.

Comparing British Colonies in North America

	Reason for Founding	Geography	Economy	Government
New England Colonies				
Middle Colonies				
Southern Colonies				

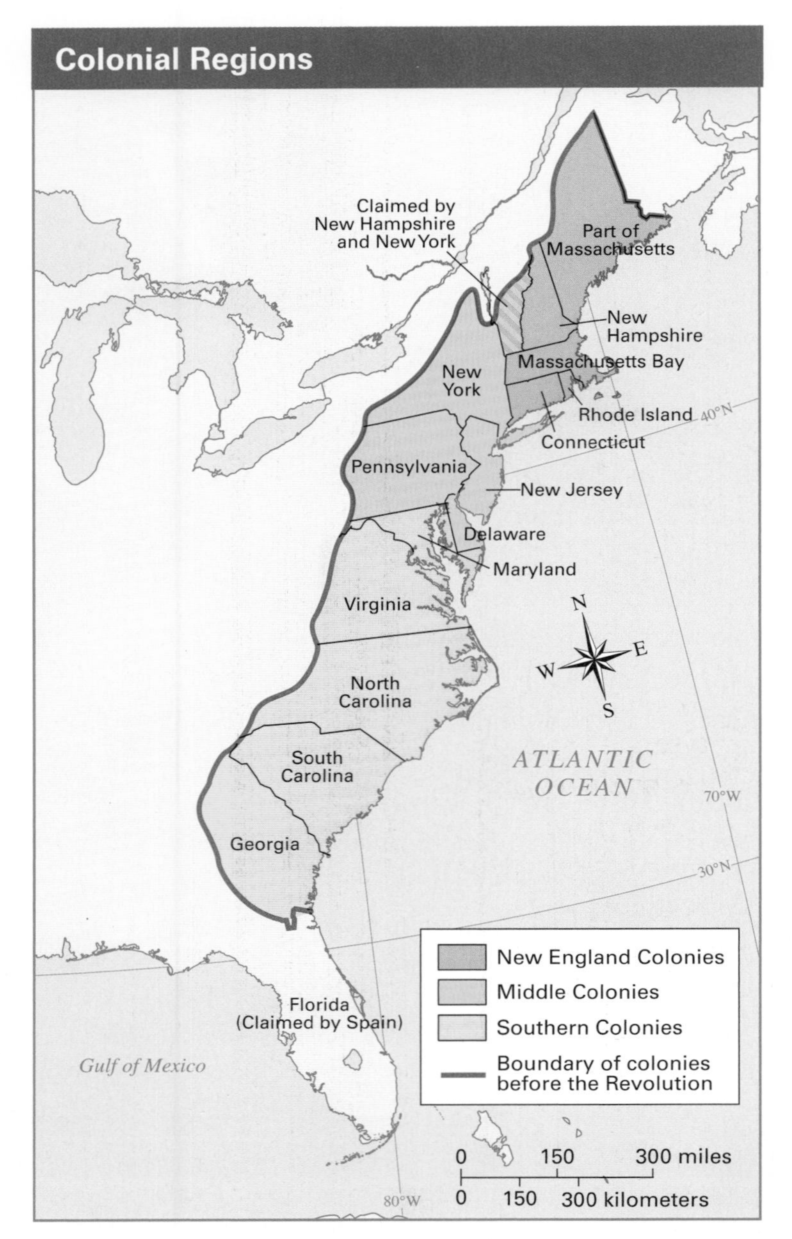

7.2 The New England, Middle, and Southern Colonial Regions

People came to each of the colonial regions for different reasons. Each region had its own geography. Each region offered settlers special choices and ways of life.

The New England region included the colonies of Massachusetts Bay, New Hampshire, Rhode Island, and Connecticut. It had rocky soil, dense forests, and natural harbors that gave easy access to the sea. New England's economy was built on small farms, lumbering, fishing, shipbuilding, and trade.

Most New England colonists were Puritans. They wanted to change the practices of the Church of England, or the Anglican Church. Religion was an important part of their lives.

The Middle Colonies included New York, Pennsylvania, New Jersey, and Delaware. This region had rich soil. Farmers raised livestock and grew crops. They sold pork, beef, wheat, and barley (a type of grain) to other colonies.

The Middle Colonies had a diverse population. The region's strong economy attracted people from other European countries besides Great Britain, such as Germany and Ireland. These people practiced many different religious beliefs.

The Southern Colonies included Maryland, Virginia, North Carolina, South Carolina, and Georgia. This region's geography favored cash crops. Rich men came to this region from Great Britain. They grew cash crops such as tobacco and rice on **plantations**.

Plantations needed many workers. At first, landowners used American Indians and **indentured servants** to plant and harvest plantation crops. Indentured servants also worked in other places in the colonies. Soon, Southern landowners began to replace these workers with enslaved Africans.

plantation a large farm on which crops are grown by free workers or slaves who live on the land

indentured servant a person who works for a period of time to pay off money owed for a debt, such as passage from Europe

7.3 Massachusetts Bay: New England Colony

You read in Chapter 6 about the Pilgrims who came to Massachusetts in 1620. They were Puritans who wanted to leave the Church of England.

Another group of Puritans also sought religious freedom. Led by John Winthrop, the group formed the Massachusetts Bay Colony. They settled in New England in 1630. These Puritans wanted to freely practice their religious beliefs in their new home.

The rugged geography of New England did not make the Puritans give up their plan. The soil was rocky, and winters could be harsh. But there were also vast forests and clean water. The winter cold killed insects and germs that caused disease. Colonists in New England often lived longer than people in other regions.

The region supported many **industries**. Colonists grew crops and raised animals on small farms. Men cut lumber from trees to build houses and trading ships. Fishing also provided food. Some colonists became skilled whalers. They made oil and candles from whale fat.

industry a group of businesses that produce certain goods or services

Massachusetts had a more democratic government than most countries in Europe. At first, only Puritan men could vote. As time passed, all men who owned land could vote. The colonists met at town meetings to solve local problems. They made decisions by majority rule. This was the first truly democratic form of local government in the colonies. Settlers elected representatives to the colony's lawmaking body. John Winthrop was elected governor 12 times between 1630 and 1649.

Puritans came to Massachusetts to practice their religion freely. Life was often hard. But there were many ways to earn a living.

Puritan leaders did not like the ideas that Anne Hutchinson preached. They put her on trial. Then they forced her to leave Massachusetts Bay. Rhode Island colonists welcomed her.

7.4 Rhode Island: New England Colony

From its start, Rhode Island offered people religious freedom. In 1631, a young minister named Roger Williams began to criticize the Puritan leaders of the Massachusetts Bay Colony. He thought that government and religion should be separate. These leaders forced him to leave the colony in 1635.

Williams spent the winter with some American Indians. In 1636, he started a town called Providence. It later became the capital of Rhode Island. Rhode Island welcomed people with different religious beliefs.

Puritan Anne Hutchinson also lived in the Massachusetts Bay Colony. She spoke out against some Puritan practices and beliefs. In 1637, she was put on trial for her religious ideas. The court found her guilty and forced her to leave the colony. She, too, moved to what became part of Rhode Island. There she could practice her beliefs.

Rhode Island's geography helped colonists build a strong economy. Narragansett Bay and local rivers provided fish and routes for travel and trade. Men trapped animals and traded the furs. The forests supplied timber. The soil in southern Rhode Island was good for farming. Winters were sometimes harsh. But summer rains helped crops grow.

Many Rhode Island colonists were farmers. They raised livestock. They grew corn, apples, and onions on small farms. Other colonists were traders. Ships from Rhode Island carried rum, wool and flax. Flax is a plant from which linen cloth and oil are made. Traders sold these goods in England and in the **West Indies**. Some colonists became rich in the trade of enslaved West Africans, even though few Rhode Island colonists themselves owned slaves.

Rhode Island was one of the most democratic colonies. At first, most men could vote for the colony's governor and local officials. Later on, only men who owned property could vote. But voters did not have to practice a certain religion.

West Indies islands that lie between southeastern North America and northern South America, and separate the Caribbean Sea from the Atlantic Ocean

7.5 New York: Middle Colony

The colony that the British named New York was first settled by people from the Netherlands. The Netherlands (often called Holland) is a country in northern Europe. Its people are the Dutch. The Dutch came to the area to set up fur-trading posts. The British, however, wanted this land for themselves so that British settlers in New England could move westward. In 1664, the British captured the colony. England's king gave the land to his brother, the Duke of York.

New York's geography made it a good place to settle. New York Harbor was ideal for shipping and trade. The valleys of the Hudson and Mohawk rivers were well suited to farming and trade. Iron, a useful mineral, was found in this region.

Winters in New York were cold, and summers were hot and humid (moist). But there were long growing seasons in the valleys and along the coast. So farming was easier here than in New England.

New York's economy offered colonists good jobs in many industries. Farmers grew wheat, corn, vegetables, and tobacco. Other colonists became miners, lumbermen, sailors, trappers, and merchants. Some workers were indentured servants or enslaved Africans.

Colonists had little power in New York's government. Governors appointed by the king were controlled by England. The governor appointed other officials and enforced the laws.

In 1664, the British took what would become New York from the Dutch. This allowed British settlers in the New England Colonies to move westward.

William Penn treated American Indians fairly. He paid them for their land. In return, they lived in peace with the Quaker colonists.

7.6 Pennsylvania: Middle Colony

grant to give something to someone of lower rank as a favor or privilege

assembly a body of lawmakers

Quakers were another religious group whose beliefs differed from those of other churches. Quakers had no priests or ministers. They would not fight in wars. English Quaker William Penn was jailed several times for his beliefs. He wanted to start a colony where Quakers could live safely. In 1681, England's King Charles II **granted** land in North America to Penn. Penn founded Pennsylvania there.

Penn welcomed people from many countries to his colony. They practiced different religions. Penn also treated American Indians with respect. Therefore, they lived in peace with the colonists. Although many Quakers opposed slavery, Penn permitted people to bring enslaved Africans to the colony.

Pennsylvania's geography provided many resources. The Delaware River Valley had rich soil for farming. There were forests for timber. Other raw materials included coal and minerals like iron and copper. Rivers offered easy transportation. Winters were cold and snowy, but the climate did not discourage colonists.

The colony developed a strong economy. There were jobs in many industries. Farmers raised dairy cattle. They also grew wheat and vegetables such as corn. People worked as miners, lumbermen, and merchants. Many Quaker merchants and farmers became rich.

The king approved Penn's appointment of the colony's governor. A General Assembly met to pass or reject laws made by a council. All men who owned property could vote for members of the **Assembly**. In 1696, the colony became more democratic when the elected members of the Assembly gained the power to write laws.

7.7 Maryland: Southern Colony

Cecilius Calvert, an English nobleman also known as Lord Baltimore, started the colony of Maryland in 1634. He hoped to make money from the colony. Lord Baltimore also wanted to provide a safe place for Catholics like himself. In England and in some of the colonies, Catholics were treated harshly.

Maryland's geography was well suited for planting and selling tobacco. This crop grew well in the hot, steamy summers. Chesapeake Bay was a route to the ocean for most settlers. Farmers near the bay could ship their crops to England and other places. Unfortunately, the climate also encouraged mosquitoes that spread deadly diseases.

There were many kinds of jobs in the colony. Most colonists worked on small farms. They grew tobacco, corn, wheat, and fruit trees. Some farmers raised cattle for beef and milk. Other industries included lumbering, shipping, and fishing. Some men made money by buying and selling slaves.

Some wealthy families owned tobacco plantations. Enslaved Africans and indentured servants did most of the work there.

This painting, *The Founding of Maryland,* shows the importance of religion to the Catholics who settled Maryland. Notice the priest at left blessing the group of settlers and American Indians.

Most colonists had little power in Maryland's government. Lord Baltimore made his brother, Leonard Calvert, the governor of the colony. At first, Calvert made the decisions. Then, in 1637, he allowed the colony to have an assembly. For the most part, only white men with property voted for members of the assembly. Over time, more non-Catholics moved to the colony. Calvert had the assembly pass a law to protect Catholics' right to vote and to serve in the government. These rights were denied to Catholics in some of the other colonies.

7.8 Georgia: Southern Colony

The Southern Colony of Georgia was started in 1732 for two main reasons. First, the British government wanted to keep Spanish troops from moving north from Florida.

Second, some wealthy British men wanted to help poor people avoid going to debtors' prison. A debtor is someone who owes something to another person. At that time, people went to jail if they could not pay their bills. Sending debtors to Georgia rather than to jail gave them a new start. They had a chance to earn a living in the new colony.

Georgia's geography was ideal for growing certain crops. Farming became the key industry in the colony. Winters were mild. Summers were long, hot, and humid. This climate was good for growing indigo, a plant used to make blue dye. The southern part of Georgia was mostly swamp. This land was ideal for growing rice. Later on, farmers grew tobacco and cotton.

People in Georgia also had other jobs. In the north, settlers cut down forests. They sold the lumber for homes. Then they used the cleared areas as farmland. Some colonists earned a living by trading goods with American Indians.

The artist made this engraving to persuade people to move to Georgia. Some rich British hoped that Georgia would be a place where poor people could seek a new and better life.

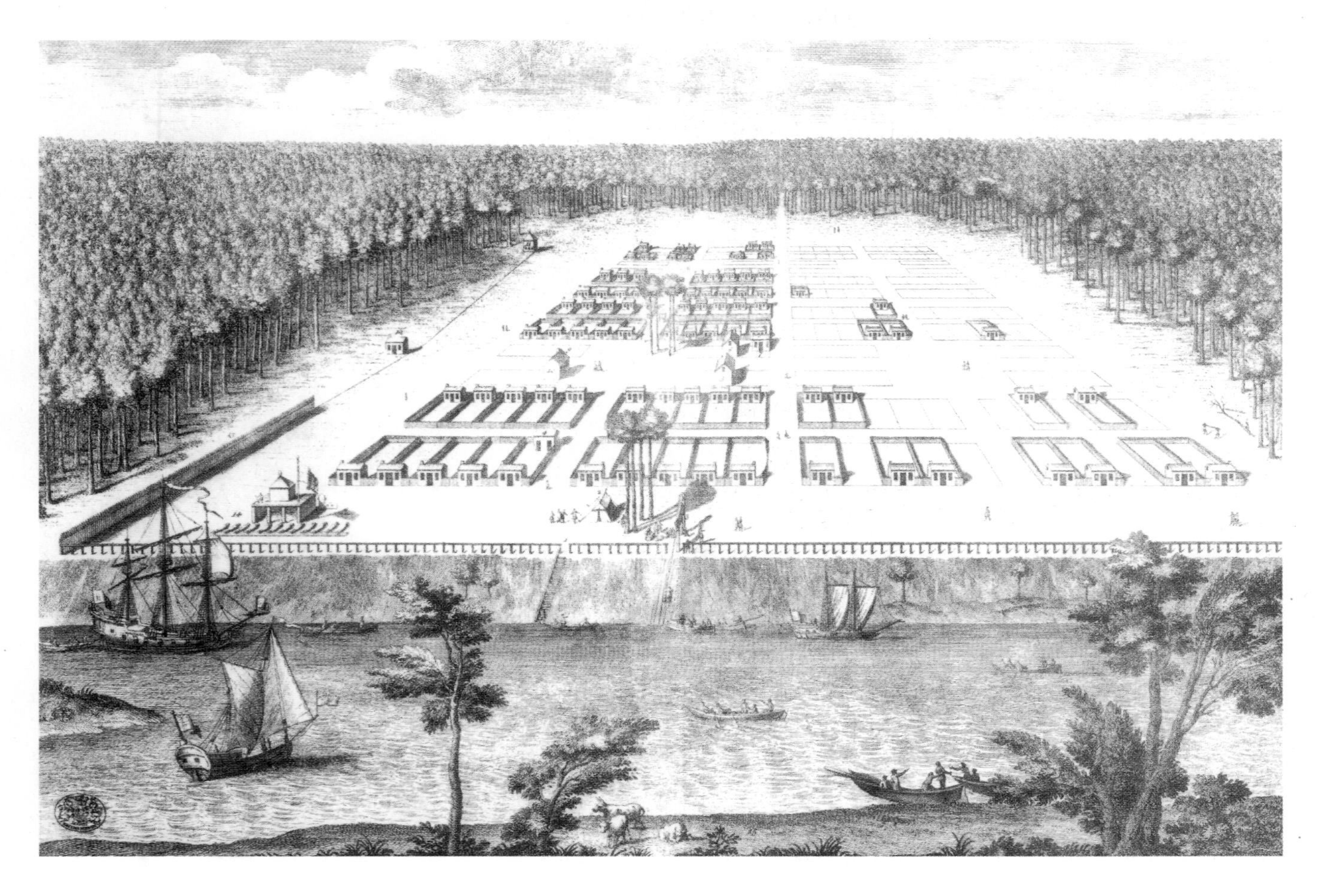

At first, only the rich men who had started the colony took part in running the government. They passed laws that they thought were best for the colony. They did not permit slavery. In 1752, however, these men turned control of the colony over to Great Britain's King George II. The king allowed white male voters to elect an assembly. However, he could overturn any law the assembly passed. New laws made slavery legal, and it soon became widespread.

Summary

In this chapter, you learned about the British colonies in what would become the United States. You used a map of colonial regions to help you organize information about the New England, Middle, and Southern colonies.

Several factors made the three regions different. Geography was one factor. The kind of climate and the type of soil in a region affected what crops could be grown there. The natural resources in each region led to the growth of certain industries.

Colonies within the same region had differences, too. Their governments and laws varied. Still, many colonists experienced more democracy than they had previously known in Great Britain and other European countries.

There were different reasons for founding each of the colonies. Some settlers sought religious freedom. Others came in search of wealth or to escape from debt. Slave traders forced enslaved Africans to come to these regions. What choices did these settlers face? How did they make their way in their new lives? You will find out in the next section.

As the colonies grew, settlers built towns with churches, schools, and government buildings.

Reading Further 7

Choosing a Career in the Colonies

The British colonies attracted hundreds of thousands of immigrants. In Europe, most people worked at the same jobs their families had always done. But in the colonies, a young man had some choices. These choices varied among regions. What kinds of jobs did each of the three colonial regions offer?

The New England Colonies

For Sam, it was an exciting time. He would soon be an adult. In the British colonies, he could decide his own future. What kind of work should he choose?

Sam lived in New England. He was part of a large family. He had seven brothers and sisters. They all worked on the family farm. It provided most of the basics the family needed.

Sam liked life on the farm. Perhaps he'd become a farmer. After all, that is what most people in New England did. He might leave his family's home to work for a time at a neighbor's farm so that he could make some money.

When he was a little older, he could marry. As a wedding present, his parents might give him a small piece of land. He and his wife could build a home and run a farm, as his parents had done. He could picture himself and his wife attending church and taking an active part in village life. And they could raise a big family. They would be comfortable, if not rich.

New England whalers remove strips of blubber, or fat, from a dead whale.

Although Sam liked farm life, he had another dream. He longed to earn a living from the sea. New England had many fine harbors. And not far off shore were some of the world's finest fishing grounds. The fishing industry provided jobs for thousands of people.

Whaling was another seafaring industry. It was hard dangerous work. But Sam was drawn by the promise of adventure. New England whaling ships sailed the world. He could travel to new and amazing places.

Young Sam had exciting options. He would choose his future soon.

The Middle Colonies

Farming was also the most common job for colonists in the Middle Colonies. There was plenty of fertile land. The climate allowed farmers to raise important crops, such as wheat.

But the Middle Colonies were known for something else, too. The region had two large cities: New York and Philadelphia. Life for residents of these places was very different from life for people in the countryside.

For one thing, the cities offered a great variety of jobs. Some people worked in the shipyards. Row upon row of workshops and stores employed many other colonists. It was in one of these enterprises that young Caleb would be seeking his future as a skilled worker.

The Middle Colonies had a strong economy. Becoming a printer was one of many jobs boys might choose.

Caleb's father had arranged for his son to become a printer. Soon, Caleb would begin training for this job. He would have to learn to perform many tasks.

To learn these skills, Caleb would need to become an **apprentice**. While still a young teenager, he would have to leave home to live with a master printer. The printer would teach Caleb all about printing. The printer would also provide food and housing for Caleb. In return, Caleb would work for the master printer as he learned the skills of printing.

apprentice a person who learns an occupation by getting experience under a skilled worker

Caleb's training would last several years. When it was finished, he could expect to get a paying job. If Caleb were ambitious, he might someday try to set up a shop of his own. It would be risky! He would need money for supplies. The business might fail. But a person who took risks could prosper. If his business thrived, he could become wealthy. And there was plenty of opportunity in the bustling big cities of the Middle Colonies. In the future, their economies would grow into the economic system that the United States uses today.

Caleb was nervous about moving away from his family. But he knew that he must get good training. He was ready to learn how to be a skilled printer and to make his place in the growing economy of colonial America.

The Southern Colonies

Thomas lived in South Carolina, one of the Southern Colonies. His family owned a large rice plantation. Carolina rice was the best. Family members were able to sell this product for a high price and earn a good income. With this money, they were able to purchase the items they needed and could not produce themselves. They could afford many luxuries, as well.

Thomas was getting older, and he had begun thinking about his future. The chances were very good that he would inherit his family's plantation. After all, he was the oldest of the surviving children of his family. He had had an older brother and sister. They had both died at an early age. Sadly, this was not uncommon in the colonial South. Disease was a serious problem in the wet, warm climate. In fact, Thomas was lucky that both of his parents were still alive. One of Thomas's friends had lost both of his parents and had had no other choice but to become a servant to another family.

But for Thomas, the future seemed bright. He would one day take control of the family plantation. He would manage the workers, most of them slaves, who produced the large rice crop. Since there were few villages or town centers, such as those found in New England, people tended to gather at each other's houses. He and his wife would entertain friends and visitors at home. And he would play games such as cards and pool with his friends. These were favorite pastimes in the colonial South.

Thomas was pleased about his future. After all, he had been raised to lead such a life. There were few other choices for wealthy young men in the colonial South. To run a large and prosperous plantation was a promising future for a Southern man.

People in the Southern Colonies raised cash crops such as rice on their farms and plantations.

Choices for Some Colonists

Unlike many men in Europe, young men in the British colonies could often choose what work they did. Many colonists worked on farms, especially in the Southern Colonies. In the Middle and New England colonies, varied industries offered more choices.

Women, however, had more limited choices. They were expected to take care of a house and a family. There were few other careers open to them. If women were paid to do a job, it was most likely a job as a household servant. Women might hold such a job until they married.

Poor people also had few choices. Some people signed agreements to work as indentured servants. This meant that they would work for a master for a period of years to pay off money they owed. The agreement might last from four to seven years. Indentured servants sometimes worked on plantations or in homes or shops in the towns. After their term of service ended, they might receive some money or land to begin a new life. Many people came to the American colonies as indentured servants. They paid off the cost of the ocean trip through work. Life for an indentured servant was hard. They often suffered harsh treatment. But they did have the hope of eventually being free to build a new life.

There were also many workers in colonial America who were enslaved. In the early colonial era, people owned slaves in all the colonies. Most slaves, however, lived in the Southern Colonies.

Almost all the slaves were from West Africa. Their white owners considered them property. Slaves had no control over their own lives. Now and then, an owner might free a slave. However, this was rare. And even former slaves had few rights. They also had fewer job choices than whites. And worse, freed slaves faced the ongoing threat of being forced back into slavery.

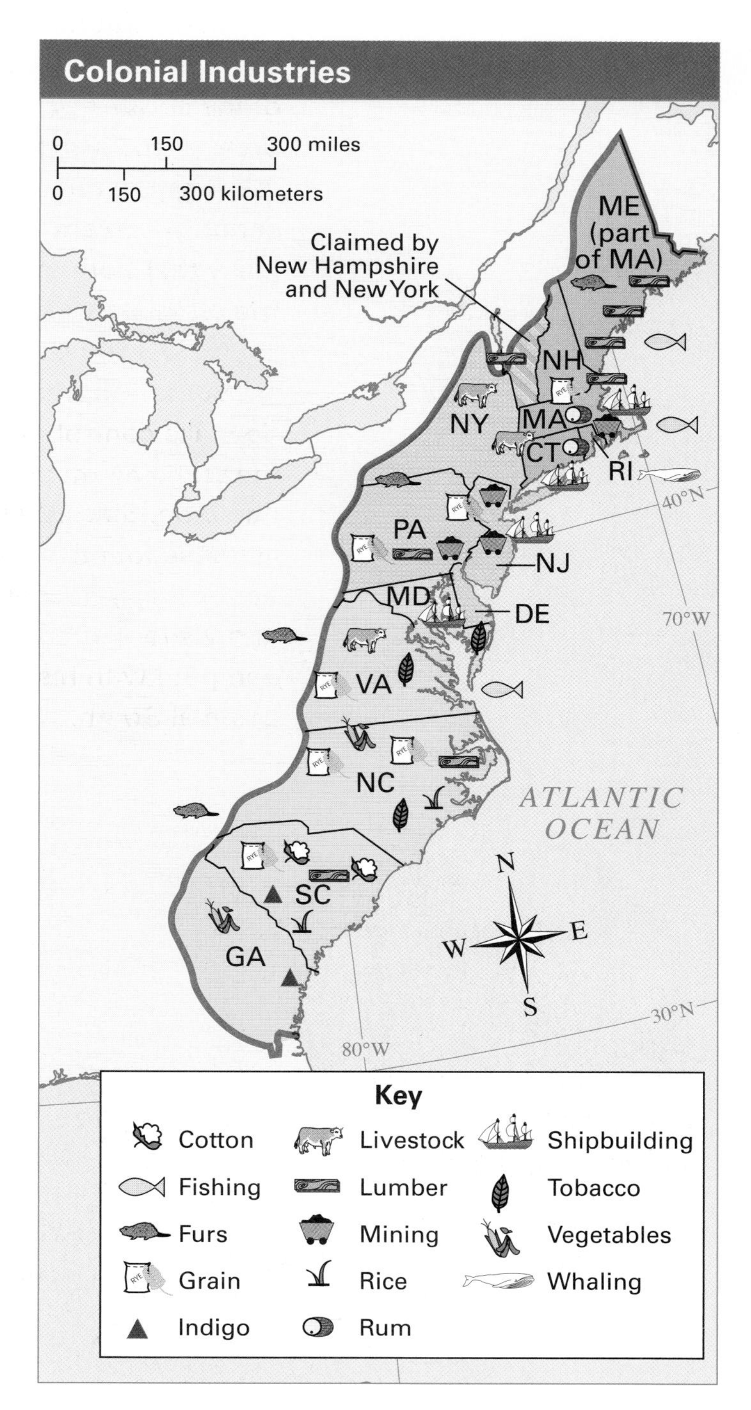

The Granger Collection, New York

What might be happening to this young girl?

What might this mother be thinking?

Why do you think this man is being whipped?

Facing Slavery

What was the impact of slavery on Africans?

8

8.1 Introduction

In Chapter 7, you read about the similarities and differences among the British colonies in North America. One difference was that the Southern Colonies used the labor of enslaved Africans. In this chapter, you will explore how the experience of slavery affected West Africans.

For hundreds of years, the **slave trade,** or exchange of captured people for goods, forced West Africans to confront dilemmas to survive. A **dilemma** is a situation in which a person is forced to make a decision even though he or she does not like any of the choices.

Starting in the late 1400s, European traders traveled to West Africa. They brought guns and other goods with them. The leaders of kingdoms and villages in West Africa wanted these things. They had to decide whether they were willing to exchange people for these goods. Many leaders chose to take part in the slave trade. Newly enslaved Africans had to find a way to live through the harsh conditions on ships crossing the Atlantic Ocean. Once Africans arrived in North America, they had to make choices about how to survive in their lives as slaves.

In this chapter, you will read about the dilemmas that West Africans faced because of the slave trade. Use the image below to help you think about what slaves went through during each part of their journey.

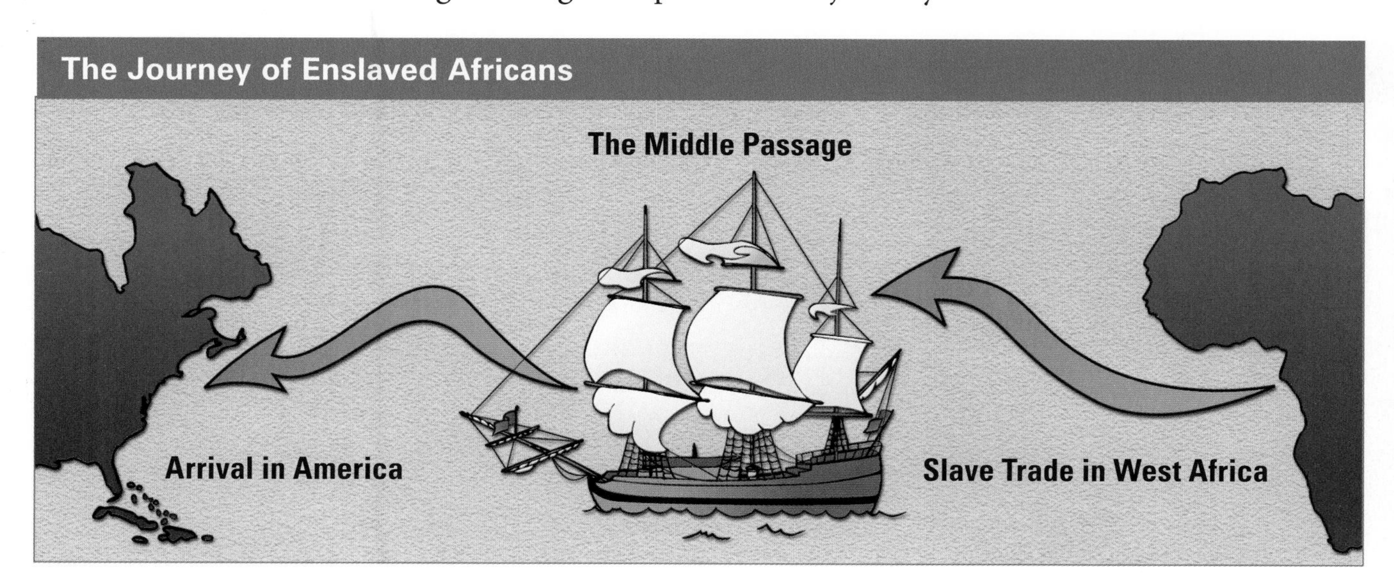

West Africa

40°N
Mediterranean Sea
Sahara
20°N
AFRICA
West Africa
0°
ATLANTIC OCEAN
N
W
E
S
20°S
0 1,000 miles
0 1,000 kilometers
INDIAN OCEAN
40°S
20°W 0° 20°E 40°E 60°E

8.2 West Africa in the 1500s

West Africa is a region of Africa. It lies near the equator and south of the Sahara, a large desert in northern Africa. To its west and south is the Atlantic Ocean. Most of West Africa is covered by grassland or rainforest.

In the 1500s, people of many cultures lived in West Africa. In many ways, West Africans were alike. Most people farmed. Some were miners, craftspeople, or traders. Traders led caravans of camels carrying gold and ivory from West Africa to countries north of the Sahara. In return, West Africans received salt, cloth, and other goods.

Throughout West Africa, society was based on the family. Relatives lived in the same village. They owned land together and shared their crops. They also worshipped the spirits of their ancestors. Villagers danced and sang chants to ask the spirits to protect them. Another one of their common traditions was storytelling. Fables, legends, and myths helped these people learn about their culture and history.

But West Africans were different in many other ways. Some lived in small villages. Others lived in large cities, such as Timbuktu. Some villages and cities were part of empires. The people of West Africa spoke many languages. Often, people from different villages could not understand one another.

Most West Africans in the 1500s lived in freedom. But that would change when slave traders from Europe came to Africa.

This scene shows daily life in a West African village.

8.3 Dilemma 1: Trading Slaves for Guns in West Africa

Some West Africans, like these men standing in the canoe, captured people. Then they traded these people as slaves to Europeans for guns, cloth, rum, and other goods.

Some people in West Africa were not free. These enslaved people were servants or workers. Some of them had been captured during wars or had been found guilty of crimes. West Africans sometimes sold these slaves to Arab traders. These traders were from countries in North Africa and Southwest Asia.

Although these slaves were not free, many of them were part of the larger family in a village. They may have had fewer rights than other villagers, but they could own land to farm. They could become skilled workers and earn money. Often, their descendants would be considered free.

Traders from Europe changed this way of life in West Africa. Europeans had sugar and tobacco plantations in the Americas that needed workers. Using slaves was a cheap way to get the work done. So traders went to West Africa. They offered cloth, rum, salt, and other goods in exchange for slaves. Many Africans became wealthy by trading slaves for goods like these.

The European traders also offered to trade guns for slaves. A village that had guns became more powerful than its neighbors. Once one village decided to make this trade, then it forced its neighbors to protect themselves by trading slaves for guns, too. Soon groups all over West Africa were capturing and enslaving people to trade them for guns.

Traders captured West Africans, put them in chains, and marched them away from their villages.

8.4 The Slave Trade: The Choices

A few West Africans refused to take part in the slave trade. But it was hard to resist the Europeans. One West African king tried. He said he would not permit slaves to be moved through his country. The Europeans tried to bribe him, but the king still refused. Then the Europeans convinced a rival group of West Africans to go to war against him. Many of the king's people were captured and then sold as slaves themselves.

Other West Africans tried to find slaves outside their own nations. Sometimes a king made war against his neighbors. He sold the people he captured to the slave traders. More often, however, a group from one West African village would raid another village. Armed with guns, the raiders would capture men, women, and children. Sometimes, they would kidnap the children while the adults were out farming in the fields.

Some West African groups did not raid other villages. Instead, they traded people who were already their slaves, such as prisoners they had captured during previous wars. These groups did not want to be a part of the slave trade, but they had little choice. Their neighbors who did trade slaves were becoming richer and more powerful and might soon try to capture and sell them as slaves.

8.5 Dilemma 2: Surviving the Middle Passage

The slaves faced a terrible journey. First, other West Africans put them in chains and marched them hundreds of miles to Africa's west coast. Many slaves died along the way or after reaching the coast. Then European traders loaded the survivors onto slave ships for the voyage to the Americas.

This voyage was called the **Middle Passage** because it was the second of three stages of the slave trade. The Middle Passage took from 21 to 90 days. In bad weather, it could take even longer. Traders sold slaves in South America, the West Indies, and the British colonies.

For the slaves, the trip was a nightmare. They were allowed little exercise. Pairs of men were chained together at the ankle and wrist, without room to sit up or to stand. Often men, women, and children were packed so closely together that they could barely move. Many were covered with sores from lying on the rough floorboards. The smell and the heat were unbearable, and the ships were full of lice, fleas, and rats. Sharks followed the ships, feeding on the dead who were thrown overboard.

No one knows how many West Africans made the Middle Passage, but the number has been estimated at 10 to 12 million. About 15 out of every 100 Africans died during the voyage.

The slave trade was part of the **triangular trade**. European traders took slaves from Africa to the Americas and sold them to owners of sugar plantations in the West Indies and tobacco plantations in the Southern Colonies.

In the West Indies, slaves grew sugarcane. It was turned into sugar and molasses. New Englanders bought these products and made them into rum. Traders took American goods, such as rum, tobacco, and lumber to Europe. Then they took goods made in Europe to Africa. There, they traded the goods for more slaves.

Middle Passage the voyage of slave ships across the Atlantic Ocean, from West Africa to the West Indies and the American continents

triangular trade the exchange of slaves and goods between Europe, the Americas, and West Africa, using shipping routes across the Atlantic Ocean

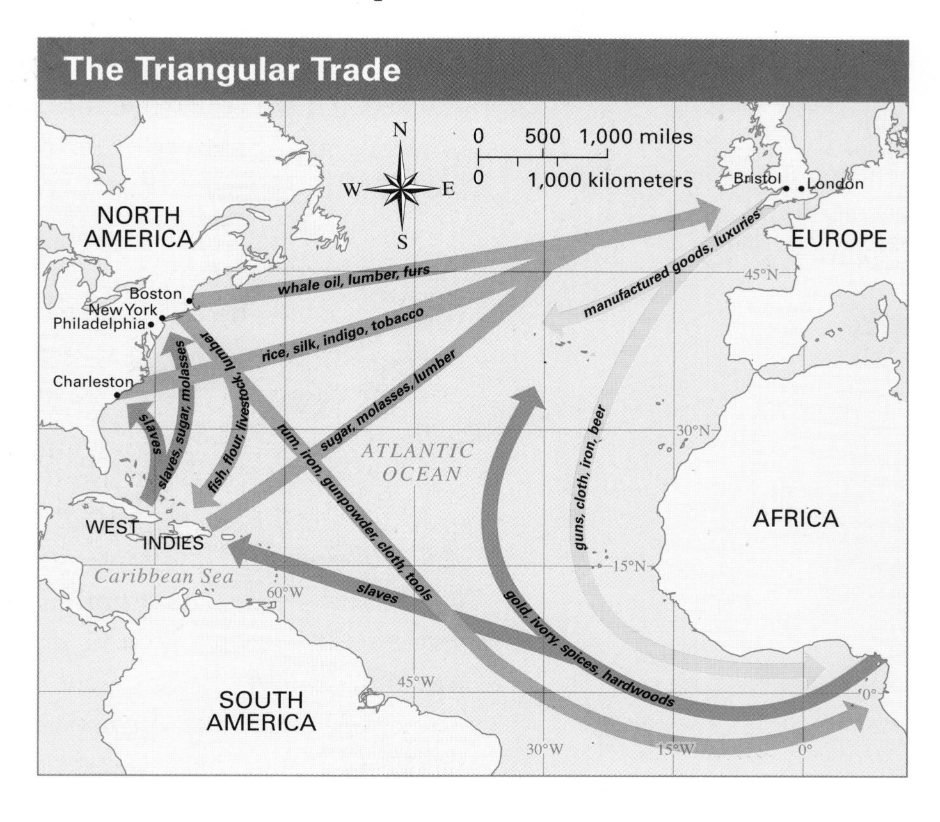

8.6 The Middle Passage: The Choices

Many of the enslaved Africans had never seen white people before. Some slaves thought that the white men wanted to eat them. None of the slaves knew where they were going or what would happen to them. They reacted in different ways to their terrifying situation.

Some slaves tried to kill themselves by refusing to eat or by jumping off the ship. But losing slaves meant losing money, so the ships' captains needed to keep the slaves alive. They used brutal methods to force slaves to eat. When slaves jumped overboard, the ships' crews went after them in rowboats. Slaves who were caught were often punished by whipping.

Some slaves rebelled by attacking their crew with crude weapons they had made. But the white men had guns and sometimes got help from the crews of other slave ships nearby. Once in a while, the slaves did win. But most slave revolts failed.

Many slaves tried to maintain enough of their strength to survive the journey. Some were too sick to resist their captors. One slave recounted his reaction when he found out that he was going to the Americas to work. He later wrote that he felt relieved and thought that being forced to work would not be so bad. But for many West Africans, life in the Americas would be even worse than the Middle Passage.

Enslaved Africans might be thrown overboard if they became seriously ill, or led a revolt, or if food was in short supply.

Slaves worked long hours in the fields, planting and harvesting crops. Here, slaves work in a cotton field. Notice the overseer on the horse.

8.7 Dilemma 3: Living as a Slave in the Colonies

When a slave ship arrived in the American colonies, the slave traders sold the West Africans to white plantation owners. Sometimes traders sold the slaves at "scrambles," or public sales, where the price was the same for each slave. The slaves were herded into a pen. When the gate was opened, buyers rushed in and "scrambled" around, grabbing the slaves they wanted.

Traders also sold slaves at **slave auctions**. The slaves stood on a platform called an auction block, while buyers bid against each other. One by one, the slaves were sold. Parents were sold separately from children, husbands from wives, and brothers from sisters. Often, they never saw each other again.

A slave's first year on a plantation was very hard. The slave had to survive a period of "breaking in," or adjusting to his or her new life. First, owners gave each slave a new name. Next, an **overseer** shouted orders at them in an unfamiliar language. The overseer gave them tools that they had never seen or used before. If the slaves did not understand what they were supposed to do, or if they disobeyed the overseer, he might have had them whipped, burned, or even killed.

Most slaves worked in the fields. They often worked 16 hours a day, planting and picking crops. Slaves sometimes had to walk for an hour to get to the fields. There was a short meal break at noon, and another one in the evening. Then the slaves walked back to their cabins. Usually, more than one family lived in one small cabin with a dirt floor. Sometimes, all they had for a bed was a bundle of straw, with some rags for a blanket.

slave auction a public sale in which slaves were sold to the highest bidders

overseer a person who was in charge of the work of slaves and could punish them for disobeying him

Most slaves lived in cabins like these. Often more than one family lived in a single small cabin.

8.8 Slave Life in the Colonies: The Choices

Slaves coped with their harsh lives in different ways. Some slaves attempted to escape. Runaways usually hid in nearby woods and tried to make their way to freedom. Sometimes, they banded together. In 1739, a group of about 60 runaway slaves in South Carolina seized guns from a warehouse and started on a march to freedom. But white owners caught up with them. In the battle that followed, the owners killed about 40 of the runaways. Most slaves who ran away were eventually caught and often severely punished by their owners.

Slaves resisted their new lives in other ways, too. One way was to pretend not to understand what they were being told to do. Another way was to pretend to be too sick or too hurt to work. Slaves sometimes broke tools or set buildings on fire. A few slaves hanged themselves. Some slaves believed that when they died, their spirits would return home to West Africa.

Many slaves chose to work hard and do what they were told. They hoped that their owners would make them house servants or skilled workers. In an owner's home, slaves had a somewhat easier life. They worked as cooks, gardeners, coachmen, and personal servants. They ate the leftovers from the master's table and wore the family's old clothing. Some slaves were taught to be carpenters or weavers. They might even earn wages for extra work done on Sundays and holidays. They wanted to save enough money to buy their freedom, but very few slaves accomplished this goal.

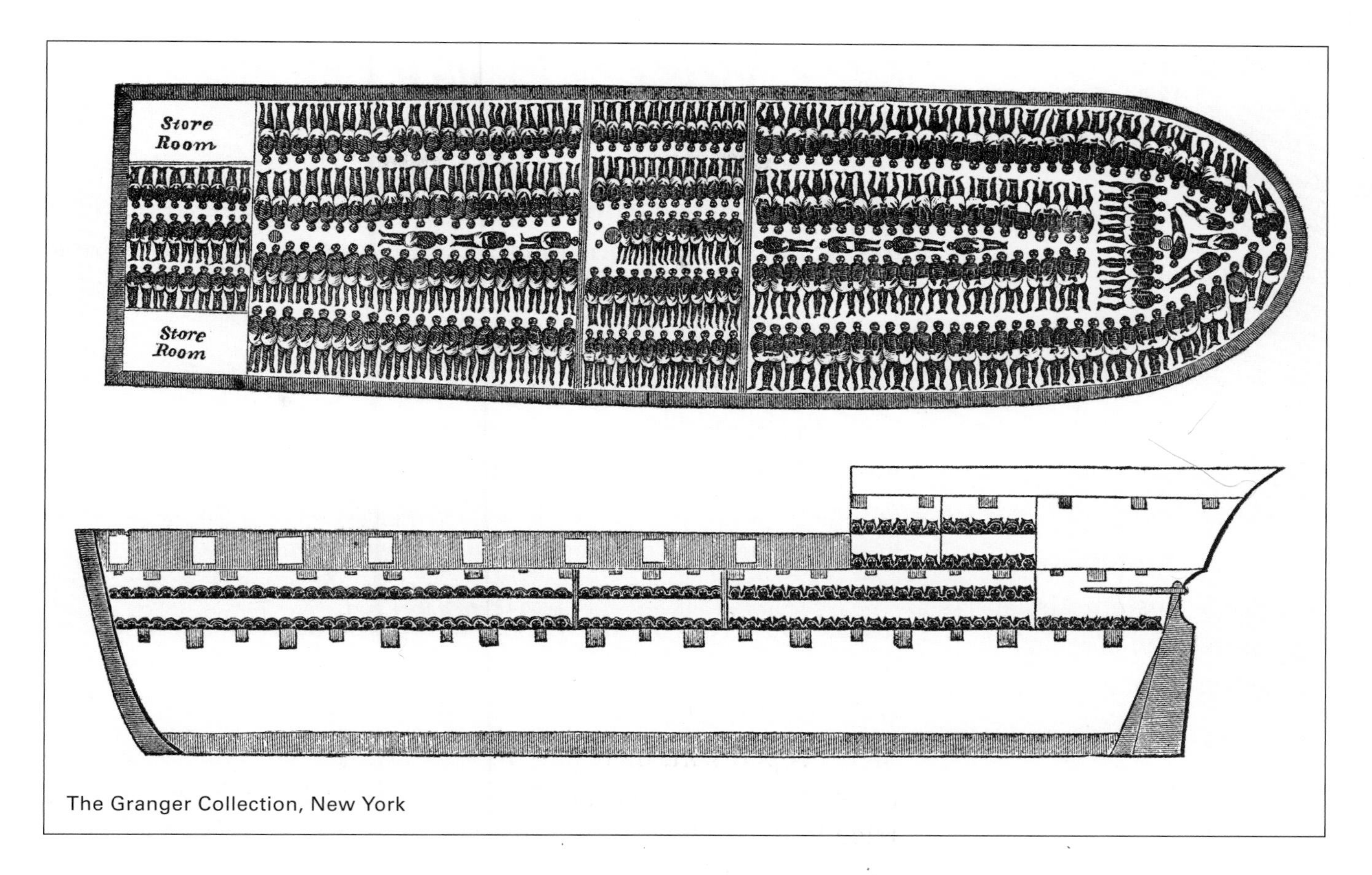

The Granger Collection, New York

This diagram shows the inhumane crowding slaves endured on ships during the Middle Passage.

Summary

In this chapter, you learned how West Africans became slaves in the Americas. You used an illustration to track how slave traders moved Africans across the Atlantic Ocean. You identified three dilemmas of slavery that faced West Africans.

In the first part of the slave journey, West Africans were captured. They had to march many miles to the coast. In the second part, these Africans endured harsh conditions as they crossed the ocean. This trip was called the Middle Passage. Finally, those who survived responded in different ways to their lives as slaves.

You also read that the slave trade was part of the triangular trade. Trade routes linked Europe, Africa, and the Americas.

In the next pages, you will learn more about the daily lives of enslaved African Americans in the colonies. How did they find hope and comfort under such difficult and desperate conditions? Read on to find out.

Reading Further 8

How Slaves Kept Hope Alive

Slavery in what was to become the United States began soon after the first Europeans arrived. It continued for 250 years. During that time, slaves struggled to keep alive memories of their proud past. They used these memories to build a new culture. How did memories and culture help the slaves survive their ordeal?

In his book *Roots,* American writer Alex Haley described the most powerful and moving moment of his life. He was in an African village, surrounded by native Africans. Somehow, Haley knew he shared a connection with these strangers.

Haley described his meeting with the village **griot** (GREE oh). It was 1967. Two hundred years earlier, Haley's relative had left this African village. Yet the griot was able to tell Haley vivid stories of his family's past. In detail, the griot explained the history of Haley's relatives. Haley was stunned at what he heard.

griot a western African storyteller who recites the history of a tribe or family

Soon, a crowd of villagers had gathered around him. Out of the crowd came a woman. She carried a small baby. The woman placed the child in Haley's arms for a moment. Then she took the baby back. Another woman did the same. This continued for some time. Before long, Haley had held about 12 of the village's babies. Later, an expert on African culture explained to Haley the meaning of this village ceremony. "In their way," the expert said, "they were telling you that 'through this flesh, which is us, we are you, and you are us.'"

This relative of author Alex Haley holds a photo of him. They met when Haley visited his ancestor's homeland.

What had drawn Haley to Africa to seek out these stories from his past? He was looking for answers to questions he had thought about since childhood.

As a young boy, Haley had listened as his older relatives told stories about the family history. Their stories were about his ancestors during the time of slavery. Haley learned where his relatives had been born, at which plantation they had lived enslaved, and more. All the stories traced his family back to one man. Haley's relatives called him "the African." His owner had given him the name Toby. The African, himself, insisted that his name was Kinte.

The Kunta Kinte–Alex Haley Memorial in Annapolis, Maryland marks the place where Haley's ancestor Kinte arrived in North America as a slave in 1767. It also honors the storytelling of Alex Haley.

Kinte had a daughter during his years in North America. He told her about his life in Africa. These stories continued to be passed down from parent to child, through the generations. Haley's family told the stories to him when he was a young boy. Haley's grandmother made sure that he listened, she said, so that he would know where he came from. But where, Haley wondered, was that?

He had a few clues. Kinte had taught his daughter some African words. These words had been woven into the old family stories. When he grew up, Haley found experts who figured out which language the words were from. He also learned that among the words was the name of a river.

With these clues—his ancestor's name and the name of a river—Haley found Kinte's home village. In 1967, he went to see it for himself. He listened in awe as the village griot told him stories of Kinte's family. He heard how the young Kinte had disappeared from his village. The stories connected with the ones his grandmother had told him.

After two centuries, Haley had reconnected his African and American families. The link had nearly been broken. Slavery had almost destroyed it. But it had endured. His family's history had lived on in a handful of words and stories, passed from parent to child. It had survived through more than 200 years.

Music provided comfort and encouragement for slaves.

Storytelling, Song, and Prayer

Haley's story shows the importance of storytelling among enslaved Africans. Storytelling was one of the ways in which families survived the ordeal of slavery. Kinte told his daughter the story of his capture. He also made sure that she knew details of his African culture.

Some slaves shared folktales from Africa. For example, a slave might tell stories of clever animals, such as rabbits, that managed to outsmart bigger, stronger creatures. Other stories might warn of how dangerous and cruel the big beasts could be. Through such stories, children could understand that, as slaves, they were like the small creatures. They needed to use their wits to survive.

Storytelling could also be a time for a family to relax together. A slave's day was filled with hard work. Adults got up before sunrise to work long hours at their tasks. Children had jobs, too. Gathering to share stories was one way in which enslaved people could build family ties. Such ties, which could be broken by an owner at any time, helped make life bearable.

Music was another source of strength and comfort for enslaved Africans. As slaves worked in the fields, they often sang songs called **spirituals**. The music did more than pass the time and provide entertainment. It also carried deep meaning. Many of the slaves' songs told of freedom in a way that did not threaten white slaveholders. The plantation owners usually allowed the singing because the words told Bible stories and encouraged the slaves to work.

Some songs carried secret messages. For example, a song might serve as a signal to slaves that an escape was planned for that night. Songs might also give instruction about how to run away and reach freedom. For example, "Follow the Drinking Gourd" is a song about a group of stars called the Big Dipper. One of the stars in the Big Dipper is the North Star. So, by following the "drinking gourd," or the Big Dipper, slaves would know that they were traveling north toward freedom. This increased their chances of escaping to places like Canada that did not have slavery.

For slaves, a preacher's message at religious services was also a source of strength and hope. He told them that life was hard, but that God had something better in store. God would deliver them from bondage. They would be free, for there would be no slaves or owners in heaven.

spiritual a type of religious song that developed among enslaved Africans and that expressed deep emotion

Slaves combined African traditions and Christian practices in their religious services.

Slaves shouted out in joy at such promises. They swayed and danced to the rhythm of the sermon. The words were like a song without music. Then they all sang, clapping and jumping. They lost themselves in their strong feelings.

Religion was a key part of life. Worship services were a community event. And the promise of freedom gave them hope. This helped them survive the harsh conditions they faced.

Enslaved Africans learned about the Christian religion from their white owners. But the slaves did not give up their African traditions. Instead, they combined the old practices with those of Christianity to make something new. The religion of the slaves was joyful, full of song and dance. It also included other features from Africa, such as the use of herbs, spells, and charms.

Slave owners had mixed feelings about the slaves' religion. Some believed that Christianity would make the slaves more willing to obey their masters. But others could see the differences in the ways in which slaves worshipped. They did not like the African traditions slaves followed. So the slave owners tried to change these rituals or to stop them.

Perhaps slave owners feared the strength their slaves drew from religion, and from the songs and stories the slaves shared. Perhaps the slave owners knew that the spirit of such people could not be defeated. It was this same spirit that Haley found on his visit to Africa. Through shared memories and culture, his family and his people survived—and thrived.

Find these people in the photograph above. What do you think each one is doing?

Life in Colonial Williamsburg

9

What were key parts of life for Southern colonists in the 1700s?

9.1 Introduction

In Chapter 8, you learned how West Africans were enslaved and brought to the American colonies. In this chapter, you will take a walking tour of an important Southern colonial town. During your tour, you will find out what life was like in Virginia for two different groups—the white colonists and the African slaves.

Williamsburg was the capital of the British colony of Virginia. As you visit this town, you will learn about Virginia's government. You will also learn about the culture, or way of life, in this colony. You will see what it was like to be a colonist going to church, school, and work. You will find out how colonists relaxed and had fun. And you will see how enslaved Africans lived and worked.

Williamsburg has been restored and preserved much as it was in the 1700s. Tourists visit it to learn about life in colonial times. As you tour the town, locate the places you visit on the map below.

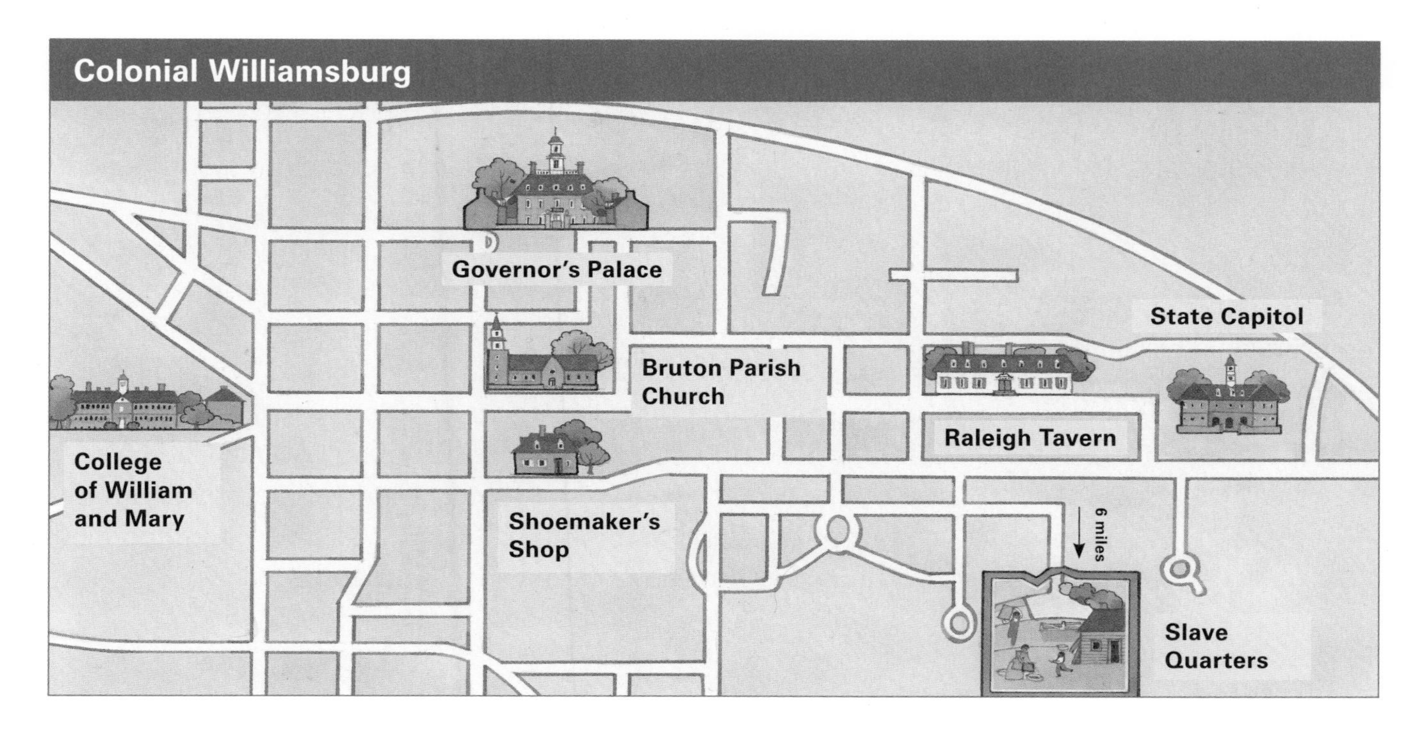

This man is dressed to look like a lawyer or a government worker in colonial Williamsburg.

9.2 Colonial Williamsburg

From 1699 to 1780, Williamsburg served as the capital of Virginia, the largest American colony. The town was named in honor of King William III of England.

Williamsburg was the center of government, education, and culture in colonial Virginia. The town was built around four main buildings. The **capitol** stood at one end of the main street. At the other end was a college. The Governor's Palace lay to the north. Near the center of the town was a church.

By 1770, about 2,000 people lived in Williamsburg. Some of them were lawyers and government workers. Some people were carpenters and cabinetmakers. Others worked in shops or served drinks and food in taverns.

Like other Virginians, the people of Williamsburg often married in their 20s. Divorce was not available in the colonies.

About half of Williamsburg's people were Africans. Most of them were slaves who worked in town or on nearby farms and plantations.

Many people visited Williamsburg. Most Virginians lived in the countryside, far from the town. But they came to the capital to shop, attend church, and take care of business at government offices. American Indians came to trade.

capitol the main government building, in which lawmakers meet

As you learn about Williamsburg, think about what it was like to live there during colonial times. Listen to the bells ringing at the college, church, or capitol building. See the people working and shopping. Hear them speaking with British accents. Listen to the languages of American Indians as they trade. See the chickens and sheep in the streets. Hear the sounds of horses as they pull oxcarts and wagons. Picture yourself walking down the main street to the College of William and Mary.

9.3 Education: The College of William and Mary, and Dame Schools

At one end of the town's main street stood the College of William and Mary. The college was named after King William III and Queen Mary II of England. In 1693, they gave the order to start a school. Work on the first building began in 1695 and was completed in 1700. It was later named the Wren Building. The town was called Middle Plantation.

In 1699, the House of Burgesses moved the capital of Virginia from Jamestown to Middle Plantation. At this time, they renamed the town Williamsburg, in honor of England's king. While the capitol was being built, the Wren Building held the government offices.

The College of William and Mary was a school for boys. It included a grammar school. Here, boys aged 12 to 15 learned to read, write, and do arithmetic. Older boys could study to become priests in the Church of England, or the Anglican Church.

In the 1700s, about 100 boys attended William and Mary each year. Many famous people studied there. In fact, four boys who later became U.S. presidents—George Washington, Thomas Jefferson, James Monroe, and John Tyler—attended the college.

Boys at the College of William and Mary had classes in rooms like this one. This classroom is in the Wren Building, the oldest college building still in use in the United States.

In this scene, two girls reenact a lesson at a colonial dame school. The woman playing the role of their teacher reads to them.

Boys and girls in the colonies were educated differently. In large towns like Williamsburg, many boys went to school. In the countryside, families with enough money might send boys to study with a local minister or priest. Or parents might hire a tutor, or private teacher, to come to their homes.

In the colonies, women usually took care of running the home. As a result, most girls did not go to school. Instead, they stayed at home. They learned cooking, sewing, and other skills from their mothers and older sisters.

Some girls attended dame schools. (*Dame* means "woman" or "lady.") Women ran these schools in their homes. Parents hired these women to teach small groups of young children. Students learned reading, writing, and arithmetic. They had lessons in civility, or manners. The girls also learned prayers, knitting, and sewing.

Few enslaved African children received a full education. African American parents who had some education might teach their children to read and write. Williamsburg did have two very small schools for nonwhite children. One was for African American boys. The other was for American Indian boys. Both schools prepared boys to be priests in the Anglican Church. Very few boys attended these schools. After some slaves revolted in 1831, Southern states passed strict laws against any further education of slaves.

Rules Learned by Colonial Children

Boys and girls in the colonies learned strict rules about how to behave. Some children studied a book titled *Rules of Civility and Decent Behaviour in Company and Conversation.* As a teen, George Washington copied 110 rules from this book. He tried to live by them all his life. Here are a few of the rules:

1st Every Action done in Company, ought to be with Some Sign of Respect, to those that are Present.

2nd When in Company, put not your Hands to any Part of the body, not usually Discovered [seen].

3rd Shew [show] Nothing to your Friend that may affright [frighten] him.

4th In the Presence of Others Sing not to yourself with a humming Noise, nor Drum with your Fingers or Feet.

Some girls went to dame schools. There they learned prayers, the alphabet, knitting, and sewing. This is a piece of embroidery called a sampler. Samplers traditionally show the alphabet and a date sewn with fancy stitches.

9.4 Trades: The Shoemaker's Shop

If you walked along the streets of Williamsburg, you would see a number of shops where **craftsmen** worked at their **trades**. These stores were called trade shops.

craftsman a person who works at a job that requires manual or artistic skill

trade a craft, or an occupation that requires manual, artistic, or mechanical skill

Craftsmen in the colonies made items that colonists needed for their homes and farms. Blacksmiths made objects such as cooking pots and plows out of iron and steel. Coopers made barrels and other containers. Millers ground grains into flour. Gunsmiths made rifles and repaired metal items like buckles, bells, and axes. Other craftsmen included carpenters, cabinetmakers, and candle makers.

Three levels of craftsmen worked in trade shops. Master craftsmen owned their shops. They were experienced at their trade. Sometimes, they hired one or two journeymen. Journeymen were skilled workers but did not own a shop. Master craftsmen also used apprentices, who were workers learning the trade. Apprentices learned by working with the more skilled craftsmen. They did tasks requiring less skill.

This man is acting as a colonial shoemaker. He is making shoes by hand.

This is the exterior of the shoemaker's shop in colonial Williamsburg, Virginia.

Apprentices worked for a period lasting from four to seven years or until they reached the age of 21. At that point they could become journeymen.

At times, enslaved African Americans were trained in a craft. Some slave owners allowed slaves to earn money by working for other people. Even so, very few slaves were able to save enough money to buy their freedom.

One of the most common crafts in Williamsburg was shoemaking. Shoemakers specialized in making either men's or women's shoes and boots. At any one time, 9 to 12 shoemakers competed with one another for business. They also had to compete with merchants, or the people who buy and sell goods. Merchants' shops sold shoes that were made in other places, including Great Britain.

Shopping for shoes in Williamsburg was not much different from buying shoes today. Customers could buy ready-made shoes in standard sizes. But if someone needed an unusual size or some other special feature, the shoemaker would make a custom pair just for that person.

Raleigh Tavern in Williamsburg is named for Sir Walter Raleigh. Raleigh had tried to start the first colony on Roanoke Island in 1585.

9.5 Social Life: Raleigh Tavern

People in the colonies worked hard. But they also enjoyed visiting with one another, sharing news, and relaxing after a long day's work.

A favorite gathering place for colonial men was a local tavern. Taverns were places that served food and drink. Many taverns also rented bedrooms so that travelers could stop to rest during their journey.

Dinner at a Williamsburg tavern might start with peanut soup. This tasty dish was made with peanut butter, celery, and cream. A popular main course was shepherd's pie, a lamb stew with a potato-and-egg topping.

After dinner, guests often drank wine or beer. They might also sing songs. Some taverns hosted balls, or fancy dances. Others had game rooms, where men played cards, dice, and board games. A favorite board game was *The Royall and Most Pleasant Game of the Goose.*

The tavern that a man visited depended on his status in the colony. Lawyers and rich planters would gather at certain taverns. Craftsmen such as shoemakers and blacksmiths would meet at other taverns.

One famous colonial tavern was the Raleigh Tavern in Williamsburg. It opened for business in about the year 1717.

It was named for Sir Walter Raleigh, an English explorer. In 1585, Raleigh had tried to start the first colony on Roanoke Island, which was part of Virginia at that time.

When the leaders of Virginia came to the capital, they often spent time at Raleigh Tavern. They ate meals in the dining room. They attended balls in the Apollo Room. They held business meetings. Most important to the history of our nation, these powerful men came to discuss **politics**. George Washington and Thomas Jefferson spent time at Raleigh Tavern with other men who were active in politics. It became a center for meetings of those who wanted independence from British rule in the years before the American Revolution.

politics the activities of governments and the people who work in them

Raleigh Tavern was a popular meeting place for important men in Virginia. Here they discussed business and politics.

royal colony a colony that is controlled directly by a king or queen, who usually appoints a royal governor

bill a draft of an idea for a law that is then considered by lawmakers

9.6 Government: The Governor's Palace

As Virginia's capital, Williamsburg was where government leaders such as the royal governor and the colony's lawmakers worked. At this time, Virginia was a **royal colony**.

Lawmakers were members of Virginia's General Assembly. The Assembly included the royal governor, his council, and the House of Burgesses. The House had two men from each county and one member each from certain towns. These men were called burgesses. The General Assembly met in the capitol building. They wrote and voted on **bills**. When they passed a bill, it went to the governor. If he approved and signed the bill, it became a law.

The royal governor of Virginia lived and worked in the Governor's Palace. He also entertained guests here. The building was designed to impress visitors and to remind them of the king's power.

Virginians became members of the General Assembly in one of two ways. Voters elected burgesses. The governor appointed his council members. But both voters and Assembly members had to be white men with property who belonged to the Anglican Church.

The British king appointed the royal governor to be the king's representative. The governor lived in a large house called the Governor's Palace.

The Governor's Palace was designed to impress visitors with the king's power. It was three stories high. It took 25 servants and slaves to care for it. Outside were large gardens and orchards. There was even a canal, or man-made waterway, on which the governor could row a small boat to admire the flowers and trees.

The governor worked in the palace. One of his jobs was to read the bills that the Assembly sent him. The governor had great power to decide which bills became laws. If he did not like a bill, he could refuse to sign it.

The palace was also the scene of official celebrations. On important occasions, like the king's birthday, the governor would invite colonial leaders to attend fancy balls.

Actions of Virginia's Royal Governor

Colonial governors were powerful. They made decisions about bills and other issues. Here are three actions taken by the royal governor of Virginia:

A Lighthouse at Cape Henry

In the 1700s, Virginia's royal governor and Maryland's governor worked to get a lighthouse built near Cape Henry in Chesapeake Bay. They hoped to make it safer for trade ships to sail between their colonies. Virginia's Assembly passed the lighthouse bill. The governor signed it in 1772. But the colonies did not have the money to build the lighthouse. In 1789, President George Washington signed a federal bill to fund lighthouses. At last, in 1792, Cape Henry lighthouse was completed.

Cape Henry Lighthouse

Voters in the Virginia Colony

The governor agreed to laws that determined who could vote in Virginia. Voters had to be white men over the age of 21 with property. They had to belong to the Anglican Church. Men without property, women, African Americans, and American Indians were not allowed to vote.

A Pardon for a Teenaged Pirate

Lawbreaking was often punished harshly in Virginia. For a minor crime, such as not attending church, people might be fined. For a major crime, such as stealing, lawbreakers could be put to death. But those found guilty could ask for a pardon, or a release from punishment. In 1727, a teenager named John Vidal was convicted of piracy—the robbing of ships at sea. Vidal begged for mercy. He said that he "never intended to go apirating." The governor pardoned him.

These women are reenacting the lives of slaves in the Virginia colony. Slaves lived in rough cabins called slave quarters. The cabins had little furniture and dirt floors. Slaves often slept on burlap mattresses stuffed with straw.

9.7 Slavery: The Slave Quarters at a Tobacco Plantation

About half the people in Williamsburg were enslaved Africans. Some worked in town. Most lived and worked on farms and plantations outside the town.

Slaves in the colonies had different roles. Some of them were house slaves. House slaves did chores in their owner's house. Some slaves were town slaves who worked in places like Williamsburg as gardeners or coachmen. Town and house slaves often worked seven days a week. A few town slaves learned a craft, such as shoemaking or blacksmithing.

But most of the slaves worked in the fields on plantations and farms. They worked six days a week, from sunrise until after sunset.

Slaves lived in rough cabins called slave quarters. In colonial days, you might have seen the slave quarters on a tobacco plantation located just outside Williamsburg. Inside these cabins, there would have been burlap mattresses stuffed with straw used for beds. Against the wall would have stood tools used for work in the fields, such as rakes, hoes, and shovels. You might have found some musical instruments, such as drums and fiddles. Since a few slaves could read, you might even have seen an old copy of the local newspaper, the *Virginia Gazette*.

Enslaved people had difficult and painful lives. They worked long, hard hours. They had to do whatever they were told. Often their owners beat them. If a slave fought back, he or she could be killed. Owners could also sell their slaves, separating them from friends and family, at any time.

As you learned in Chapter 8, slaves survived these terrible conditions by relying on one another. They worked to create strong family ties. They looked after their family members.

Slaves also had their own Christian preachers. These preachers spoke in their sermons, or religious talks, about the equality of all men. And as in West Africa, music played an important part in their religious services.

Just as their West African ancestors did, slaves in the colonies used songs to express themselves. As you have read, they sang spirituals. Another common type of song was the call-and-response. In these songs, a leader would sing a line (the call) and then everyone would repeat it (the response). The enslaved Africans sang of their anger and pain. They also sang of their hope for freedom.

"Juba": A Call-and-Response Song

The word *juba* refers to a call-and-response song with clapping. It can also mean leftover food, such as bread crusts, and the skin from cooked meat. Owners fed their house slaves such scraps.

One African American woman's father told her that his mother had added milk to food scraps to make his family's meal. While she and his sisters prepared food for their owner, his mother had sung the words below. The song expressed her wish to give her family good, hot food, like the food she made for the slave owner. Instead, she could only give her family leftovers, or juba.

Call: Juba this and juba that
Response: Juba this and juba that

Call: And juba killed a yellow cat
Response: And juba killed a yellow cat

Call: And get over double trouble, juba
Response: And get over double trouble, juba

Call: Ah, ah, juba
Response: Ah, ah, juba

Call: You sift-a the meal
Response: You sift-a the meal

Call: And you give me the husk
Response: And you give me the husk

Call: You cook-a the bread
Response: You cook-a the bread

Call: You give me the crust
Response: You give me the crust

Call: We fry the meat
Response: We fry the meat

Call: You give me the skin
Response: You give me the skin

Call: Juba this and juba that
Response: Juba this and juba that

Call: Juba killed a yellow cat
Response: Juba killed a yellow cat

9.8 Religion: Bruton Parish Church

In some colonies, people had religious freedom. But in other colonies, they had to attend the churches that were supported by the government.

In Virginia, as in England, religion and government were not separate from each other. England's king was the head of the Church of England, also known as the Anglican Church. In a similar way, the royal governor was the head of Virginia's official Anglican Church. Only Anglicans could vote or hold government positions. And the law required that all white colonists attend church. Virginians also had to pay taxes to support the official church.

At first, the Anglican Church leaders tried to prevent people from practicing other religions. Over time, some colonists demanded the right to worship in other churches. The Anglican Church began to allow colonists to join other Protestant groups. Throughout the 1700s, Virginia gradually allowed more freedom of religion.

The Bruton Parish Church was the Anglican Church building in Williamsburg. It was located near the center of the town.

As in most colonial towns, the local church was the center of religious activity in Williamsburg. Many famous Virginians, such as Thomas Jefferson and George Washington, attended services at Bruton Parish Church.

In Virginia, the Church of England, or Anglican Church, was the official church. Bruton Parish Church was the Anglican Church building. It still stands today in the center of colonial Williamsburg.

On Sundays, people often arrived early at church to meet and talk. Many of them only came to town once every few weeks. Outside the church, people discussed the latest news. They also read and posted announcements. At times, these gatherings were as lively as town fairs.

Once inside the church, people sat in different places, depending on their position in the community. The important people sat close to the pulpit—the platform or raised desk where the minister stood during services. Those with less influence in the colony sat farther away.

In Bruton Parish Church, the governor's family sat directly across from the pulpit. In the early years of the church, men sat on one side, and women on the other. Later, families sat together. Important men of the area sat in the front rows. Their house slaves might sit with them. Students from the College of William and Mary sat in the balcony, far from the pulpit. Most Africans stood in the back or looked in through the windows.

When the services ended, the colony's most important people left the church first. Before the women and the less poswerful and wealthy men could go outside, they had to wait for the rich men who had influence, such as plantation owners, to leave.

Summary

In this chapter, you learned about life in Williamsburg, the colonial capital of Virginia. A map of the town helped you to locate six places as you read about the activities in the town.

At schools like the College of William and Mary, boys learned to read and write. Many girls learned skills at home. Some children went to dame schools. In trade shops, skilled craftsmen made items to sell. In taverns, men gathered to relax and discuss current events. At the capitol and the Governor's Palace, men made laws for the colony. Meanwhile, enslaved Africans lived in slave quarters. They worked long hours as house servants or as field workers.

The parish church was the center of religious activity. It was also a place where colonists gathered to share news.

In the 1700s, some colonists began to worship in a different way. This affected other aspects of colonial life. Read on to learn how the change in religious ideas led to other changes in colonial society.

Reading Further 9

A Religious Revival in the Colonies

Bruton Parish was like other town churches throughout the colonies. But many farmers lived too far away to attend services. To reach these people, a new religious movement arose in the 1730s and 1740s. It was called the Great Awakening. How would this change affect the future of the colonies?

Nathan Cole, a Connecticut farmer, had waited for this moment for a long time. He had heard about the preaching of Great Britian's George Whitefield. He longed for the chance to hear the great minister deliver one of his fiery sermons. Just the thought of it caused Cole to feel closer to God.

Then, this morning, Cole was at work in his fields when he heard the startling news. Whitefield was to preach in a nearby town. The service would begin in less than two hours!

Cole stopped his work at once and rushed to fetch his wife. The two mounted a single horse and set out at a run for the town of Middletown, 12 miles away. The horse soon tired. Anxious not to slow down, Cole got off the horse to lighten its load. He then ran alongside his wife and the exhausted animal.

George Whitefield traveled through the colonies in the 1700s preaching the religious ideas of the Great Awakening.

Cole and his wife passed empty fields. It seemed everyone had dropped what he or she was doing to attend the meeting. He also noticed that the sky was filled with what he first thought was fog. But it was actually clouds of dust kicked up by others racing along the dirt roads to see the great minister.

Soon, the road to Middletown became clogged with riders. All were rushing to the town for the chance to hear the preacher Whitefield.

Fortunately for Cole and his wife, they were not disappointed. They arrived in time to hear the sermon. Along with three to four thousand other worshippers, the Coles listened to Whitefield's words. "My hearing him preach gave me a heart wound," reported Cole. "By God's blessing, my old foundation [set of beliefs] was broken up."

Before men such as Whitefield arrived, religion in the colonies did not cause much excitement. Church services were quiet, formal events. People did not show deep feeling during services. Neither did ministers. They spoke calmly but sternly. They wanted their followers to listen to what they said. Followers believed that God spoke through the ministers.

Colonial church services in the early 1700s were quiet and formal. Churches, such as this one in Boston, focused on the rich and powerful people in the congregation.

Indeed, churches in the colonies held great power. As you have read, some colonies had official churches. People in those colonies were required to pay taxes to support the church.

However, early colonial churches did not serve all people equally. Attendance among some groups was low. Many farmers lived too far from any town to attend services. Churches also focused on the rich and powerful. Town leaders held high positions in the church as well as in the larger community. The less wealthy and powerful often felt left out. Other colonists simply did not accept the church's authority.

Over time, the early colonial churches began to lose their power. Preachers began to complain about bad behavior among the colonists. They were troubled by the spread of sinful habits. Young people were of special concern. They seemed, some preachers thought, more interested in having fun than in living a good life.

Some leaders worried that churches were losing their influence on the people. This threatened the very future of the colonies. In Massachusetts, leader William Stoughton made this complaint: "O, what a sad [change] hath of later years passed upon us in these churches and plantations. Alas! How is New England in danger to be buried in its own ruins." Stoughton spoke these words in 1688. The problem that upset him grew worse in the following years. By the 1730s, religious life was in need of revival. This was soon to come.

New Bedford Whaling Museum, New Bedford, Massachusetts

Some preachers during the Great Awakening drew large crowds that gathered outside. People became very emotional during the services.

Colonial religious life underwent a big change in the 1730s. In fact, historians call the movement that began at this time the Great Awakening.

The Great Awakening started with preachers such as George Whitefield. They brought a new type of message to the people. These preachers did not stress following rules. Instead, they seemed to speak to each person. They told each man and woman to build his or her own relationship with God.

The impact of this message was dramatic. For one thing, church services changed. Before the Great Awakening, meetings were mostly calm and quiet. But as Massachusetts minister Jonathan Edwards noted, during the Great Awakening "It was a very frequent thing to see a house full of outcries, faintings, and convulsions [violent shaking]." Some people shouted with joy. Others cried out in fear and shame. At times, people were completely overcome with emotion. They became so exhausted that they could not return home. It was common for people to stay all night at the church.

Jonathan Edwards had his own church. But many Great Awakening preachers traveled from town to town. George Whitefield was one example. Wherever he went, he drew huge crowds. He once spoke before 30,000 people. Unable to fit in a church building, the people would gather in open fields. They were drawn by his message—and also his dramatic style.

The Great Awakening changed more than church services. Edwards also noted a change in people's actions. "There has been vastly more religion kept up in the town, among all sorts of persons," he wrote. People who had never attended church became religious. Neighbors on the street talked openly about religion. Young people gave up some of the bad habits that had once troubled religious leaders. Concern for the poor also increased.

The Great Awakening had a major effect on colonial life. In fact, it helped change the course of American history.

For one thing, the Great Awakening weakened the once powerful churches. Many colonists joined new churches. Groups such as the Baptists and the Methodists grew quickly. Over time, the Anglicans and the Puritans lost their special place in colonial life. The practice of making taxpayers support a church came to an end. Church and government separated. People enjoyed more options for worship. Religious freedom grew during the mid-1700s.

The Granger Collection, New York

Princeton was one of several colleges built during the Great Awakening. This is how the school looked in 1764.

The Great Awakening led to the founding of new colleges. Harvard College and the College of William and Mary had trained ministers for the older churches. Now, new colleges such as Princeton and Brown were built. These colleges helped train ministers to teach the new ideas of the Great Awakening.

For many colonists, the Great Awakening also changed some of their basic ways of thinking. Recall that at Bruton Parish Church, town leaders, such as the governor, sat in the front rows. Important people held a special place. Africans sat in the back—or outside. The Great Awakening challenged such practices. Many preachers began to recognize the religious needs of all people. This included enslaved Africans and American Indians. Dartmouth College was founded, in part, to educate American Indians.

The Great Awakening did not bring an end to slavery. But it did change the way people thought about their leaders. It taught that God loved the weak and the poor just as much as the powerful. No group or class should enjoy special favor. Such teachings helped create an independent spirit. This spirit would grow over time. Within a few years, it would change the colonies' relationship with Great Britain.

How might each picture be an example of the colonists' protests against the British?

Tensions Grow Between the Colonies and Great Britain

10

What British actions angered the colonists in the 1700s?

10.1 Introduction

In Chapter 9, you read about life in the American colonies in the early 1700s. At that time, the colonists were content with the rule of Great Britain. They supported the British king. In this chapter, you will learn about events that changed how the colonists felt.

During the 1750s and 1760s, Great Britain and the colonists joined forces against the French. This conflict was called the French and Indian War. The war left Great Britain with huge debts and new lands to protect in North America. To solve its problems, the British government passed a number of **acts,** or laws. Some of these laws ordered the colonists to pay new taxes. The colonists became angry because they had no representatives in the British government to vote on these laws. They said that this **taxation without representation** was unfair. Many colonists began to **protest,** or object to, British rule.

Look at the drawing of the parent and child to the right. Some people have compared Great Britain and the colonies to a parent and a child. Great Britain was like a parent because it created the colonies and expected them to respect its authority. The colonies were like a child who sometimes refused to obey the parent. Such a comparison is called a metaphor.

As you read this chapter, think about the metaphor of the bond between a parent and a child. What can a parent do when a child disobeys? What may happen to the bond when the parent makes new rules, or punishes the child?

A Strained Relationship

British troops captured the Canadian city of Quebec in 1759. This victory helped the British win the French and Indian War.

10.2 The French and Indian War

During the 1600s and 1700s, Great Britain, France, and Spain often fought one another to gain lands. They clashed in Europe, Asia, and the Americas.

In North America, Great Britain and France both claimed the Ohio River Valley. British settlers wanted to farm the rich soil there. The French wanted to trap beavers and trade the furs.

In 1754, the contest over the land along the Ohio River began a war that lasted almost 10 years. Thousands of British soldiers, with many colonists, fought against the French. Because many American Indians were allies of the French, the British colonists called the conflict the French and Indian War. Some American Indians, however, did fight alongside the British.

At first, Great Britain lost many battles. The British soldiers' bright red uniforms helped make them easy targets. But things changed in 1759 when British troops captured the city of Quebec in Canada. By 1760, the French had lost control of Canada. In 1762, they asked for peace. Under the terms of the peace agreement in 1763, France gave up its land claims in present-day Canada to Great Britain. The British also won the land between the Mississippi River and the Appalachian Mountains.

The war gave Great Britain more land. But it also created huge problems. Most important, it left Great Britain with debts, or unpaid bills. The British national debt had almost doubled by the end of the war.

10.3 The Proclamation of 1763

proclamation an official public announcement

After the French and Indian War, many British settlers moved west. They built homes on the land that Great Britain had won from the French. American Indians feared that this movement of people would destroy their way of life. Some American Indians tried to drive the settlers away by attacking their homes and the British forts. By the time this fighting ended, nearly 2,000 settlers, soldiers, and traders had died.

To stop the attacks and to protect the colonists, Great Britain announced a law called the Proclamation of 1763. This **proclamation** declared that American Indians could have much of the land west of the Appalachian Mountains. It also said that settlers could not move to these areas.

The colonists disliked this law. They did not like the way in which Great Britain was trying to control the colonies. Many colonists simply ignored the law and moved west.

North America in 1763

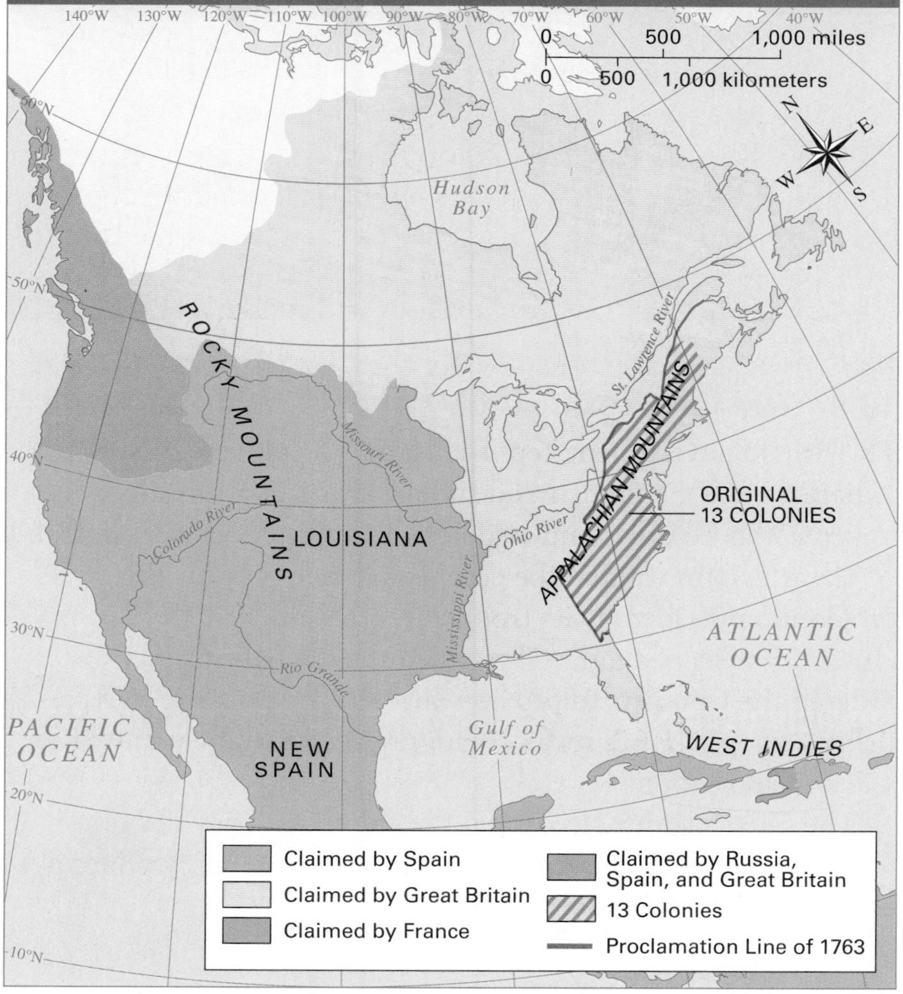

Claimed by Spain
Claimed by Great Britain
Claimed by France
Claimed by Russia, Spain, and Great Britain
13 Colonies
Proclamation Line of 1763

The Quartering Act forced colonists to house and feed thousands of British troops. This law angered the colonists.

The Granger Collection, New York

10.4 The Quartering Act

The British government kept thousands of soldiers in North America after the French and Indian War. Great Britain wanted to protect its colonies and also keep them under closer control.

Great Britain wanted the colonists to help pay for the protection provided by its troops. In 1765, the British **Parliament** passed a new law called the Quartering Act. It ordered the colonists to provide quarters, or places to live, for British troops. Colonists also had to give the soldiers food, fuel, and transportation.

Parliament the lawmaking part of the British government, similar to the Congress in the United States

The Quartering Act angered the colonists. They did not want to pay for British troops in the colonies. Therefore, many colonists treated the soldiers badly.

10.5 The Stamp Act

After fighting the French and Indian War, Great Britain needed money to pay its debts. It also had to pay for the army in the colonies. In 1765, to raise money, Parliament passed a new tax law called the Stamp Act.

The Stamp Act said that the colonists had to pay a tax on printed papers. Newspapers, pamphlets, marriage licenses, and playing cards were taxed. When a colonist paid the tax, an official would mark the printed paper with a large stamp.

The Stamp Act forced colonists to pay a tax on printed papers. When a colonist paid the tax, an official marked the printed paper using a stamp like the one shown here.

This new tax angered the colonists. They did not want to pay more money for things they used every day. They did not want to pay another tax to the British government. But they were mostly angry because they had no say in making the law.

Colonists showed their anger in many ways. Some colonists refused to buy the stamps. Some of them protested in the streets and town squares. And some tried to scare off the tax collectors. At times, groups of colonists even attacked the tax collectors and their homes.

Groups from different colonies joined together in protest against the Stamp Act. In some colonies, merchants agreed not to buy any British goods. Many women, such as the Daughters of Liberty in Rhode Island, refused to buy British cloth. They wove their own cloth instead.

In October 1765, nine colonies sent **delegates** to a special gathering in New York. This meeting became known as the Stamp Act Congress. The delegates thought that all British subjects had a right to vote on taxes through representatives. But the colonies had no representatives in Parliament. The delegates said that it was unfair for Parliament to pass tax laws like the Stamp Act. To them, such laws were an example of taxation without representation.

The colonists' angry protests surprised King George III and Parliament. However, British leaders knew that they could not force the colonists to obey the Stamp Act. In March 1766, Parliament **repealed** the law. But Parliament let the colonies know that it still believed in its right to tax them.

In 1767, Parliament again passed tax laws to raise money from the colonies. These laws, called the Townshend Acts, taxed several goods that the colonies **imported**. These goods included lead, glass, paint, paper, and tea. In protest, the colonists again stopped buying British goods.

delegate a person who represents others at a convention or conference

repeal to cancel, or undo, a law

import to bring into a country, especially for sale

10.6 The Boston Massacre

In 1770, the colonists remained angry that British troops were living in their towns and cities. They thought that the soldiers were rowdy and rude. It was also upsetting to the colonists when soldiers took jobs away from them. The British soldiers could work for low pay in their spare time.

The soldiers weren't content, either. They were far from their homes. The colonists' anger made their jobs more difficult.

As time went on, the relationship between the soldiers and the colonists worsened. Things were especially tense in the city of Boston. The colonists showed their hatred for the soldiers by making fun of their red coats. They called them names like "lobsterback." And some soldiers went out of their way to annoy local citizens. Soon, name-calling and fistfights in the streets were common.

Paul Revere's famous engraving shows his version of the Boston Massacre. In it, soldiers fire at a peaceful crowd. But that was not what actually happened.

On the cold night of March 5, 1770, violence erupted in Boston. A British soldier was standing guard at the Customs House, a building where the disputed taxes were collected. A crowd began to gather. People called the soldier names. Some of them threw stones and snowballs. Captain Thomas Preston and seven other soldiers hurried to the guard's defense. They loaded their muskets, a type of gun.

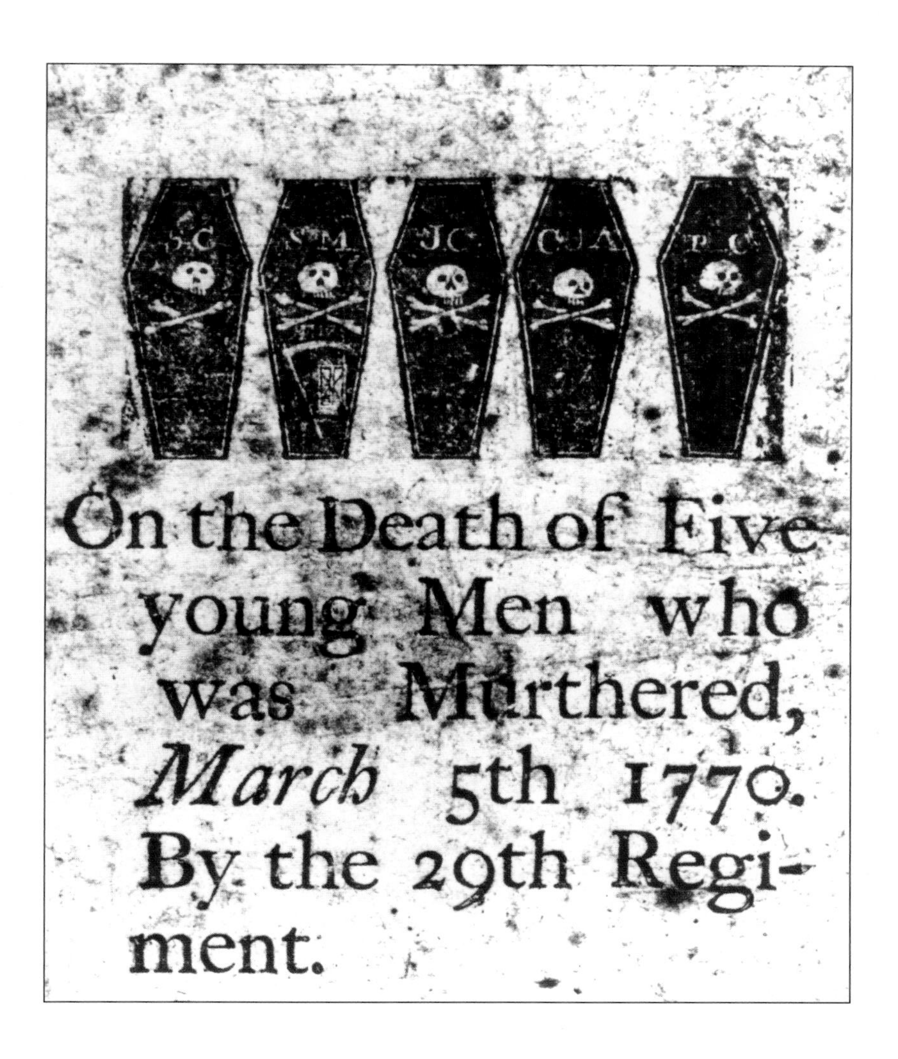

Paul Revere created this picture. It reminded colonists about the Boston Massacre.

The crowd kept taunting the soldiers. The colonists threw more snowballs and chunks of ice. No one is sure about what happened next. Some people said that Captain Preston told his soldiers not to fire their guns. But one soldier thought that he heard the command "Fire!" He shot into the crowd. When the crowd moved toward them, the soldiers panicked and fired more shots. Within moments, five people lay dead or dying. Six more were wounded.

The colonists called this tragic event the Boston Massacre. A silversmith named Paul Revere made an engraving, or an image etched into metal, of the **massacre**. The engraving shows soldiers firing at a peaceful crowd, although that was not what actually happened.

massacre the murder of several or many people who cannot defend themselves

Colonists shared news in letters, or correspondence. Colonial governments had begun to set up informal Committees of Correspondence in the 1760s. Members of these groups let one another know what was going on in their regions. Samuel Adams was a leader of protests against the British. He made sure that the news of the massacre spread throughout the colonies. In 1772, Adams helped form a permanent Committee of Correspondence in Massachusetts. This group wanted to unite the colonists to protest against British actions.

Colonists dressed as American Indians threw tea into Boston Harbor. This was known as the Boston Tea Party. It was a protest against the Tea Act.

10.7 The Boston Tea Party

In response to the Boston Massacre, Parliament repealed all the taxes on the colonies, except the tax on tea. Although the colonists loved tea, many **boycotted** it because of the tax.

The largest British tea company, the British East India Company, lost a great deal of money. To save the company, Parliament passed the Tea Act in 1773. It said that only this company could sell tea to the colonies. The British hoped to force the colonists to again buy British tea.

boycott to protest by refusing to use or buy a good or service

The Tea Act did, in fact, lower the cost of tea. But the colonists were still angry. This was another unfair law passed without their approval. And they didn't like being forced to buy tea from only one company. What if Parliament decided to let certain companies control other imported items?

Again, the colonists protested. Some spoke out. Others again boycotted tea. In Boston, some local citizens acted. On December 16, 1773, a group of men dressed as American Indians boarded ships in Boston Harbor. They opened 342 chests of tea and dumped the tea into the water.

Afterward, the colonists called this incident the Boston Tea Party. Soon, people began to sing about it in the colonies. "Rally, Mohawks [an American Indian tribe]," they sang. "Bring out your axes / And tell King George we'll pay no taxes / On his foreign tea." But in Great Britain, people were shocked and angry. And King George was furious.

10.8 The Intolerable Acts

After the Boston Tea Party, Parliament passed several laws called the Coercive Acts. The British wanted to coerce, or force, the colonies to obey Great Britain. Many colonists said that they could not tolerate, or accept, these harsh laws. The colonists called these laws the Intolerable Acts.

One law, the Boston Port Act, closed Boston Harbor. Trade ships could not enter or leave the harbor until Boston paid for the lost tea. Many workers lost their jobs. Some people feared that the citizens of Boston would starve.

The other colonies helped by sending money, food, and supplies to Boston. In addition, in September 1774, the **First Continental Congress** was held. Leaders from every colony except Georgia met in Philadelphia. They discussed their complaints about Great Britain. The angry delegates agreed to fight against the Boston Port Act and the other Intolerable Acts.

This picture shows colonists attacking a tax collector. They have tarred and feathered him and are making him drink tea. Parliament passed the Intolerable Acts to punish the colonists for actions like this and the Boston Tea Party.

Summary

In this chapter, you read about some of the events, from 1754 to the end of 1774, that created tension between the colonies and Great Britain. You used the metaphor of a parent and a child to describe this relationship.

The British behaved like concerned parents who protected the colonists, their children. Great Britain thought that the colonists should be grateful and respect British authority. But, like growing children, the colonies wanted to have a greater role in making their own decisions. They did not like Great Britain's efforts to control them. When Great Britain ignored their complaints, the colonists protested, sometimes violently. By 1775, people on both sides were very angry.

In the next pages, you will learn more about King George III. He ruled Great Britain during this time. How did the king's personality and beliefs affect events in the colonies? Read on to find out.

First Continental Congress a meeting of delegates from 12 colonies, held to present complaints to King George III, to set up a boycott of British goods, and to arrange a second meeting if needed

Reading Further 10

King George III and His Colonies

In 1760, King George III took the throne in Great Britain. He came to power just as conflicts with the colonies began to grow. His personality traits and attitudes increased tensions. How did the king's point of view contribute to the break between his country and its American colonies?

In 1748, a ten-year-old British boy named George acted in a play. He took the role of a noble hero, Cato. In the play, the ruler of Cato's country has become a tyrant. He has stopped listening to the people and has begun to behave as a dictator. But Cato believes deeply in the people's right to freedom. Rather than give in to a tyrant, Cato chooses to fight and die. "A day, an hour, of . . . liberty," he says, "is worth a whole eternity in bondage."

The Granger Collection, New York

Young Prince George worked hard to prepare himself for his future role as king.

The play was popular in Great Britain at the time. Many people agreed with its ideas about liberty. Young George also believed in these ideas. He knew that he would one day be the king of Great Britain. He would have great power. But he believed that he must use his power for the good of the country. He realized that it would be his job to ensure the freedom and well-being of his people. The young man took these duties very seriously.

At that time, becoming king might have seemed in the far distant future to Prince George. His grandfather, George II, sat on the royal throne. His father, Prince Frederick, was next in line to be the king of Great Britain. Prince Frederick was just 41 years old. It appeared likely that George would have to wait many years to become king.

But George's time arrived much sooner than he expected. In 1751, Prince Frederick died suddenly. George was only 12 years old. And now, he was next in line for the throne.

For the next several years, George prepared himself to rule his kingdom. He studied languages and math. He learned about science and other subjects. Prince George worked hard to prepare himself to be a good king. He wanted desperately to be a worthy ruler of his people. In short, he was very tough on himself. While the young prince looked forward to becoming king, he was also painfully aware of his own failings. "I am young and inexperienced and want advice," he once wrote to his tutor.

The young prince was also very hard on others. He was quick to judge people's behavior. He often reacted badly to criticism and took it personally. He stubbornly held on to grudges against those who had insulted him or his family.

Prince George's personal traits were probably not unusual for a young person. But Prince George was not just any young man. For in 1760, his grandfather, King George II, died. Now, Prince George was king and ruler of Great Britain. At the age of 22, he had to lead his country. More important, he had to learn to deal with those who opposed him. Challenges came from within Great Britain. And as the 1760s wore on, challenges also came from across the ocean. The colonies in North America were growing increasingly dissatisfied with how Great Britain was treating them.

This painting shows King George dressed for the ceremony that recognized him as king of Great Britain. He was 22 years old.

The Granger Collection, New York

In this 1774 colonial political cartoon, the Intolerable Acts fan the flames of anger burning in the colonies. While some men try to put out the fire, King George III looks on at right.

In 1760, the young king was ready to begin his new duties. In his first speech from the throne, he declared, "I glory [take pride] in the name of Britain." His greatest satisfaction, he said, was to serve the people. It was their love and support that would protect him. The public seemed to welcome this patriotic new king.

But Parliament felt otherwise. King George had hoped to be able to work with all the members of Parliament. But many of the members did not want to work with the king. They did not like his ideas. They thought that government worked best when Parliament was not under the king's control. They were worried that King George wanted too much power.

King George's strong personality began to cause trouble. The king believed deeply in doing what he thought was right. Therefore, he held firmly to his ideas. He was very critical of those who did not agree with him. He found it difficult to work out compromises. His rigid attitude created many enemies in the government. He considered opposing ideas and criticisms to be personal attacks against him. One member of Parliament noted that the king was "capable of great resentment . . . and . . . of [holding on to] it."

The king's personality also caused problems with the American colonies. During the 1760s, relations between Great Britain and the colonies became tense. As the conflict grew, the king would not even consider changing his views. He refused to listen to the colonists' concerns and frustrations. He did not believe that they had any right to protest against his actions. He felt that their complaints were an insult to him. He saw no merit in their point of view.

At first, the colonists hoped that they could persuade the king to be reasonable. After all, they had succeeded in persuading King George and his government to repeal the Stamp Act. In New York, colonists even built a statue to thank the king for repealing several taxes in 1770.

But the king had had his own reasons for dropping the taxes. His reasons had little to do with the colonists' unhappiness. George had realized that enforcing the taxes would be costly. It made little sense to have taxes that lost money for the British government. George did not think that the British government was in any way wrong to tax the colonies. He did not agree with the colonists' angry protests against taxation without representation. Parliament would soon create new taxes, with George's full support. The king thought that this was fair and proper.

The Granger Collection, New York

In this British political cartoon from about 1776, members of Parliament argue about colonial policies while the American colonies burst into flames of revolution.

Indeed, George believed that the colonists' demands were outrageous. The more the colonists acted out in protest, the angrier King George became. Members of his government could see trouble coming. Some members even agreed with the American rebels and suggested that the king consider a compromise. George refused. He felt that it was his duty to hold on to his nation's colonies. He was furious that the colonists dared to challenge his power and his government. This anger clouded the king's judgment.

King George III had set Great Britain on a collision course with the American colonies. He would never give in to them. This attitude would lead to a break between the colonies and his nation.

Patriots cheer as people pull down a statue of King George III, the ruler of Great Britain.

This statue of King George III was in New York City.

Loyalists look on in dismay as the statue of their king is torn down by excited Patriots.

To Declare Independence or Not

What were the arguments for and against colonial independence from Great Britain?

11.1 Introduction

In Chapter 10, you learned that tensions between Great Britain and the American colonies had grown between 1754 and 1775. In this chapter, you will read about colonists who argued for and against **independence,** or separation from Great Britain.

People for independence no longer wanted Great Britain to rule the colonies. These colonists were called **Patriots**. Some Patriots argued for their cause in speeches and newspaper articles. Others took stronger actions, such as joining mobs that attacked the homes and businesses of those who disagreed with them.

Colonists who remained loyal to Great Britain were called **Loyalists**. Some Loyalists gave speeches arguing that the colonies should remain under the rule of Great Britain. Other Loyalists took stronger actions, such as armed attacks against Patriots.

Many colonists remained **neutral,** or did not take sides. They were neither Loyalists nor Patriots.

As you read this chapter, use this T-chart to track how six important colonists felt about independence. The Loyalists on the left-hand side of the T-chart argued against independence. The Patriots on the right-hand side of the T-chart argued in favor of becoming a country separate from Great Britain. Why did some colonists want to remain under the rule of Great Britain and its king? Why did others want the colonies to be independent?

11.2 Who Were the Loyalists and Patriots?

The colonies were divided over the question of independence. Historians disagree about how many colonists chose each side. Some believe there were more Patriots than Loyalists. But probably less than half of the colonists were Patriots, and less than half were Loyalists. The rest were neutral.

The Granger Collection, New York

Some historians think that less than half of the colonists supported King George III, shown here.

The Loyalists included many kinds of people. Some were rich landowners. They feared that Patriot mobs might take their property.

Some Loyalists were governors who had been appointed to their jobs by King George III. These men liked their government, and they felt that it was their duty to make sure that British laws were obeyed in the colonies.

Other Loyalists were religious leaders who believed that the king's power came from God. Many of them were members of the Church of England, Great Britain's official church. They believed that it was wrong to oppose the king. They told their followers, "You have a duty to be loyal to the church and to the king!"

Many colonists were Patriots. This group included merchants who lived in and around the city of Boston. They were angry about British taxes on goods such as tea and paper. The taxes hurt their businesses because many colonists boycotted the taxed goods.

Some Patriots were lawyers. They fought in the courts against British laws that they thought were unfair. They believed that the colonists should have more say in making laws that directly affected them.

Some Patriots were farmers. Others were people who worked at crafts such as printing, shipbuilding, and making clothes. They agreed with Patriot leaders who said that independence would bring more freedom and wealth to the colonies.

In this chapter, you will learn about three Loyalists and three Patriots. As you read about these people, think about why they felt the way they did. What reasons did each give for being a Loyalist or a Patriot?

11.3 Thomas Hutchinson: A Loyalist Governor

Thomas Hutchinson was a Loyalist who lived in Massachusetts. The king named him the royal governor of Massachusetts in 1771. He was a dedicated official. But over time, Hutchinson became one of the most hated men in the colonies because he always sided with the British against the Patriots.

Hutchinson was a thin, serious man who rarely smiled. He didn't like to show his feelings. Although he was a successful businessman, he didn't wear fancy clothes.

As an official serving the king, Hutchinson firmly believed in enforcing British laws such as the Stamp Act of 1765. Patriots were furious about the Stamp Act. One night, an angry mob burst into Hutchinson's house. The mob stole money and broke furniture. They also destroyed his prized collection of books. From then on, Hutchinson was a bitter enemy of the Patriots.

As a Loyalist, Hutchinson believed that the colonists could not govern themselves without the British king to guide them. He thought that King George III knew what was best for the colonists because the king was wise and experienced. Hutchinson also wrote that British people who lived overseas, such as the colonists, could not expect to have the same freedoms that British people in Great Britain enjoyed.

In 1774, some Patriots embarrassed Hutchinson by printing some letters that he had written to the British government. The letters said that Great Britain should be tougher on the colonists. When colonists read his letters in the newspaper, many more of them turned against him. And they became convinced that getting fair treatment for the colonies from Great Britain was not possible.

Thomas Hutchinson was a Loyalist. The king named him the governor of Massachusetts. He enforced British laws that were not popular in the colonies.

11.4 Jonathan Boucher: Loyalist Religious Leader

Reverend Jonathan Boucher was a British religious leader. He used his sermons to spread his Loyalist beliefs.

Boucher first came to the colonies as a young man in 1759. Later, he went back to Great Britain. There he became a priest in the Church of England. Then he returned to the colonies. He became a well-known religious leader in Maryland.

Many people in the colonies liked Boucher because he was intelligent and full of charm. He was balding and usually wore spectacles, or glasses.

Boucher was full of energy and ambition. He was a forceful man who was comfortable talking in front of large groups. Boucher was never afraid to speak his mind, no matter how many people disagreed with him. As a minister, he expected everyone to obey his teachings. He used his talents and his occupation to argue for the Loyalists' cause.

Jonathan Boucher was a British religious leader. He lived in Maryland. His sermons spread his Loyalist beliefs.

The Granger Collection, New York

Boucher preached that the king's power came from God. He said that Christians had a special duty to obey British laws. Disobeying the king was like disobeying God.

Boucher did not believe that common people were capable of ruling. He argued that the colonists should obey British laws for their own good. He said that these laws came from God and made life safer and better for most colonists.

Finally, Boucher warned that working for independence was dangerous. These actions could lead to a war with Great Britain. Such a war would hurt thousands of people far worse than living with a few unfair laws would.

Boucher's Loyalist sermons made some Patriots angry. They threatened to hurt him. Realizing that he was in danger, Boucher began keeping loaded pistols nearby when he gave his sermons.

11.5 Lord Dunmore: Loyalist Governor of Virginia

John Murray was a fierce Loyalist leader. His British title was Lord Dunmore. He came from a royal Scottish family and was elected to the British Parliament at the age of 29. In 1771, King George III appointed Dunmore to serve as royal governor of the colony of Virginia.

Dunmore was a proud and wealthy man. He dressed in fancy clothes that showed off his wealth and importance. He was stubborn and sometimes bad-tempered. And he was very loyal to Great Britain.

Dunmore pointed out that Great Britain started the colonies and continued to protect them. Therefore, he felt it had the right to rule them and to make them pay taxes on British goods.

Dunmore also argued that fighting for independence would hurt the economy and make many colonists poor. He strongly believed that the colonists had a duty to obey British laws. The colonies, he said, must depend on Great Britain. Colonists who would not fight for the king were **traitors**.

As governor, Dunmore thought that being tough would frighten the colonists into accepting British rule. Instead, his firm actions angered many people in Virginia.

Dunmore began to fear for his family's safety. In June 1775, he moved them onto a British warship. He then gathered a number of warships. He sent the ships to attack Patriots' homes and plantations along the Elizabeth River. He promised to free any slaves owned by the rebels if the slaves fought against the Patriots. A number of enslaved Africans joined him to gain their freedom.

In the end, Dunmore's harsh actions only made the views of the Patriots more popular. Because of him, many who had been neutral began to think that they should fight for independence from Great Britain.

traitor a person guilty of betraying or acting against his or her own country

John Murray, or Lord Dunmore, was a Loyalist leader. In 1775, he launched a naval attack on the homes of Patriots along the Elizabeth River in Virginia.

The Granger Collection, New York

11.6 Benjamin Franklin: The Thoughtful Patriot

Benjamin Franklin was a popular and respected Patriot. At first, he did not favor independence. He hoped that Great Britain would start to treat the colonies more fairly. When that didn't happen, Franklin sided firmly with the Patriots.

Franklin had many talents. He was a successful writer, printer, inventor, and scientist. He lived in the city of Philadelphia, in the colony of Pennsylvania. There, he helped to start a library, a hospital, and a college.

Although he was an important man, Franklin often dressed in plain suits. He sometimes wore spectacles. He often wore a little fur cap to keep his head warm in winter.

People liked and admired Franklin. He was knowledgeable, funny, and wise. He could stay calm when other people grew angry. He was good at helping people to understand one another's ideas during arguments.

These abilities made him a skilled statesman. He had a leading role in shaping American policy at home. He was also a key diplomat who represented American ideas in Europe.

From 1757 to 1775, Franklin represented the point of view of the colonies in Great Britain. Patiently, he tried to persuade the British government to stop making laws that the colonists thought were unfair. He did help convince the government to repeal the Stamp Act. But Great Britain continued to pass unfair laws. At last, Franklin went home and became a Patriot leader.

Franklin favored independence for several reasons. He thought that Great Britain would keep making unfair laws. He believed that the colonists could no longer trust the British government. Finally, Franklin believed that the colonists had the ability to govern themselves. By 1775, he was ready to help them prove that he was right.

The Granger Collection, New York

At first, Benjamin Franklin tried to reach agreement with Great Britain. But, by 1775, he fully supported independence. He became a Patriot leader.

11.7 Mercy Otis Warren: Patriot with a Pen

Patriot Mercy Otis Warren was a Massachusetts writer and poet. Patriots shared their ideas at meetings in her home. Among those who attended were John and Abigail Adams, Samuel Adams, and Otis's husband James. Some historians believe that the idea for the Committees of Correspondence was first discussed in her home.

Warren was thin, with dark eyes and dark hair. She was very religious and cautioned her friends against wearing the latest fashions. She felt that doing so would offend God.

Even as a girl, Warren loved reading, writing, and discussing politics. She became upset by Great Britain's harsh treatment of the colonies. She felt that taxes were too high and that workers were paid too little.

In both her writings and discussions, Warren made several arguments in favor of independence. She said that British laws and taxes were unfair. Families in the colonies had a hard time earning enough money to pay for expensive British goods. Therefore, the colonies would be better off with their own government.

Warren also believed that women had a duty to speak out against Great Britain. And while she thought that women didn't have the strength to fight on the battlefields, their minds could be quite powerful. She believed that women should have the same choices as men to get an education and to take an active role in politics.

Bequest of Winslow Warren, Courtesy, Museum of Fine Arts, Boston

Patriot Mercy Otis Warren was a writer from Massachusetts. She wrote plays and poems supporting independence.

Warren expressed her ideas through her writing. Two of her plays cleverly attacked Loyalists such as Thomas Hutchinson. Her writings helped to encourage many people in Massachusetts to become Patriots.

11.8 Samuel Adams: True Patriot

Deposited by The City of Boston Courtesy, Museum of Fine Arts Boston

Samuel Adams was an active Patriot in Massachusetts. In 1765, he helped to organize the Sons of Liberty. This group led colonists in resisting unfair British laws.

Samuel Adams was a leading Patriot in Massachusetts. Adams believed that the British were harsh and unfair rulers. He called on the colonies to fight for their independence.

Adams was always interested in politics. He went to Harvard University in Massachusetts. There he wrote a paper on people's right to fight against unfair government. Other local Patriots saw him as a leader. By the mid-1760s he was a full-time politician.

Adams was born into a wealthy Boston family, but he didn't always manage his money wisely. When he began his life as a politician, his friends had to buy him a new suit, a wig, and other clothing many politicians wore at that time.

Adams was devoted to politics. He was a dramatic speaker and a persuasive writer. And he was a master at using these talents to gain public support. His enemies called him a troublemaker.

Adams argued for independence by writing newspaper articles. He also gave speeches and frequently spoke at town meetings. Adams believed that colonists should not have to pay the high taxes on British goods. He also said it was unfair that the king chose governors for the colonies. The colonists, he argued, should be able to elect their own governors. Adams also thought that the colonists should have the power to change unfair laws. If Great Britain refused to give them this power, then they should become a separate country.

In 1765, Adams helped to organize a group called the Sons of Liberty. The Sons were a secret group of Patriots. They encouraged colonists to disobey laws like the Stamp Act. In 1773, Adams and the Sons led the Boston Tea Party to protest British taxes on tea.

Adams also helped to set up the Committees of Correspondence. These groups helped Patriots in all the colonies share news and plans with one another. Before long, Samuel Adams was working day and night to help the colonies win their independence.

The Granger Collection, New York

In this 1776 scene, the Sons of Liberty raise a Liberty Pole in a town square. Colonists would put a symbol such as a flag at the top. Patriots met around these poles to discuss ways to resist British laws they thought were unfair.

Summary

In this chapter, you read about six colonists who had ideas about independence. You used a T-chart to identify these six colonists as either Loyalists or Patriots.

Loyalists supported the British king. Some, like Thomas Hutchinson and Lord Dunmore, were royal governors. They believed in Great Britain's right to make laws for the colonies. Some, like Jonathan Boucher, were religious leaders. They thought the colonists had a duty to obey the king. Some landowners feared losing their property.

Patriots wanted independence from Great Britain. Some, like Benjamin Franklin, became Patriots only after trying to persuade the British to change their actions. Others, like Mercy Otis Warren and Samuel Adams, strongly protested against British laws and taxes. Soon, some Patriots were openly calling for independence.

In 1775, many colonists were not ready to take such a bold step. What convinced more colonists to support independence? Read on to find out.

Reading Further 11

Patrick Henry, Radical Revolutionary

Patrick Henry lived in Virginia. He was an early Patriot. At first, colonists thought his ideas were radical, or extreme. But his fiery speeches won him many followers. What role did Henry play in the march toward independence?

tyrant a ruler who uses his power harshly

treason the crime of acting to overthrow your ruler or betray your country

The year was 1763. The scene was a county courthouse in Virginia. The judge and jury were listening to evidence. The case was about a 1755 Virginia law. It dealt with how much money church ministers should be paid. Many ministers did not like this law. They felt that their pay was too low. They had complained to the British king. The king had overturned the Virginia law. Now a minister named James Maury was in court. He wanted money to make up for the low pay he had received under the old law.

Arguing against Maury was a young lawyer. His name was Patrick Henry. He certainly did not look impressive. His clothes were plain. He did not wear a wig, which fashionable men of the time often wore at court. But Henry took a daring approach to the case. He argued that the king had no right to overturn the law. The people of Virginia had agreed to the law, Henry argued. They had a right to make their own laws and rules.

But Henry did not stop there. He said that the king's actions made him a **tyrant**. The people of Virginia did not have to obey a tyrant, Henry declared.

Some people in the courtroom were shocked. Maury's lawyer said that Henry had committed **treason**. This crime could be punished by death. The jury, however, agreed with Henry. They decided to award Maury just one penny to show they did not think the king should have overturned the Virginia law.

Henry's performance impressed more than the jury. By standing up to the king, he had become a hero to many colonists in his community.

Patrick Henry became a successful lawyer and a powerful voice for the Patriot cause.

Patrick Henry first gained widespread notice when he argued a court case in 1763.

The Early Years

Patrick Henry was born in 1736. His family was prosperous, but they were not among the wealthiest in Virginia. Young Henry received a good education. He went to a local school until he was ten. Then his father taught him at home. By the age of 15, he had finished his education. He did not go to college.

Though he was bright, Henry had several failures. First, he opened a store with his brother. It was closed within a year. Next, Henry tried farming. A terrible fire put an end to that enterprise. Henry again tried running a store—and again was unsuccessful.

Then, Henry decided to seek a career in the law. He studied on his own for six weeks. He barely passed the exam for his law license. He began his law practice in 1760. At this, he was an immediate success. His business grew with each year.

Henry worked hard at his new profession. He traveled widely in order to build his practice. He also proved to be highly effective in court. His speaking style was compelling. He connected with his listeners. This skill helped him to win judgments in court and followers among Virginians.

Henry's popularity reached a high point after his work on the James Maury case. His victory helped him win a seat in Virginia's House of Burgesses. From this new position, he quickly built his reputation as a powerful voice for the people.

This painting shows Patrick Henry making his famous speech against the Stamp Act. Some say he replied to cries of treason with these words: "If this be treason, make the most of it."

The Granger Collection, New York

resolution a statement that expresses the wishes or decisions of a group

Inspiring Words

Patrick Henry entered the House of Burgesses on May 20, 1765. Less than two weeks later, he gave one of his fiery speeches. His words alarmed Loyalists but inspired the Patriot spirit throughout the colonies.

The topic of Henry's speech was the Stamp Act. Recall that many colonists hated this law. They believed it was taxation without representation.

For two days in May 1765, the House of Burgesses discussed the Stamp Act. Henry led the debate. He wrote five **resolutions,** or statements, of his views. Henry's resolutions challenged the power of the British government. They declared that only Virginia could tax the people of the colony. Colonists, Henry argued, did not have to obey the hated law.

Henry wanted the burgesses to agree with his ideas. He made a speech in hopes of winning their support. As he spoke, Henry hinted at a daring threat. He listed the names of some rulers from history—and the people who had killed them. King George III, Henry warned, should learn from these examples.

Some members of the House of Burgesses were horrified. They cried out that Henry was guilty of treason. But most members were won over by his speech. The House of Burgesses agreed to his resolutions. Henry had been a burgess for just a few days. But he was already a leading figure.

Word of Henry's actions spread quickly. Newspapers printed his resolutions. Other colonial governments passed their own, similar statements. Colonists took to the streets to protest the Stamp Act. The spirit of independence was growing.

Henry's Stamp Act speech and resolutions gained attention throughout the colonies. His fame as a leading Patriot grew.

Henry was known for his skill as a speaker. He spoke with great feeling and intensity. His speeches had a powerful impact on the emotions of his listeners. One man compared Henry's words to "the mountain torrent [rushing stream] that swept away everything before it."

Patrick Henry made his "give me liberty" speech in St. John's Church (above) in Richmond, Virginia.

Henry did not follow the rules of debate that many other leaders of his day did. He used simple terms. He relied on emotion rather than complex ideas to make his points. Some people made fun of his plain style. But he was able to communicate with all kinds of people. This included people with little education. One of his friends noted that Henry "trampled upon rules [of speech] and yet triumphed."

Henry gave his most famous speech at St. John's Church in Richmond, Virginia, in March 1775. By this time, the colonies' relationship with Great Britain had become very strained. Still, many people did not want to go to war against the king and Great Britain. Henry was ready to fight to win freedom. In a stirring performance, he called on Virginia to get ready for war. His words are among the best known in American history: "Gentlemen may cry, Peace, Peace—but there is no peace.... I know not what course others may take; but as for me, give me liberty or give me death!"

Henry's speech was convincing. And again, news of his words traveled far from Virginia. Soon colonists everywhere were repeating his call for freedom. It would not be long before his cry for war would be fulfilled in the colony of Massachusetts.

This plaque honors the men who planned the Continental army. Why do you think their plan was important?

This plaque honors the men who selected the leader of the Continental army. What kind of leader do you think they chose?

This plaque honors the men who debated independence. What do you think they decided?

The Declaration of Independence

12

What are the main ideas in the Declaration of Independence?

12.1 Introduction

In Chapter 11, you read about the colonists' debate over whether they should declare their independence from Great Britain. In this chapter, you will learn about the point of view of Patriot leaders, such as Thomas Jefferson. These men wanted to form a new country. Jefferson wrote a document that told why the colonies should no longer be under British rule. It is called the **Declaration of Independence**.

In May 1775, fighting between the colonies and Great Britain had already begun in Massachusetts. Each colony sent delegates to the **Second Continental Congress** in Philadelphia. This Congress became the government for the colonists. It had to decide whether to declare independence. It had to make a plan to fight the war.

By early 1776, the number of colonists who favored independence had grown. Patriot Thomas Paine had written a booklet, called *Common Sense,* that had influenced them. In it, Paine argued persuasively for independence. He used simple words that everyone could understand.

In June, the Congress decided it needed to write a document that told why the colonies had the right to be free from British rule. It chose five delegates to do this, including young Thomas Jefferson. At a portable desk, Jefferson wrote the first draft of the Declaration of Independence.

Look at this drawing of the desk. Think about Jefferson writing here. What objects does he see? What might they tell us about the ideas he included in the Declaration of Independence? What had caused the Congress to ask for this document?

Thomas Jefferson's Desk

This engraving shows a colonial militia attacking British soldiers in 1775.

Minuteman a Patriot volunteer who was paid and trained to be ready to fight at a minute's notice

militia a body of mostly untrained part-time soldiers who did required military service and were available for full-time paid duty when needed

12.2 The Second Continental Congress

On May 10, 1775, leaders met in Philadelphia for the Second Continental Congress. George Washington arrived from Virginia in his blue and tan uniform. John Adams came from Massachusetts. Benjamin Franklin sailed back from Great Britain to represent Pennsylvania. In all, 65 delegates took part in the Congress. They came from all 13 colonies. These men were soon acting as the new government.

The first Continental Congress had met in 1774 to protest the Intolerable Acts. This second Congress faced three key tasks. The most urgent task was to organize the colonies for war against the British. Just before the Congress met, British troops had fought against local **Minutemen** and **militia**. The battle took place in the towns of Lexington and Concord in Massachusetts. The Congress knew that the colonies needed a more organized military to fight the powerful British forces. It created the Continental army and navy.

The next task was to decide who should lead the new army. Congress quickly chose a good soldier and a strong leader—George Washington.

The third and hardest task was to decide whether to declare independence from Great Britain. Some Patriots, such as John Adams, were ready to take this step. But there were still delegates loyal to King George III. They continued to hope the colonies could make peace with Great Britain.

12.3 Thomas Paine and *Common Sense*

Many colonists, too, were not sure about independence from Great Britain. They wanted the king to listen to their complaints, but they were still loyal British citizens. And they feared that the colonies could not win a war against the strong British army.

In the mid-1700s, people in Europe were exploring new ideas about science, government, and human rights. One key idea was that all people should have freedom and fair treatment under the law. This time is called the Age of Enlightenment, or the Age of Reason. Writers of the period published their ideas in newspapers, pamphlets, and booklets. These ideas spread through Europe and the American colonies.

One man who believed in these new ideas was Thomas Paine. He came to the colonies from England in 1774. Paine published a booklet, in January of 1776, called *Common Sense*. In it, he argued that people should rule themselves rather than be ruled by a king. America, he said, could show the world a better form of government.

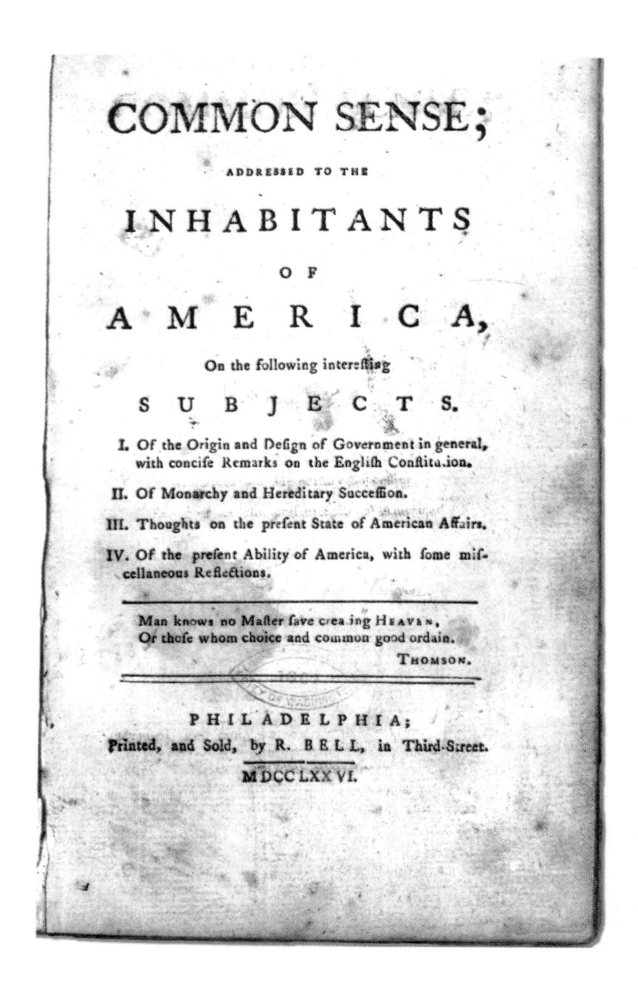

COMMON SENSE;

ADDRESSED TO THE

INHABITANTS

OF

AMERICA,

On the following interefting

SUBJECTS.

I. Of the Origin and Defign of Government in general, with concife Remarks on the Englifh Conftitution.

II. Of Monarchy and Hereditary Succeffion.

III. Thoughts on the prefent State of American Affairs.

IV. Of the prefent Ability of America, with fome mifcellaneous Reflections.

Man knows no Mafter fave creating HEAVEN,
Or thofe whom choice and common good ordain.
THOMSON.

PHILADELPHIA;
Printed, and Sold, by R. BELL, in Third-Street.
MDCCLXXVI.

Thomas Paine's booklet *Common Sense* convinced many colonists to support independence.

Common Sense swayed many people. Paine wrote simply, in words that all could understand. Many colonists still thought of Great Britain as their parent country. But Paine said that parents do not "make war upon their families." The blood of the Patriots killed in Massachusetts, he wrote, cried out that it was time to separate from Great Britain. He said the colonists could defeat the British army.

Soon, more than 500,000 copies of *Common Sense* had been sold. Never before had so many copies of one book been published in the colonies. People everywhere read it, including soldiers in the Continental Army. George Washington wrote that *Common Sense* was changing minds. By the spring of 1776, many people were ready to support a vote for independence.

12.4 Writing the Declaration of Independence

The Second Continental Congress began to move toward independence. On June 7, 1776, delegates from Virginia proposed a resolution. It said that "these United Colonies are, and by right ought to be, free and independent States."

Thomas Jefferson wrote the first draft of the Declaration of Independence. The committee reviewed the draft. Then they presented it to the entire Second Continental Congress.

The Congress agreed to think about whether to accept this resolution. It chose five men as a committee to write a document to explain why the colonies should be independent. John Adams and Benjamin Franklin were part of this group. A studious, redheaded Virginian named Thomas Jefferson was also a member.

Jefferson was only 33 years old, but he was already known as a fine writer and thinker. His fellow committee members asked him to write a draft of a declaration of independence.

Jefferson set up a folding desk in his room. Then he began to write. For about a week, he wrote and rewrote his draft. Finally, he showed his draft to the other committee members. Adams and Franklin made a few changes to it. Then they gave the document to the Congress.

For a few days, the members of the Congress argued about independence. Then, on July 2, the delegates voted to separate from Great Britain.

The Congress spent the next two days discussing each word of the declaration. They voted to make a number of changes. Delegates from two southern colonies, where plantation owners used slaves, objected to statements about slavery. Several other delegates agreed. Jefferson had called slavery a "cruel war against human nature." The Congress took out these words. Some of the changes angered Jefferson. But everyone knew that all the colonies had to agree in order for them to become a united country. Finally, on July 4, 1776, Congress approved the Declaration of Independence.

After much discussion and a number of changes, the delegates signed the declaration.

12.5 Approving the Declaration of Independence

The delegates approved a handwritten copy of the declaration. They knew that this was an act of treason toward the king. John Hancock was the president of the Congress. He warned the delegates that they must "all hang together," or stay united. Benjamin Franklin replied, "We must all hang together, or assuredly we shall all hang separately." The punishment for treason was death by hanging.

When the time came to sign the Declaration, Hancock signed first, writing his name in large bold letters. His signature became famous. To this day, people call their signature a "John Hancock." Then Jefferson and the other delegates signed, too.

Congress sent copies of the document to each of the colonies and to the Continental army. Excited Patriots celebrated when they heard the news about the declaration. A crowd in Philadelphia cheered when it was read in public for the first time, on July 8. General Washington's troops heard it the next day. Then soldiers and citizens tore down a statue of King George III. They melted the metal to make bullets. Patriot troops in Boston fired guns and cannons to honor the event.

Everywhere, church bells rang. There were parades and bonfires. Today, Americans still mark the birth of our country on the Fourth of July. On this date the delegates to the Second Continental Congress adopted the Declaration of Independence.

12.6 The Declaration of Independence

The delegates to the Second Continental Congress wanted to explain why the colonies wished to form a separate nation. The following excerpts from the Declaration of Independence are part of this explanation. The entire Declaration of Independence can be found at the back of this book.

The first excerpt tells why the colonists felt they needed to write the document.

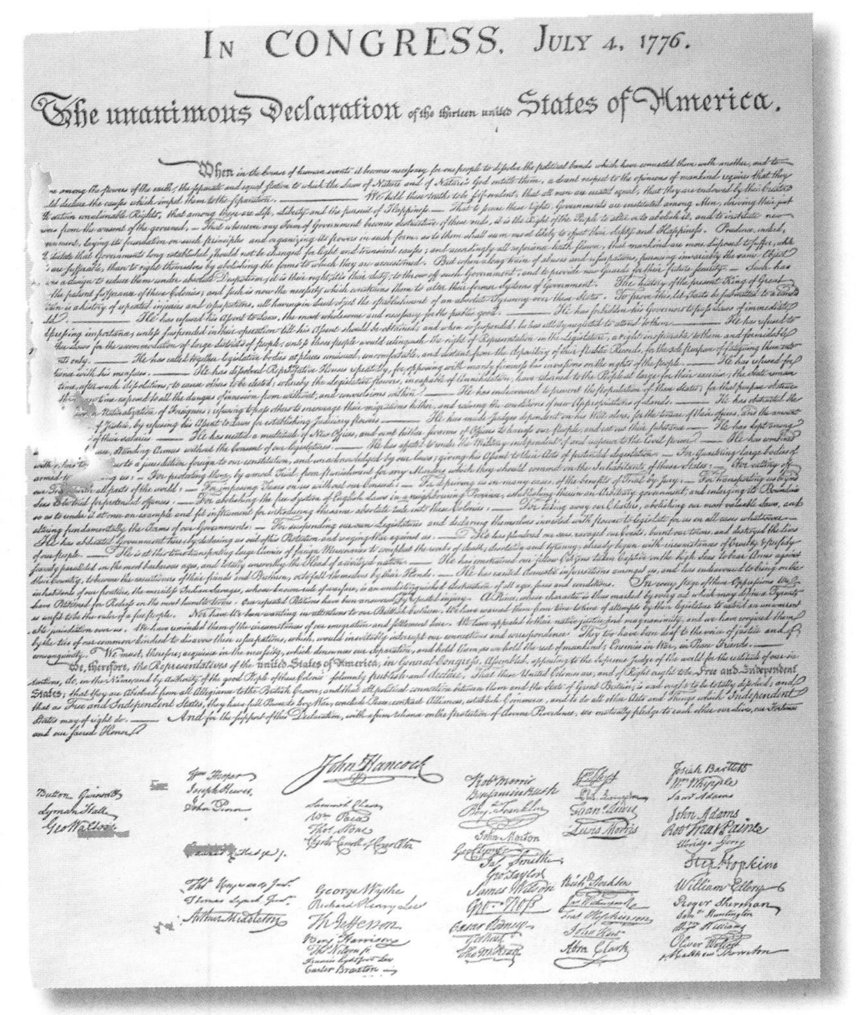
IN CONGRESS, JULY 4, 1776.

The unanimous Declaration of the thirteen united States of America.

The Declaration of Independence explains why the colonists wanted to form a separate nation.

When in the Course of human events it becomes necessary for one people to dissolve the political bands which have connected them with another, . . . a decent respect to the opinions of mankind requires that they should declare the causes which impel them to the separation.

The second excerpt lists some of the rights all people should have.

We hold these truths to be self-evident, that all men are created equal, that they are endowed by their Creator with certain unalienable Rights, that among these are life, liberty and the pursuit of happiness.

The third excerpt explains why government exists. It also describes citizens' rights if the government acts unfairly.

That to secure these rights, Governments are instituted among Men, deriving their just powers from the consent of the governed. That whenever any Form of Government becomes destructive of these ends, it is the Right of the People to alter or to abolish it, and to institute new Government.

The fourth excerpt presents a general complaint against King George III.

The history of the present King of Great Britain is a history of repeated injuries and usurpations, all having, in direct object, the establishment of an absolute Tyranny over these States. To prove this, let facts be submitted to a candid world.

The fifth excerpt declares the colonies' independence.

(We) solemnly publish and declare, That these United Colonies are, and of right ought to be Free and Independent States; that they are Absolved from all Allegiance to the British Crown, and that all political connection between them and that State of Great Britain, is and ought to be totally dissolved.

Summary

In this chapter, you read about the Second Continental Congress. It governed the colonies. It formed an army and picked George Washington as the new nation's military leader. It took steps to separate from Great Britain.

You learned that young Thomas Jefferson wrote the first draft of the Declaration of Independence. You saw items that he might have looked at as he worked. These included an invitation to the Congress and a copy of the booklet *Common Sense*. You read about some of the changes delegates of the Second Continental Congress made to the declaration before approving it on July 4, 1776.

In the next pages, you will learn more about Jefferson and the ideas of his time. What were the complex views about slavery? How did the ideas in the Declaration of Independence reflect the treatment of American Indians and women? Read on to find out.

Reading Further 12

Jefferson's Conflict: Ideas vs. Reality

The Declaration announced the start of a new nation. It also had bold ideas about equal rights for all people. These ideas were hard to put into practice. How did Thomas Jefferson's words differ from the reality of his life and the times in which he lived?

In 1776, Thomas Jefferson was a young man. And he was feeling proud. For about a week in June, he had worked hard on the draft of the Declaration of Independence. He had included ideas in which he deeply believed. But now, his work was being torn apart. The other members of the Second Continental Congress were making changes to his draft.

Line by line, the delegates studied Jefferson's words. Here they cut a word or sentence. There they added one. His strongest statements were weakened. Others were entirely removed. Jefferson was troubled. It seemed to him that the delegates were overly afraid of angering the British government. Yet the young Virginian said nothing. He sat in silence. But he felt angry and ashamed.

Jefferson and the other committee members presented a draft of the declaration to the rest of the Continental Congress. The Congress made a number of changes to the document.

The Granger Collection, New York

Jefferson owned slaves throughout his life. His slave Sandy was a carpenter and a shoemaker. The entry above, in Jefferson's account book for January 29, 1773 begins, *sold Sandy to Col. Chas Lewis for 100 £.* This £ symbol stands for a pound, or a unit of British currency.

Ideals and Reality

Jefferson was most upset about the changes related to slavery. His draft of the Declaration had strong language on the subject. The king, Jefferson wrote, had denied the "sacred rights of life and liberty . . . of a distant people who never offended him, captivating and carrying them into slavery. . . ." Jefferson blamed the king for refusing to let the colonies pass laws ending the slave trade.

The delegates took out this part of the draft. No one argued in favor of Jefferson's wording. The final Declaration of Independence would state that "all men are created equal." But it would say nothing about slavery.

Jefferson thought slavery was wrong. He believed that it hurt whites as well as enslaved Africans. "There must doubtless be an unhappy influence on the manners of our people produced by the existence of slavery among us," he wrote. From slavery, whites learned to be tyrants. He looked forward to the day when slavery would end.

Jefferson took steps against slavery. In the 1760s and 1770s, he helped lead efforts to end the importing of slaves into the colonies. In 1774, he wrote, "The abolition of domestic slavery is the great object of desire in these colonies." Later, he created a plan for freeing enslaved Africans. He opposed the spread of slavery beyond the South. Few white men of his time and place held similar views.

Yet Jefferson's actions regarding slavery were not so clear in his personal life. During his lifetime, he owned about 600 slaves. At any one time, 200 slaves worked for him. He earned money from slave labor. He sold slaves to pay off debts.

Jefferson also believed that freed slaves could not live side-by-side with whites. He thought that they must be sent far away. "Nothing is more certainly written in the book of fate that these people are to be free," he wrote late in his life. "Nor is it less certain that the two races, equally free, cannot live in the same government."

Conflicting Views on Slavery

Jefferson wrote in the Declaration of Independence that "all men are created equal." And the delegates of the Second Continental Congress approved these words.

equality the state of having the same rights and privileges as others

A belief in **equality** was at the heart of the Declaration. Because Jefferson felt that all men were equal, he believed they had certain rights. If a government denied those rights, he thought, the people could reject that government.

Jefferson had learned about many of these ideas from the writings of some of the great thinkers of Europe in the 1600s and 1700s. This period is called the Age of Enlightenment. John Locke was one such man whom Jefferson admired. Jefferson was also influenced by Thomas Paine, the author of *Common Sense*.

But what about the equality and rights of enslaved Africans? British writer Samuel Johnson saw the conflict between the ideas of some American leaders and their actions. "How is it," he wrote, "that we hear the loudest yelps for liberty among the drivers of negroes [slave owners]?" Some colonists also saw the problem. John Adams' wife Abigail wrote to her husband about it. She wondered how the colonists could fight "for what we are daily robbing and plundering from those who have as good a right to freedom as we have."

Abigail Adams knew that the words of the Declaration did not reflect how slaves lived in the colonies.

There was much disagreement over slavery in the colonies. Some colonists did not think that Africans were equal to white people. Others, like Abigail Adams, felt that slavery was wrong and that all people should have the same rights. In the middle were men such as Jefferson. He saw the need to end slavery. But he thought it would take time. He also believed that freed Africans would need to learn new skills and should move to some other place where they could thrive.

For now, Jefferson knew, slavery would remain an unfortunate part of American life. "As it is, we have the wolf by the ears," he once wrote on the subject of slavery. "We can neither hold him nor safely let him go." For years, the idea of equality between black and white people would remain only words on a page. Yet they were powerful words. And they would not be forgotten.

Jefferson believed that women should be wives and mothers. He did not think they should take part in politics.

Other Inequalities

Many people realized, as Jefferson did, that the treatment of slaves fell far short of the idea behind the words "all men are created equal." But they felt less concern for the unequal treatment of other groups in the colonies.

American Indians were one example. Their rights mattered little to most white people. Jefferson admired American Indians. He believed in treating them fairly. But he did not think they should be equal to white men in the new nation. And he felt that American Indians should give up their traditions and way of life. He wanted them to live more like white people.

Another group not included in the ideal that "all men are created equal" was women. Like many men of his time, Jefferson believed a woman's purpose was to be a wife and a mother. Women had few legal rights. They could not vote. Jefferson saw no need for women to have the same education that men did. Most men agreed with these limits for women.

Jefferson felt that men and women had different roles in the world. For example, women had no place in politics. Jefferson had lived in France. There, women were active in matters of government. This horrified Jefferson. He preferred the American way. In the new United States, many women took little interest in political issues or actions.

Indeed, it would be a number of years before many American women began to fight for equality. It would take even longer for them to reach their goal. In 1776, the statement "all men are created equal" purposely left women out. In truth it applied only to white men.

Yale University Art Gallery, Trumbull Collection

On which side do you think these men are fighting? How can you tell?

On which side do you think these men are fighting? How can you tell?

The American Revolution

13

How did the colonists win the American Revolution?

13.1 Introduction

In Chapter 12, you learned how the American colonies declared their independence from Great Britain. From 1775 to 1783, colonists fought in the American Revolution to win their freedom. A **revolution** is the overthrow of one government and its replacement with another.

The two sides in the war used different **strategies,** or overall plans, to try to win the war. At first, Great Britain seemed sure to succeed. It had a large navy. Its army was made up of skilled, full-time soldiers. The Continental army of the colonies was small and untrained. The British won most of the early battles.

The colonial soldiers, or Continentals, had some advantages. They had stronger reasons for wanting to win. They were defending their homes and their rights. Unlike the British, they were fighting on familiar lands. Also, foreign countries that were allies of the colonies sent aid to the struggling Americans.

Look at the visual metaphor below. The American Revolution can be compared to a tug-of-war between two unequal teams. The British army was like the team on the right, strong and confident. The Continental army was like the team on the left, small but motivated. As you read this chapter, think about how the smaller team might be able to win this tug-of-war. How did the Patriots defeat the British?

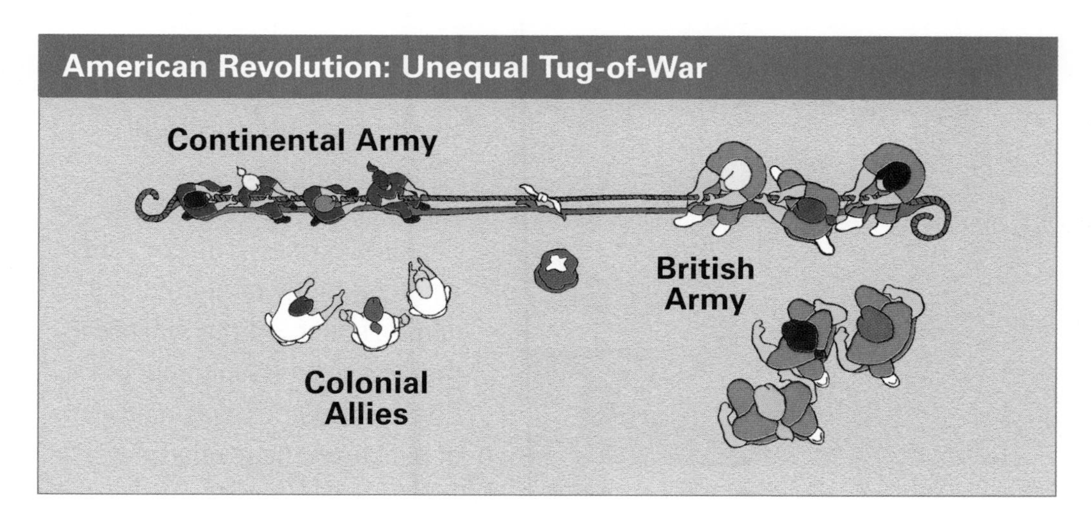

13.2 The Continental Army

When the war started, there was no American army. Instead, colonies had their own militias. These were made up of part-time soldiers, like those who fought the British soldiers at Lexington and Concord.

volunteer a person who performs a service for free

enlist to agree to serve in an army or a navy

In 1775, the Second Continental Congress asked George Washington to lead a new army. This Continental army was made up of **volunteers**. Most of these men were poor farmers, merchants, and workers. At the start of the war, they **enlisted** in the army for about one year at a time. Then they returned home to take care of their families.

Historians estimate that 8,000 to 24,000 men were in Washington's army at any one time, including many African Americans. Women took part as well. They cooked for soldiers, mended uniforms, and cared for the sick and wounded. Some women even fought in battles.

But the Continental army had a number of serious problems. Congress had little money to pay the soldiers or buy supplies for the army. As a result, the volunteers were poorly supplied with uniforms and guns. In addition, these men knew very little about being soldiers.

Washington worked hard to train his men. He taught them to obey orders and to fight together. In speeches and written messages, he encouraged them to believe that they could beat the mighty British military forces.

Like the Continental army, the colonial navy was small. It was made up of trade and fishing ships that carried little cannons. With their inexperienced army and tiny navy, the colonies were like a weak man about to fight a powerful giant.

The Granger Collection, New York

These Minutemen of Concord could be ready to fight in a minute's time. At the start of the American Revolution, the Continental army was made up of such untrained volunteers.

The Granger Collection, New York

The British troops had training and discipline. Their government gave them food and weapons. They were well supplied at the Battle of Bunker Hill, shown here.

13.3 The British Army

At the start of the war, Great Britain was confident that it would soon end the revolution. It had one of the strongest military forces in the world. The British navy's 270 warships controlled the seas. British shipyards built another 200 warships during the war.

Great Britain's army was large and well trained. Its soldiers were paid, and serving in the army was their full-time job. Most soldiers were experienced fighters. Their leaders disciplined them harshly. A soldier could be whipped for using bad language.

Unlike the American Congress, the British Parliament had money to buy food and weapons for its army. Each soldier was given a uniform, a musket, a short sword, and a bayonet, or sharp blade. Soldiers attached the bayonets to the front ends of their muskets to use in close fighting.

There were about 48,000 soldiers in the British army. Most were poor men who earned low pay. Some were from other countries. Great Britain hired about 30,000 **mercenaries** from Germany to fight in America.

mercenary a soldier hired to fight for a foreign army

Thousands of American Indians joined the British as well. They sided with Great Britain because, since 1763, the British had helped protect their lands from settlers. Thousands of Loyalists also fought for Great Britain. New York's many Loyalists joined the British side at the start of the war.

13.4 The British Army Is Far from Home

The British army and navy were strong. But the British had a major problem. They were far from home. Supplies, military orders, and soldiers had to travel 3,000 miles by sea across the Atlantic Ocean. The trip from Great Britain to America could take three months.

The Granger Collection, New York

The small Continental navy won a few sea battles. Captain John Paul Jones defeated the British warship *Serapis.* During this clash, Jones said the famous words, "I have not yet begun to fight!"

Once British ships crossed the ocean, it was often hard to get the cargo ashore. The Continentals had few naval ships to attack the British warships. But they did call on hundreds of privateers. Privateers were small, fast ships with a few light cannons. Congress gave the captains of the privateers permission to attack British supply ships. Ship captains could keep most of the goods they captured. Later in the war, French warships also attacked British ships.

Unlike the British, Continental troops were fighting in their home country and could get supplies more easily. In addition, as the war went on, the Continental army found new ways of getting weapons and supplies. Often, local citizens sold or gave the army food. American troops captured cannons and muskets from the British.

American women also helped the Continental army. They ran the farms and businesses while the men were away fighting. Women brought supplies to the camps, made uniforms, and worked as nurses. They also spied among the British.

In contrast, the British had to fight in a country that was not their home. Most colonists refused to give them food or supplies. The British often felt as though they were surrounded by people who disliked and even hated them. These feelings made the troops less eager to fight.

During the winter at Valley Forge, the men in Washington's army suffered from starvation and bitter cold. But they refused to give up.

13.5 The Continental Army Is Motivated to Win

Continental soldiers had a special advantage over the British—a stronger motivation, or desire, to win.

Continental soldiers believed that they were defending the rights described in the Declaration of Independence. They were fighting to make a better future for themselves and their families. Many thought that these were goals worth dying for.

Washington's troops showed this strong motivation at Valley Forge, Pennsylvania, in the bitterly cold winter of 1777–1778. They were tired and starving. Many didn't have warm clothing or even shoes. More than 2,500 men died that winter from cold and sickness. Yet the army didn't give up.

The British soldiers had less motivation. Most of them fought because it was their job. They were not defending their homes or their freedoms. And Parliament had other problems besides the war. It had colonies to protect in places outside North America. It had strong enemies like France and Spain. And many people in Great Britain didn't want to pay for a war in distant North America.

Of course, not all Americans wanted to fight the British. Loyalists still believed that independence was unwise. In addition, the British sometimes promised to free slaves who joined their side. As a result, some African Americans fought for the British. As you have read, many American Indians also fought for the British in hopes of protecting their lands.

Washington Crossing the Delaware by Emmanuel D. Leutze, (97.34) The Metropolitan Museum of Art, Gift of John Stewart Kennedy, 1897

On a winter night in 1775, Washington led his troops across the Delaware River to New Jersey. There, in the Battle of Trenton, they defeated German mercenaries to win a key early Patriot victory.

13.6 Different War Strategies

The British and the American armies used different war strategies. Each tried to use its strengths. The British fought an offensive war. They attacked the Continental army. Their aim was to control key cities and the countryside. The Continental troops fought a defensive war. Their goal was to protect themselves from attacks by the British army, rather than to destroy it.

At first, the British tried to end the war quickly. They won the Battle of Bunker Hill near Boston in June 1775. They kept control of Boston, the city they thought was the main Patriot stronghold. But they soon learned that men across the colonies would fight for independence.

tactic a planned action, such as a way of moving or using troops, aimed at reaching a certain goal

In August 1776, the British took control of New York City after the Battle of Long Island. Washington moved his men into the countryside. From there, the Continental army used **tactics** not common for that time. Patriot troops made surprise attacks on small groups of British soldiers, and then retreated. Sharpshooters hid in the woods and shot British soldiers, one by one. These tactics puzzled British troops, who preferred to meet their enemy face-to-face.

So the British changed their strategy. They tried to use their better-trained troops to openly engage Washington's troops in battle. But one night in December 1776, Washington sneaked his troops across the Delaware River, from Pennsylvania to New Jersey. There, in the Battle of Trenton, they surprised and defeated German mercenaries who were celebrating Christmas. This was a key early Patriot victory.

By 1777, the British generals were determined to force Washington's army into the open. To do this, the British took the key city of Philadelphia.

But Washington wanted to protect his soldiers. Rather than risk losing men in a direct battle, he let the British take the city. He then moved his men to Valley Forge to train and to avoid the British for the winter. This location was easy to defend. It was also close enough to York, Pennsylvania, to protect Congress as it met there.

13.7 The Continental Army Gains Allies

Patriot leaders needed allies to win the war. In 1776, Congress had sent Benjamin Franklin to Paris, France, to seek help.

France agreed to supply arms and to loan money to Congress. Some European soldiers also joined the Patriot cause. A 19-year-old Frenchman, the Marquis de Lafayette, became a general in the Continental army. Baron Friedrich von Steuben, a German soldier, played a key role in training colonial troops.

turning point an event that leads to a dramatic change

In mid-1777, about 9,000 British troops crossed the border from Canada. About 2,000 Vermont and New Hampshire soldiers attacked them. Other Continental troops rushed to help. That October, with his army trapped at Saratoga, New York, British General John Burgoyne surrendered to American General Horatio Gates.

The Battle of Saratoga was a **turning point** in the war. The colonists had defeated British troops. France now sent troops and ships to help the colonists. Spain pledged to support France. Since Dutch merchants were trading with the Americans, Dutch banks loaned the Americans money. The Continental army now had strong allies.

The British again tried a new strategy. For the next three years, they fought in the Southern Colonies, where Loyalists would help them. But the war did not go well there for Great Britain. In 1781, Spain captured a British fort at Pensacola, Florida.

At Saratoga, the Continental army defeated British troops. The Battle of Saratoga, in October 1777, was a turning point of the war.

Then, that summer, a large British force marched to the Virginia coast. But the French navy stopped enemy ships from bringing the British support from New York. And Washington's army and thousands of French soldiers arrived from the north. They trapped the British in the port of Yorktown. For more than two weeks, they pounded the British with cannon fire. Finally, British Lieutenant General Charles Cornwallis surrendered.

The Battle of Yorktown was the last big battle of the war. With the help of their French allies, the Continentals had won a key victory.

treaty a formal agreement between two or more nations

13.8 The Treaty of Paris, 1783

After their defeat at Yorktown, the British were ready to end the war. They were now fighting France and Spain, as well as their former American colonies. Representatives from all these countries met in Paris to work out a peace **treaty**.

Meanwhile, the fighting went on. The British navy shut down American shipping on the seas. On land, the British still controlled New York City; Charleston, South Carolina; and Savannah, Georgia. To the west, small but bloody battles were fought in Ohio, Kentucky, and western New York. Continental soldiers fought against British soldiers, Loyalists, and American Indians. Villages burned. Women and children on both sides were killed.

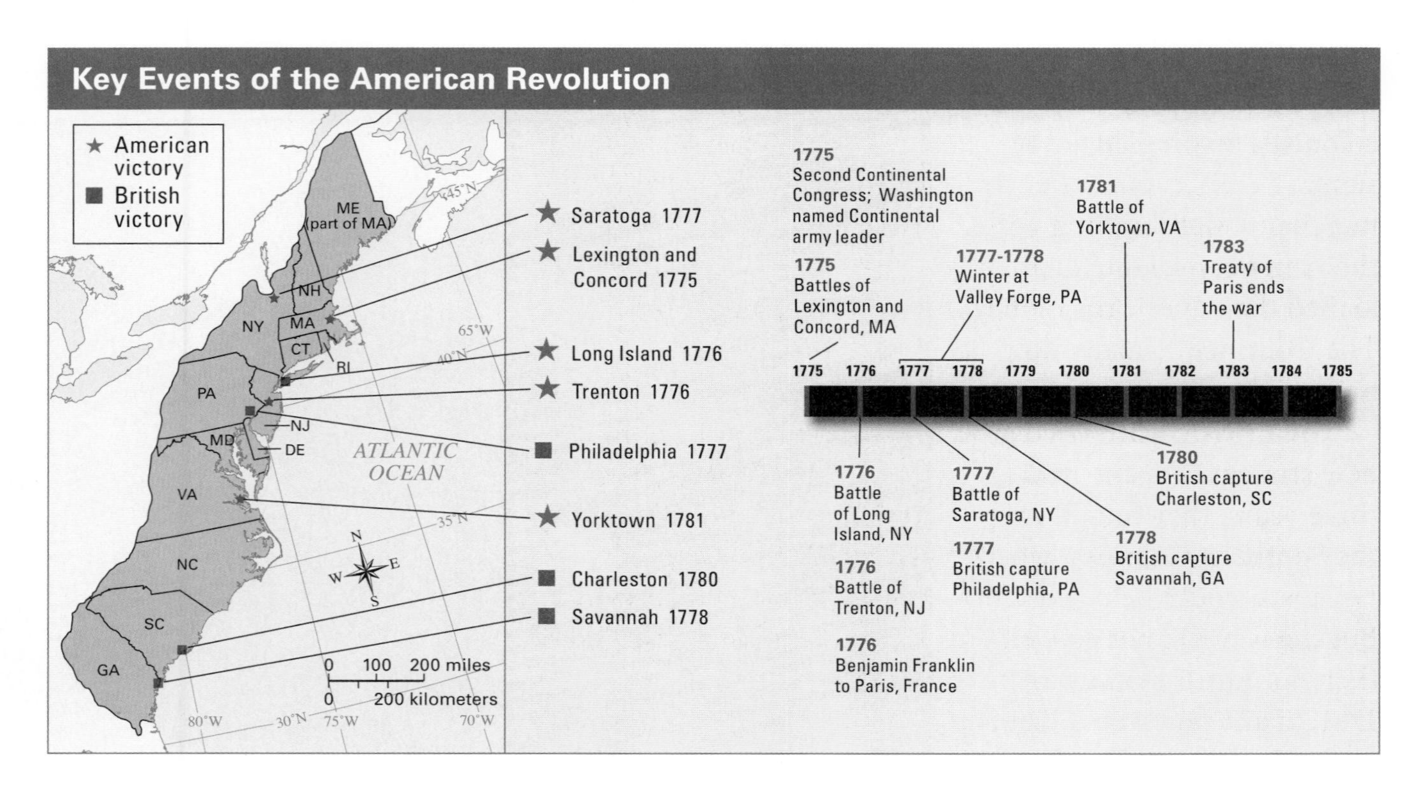

In September 1783, the war finally ended with the Treaty of Paris. In this set of agreements, Great Britain agreed to recognize the United States of America as an independent nation. Great Britain also gave the new country a huge amount of land. This included all the territory that was east of the Mississippi River, south of Canada and the Great Lakes, and north of Florida. This area included land that the British had promised to American Indians. The British kept control of their lands in Canada but returned Florida to Spain.

In the treaty, the United States promised to restore the rights and property of Loyalists. But many of the new nation's citizens did not keep this part of the agreement. This caused thousands of Loyalists to flee to Great Britain, Canada, and other places. Many African Americans who had fought for the British also escaped to other countries.

The Patriots had won the war. From this time forward, the former colonists would be known simply as Americans.

Summary

In this chapter, you learned how the colonists defeated the British to become a new country. You compared the war to a game of tug-of-war between two unequal teams. The weaker side won because of some special advantages.

The Continental army and navy were weaker than those of the British. But, unlike the British, the Continentals were fighting at home. They had a stronger motivation to win. And they could fight a defensive war. In contrast, the British had to try to control large amounts of territory as well as defeat the Continental army.

When the Continentals won the Battle of Saratoga, powerful allies joined them. In the decisive Battle of Yorktown, French soldiers and ships helped the Continentals defeat the British. The Treaty of Paris recognized American independence. It also gave a huge amount of land to the United States.

How did the widespread fighting affect Americans who were not in the military forces? What happened to groups of people such as women, African Americans, and American Indians? Read on to find out.

Reading Further 13

The Revolution's Home Front

The American Revolution played out on many battlefields. But soldiers were not the only ones to take part. The war had many heroes. It also had many victims. Women gave much to the cause. Enslaved Africans and American Indians were also involved. What was the war's impact on these people?

Rachel Wells lived in New Jersey at the time of the American Revolution. She never took part in any battles. But she played a role in the war. And she suffered the dangers of wartime.

home front areas away from the fighting in a country at war

Wells was a widow. But she was willing to do her part to support the war effort. She lent money to the government of New Jersey. Her funds helped supply the soldiers fighting the British. As she later wrote, she "threw in all her might which bought . . . clothing and let them have blankets." Even with help like hers, however, the Patriots could not hold off the British. At one point, British soldiers came through Wells's town. Before leaving, they robbed Wells of a very large sum of money. She was forced to flee to Philadelphia to try to rebuild her life. But by the war's end, she was living in poverty. She had to beg the Continental Congress to help her get her money back. "Pray forget not the poor weaklings," she wrote in her plea.

Wells's story shows that the American Revolution was about more than soldiers and guns. It affected people all over the colonies. While many men marched off to battle, life went on for the people they left behind. Life on the **home front** could be complicated. And, as Wells found out, it could sometimes be dangerous.

While the men fought in the army, the women were left to defend their homes and care for their children.

Women and the War

Attacks such as the one Wells suffered were common during the war. Soldiers on both sides often raided towns. In addition to taking money, they stole food, clothing, firewood, and other supplies. Many women saw their homes destroyed. "Families flying from the [houses]," wrote one Virginia woman describing an attack on her town. "Oh shocking! Oh horrible! Surely any spot of earth on this globe, where freedom and peace can be enjoyed would now be more desirable than living here."

Women faced other hardships, too. Finding food was a challenge. Supplies were short. Prices were high. Many families went hungry. And poor nutrition put people at risk for disease. Many women and children died from illness.

Still, the women carried on. They ran family businesses. They planted and harvested crops. They did their best to take care of their children.

Many women did even more. A few served as spies. Others nursed the sick and wounded. A nurse had a greater chance of dying from disease than a soldier had of dying in battle.

Some women used their household skills for the war. For instance, women in Philadelphia led an effort to raise money and make clothing for the troops.

Women helped win public support for the war. Writer Mercy Otis Warren, whom you read about in Chapter 11, was one example. So was Mary Katherine Goddard of Maryland. Goddard helped publish a newspaper.

The Granger Collection, New York

Women had many roles in the war. Molly Pitcher took her wounded husband's place as a gunner during one battle.

Some women traveled with the troops and cared for them. And in a few cases, they took part in combat. Anna Lane was wounded at the Battle of Germantown in 1777. Deborah Sampson dressed as a man and fought in several battles. Only when she was wounded did an army doctor discover her secret. Mary Ludwig Hays McCauley, known as Molly Pitcher, took her husband's place as a gunner when he was hurt at the Battle of Monmouth in 1778.

This painting shows a black soldier (at left) protecting his American commander by firing at British soldiers.

African Americans and the War

In 1776, 500,000 slaves lived in the colonies. The war brought them challenges, choices, and opportunities.

The British offered freedom to slaves who joined their side. Tens of thousands of enslaved African Americans took this offer. They ran away from their owners. Many slaves gave valuable service to the British. They fought in battle. They served as spies. They performed many jobs in army camps. Many slaves did, in fact, win their freedom.

But running away was risky. Sometimes, the British turned away slaves who wanted to join them. During the Battle of Yorktown, the British forced away many escaped slaves. Many of them starved or died from disease. Others were caught and returned to their owners.

Some African Americans fought for the Patriot cause. For example, Salem Poor was a hero of the Battle of Bunker Hill. This battle was fought at Boston in 1775. Early in the war, African Americans could not join the Patriot ranks. Some white colonists did not want to arm slaves. This worry faded, however, as the war dragged on.

African Americans found ways to help the Patriots off the battlefield, too. One example is James Armistead. He pretended to serve the British. Instead, he spied on them. For his work, Armistead won his freedom.

African American women also helped the Patriot cause. Phillis Wheatley was a slave. She was also a talented writer. She wrote a stirring poem that honored George Washington. Such efforts raised people's spirits. This was vital during the long, difficult struggle.

American Indians and the War

American Indians were another group affected by the American Revolution. They saw both the colonists and the British as a threat. And both the colonists and the British sought to use American Indians to their own advantage.

Some tribes sided with the British. They thought that the British were less of a threat to their way of life than the colonists were. A few tribes helped the colonists.

Many American Indians, however, tried to stay out of the war. In fact, they hoped that the two sides would weaken each other. This, in turn, would help American Indians.

Staying out of the war proved very hard. Few tribes, in fact, could avoid being caught up in the fighting. Neither the British nor the Americans fully trusted the American Indians. They each punished them harshly for helping the other side. Both sides often raided American Indian villages and took food supplies. Hunger among the American Indians was widespread.

By the war's end, many tribes were struggling to survive. The Patriot victory had only made things worse. The British had previously tried to slow western settlement. Now, the British were gone. Soon, white settlers were again pushing west. They moved in large numbers onto American Indian lands. The Patriots had won independence. The future of the American Indians was once again in doubt.

The British sought to persuade American Indians to fight on Great Britain's side.

The Granger Collection, New York

George Washington

James Madison

Benjamin Franklin

Find each of these men in the painting above. What role do you think each of them played as delegates at the Constitutional Convention?

The Constitution

What are the key features of the U.S. Constitution?

14.1 Introduction

In Chapter 13, you read about how Americans won their independence. Now that the United States was a separate nation, it needed a government to protect its citizens and to maintain order. Many leaders saw the need for change. In this chapter, you will learn how the young nation's leaders formed a new national government.

The **Articles of Confederation** was a document that set up the nation's first central government. This government had limited powers, and it was too weak to keep order. In 1787, the states called a meeting to improve the Articles of Confederation. This meeting was called the **Constitutional Convention**.

Instead of revising the Articles, the convention delegates wrote a new **constitution**. This document describes how the new government would work. It also sets up rules and laws. The United States Constitution creates a strong central government. It divides the government into three parts, or branches. Each branch has its own powers and responsibilities. To keep any one branch from becoming too powerful, the Constitution includes a system of **checks and balances**. Under this system, each branch limits, or checks, the powers of the others. The Constitution also set up a federal system in which power was divided between the national and the state governments.

Some say the Articles of Confederation were as unsteady as a one-legged stool. Look at the drawing of the stool at the right. As you read this chapter, think about how this three-legged stool can be compared to the government set up by the Constitution.

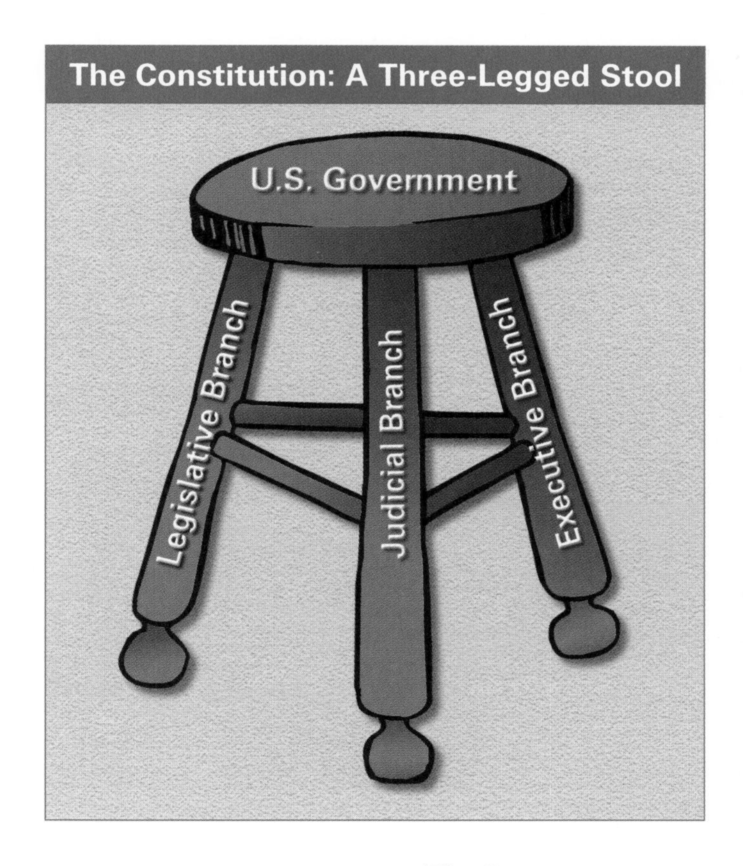

14.2 The First Government: The Articles of Confederation

After declaring independence from Great Britain, the Second Continental Congress approved a document called the Articles of Confederation. The Articles created a weak government called the Confederation Congress. This Congress managed the war against Great Britain. It also worked to solve common problems.

The Congress could declare war and pass laws. But every law had to be approved by at least 9 of the 13 states. The new government had no president and no court to settle disputes between states.

Once the American Revolution ended, the Congress had a hard time solving the new country's problems. Most of the powers were held by the states. Each state still issued its own money. The Congress had no power to collect taxes or to force the states to give it funds. It could not support a national army to protect American citizens. It could not even pay the soldiers who had fought in the war.

Here a farmer attacks a government official during Shays' Rebellion as others cheer him on. This uprising frightened many leaders. They saw the need for a change.

Times were hard. Many former soldiers and poor farmers lost their homes because they could not pay their bills. Some of them were jailed. One farmer complained, "The great [rich] men are going to get all we have, and I think it is time for us to rise and put a stop to it."

In Massachusetts, a former soldier named Daniel Shays agreed. He and hundreds of other men took part in an armed revolt. They tried to stop the state courts from taking people's property. Their fight against the government became known as Shays' Rebellion.

This violence worried the nation's leaders. Some saw the need for a stronger government that could pay the nation's bills, settle disputes between states, and maintain order.

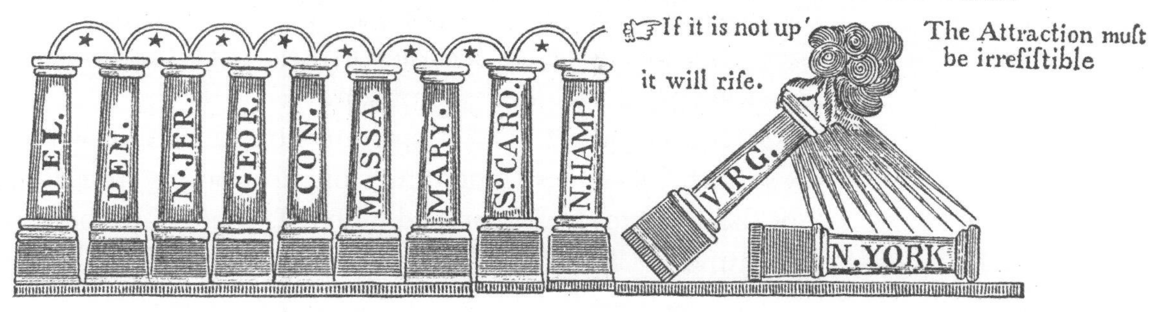

The Granger Collection, New York

This 1788 cartoon shows that nine states had approved the Constitution. New York and Virginia were about to add their votes. As you read the words, note that the letter *s* sometimes looks like the letter *f*.

14.3 A New Government: The Constitutional Convention

In May 1787, 55 delegates met in Philadelphia. Their plan was to improve the Articles of Confederation. Instead, they wrote an entirely new document. Today, their meeting is known as the Constitutional Convention.

The delegates came from all the states except Rhode Island. They were some of the best-known leaders in the nation. As a group, they were better educated and richer than most Americans. All were white men. Many were lawyers. There were also doctors, merchants, farmers, and former soldiers.

Several delegates played key roles. As president of the convention, George Washington kept the debates respectful. Benjamin Franklin, then 81, calmed heated tempers. James Madison of Virginia designed a plan for a strong national government. Gouverneur (his first name) Morris of Pennsylvania wrote much of the final draft of the Constitution.

The men worked hard during that hot summer. Some, like Madison, wanted a strong central government. Others feared losing freedoms if the government had too much power.

In the end, the delegates agreed to a federal system. This meant that power was divided between state governments and a strong national government. They separated the power of the national government into three parts, or branches. The **legislative branch** would make the laws. The **executive branch** would carry them out. The **judicial branch** would settle disputes over the meaning of the laws.

legislative branch the branch that makes laws; to legislate is to make laws

executive branch the branch that carries out, or executes, laws

judicial branch the branch that interprets laws and settles disagreements about them; "judicial" comes from the word *judge*

compromise an agreement in which each side gives up some of what it wants

One fierce debate was about the number of representatives in the legislative branch. Larger states wanted the number to reflect how many people lived in each state. Smaller states feared they would have little power under such a plan. They wanted each state to have the same number of votes. At last, the two sides reached a **compromise**. They accepted Roger Sherman's idea for a legislature with two parts, or houses. This idea was called the Great Compromise.

On September 17, 1787, after four months of hard work, most of the delegates signed the Constitution. By June 1788, 9 of the 13 states had approved it. The United States had a new government.

14.4 Making the Laws: The Legislative Branch

The Constitution is organized into seven main parts, or articles. Article I describes the legislative branch, or Congress. Congress makes the laws.

Congress is made up of two houses, the Senate and the House of Representatives. Every state elects two members, called senators, to the Senate. In the House, the number of representatives depends on the number of people who live in a state. States with more people have more representatives in the House.

This joint meeting of members of both the Senate and the House is taking place in the chamber of the House of Representatives in the Capitol.

Congress meets in the U.S. Capitol building in Washington, D.C., shown here.

To make laws, members of Congress write bills. If a majority in both houses of Congress votes to pass a bill, it is sent to the head of the executive branch, the president. If the president signs the bill, it becomes a law.

If the president refuses to sign a bill, Congress can overrule the president's decision. A two-thirds majority of both houses must vote to overrule the president. Otherwise, the bill does not become a law.

The legislative branch has many other powers. The Senate approves or rejects the people the president chooses to fill key jobs. The Senate must approve the president's choices for ambassadors. Ambassadors represent the United States in foreign countries. The Senate must approve the president's choice of federal judges. It also approves members of the president's **cabinet**.

Congress has some powers in foreign affairs, or the business that the United States conducts with other countries. Two-thirds of the Senate must vote to approve a treaty between the United States and another country. And both houses of Congress must give approval before the United States can declare war on another country.

The Constitution also gives Congress ways to remove people in the other branches who abuse their powers. The House can **impeach** the president, judges, and other officials. The Senate can put an impeached official on trial. If the Senate finds the person guilty, that official must resign from his or her job.

Article I gives other powers to Congress. It can collect taxes. It can also create a national currency, or system of money.

cabinet a group of advisors to the president, including the heads of important departments in the executive branch

impeach to accuse or charge a government official, such as the president, with a crime or misconduct

The president is the head of the executive branch and lives in the White House, shown at center. Beyond the White House are many office buildings. Some of these are used by government officials.

14.5 Carrying Out the Laws: The Executive Branch

Article II of the Constitution explains the powers of the executive branch. This branch carries out, or executes, the nation's laws.

The head of the executive branch is the president, or chief executive. Working for the president are the people and organizations that help to carry out the laws written and passed by Congress.

The men who wrote the Constitution did not want the United States to have a leader with too much power, like a king. So, they limited the president's power. For example, the Constitution gives the president the power to either sign or **veto** the bills passed by Congress. But Congress can overrule the president's veto by a two-thirds vote of both houses.

Presidents cannot make laws, but they can lead the country by making proposals, or offering ideas, to Congress. One way that presidents do this is by giving a State of the Union speech every year to both houses in the House Chamber. In these speeches, they may suggest ideas for new laws.

The president can call Congress together for a special session, or meeting. This power is a useful tool when a president believes that there is a national emergency.

The president shares power over foreign affairs with Congress. The president can sign a treaty with another nation, but two-thirds of the Senate must approve it. As commander in chief, the president is in charge of the nation's armed forces, such as the army and navy. But only Congress can declare war.

As chief executive, the president nominates, or suggests, people for key jobs in the government. For example, the president nominates cabinet members, ambassadors, and federal judges. However, the Senate has to accept or reject the president's choices.

The president has the power to grant pardons to people who have been found guilty of crimes against the nation. A pardon is a release from punishment. But the president cannot give pardons in cases of impeachment.

The president is only the head of the executive branch and not a king. But most people view the president as the leader of the country. In many ways, such as in discussions with other countries, the president represents the United States.

veto to reject a bill and prevent it from becoming a law, a power that belongs only to the president

14.6 Interpreting the Laws: The Judicial Branch

Article III of the Constitution describes the judicial branch. This branch interprets the nation's laws, settles disputes between states, and protects the Constitution.

The judicial branch is headed by the Supreme Court. Congress has used its power to create other federal courts under this Court. The Supreme Court has nine judges, or justices. The Court's leader is the chief justice. Justices are appointed by the president and approved by the Senate. They serve for life, or until they choose to retire.

The judicial branch has some important powers. It decides whether a national or state law conflicts with the Constitution. Such a law is called unconstitutional. Because the Constitution is the basic law of our country, the judicial branch can overrule unconstitutional laws.

The judicial branch also has the power to review and comment on treaties. If it finds that a treaty violates the Constitution, then the treaty is not put into effect.

The judicial branch interprets the law. That is, the courts settle disagreements about what a law means or how it applies to a particular situation.

The judicial branch has power during impeachment trials. Most notably, the chief justice is the judge in such trials.

By using its powers, the judicial branch protects the Constitution and the rights of Americans. If the actions of the other branches conflict with the Constitution, the judicial branch acts to enforce the Constitution.

In this Supreme Court building, the nine Supreme Court justices make many important decisions.

14.7 Limiting Power: Checks and Balances

The men who wrote the Constitution wanted a strong and lasting government. To achieve this goal, they designed a system of checks and balances. The Constitution gives each branch of government the power to check, or limit, certain actions of the other branches. It also balances each branch's powers with the powers of the other branches.

Checks and balances ensure that no one branch becomes too powerful. For example, Congress can pass laws, but the president can approve or veto them. The president's power is a check on the power of Congress.

What if Congress and the president agree on a law that conflicts with the Constitution? If the law is challenged in court, the judicial branch decides whether it is unconstitutional. The court's power is a check on the power of the other two branches.

How are the powers of the different branches balanced? Suppose the president wants one thing and Congress wants another. Congress cannot make laws without the president's review, and the president needs Congress to pass the laws he or she wants. Their powers balance each other. And while the courts can declare laws unconstitutional, federal judges are appointed by the president with the approval of the Senate.

The Constitution gives each branch of the government the power to check, or limit, some actions of the other branches. The men who wrote the Constitution wanted a balance of power among the branches. They did not want any one branch to become too strong.

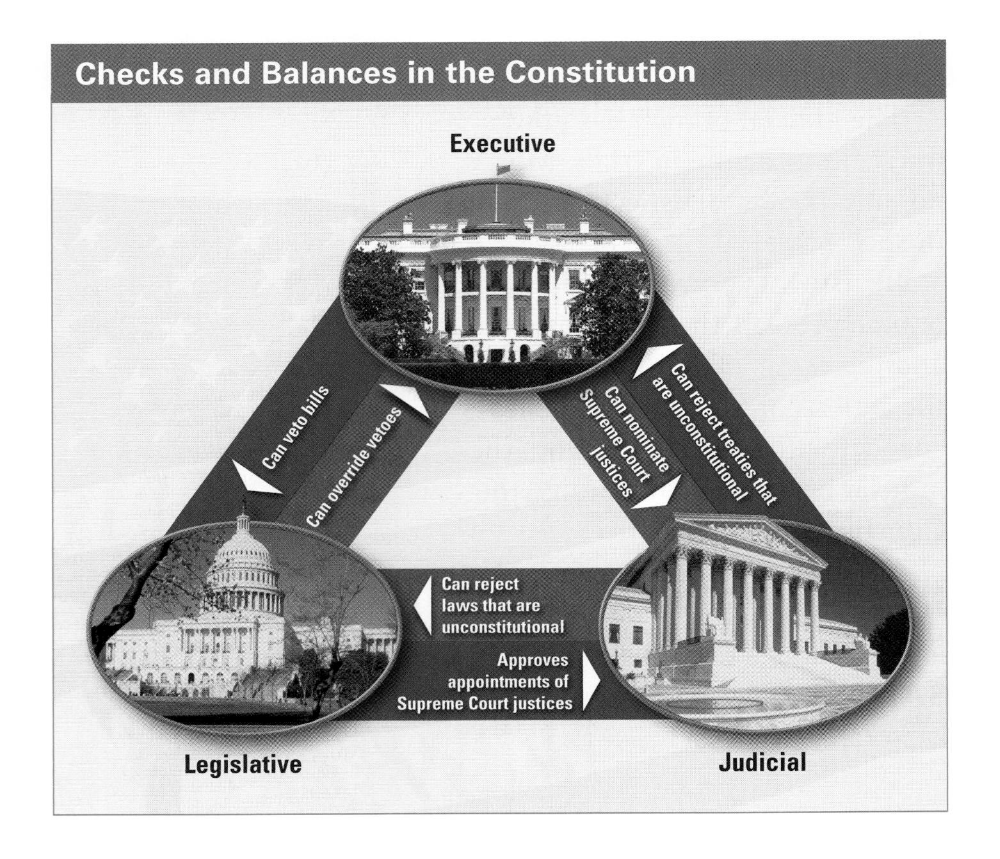

Another example of checks and balances is impeachment. Suppose members of the executive or judicial branch misuse their power. Congress can impeach them, try them, and remove them from office if they are found guilty. In these ways, the Constitution works to make sure that no one branch of the government becomes more powerful than the others.

Summary

In this chapter, you used a metaphor of two stools. This helped you contrast how the government worked under the Articles of Confederation and under the Constitution.

You learned about some weaknesses of the Articles of Confederation. This document set up the first U.S. government. After the American Revolution was over, events such as Shays' Rebellion showed that the nation needed a stronger government.

After much debate and compromise, the delegates at the Constitutional Convention set up a federal system. They divided powers among a strong national government and the state governments. The delegates wrote the rules for this new central government in the Constitution.

The Granger Collection, New York

Here we see the first page of the Constitution.

The writers of the Constitution separated the national government's powers into three branches. They used a system of checks and balances to make sure that no one branch had too much power. In this way, they tried to form a strong and lasting government that would respect Americans' rights and freedoms.

How did the delegates come to agree on a Constitution that formed a new kind of government? What did they argue about? How did they resolve their differences? Read on to find out.

Reading Further 14

Inside the Constitutional Convention

The convention got off to a rough start. The meeting room was hot and humid. The arguments among the delegates were also heated. But in the end, the results were glorious. How did the men who wrote our Constitution complete their complex task?

The Constitutional Convention was set to begin on May 14, 1787. James Madison was eager to get to work. Virginia had chosen him as a delegate to the convention. He arrived in Philadelphia days ahead of time. He was interested in history and politics, and for years he had studied different types of government. He had lots of ideas about how to improve on the Articles of Confederation. He hoped to help create a stronger national government. This, he felt, was the best way to ensure the liberty of Americans.

But few other delegates shared Madison's excitement. When May 14 arrived, only about a dozen of them were in town. Only two states were represented by most of their delegates. Madison and the others had to wait. They agreed to gather each day to see if enough men had arrived to begin their important meeting.

As the days passed, some delegates grew annoyed. "These delays greatly impede [slow] public measures," wrote George Washington. He had arrived on schedule. Now, he became angry at the wasting of his valuable time.

Finally, near the end of May, enough delegates had trickled into the city. Most states had enough men on hand to vote and make decisions. At last, after a delay of nearly two weeks, the convention could begin.

Delegates created and signed the U.S. Constitution in this Assembly Room in what is today called Independence Hall.

Once they began to talk, the delegates agreed on some key issues. They felt that the people should be free to form their own government. And they all believed that government existed to serve the people. The delegates did not want to live in a **monarchy** again under an all-powerful ruler like the British king. They wanted a government with limited powers.

The delegates also agreed on the **rule of law**. They said that no one should be able to ignore the law. Toward this goal, each state already had its own constitution. Each one set down the basic rules and laws of that state's government. The state constitutions placed limits on the power of their governments. They also protected each person's basic rights.

The delegates wanted to create a **republic**. In this kind of government, the people hold the power to elect representatives. People live under the rule of law and their rights are protected.

Though the delegates agreed on these basic matters, they disagreed on much else. And not everyone shared the same ideas about how to govern the new republic.

Some men thought that the country needed a stronger central government. Such a government could end the squabbles among the states. It could stop each state from issuing its own money. These delegates felt that the Articles of Confederation did not have the power to keep order.

Other delegates feared a strong central government. They worried that it would put their freedom at risk. Patrick Henry refused to attend the convention, saying he "smelt a rat." Men like Henry wanted the states to keep most of the power. Rhode Island agreed and did not send any delegates.

Many conflicts divided the delegates at the Convention. Reaching agreement would not be easy.

monarchy a form of government in which a ruler holds power for life

rule of law a set of public laws that apply to all people equally, with no one getting special treatment

republic a form of government in which citizens elect representatives who are responsible to the people

These coins were issued by the new nation in 1776. The Constitution later gave this power to issue money solely to the national government.

Benjamin Franklin was, at 81, the oldest delegate at the Convention. He tried to calm delegates' tempers during heated debates.

On a rainy day, the delegates met to begin their work. The wet weather soon gave way to brutal heat. Pesky flies swarmed everywhere. The delegates suffered in the stifling Assembly Room in the Pennsylvania State House. James Madison attended every meeting. He later claimed that being cooped up in the heat all summer nearly killed him. The delegates would not open the doors or windows. They did not want people on the street to listen to their debates. They wanted the freedom to share new ideas and to change their minds. They worried that newspapers might report their discussions, and then delegates might not speak openly.

And the delegates had a lot to discuss. How strong should the national government be? How could they balance power among the states? The states with few citizens feared the power of the larger states. The larger states felt that they should have more say in the way the government worked.

Another debate had to do with how to choose leaders. How much power should the voters have? Many delegates feared that ordinary citizens would make bad choices. These delegates did not want the people's votes to directly choose people for key offices, such as president.

Delegates also debated how long a term, or period of time, men should hold an office. Would it be better to have people serve for many years? Or should they face election more often? Long terms might give officials too much power. Having elections too often might make them more concerned about winning votes than making good decisions.

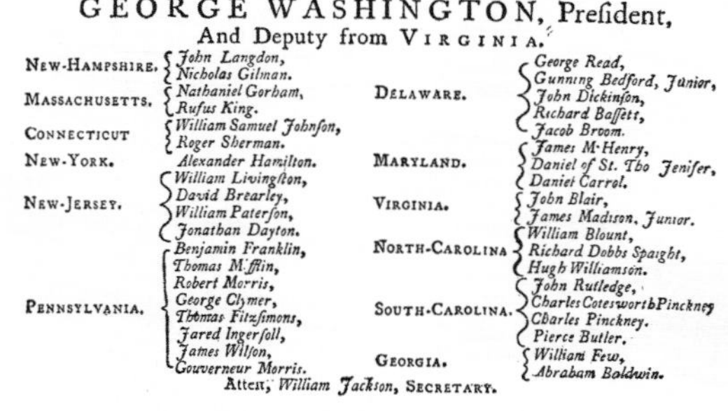

[5]

The ſenators and repreſentatives beforementioned, and the members of the ſeveral ſtate legiſlatures, and all executive and judicial officers, both of the United States and of the ſeveral States, ſhall be bound by oath or affirmation, to ſupport this conſtitution; but no religious teſt ſhall ever be required as a qualification to any office or public truſt under the United States.

VII.

The ratification of the conventions of nine States, ſhall be ſufficient for the eſtabliſhment of this conſtitution between the States ſo ratifying the ſame:

Done in Convention, by the unanimous conſent of the States preſent, the ſeventeenth day of September, in the year of our Lord one thouſand ſeven hundred and eighty-ſeven, and of the Independence of the United States of America the twelfth. In witneſs whereof we have hereunto ſubſcribed our Names.

GEORGE WASHINGTON, Preſident,
And Deputy from VIRGINIA.

NEW-HAMPSHIRE.	*John Langdon,* *Nicholas Gilman.*	DELAWARE.	*George Read,* *Gunning Bedford, Junior,* *John Dickinſon,* *Richard Baſſett,* *Jacob Broom.*
MASSACHUSETTS.	*Nathaniel Gorham,* *Rufus King.*	MARYLAND.	*James M'Henry,* *Daniel of St. Tho Jeniſer,* *Daniel Carrol.*
CONNECTICUT	*William Samuel Johnſon,* *Roger Sherman.*	VIRGINIA.	*John Blair,* *James Madiſon, Junior.*
NEW-YORK.	*Alexander Hamilton.*	NORTH-CAROLINA	*William Blount,* *Richard Dobbs Spaight,* *Hugh Williamſon.*
NEW-JERSEY.	*William Livingſton,* *David Brearley,* *William Paterſon,* *Jonathan Dayton.*	SOUTH-CAROLINA.	*John Rutledge,* *Charles Coteſworth Pinckney* *Charles Pinckney.* *Pierce Butler.*
PENNSYLVANIA.	*Benjamin Franklin,* *Thomas Mifflin,* *Robert Morris,* *George Clymer,* *Thomas Fitzſimons,* *Jared Ingerſoll,* *James Wilſon,* *Gouverneur Morris.*	GEORGIA.	*William Few,* *Abraham Baldwin.*

Atteſt, *William Jackſon*, SECRETARY.

IN CONVENTION, Monday September 17th, 1787.
PRESENT
The States of New-Hampſhire, Maſſachuſetts, Connecticut, Mr. *Hamilton* from New-York, New-Jerſey, Pennſylvania, Delaware, Maryland, Virginia, North-Carolina, South-Carolina and Georgia:

RESOLVED,

THAT the preceding Conſtitution be laid before the United States in Congreſs aſſembled, and that it is the opinion of this Convention, that it ſhould afterwards be ſubmitted to a Convention of Delegates, choſen in each State by the People thereof, under the recommendation of its Legiſlature, for their aſſent and ratification; and that each Convention aſſenting to, and ratifying the ſame, ſhould give Notice thereof to the United States in Congreſs aſſembled.

Reſolved, *That it is the opinion of this Convention, that as ſoon as the Conventions of nine States ſhall have ratified this Conſtitution, the United States in Congreſs aſſembled ſhould fix a day on which Electors ſhould be appointed by the States which ſhall have ratified the ſame, and a day on which the Electors ſhould aſſemble to vote for the Preſident, and the time and place for commencing proceedings under this Conſtitution. That after ſuch publication the Electors ſhould be appointed, and the Senators and Repreſentatives elected: That the Electors ſhould meet on the day fixed for the Election of the Preſident, and ſhould tranſmit their votes certified, ſigned, ſealed and directed, as the Conſtitution requires, to the Secretary of the United States in Congreſs aſſembled, that the Senators and Repreſentatives ſhould convene at the time and place aſſigned; that the Senators ſhould appoint a Preſident of the Senate, for the ſole purpoſe of receiving, opening and counting the votes for Preſident; and, that after he ſhall be choſen, the Congreſs, together with the Preſident, ſhould, without delay, proceed to execute this Conſtitution.*

By the unanimous Order of the Convention,
GEORGE WASHINGTON, Preſident.
William Jackſon, Secretary

This resolution of the delegates of the Convention asked the states to vote to approve the new Constitution.

An intense dispute involved the practice of slavery. What was its future? How would slaves be counted in deciding the number of representatives each state would have in Congress? This was a major concern in states where a large part of the population was enslaved Africans.

All summer long, the delegates argued. Tempers grew short. Even George Washington became angry. At one point, he wrote that he wished he had not gone to the convention at all. He was writing to New York delegate Alexander Hamilton. Hamilton had become frustrated at losing so many arguments and had gone home. He told Washington he would return only if he felt his time would not be wasted.

Things got so bad that Benjamin Franklin proposed an idea. It was clear, he said, that the delegates could not solve all the problems facing the convention. He suggested that they pray to God for help. Even this idea drew debate. One delegate said that the convention had no money to pay a minister. Franklin's idea was rejected.

Still, many delegates kept working. They found ways to resolve conflicts. For example, Roger Sherman of Connecticut offered an idea that became known as the Great Compromise. The delegates agreed to have a Congress with two houses. In the Senate, each state would have the same number of seats. In this way, the small states would have as much power as the big states. In the House of Representatives, the larger states would have more seats, and so more power. This plan settled the debate between the small and large states.

There were other compromises, too. Most delegates gave up something and got something they wanted in the new Constitution. No group or interest got too much power. When the document was finished, Benjamin Franklin asked the delegates to sign it. It was not perfect, he said. But it was close. Most of the delegates agreed. All but three of the men present on the final day signed the Constitution.

Now the nation would have to decide whether to accept it.

Congress of the United States
begun and held at the City of New-York, on
Wednesday the Fourth of March, one thousand seven hundred and eighty nine

THE Conventions of a number of the States, having at the time of their adopting the Constitution, expressed a desire, in order to prevent misconstruction or abuse of its powers, that further declaratory and restrictive clauses should be added: And as extending the ground of public confidence in the Government, will best ensure the beneficent ends of its institution

RESOLVED by the Senate and House of Representatives of the United States of America, in Congress assembled, two thirds of both Houses concurring that the following Articles be proposed to the Legislatures of the several States, as amendments to the Constitution of the United States, all, or any of which Articles, when ratified by three fourths of the said Legislatures, to be valid to all intents and purposes, as part of the said Constitution; viz.

ARTICLES in addition to, and Amendment of the Constitution of the United States of America, proposed by Congress, and ratified by the Legislatures of the several States, pursuant to the fifth Article of the original Constitution.

Article the first.... After the first enumeration required by the first article of the Constitution, there shall be one Representative for every thirty thousand, until the number shall amount to one hundred, after which, the proportion shall be so regulated by Congress, that there shall be not less than one hundred Representatives, nor less than one Representative for every forty thousand persons, until the number of Representatives shall amount to two hundred, after which the proportion shall be so regulated by Congress, that there shall not be less than two hundred Representatives, nor more than one Representative for every fifty thousand persons.

Article the second... No law, varying the compensation for the services of the Senators and Representatives, shall take effect, until an election of Representatives shall have intervened.

Article the third.... Congress shall make no law respecting an establishment of religion, or prohibiting the free exercise thereof; or abridging the freedom of speech, or of the press, or the right of the people peaceably to assemble, and to petition the Government for a redress of grievances.

Article the fourth... A well regulated militia, being necessary to the security of a free State, the right of the people to keep and bear Arms, shall not be infringed.

Article the fifth..... No Soldier shall, in time of peace be quartered in any house, without the consent of the Owner, nor in time of war, but in a manner to be prescribed by law.

Article the sixth..... The right of the people to be secure in their persons, houses, papers, and effects, against unreasonable searches and seizures, shall not be violated, and no Warrants shall issue, but upon probable cause, supported by oath or affirmation, and particularly describing the place to be searched, and the persons or things to be seized.

Article the seventh... No person shall be held to answer for a capital, or otherwise infamous crime, unless on a presentment or indictment of a Grand Jury, except in cases arising in the land or naval forces, or in the Militia, when in actual service in time of War or public danger; nor shall any person be subject for the same offence to be twice put in jeopardy of life or limb, nor shall be compelled in any criminal case to be a witness against himself, nor be deprived of life, liberty, or property, without due process of law; nor shall private property be taken for public use without just compensation.

Article the eighth... In all criminal prosecutions, the accused shall enjoy the right to a speedy and public trial, by an impartial jury of the State and district wherein the crime shall have been committed, which district shall have been previously ascertained by law, and to be informed of the nature and cause of the accusation; to be confronted with the witnesses against him; to have compulsory process for obtaining witnesses in his favor, and to have the assistance of counsel for his defence.

Article the ninth... In suits at common law, where the value in controversy shall exceed twenty dollars, the right of trial by jury shall be preserved, and no fact tried by a jury shall be otherwise re-examined in any Court of the United States, than according to the rules of the common law.

Article the tenth... Excessive bail shall not be required, nor excessive fines imposed, nor cruel and unusual punishments inflicted.

Article the eleventh... The enumeration in the Constitution, of certain rights, shall not be construed to deny or disparage others retained by the people.

Article the twelfth... The powers not delegated to the United States by the Constitution, nor prohibited by it to the States, are reserved to the States respectively, or to the people.

Frederick Augustus Muhlenberg Speaker of the House of Representatives.
John Adams, Vice President of the United States, and President of the Senate.

ATTEST,

John Beckley, Clerk of the House of Representatives.
Sam. A. Otis Secretary of the Senate.

The Granger Collection, New York

Congress shall make no law respecting an establishment of religion, or

...No Soldier shall, in time of peace be quartered in any house, without the consent of the Owner, nor

the right of the people to keep and bear Arms, shall not be infringed.

Why did Americans feel that they needed to protect their rights?

The Bill of Rights

What are the basic rights and freedoms of the American people?

15.1 Introduction

In Chapter 14, you learned how the Constitution creates a strong central government for the United States. In this chapter, you will read about the first 10 **amendments,** or changes, to the Constitution. They protect the rights and liberties of American citizens. Together, these amendments are called the **Bill of Rights**.

The Constitution described how the nation's new national government would work. But the Constitution did not say how citizens would be protected from the government's power. Many Americans wanted the Constitution to include a bill, or list, of rights for citizens that the government would always have to respect.

The Bill of Rights is like a shield that protects all citizens. For example, the Fifth and Sixth Amendments describe the rights of those accused of a crime. Among these rights are the right to a lawyer and the right to a fair trial by a **jury.** A jury is a group of citizens who are chosen to decide the outcome of a trial.

Look at this drawing. As you learn about the Bill of Rights, think of it as a shield. Why did Americans in 1789 want a shield to protect them from a strong central government? What rights and freedoms are protected by the Bill of Rights? How do these rights affect the lives of American citizens today?

The Bill of Rights: A Protective Shield

ratify to approve; to make a written document official by signing it

15.2 The Need for a Bill of Rights

The Constitution was completed in 1787. Then it had to be **ratified** by at least nine states. Americans fiercely debated whether to approve the Constitution. Many people were afraid that it made the national government too strong. They had already fought a war because British rule had not respected their rights. Americans did not want this to happen again under their new government.

In several states, the vote on the Constitution was very close. Supporters James Madison, Alexander Hamilton, and John Jay gained votes by publishing essays called *The Federalist Papers*. In these essays the three men explained why a strong central government would be good for the nation.

James Madison proposed to Congress the set of amendments that became known as the Bill of Rights.

Madison and others also proposed adding a bill of rights to the Constitution. It would list rights and freedoms that the government could not take away from American citizens.

This proposal helped win approval for the Constitution. By July 1788, nine states had ratified the document. The following March, the new national government gathered for the first time in New York City.

The first Congress faced the important task of considering changes to the Constitution. The men who wrote the Constitution had included a process for adding amendments. The states had sent Congress ideas for these first changes. A number of the ideas concerned a bill of rights. Madison sorted through the many suggestions. Then he proposed the first set of amendments to Congress.

On September 25, 1789, Congress voted to approve the 10 amendments now known as the Bill of Rights. These amendments were then sent to the states for ratification. By December 15, 1791, enough states had approved them. The amendments became part of the Constitution.

Over time, the courts have interpreted how the Constitution applies to various situations. In this way, the meaning of the Bill of Rights has grown in the years since 1791.

15.3 The First Amendment

The First Amendment stops Congress from making laws that take away basic freedoms. These include freedom of religion, speech, and the press.

Many early Americans sought freedom of religion. For example, the Pilgrims left England because the king had forced them to worship in the Church of England. Some American colonies had also demanded that people join one church.

The First Amendment protects Americans' freedom to choose their religious beliefs and practices. Americans worship in many ways. Some people don't practice any religion. To protect the people's right to choose, the courts have said that public schools cannot require students to say prayers in school.

Freedom of speech protects the people's right to give opinions. Americans can criticize the government and express unpopular ideas. Americans wanted this right because many colonists had been arrested for criticizing British laws. In modern times, leaders like Martin Luther King Jr. spoke out for laws that protect the rights of all people. Without the First Amendment, King might have been put in jail for his words.

Freedom of speech does have limits. People cannot use this right to harm others or to break the law. For example, suppose someone yelled "Fire!" in a crowded theater when there was no danger. Because people might get hurt in the rush to escape the theater, this kind of speech is not protected.

Freedom of the press protects the right to report news and give opinions in newspapers and in other forms. Americans wanted to guard this right because the British had jailed newspaper writers and editors for printing complaints about British actions. But freedom of the press also has limits. For example, it does not include the freedom to write lies about people.

The First Amendment also protects people's right to assemble, or gather in groups. And it gives Americans the right to petition, or ask the government to correct injustices.

The First Amendment protects citizens' rights to speak out against the government. These students are exercising their right of freedom of speech as the Supreme Court considers a case involving freedom of speech in schools.

The Granger Collection, New York

Minutemen, like this farmer, had fought for independence. In 1789, people wanted to protect their right to use guns to defend and provide for their families. The Second Amendment gave them the right to "keep and bear arms."

15.4 The Second Amendment

The Second Amendment says that each state needs a militia, or an army of citizens. Therefore, the government cannot take away the people's right to "keep and bear arms."

Americans in 1789 wanted to be able to defend themselves. Men had used their muskets against British troops in the American Revolution. People remembered how these citizen soldiers had bravely fought for their rights. At this time, people also used guns in everyday life, to hunt for food and to protect their families. And there were no police to keep order. Since many people lived in the countryside with few neighbors nearby, they feared attacks by outlaws or American Indians.

Today, the Second Amendment protects the right to own guns. But people disagree about whether every person should be allowed to own any type of gun. Many people say no. They are disturbed by events, such as violent crimes and accidental shootings involving guns. They think that laws should control who can own and carry guns. They want laws that restrict the right to own some kinds of weapons. Others argue that the Second Amendment does not allow such laws. These people do not think that citizens should lose the right to have any type of gun just because some people misuse them.

Before the war, British officials could search colonists' homes or shops and take what they wanted to use as evidence in court. The Fourth Amendment protects people from such acts.

15.5 The Fourth Amendment

The Fourth Amendment forbids unreasonable searches and seizures by government officials. Seizure means taking away property. The Fourth Amendment says that officials cannot perform searches and seizures without a good reason.

In 1789, Americans wanted to protect their right to safety and privacy. British officials had gone into colonists' homes, shops, and barns. They had not needed a good reason to suspect the owners of a crime. They had felt free to seize what they liked and use it as evidence in court.

The Fourth Amendment limits the power of the government to search people's homes and businesses. Most searches require a warrant. This is an order from a judge. Officials must show probable cause, or a good reason, to get a warrant. They must convince a judge that the search is likely to uncover evidence of a crime. Also, they can search only for the specific items that are listed in the warrant.

Today, the Fourth Amendment protects citizens from the power of the police and others who enforce laws. If a search or seizure violates the Fourth Amendment, any evidence that was found cannot be used in court.

Over the years, the courts have said that some reasonable searches do not require a warrant. For example, to protect public safety, airport officials can search people's carry-on luggage for weapons. Police can search cars for drugs and stolen goods. But police must have good reason to believe that the car can be linked to a crime.

The Fourth Amendment limits the power of police to search people. The officer shown here must have either a search warrant or probable cause to conduct this search.

A person accused of a crime is protected by the Fifth Amendment from having to give evidence against himself or herself in court. The expression "I take the Fifth" means "I choose to remain silent."

15.6 The Fifth Amendment

The Fifth Amendment protects the rights of Americans who are suspected of a crime. British laws also did this, but courts in the colonies did not always follow these laws. Americans wanted to make sure that the courts treated people fairly.

The Fifth Amendment protects citizens against double jeopardy. Jeopardy means danger, such as the danger of being put in jail. The courts cannot put someone on trial or punish a person twice for the same crime. When a jury finds a person not guilty, he or she goes free. The government cannot try the person again for the same crime in front of another jury. The government can ask for another trial only if a jury cannot reach a decision.

The Fifth Amendment also says that the government cannot force people to be witnesses against themselves. Witnesses are people who give evidence. The amendment says that people do not have to say things that can be used against them in court. In the United States, confessions must be given freely. People accused of a crime have the right to say nothing. They can have a lawyer present when police ask questions. Today, police officers must tell citizens during an arrest that they have these legal rights. This information is called the Miranda warning. It is based on a Supreme Court ruling made in 1966.

due process proper legal procedures, such as a fair trial

The Fifth Amendment also says that the government cannot punish people without **due process** of law. The government must also offer fair payment for property taken for public use.

15.7 The Sixth Amendment

The Sixth Amendment describes more rights of those accused of crimes. It says that they have the right to a fair trial.

Both British law and the U.S. Constitution include the right to a trial by jury. Americans wanted to make sure that a jury trial was also a fair trial. To ensure this, the Sixth Amendment says that trials must be speedy and public. This means that people cannot be kept in jail for a long time while they wait for their trial. Trials cannot take place in secret. Accused persons also have the right to present witnesses and to question those who testify against them.

The amendment also says that juries must be impartial. This means that jury members must not be **prejudiced** against the accused person. Courts have applied this rule in a number of ways. For example, an all-white jury in Mississippi found a black man guilty of killing a white man. Later the Supreme Court threw out the jury's decision. The Court said that the man's lawyer had not been allowed to question whether the all-white jury was fair and impartial.

prejudice having a negative judgment or opinion of something or someone that is not based on facts

Finally, the Sixth Amendment says that accused people have the right to a lawyer. Courts have extended this protection to people who cannot afford to hire a lawyer. The government must provide a lawyer if an accused person does not have the money to pay for one.

The Sixth Amendment guarantees the rights of people who are accused of a crime. These people have the right to a fair, speedy, and public trial. They have the right to a lawyer. Here, a lawyer talks to a jury.

The Eighth Amendment protects citizens' rights to fair and reasonable punishment when they break the law. Courts can sentence criminals to time in a jail cell, like this one. But this amendment forbids cruel and unusual punishments, like cutting off a thief's hand.

15.8 The Eighth Amendment

The Eighth Amendment protects the people's right to fair and reasonable punishment when they break the law. It says that punishments cannot be so harsh that they are unfair.

Courts can make people pay fines, or money, for breaking the law. But these fines cannot be excessive, or too high. For example, making someone pay $1,000 for a parking ticket would be excessive.

The Eighth Amendment also forbids excessive bail. Bail is the money someone has to pay to get out of jail while awaiting a trial. But the amendment does not say that courts must allow bail in all cases. For instance, a judge can deny bail to someone accused of murder. Then that person must await trial in jail.

Most important, the Eighth Amendment forbids cruel and unusual punishments. Americans wanted this protection because punishments for crimes in the 1700s were often very harsh. For example, the government could sentence people to whippings. A court could send someone who owed money to jail. Once in jail, it would be almost impossible for people to earn money to pay off their debts.

Over the years, courts have applied this same protection to people serving time in prison. For instance, not giving prisoners medical care when they are seriously ill is considered cruel and unusual punishment.

Americans sometimes find it hard to decide whether a punishment is cruel and unusual. For example, they disagree about the death penalty, or sentencing people to die for their crimes. Some people think that this is a fair punishment for very serious crimes, such as murder. Other people argue that taking someone's life is always too harsh a sentence.

Courts have ruled that the Eighth Amendment does not forbid the death penalty. Even so, some states do not allow it.

15.9 Other Rights Protected by the Bill of Rights

The Bill of Rights also protects other rights and liberties. The Third Amendment says that the government cannot force citizens to let soldiers live in their homes. The Seventh Amendment protects the people's right to settle **civil** disputes in a jury trial. For example, someone hurt in a car accident might want the driver to pay for hospital costs. The amendment allows the driver to have a jury trial to decide who has to pay.

The Ninth Amendment says that the Constitution's list of rights is not complete. Americans have other rights, such as the freedom to choose where to live and what job to do.

The Tenth Amendment restates the limits on the U.S. government's power that are set out in the Constitution. The national government has only those powers that are clearly listed in the Constitution. All other powers belong to the states or to the people.

civil noncriminal cases involving disputes among individuals about property, money, or other personal matters

Summary

In this chapter, you learned why Americans wanted a bill of rights added to the Constitution. You compared the Bill of Rights to a shield that protects citizens from the power of the central government.

The ten amendments in the Bill of Rights protect important rights and liberties. For example, Americans are free to choose their religion. They can speak about and publish their opinions. They can own guns. They have protection against unreasonable actions by the police and the courts.

Many Americans take the Bill of Rights for granted. But in 1789, few people in the world had these rights and freedoms. Even today, many governments around the world do not protect the rights and freedoms of their citizens.

When the Bill of Rights was written, the United States was a new country. The men who set up the government tried to create a system that would protect both the people and the nation. Did they succeed? How did their ideas balance the rights of each person with the needs of the country? Read on to find out.

Reading Further 15

Individual Rights vs. Society's Needs

The Bill of Rights guarantees people the freedom of speech. But that freedom is not without limits. There are times when the needs of society are greater than a person's right to say what he or she wants. How do we guard individual rights while also protecting the needs of all people?

John and Mary Beth Tinker and their friend Christopher Eckhardt wore the black armbands as a sign of protest. The year was 1965. John was 15; his sister Mary Beth was 13; and his friend Christopher was also 15. Their country, the United States, was at war in the faraway country of Vietnam. These teenagers wanted the fighting to stop. To express their concern, each came to school wearing a strip of black cloth on one arm. They hoped that the black bands would make people think about those who were dying in the war.

Many other students at the school paid little attention to the Tinkers and Eckhardt. A few made fun of them. Some criticized them. One student stood up for them and told the others to leave them alone. Mary Beth's teacher did complain of a disruption to his class. But most people agreed that this school day progressed much like any other day. Teachers taught and students learned.

School officials had a different view. They had found out in advance about the students' plan to wear armbands. They thought the protest would cause problems. It might be a distraction in classes, and students might have trouble focusing on their work. To prevent these difficulties, school officials had made a new rule. Students could not wear armbands to school. When the Tinkers and Eckhardt arrived, school officials asked them to take off the black bands. The students refused, and the officials sent them home. They could not return to school until they came without the armbands.

Mary Beth and John Tinker were suspended from school for wearing armbands as a war protest. The original bands were entirely black. The peace signs were added later.

The Tinkers and Eckhardt went home. They stayed there for about two weeks—the length of time they had planned to wear the armbands. Then the students ended their protest. They returned to school and continued their studies.

The dispute, however, was far from over. The students believed that the school had violated their constitutional rights. They and their parents decided to start a legal case against the school. They wanted to prove a point about the rights protected by the First Amendment.

Mrs. Lorena Tinker (left) supported her daughter, Mary Beth Tinker (right), in the court case.

Recall that the First Amendment says that government cannot take away certain basic freedoms. Among these is the freedom of speech.

It may seem strange to charge that the school had taken away the students' right to free speech. After all, the Tinkers and Eckhardt had not said a word. But they believed that the First Amendment protects the right to express ideas in many different ways. In fact, the United States Supreme Court had ruled that such actions as waving or saluting to a flag could be thought of as types of speech. These other types were known as symbolic speech.

The case was called *Tinker v. Des Moines*. The first court to hear the case was a U.S. District Court. It sided with the school. The Tinkers and Eckhardt **appealed** this decision. The case moved to a U.S. Court of Appeals. This court was split—half the judges sided with the school, and half with the students. So the students appealed to the United States Supreme Court. The Supreme Court agreed to hear the case in 1968.

appeal to request that a case or a decision be reviewed by a higher court

The Case Moves Through the Courts

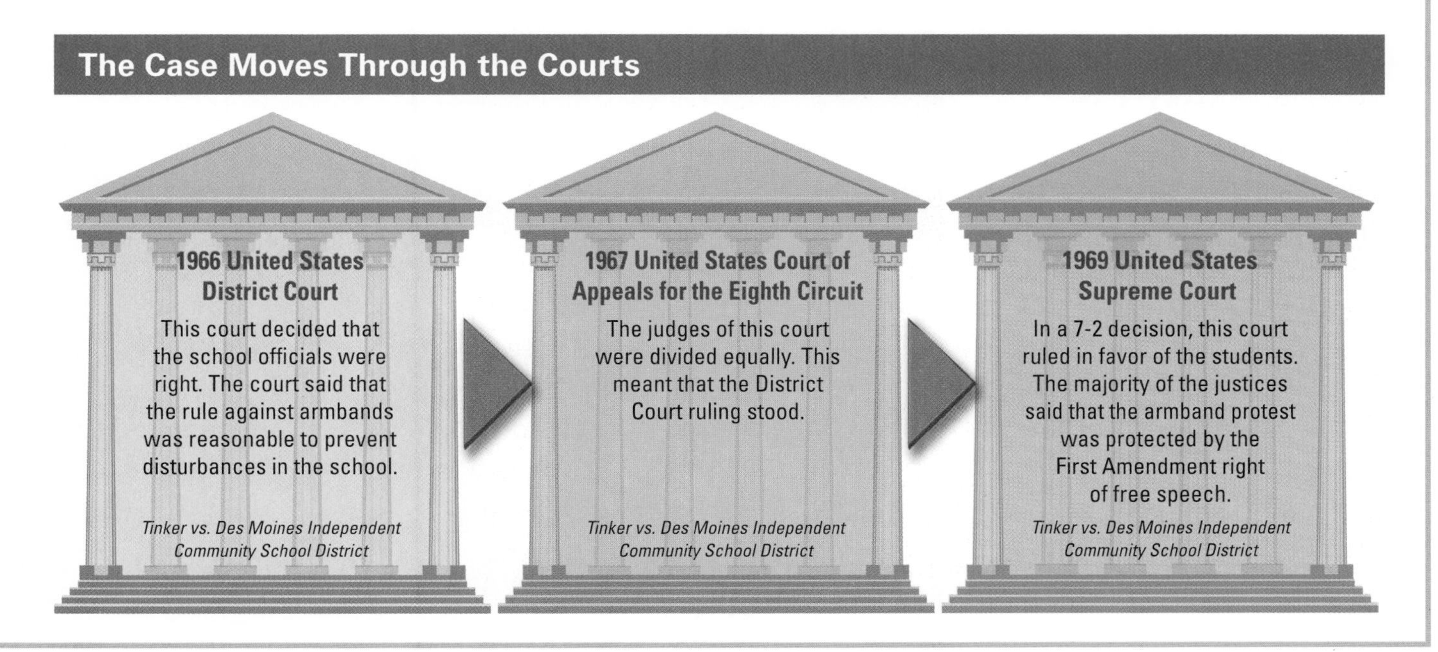

In the 1960s, Americans were divided in their opinions about the Vietnam War. The protesters shown here want the war to end.

The Supreme Court justices had a lot to consider in the Tinker case. The First Amendment protects the freedom of speech. And the Court had ruled that symbols such as black armbands could be viewed as a type of speech. Still, all the justices agreed that there were times when government could limit free speech. Was this such a case? Did the school have the right to tell students that they could not wear armbands in silent protest against a war?

Some justices did not think that the school had this right. Justice Abe Fortas wrote, "It can hardly be argued that either students or teachers shed [give up] their constitutional rights to freedom of speech or expression at the schoolhouse gate."

Justice Fortas agreed that schools might need to limit the freedom of speech at times. But, he wrote, they could only do so when there was real danger of a major disruption. It is not enough, he argued, that schools fear a minor disturbance. "Any word spoken, in class, in the lunchroom, or on the campus . . . may start an argument or cause a disturbance," he wrote. "But our Constitution says we must take this risk."

Justice Fortas also wrote that being able to share ideas—even upsetting ones—is part of how students learn. There would be no true freedom of speech if people could be kept from sharing ideas that might prove troublesome. The actions of the Tinkers and Eckhardt did not get in the way of school activities. The Constitution, Fortas wrote, protected such speech.

Not every justice agreed with Fortas. Justice Potter Stewart thought that children do not have the same rights to freedom of speech as adults. But the strongest argument came from Justice Hugo Black.

These Supreme Court justices ruled on *Tinker v. Des Moines*. Justices Fortas and Stewart stand at the far left. Justice Black is seated, second from the left.

Today, students continue to express their opinions in and out of school.

Black said that the school had treated the students fairly. "I have never believed," he wrote, "that any person has a right to give speeches or engage in demonstrations where he pleases and when he pleases." Black believed that students should be limited in what they can say in class. The purpose of schools is to teach children. School is not, Black wrote, a place for children to share their own views.

Justice Black agreed that the armbands caused few problems at the school. But he said that the school still had a good reason to outlaw them. To Black, even a mild disruption was too much. "I think the record overwhelmingly shows that the armbands did exactly what the elected school officials and principals foresaw they would," he wrote. The protest "took the students' minds off their class work and diverted them to thoughts about the highly emotional subject of the Vietnam War." School discipline was already lacking in the country, Black wrote. If the Court supported the armband protest, "some students . . . will be ready, able and willing to defy their teachers on practically all orders."

Justices Fortas and Black had strong opinions in this case. But what did the other justices think? How did the Supreme Court rule in *Tinker v. Des Moines*?

In the end, seven justices sided with the students. This became the Court's ruling. One justice joined with Black. These two believed that the school had acted properly.

The Court's ruling in 1969 affected more than the Tinkers and Eckhardt. It meant that all American students, everywhere, have the right to freedom of speech. This freedom has limits. But the Constitution does protect even a young person's right to share his or her views in a calm and peaceful way.

The Granger Collection, New York

What changes did settlers bring to the West in the early 1800s?

What might these people already living in the West be thinking about the changes?

Manifest Destiny and Settling the West

16

How did the expansion of the United States affect people inside and outside the country?

16.1 Introduction

In Chapter 15, you learned how leaders of the young nation added the Bill of Rights to the Constitution to protect the rights and freedoms of Americans. At that time, the United States stretched from the Atlantic Ocean to the Mississippi River. In this chapter, you will read about how the United States spread west across North America by taking control of **territories,** or large regions of land.

In the 1800s, the lands west of the Mississippi River were claimed by several nations. Many Americans wanted these lands. Some people believed that it was their natural right to take these territories for the United States. They said that expanding westward was the nation's fate.

American leaders used a variety of methods to **annex,** or add, territory to the United States. Sometimes they bought land. Sometimes they made agreements with other countries for land. One time, the United States was able to add land after fighting a war.

Many Americans thought that expanding the United States was good for the country. But as you will see, it was not good for everyone.

The map to the right shows the United States' **acquisitions,** or lands gained, between 1783 and 1853. As you read this chapter, look back at this map. How did the United States gain control of each territory? What happened to the people who already lived there?

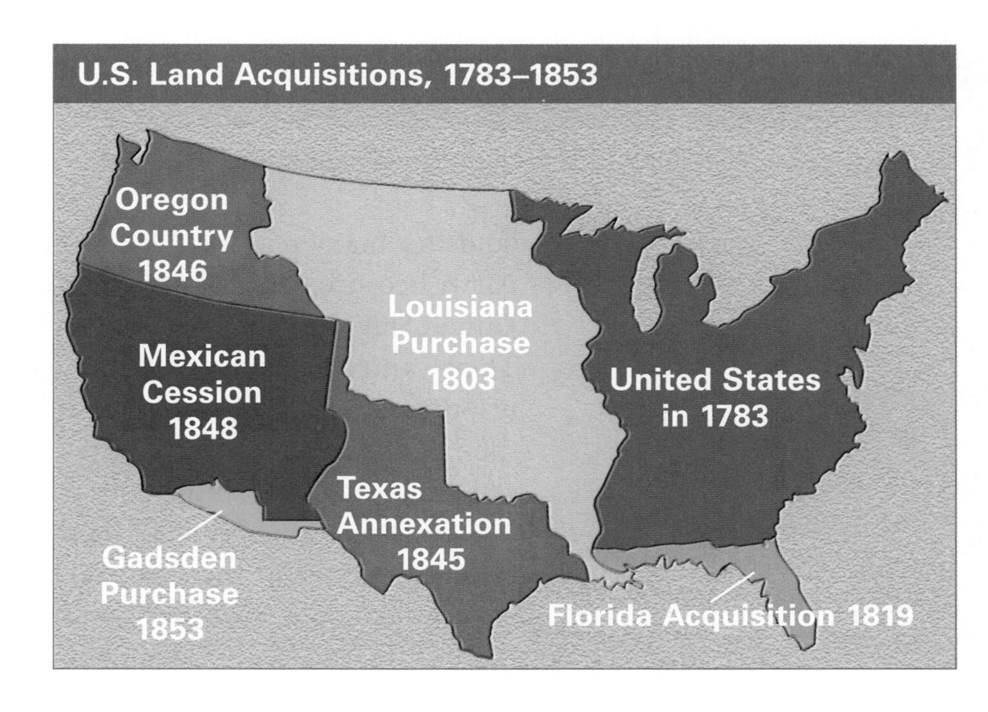

16.2 The United States in 1783

When the American Revolution ended in 1783, the original 13 colonies along the Atlantic Coast became the United States. The new nation also gained most of the land that stretched from the colonies to the Mississippi River, which had previously been under British control. Soon, more settlers began moving west into this territory, where only American Indians had lived before. Some settlers wanted to go even farther, across the Mississippi River.

This painting by John Gast is called *American Progress*. In it, the United States is portrayed as a woman. She floats west toward her manifest destiny. She brings the railroad and telegraph lines. Settlers also move with her. The American Indians seem to retreat.

Several nations claimed territories that Americans wanted for themselves. In the Southeast, Spain controlled Florida. France claimed much of the land west of the Mississippi River. Farther west, first Spain and then Mexico controlled huge territories. These territories included the places we know today as Texas, the Southwest, and California. Great Britain still claimed large areas in the Northwest. These included the present-day states of Oregon and Washington. Russia claimed a part of the Northwest, too.

Americans wanted these lands for many reasons. The U.S. population was growing, partly because people from other countries were moving to the United States. Settlers wanted land on which to live and farm. They wanted to work and to build homes. Businesses wanted resources, like wood and minerals, as well as new places to sell their goods. Leaders wanted the United States to be strong—and safe from attacks by other countries.

Americans were proud of their new country. Many Americans believed that it was their natural right to spread their religions, government, and ways of life westward across North America to the Pacific Ocean. In 1845, a newspaper writer called this idea the **manifest destiny** of the United States.

manifest destiny
an American belief in the 1800s that it was the natural right of the United States to expand westward to the Pacific Ocean

In this scene, James Monroe (left) and Robert Livingston (center) discuss the Louisiana Purchase with French statesman Charles Talleyrand (right).

16.3 Louisiana Purchase (1803)

The first land added to the nation was the Louisiana Purchase of 1803. The United States bought most of the land between the Mississippi River and the Rocky Mountains from France.

This was important because Americans had interests in this area. People shipped goods down the Mississippi River to the port city of New Orleans. From there, ships took goods to the Atlantic Coast. This was easier and cheaper than moving goods by land over the Appalachian Mountains.

But New Orleans was controlled by France. To ensure that Americans could move their goods, President Thomas Jefferson wanted to buy New Orleans. He was willing to pay up to $10 million for the port city.

At this time, France feared a possible war with Great Britain. The French needed money for their army. And they were ready to give up their claims in North America. They surprised Jefferson by offering to sell all of the Louisiana Territory for $15 million. American representatives James Monroe and Robert Livingston agreed to the sale. This land doubled the size of the nation.

But the Louisiana Purchase was not good for everyone, especially American Indians. For years, settlers had wanted to push American Indians westward. Now, there was a place to put them. In the 1830s, the U.S. government forced several tribes from their homelands in the South. Thousands of Choctaws, Creeks, Chickasaws, and Cherokees had to move onto **reservations** in what is now Oklahoma. Many starved, froze to death, or died from diseases on the brutal trip west.

reservation an area of land set aside by the United States government for American Indians to live on

expedition a group of people sent to explore unknown places

16.4 Lewis and Clark Expedition (1804 to 1806)

Shortly before he completed the Louisiana Purchase, President Jefferson made plans for an **expedition** to explore the huge territory. Two former soldiers, Meriwether Lewis and William Clark, led the group. They would map the Louisiana Territory. They would also look for a Northwest Passage to the Pacific Ocean. Jefferson asked them to take notes on the soil, plants, animals, and American Indian tribes that they came across in their travels. He also wanted the explorers to scout locations for trading posts and settlements.

In May 1804, Lewis and Clark started up the Missouri River from St. Louis, Missouri. They took more than 40 other men with them. One of these men was Clark's slave, York. York would become the first black man to cross North America.

As the expedition moved along the Missouri, the men found high, cold plateaus. The explorers spent the winter with a group of American Indians, the Mandans, in what is now North Dakota.

There, Lewis and Clark met Sacagawea (sah-keh-jeh-WEE-uh), a young Shoshone woman. The next year, she joined the group as they crossed the Rocky Mountains and struggled through early snows. She helped them speak with tribes they met along the way. The group followed the Snake and Columbia rivers, finally reaching the Pacific Ocean in November 1805.

On their return journey, Lewis and Clark mapped two more routes across the Rocky Mountains. In 1806, they returned as heroes. Now settlers could move even farther west.

This painting shows members of Lewis and Clark's expedition. The woman is Sacagawea. To her right is Meriwether Lewis, and then William Clark. York, Clark's African slave, is to Clark's right.

This painting shows Seminoles from Florida attacking a Georgia settlement. General Andrew Jackson used these raids as an excuse to attack Florida.

16.5 Florida Acquisition (1819)

In the early 1800s, most of the land we know today as Florida was under Spanish rule. Americans in the Southeast wanted this land. Slave owners in Georgia were angry because some slaves were escaping to Florida. Often, the runaways hid with the Seminoles, a tribe of American Indians. Some runaway slaves even became members of the tribe.

Also upsetting were the raids, or attacks, by the Seminoles on settlements in Georgia. The Seminoles made these raids out of fear that the white settlers would eventually attack them.

In 1817, General Andrew Jackson marched his army into Florida. He ended the Seminole raids. And he captured two Spanish forts, including the one at Pensacola, the capital of Spanish Florida. President James Monroe did not fully support General Jackson's actions. But Monroe wanted Florida and he did not stop Jackson.

Spain soon realized that it could not defend its land from U.S. attacks. In 1819, Spain agreed to give Florida to the United States. In return, the United States agreed to give $5 million to the settlers in payment for slaves lost and property damaged in the Seminole raids.

Within 10 years, many Americans had moved to Florida. The U.S. government ordered the Seminoles to leave, but many refused. The tribe fought one more war against the United States before most of its members were either killed or forced to move to the West.

16.6 Texas Annexation (1845)

Santa Anna led his 7,000 Mexican troops in an attack on 200 Texans and Americans at the Alamo.

In the early 1800s, Spain ruled Mexico and most of what are now the southwestern and western parts of the United States. In 1821, Mexico gained its independence from Spain and took control of this land. Part of the region was known as Texas.

Many of the people in Texas were American Indians, including Apaches and Comanches. The Mexican government wanted more settlers in Texas who would raise crops and animals, pay taxes, and follow the Catholic religion. Mexican officials offered free land in Texas to Americans. The settlers had to promise to obey Mexican laws and to become Catholic.

By 1830, about 16,000 white Americans lived in Texas. They outnumbered the Mexicans. Soon, tensions grew between the settlers and the Mexican government. One issue was slavery. Mexico had outlawed slavery, but many of the American settlers owned slaves. Mexico allowed settlers to own some slaves in Texas. But the American slave owners worried that Mexico might one day free the slaves. Another issue was that most of the settlers wanted Texas to join the United States. Many settlers did not even speak Spanish. Mexico passed a law to stop more Americans from settling in Texas.

In 1833, a group of settlers asked the Mexican government to allow Texas to have its own government. Stephen Austin, who had been a loyal Mexican citizen, gave the group's message to the government. The Mexican government angrily refused.

By 1835, groups of Texans and Mexican soldiers were fighting. In 1836, Texas declared independence. In response, the president of Mexico, Antonio López de Santa Anna, led an army into Texas. He planned to punish the American settlers for trying to break away from Mexico.

When the Mexican army reached the town of San Antonio, Santa Anna found fewer than 200 Texans and other Americans who had come to help them. These men took a stand at an old mission, or church, called the Alamo. Santa Anna demanded that they give up. They replied by firing a cannonball. "Victory or death!" was their message.

For more than 10 days, the small group fought off Santa Anna's large army. Then, the Mexicans climbed the walls and took over the Alamo. Nearly all the Americans were killed, including Jim Bowie and Davy Crockett, two famous pioneers.

During the battle at the Alamo, a group of Texans met in another town and organized a temporary government. They appointed Sam Houston to lead the Texas army.

Dan Mieduch

Six weeks later, in April 1836, General Houston led more than 800 Texans in a surprise attack against Santa Anna's army at San Jacinto. The Texans charged the Mexican troops, shouting, "Remember the Alamo!" They won the battle and captured Santa Anna. The Texans let him go when he promised to give Texas its independence.

Texans approved a new constitution for the Republic of Texas. They chose Houston as their president. For nine years, Texas ruled itself. Its flag showed one white star on a red, white, and blue background. People called Texas the Lone Star Republic. Some Mexicans moved away to Catholic, Spanish-speaking Mexico. Others stayed on to marry and do business with American Texans. They worked in the government. But, in time, most of the Mexicans lost their lands and government positions.

Many Texans still wanted the United States to annex Texas. U.S. President John Tyler agreed. In 1845, Congress made Texas the 28th state.

Mexican troops fought and killed a group of Texans at the Alamo. Six weeks later, Sam Houston led Texans against Santa Anna's Mexican army. The Texans yelled, "Remember the Alamo!" as they attacked. They defeated the Mexicans.

The Granger Collection, New York

Oregon City was just south of Portland, on the Willamette River. This city was the capital of Oregon Country until 1852.

16.7 Acquisition of Oregon Country (1846)

From the early 1800s, Americans had dreamed that their nation would control the territory called Oregon Country. This northwestern area included the present-day states of Washington and Oregon, as well as parts of other states and western Canada. For years, Oregon Country had been occupied by both Great Britain and the United States. To the north of this region, Russia controlled Alaska.

boundary the geographic line between two places, such as two countries

In 1844, James Polk was elected president of the United States. He promised to take control of all of Oregon Country, from the northern border of California to the southern edge of Alaska. This area's northern **boundary** was deep in British-controlled territory. The boundary was located at latitude 54°40' north. Polk's supporters demanded, "Fifty-four forty or fight!"

Neither Great Britain nor the United States wanted to fight a war over Oregon Country. Great Britain knew that the southern part of the territory already contained more Americans than British and Canadians. Besides, most of the British in the area trapped beavers or traded beaver furs. By the mid-1840s, few beavers were left.

In 1846, Great Britain agreed to a boundary drawn at latitude 49° north. It reached from the Rocky Mountains to the Pacific Ocean. The British gave up any land claims south of this line.

The lives of American Indians in Oregon Country soon began to change for the worse. By 1850, Congress was giving away tribal lands to American settlers. The settlers took American Indian hunting lands and turned them into farms and ranches. For many years, there were wars between American Indians and U.S. settlers and soldiers. But in time, most tribes were forced onto reservations.

16.8 Mexican Cession (1848) and Gadsden Purchase (1853)

The next large addition to the United States came as a result of what Americans now call the Mexican War. One cause of this war was that the United States had annexed Texas. The Mexican government wanted Texas back. And Mexico knew that many Americans wanted other Mexican lands, including California.

The two countries also disagreed about the southwestern boundary of Texas. Americans wanted the boundary to be the Rio Grande. Mexico wanted it to be about 150 miles farther north and east.

In 1846, President Polk sent an army, led by General Zachary Taylor, to protect the Rio Grande. A group of Mexican soldiers tried to defend the area, believing that it belonged to Mexico. Crossing the river, they fought a small group of Americans. "American blood has been spilled," General Taylor wrote to President Polk. Now the president had an excuse to go to war. Mexico, he told Congress, had started the fighting. On May 13, 1846, Congress voted to declare war.

Many Americans were against the war. They felt that the United States was just trying to get more land. Others supported President Polk and cheered each U.S. victory.

American troops landed at the Mexican seaport of Vera Cruz in 1847. They then began the march to Mexico City.

The war went on for nearly two years. The United States won the first battle at Santa Fe easily. But Mexico did not give in. President Polk then ordered U.S. troops to capture Mexico City, the capital.

Mexican soldiers battled fiercely to defend their country. Both sides suffered great losses. In one battle at Mexico City, about 800 U.S. soldiers and 3,000 Mexican soldiers died or were captured. Even when U.S. soldiers captured the capital, Mexico did not admit defeat. Volunteer American soldiers continued to attack, rob, and kill Mexican citizens.

cede to give up territory, usually as the result of a treaty

Finally, the Mexicans surrendered. In February 1848, Mexico signed the Treaty of Guadalupe Hidalgo. In this agreement, Mexico **ceded** a huge amount of territory to the United States. This land was called the Mexican Cession. It included the present-day states of California, New Mexico, Utah, and Nevada, as well as parts of four other states. Mexico also agreed to the Rio Grande as the border of Texas. The United States paid Mexico $15 million for this land.

Five years later, in 1853, Congress bought one last piece of Mexican land for $10 million. It was an area south of the Gila River, in present-day Arizona and New Mexico. This land contained a pass through the mountains. The pass would make it easier to build a railroad across the southern United States. This land sale became known as the Gadsden Purchase. It was named for the American who had worked out the agreement.

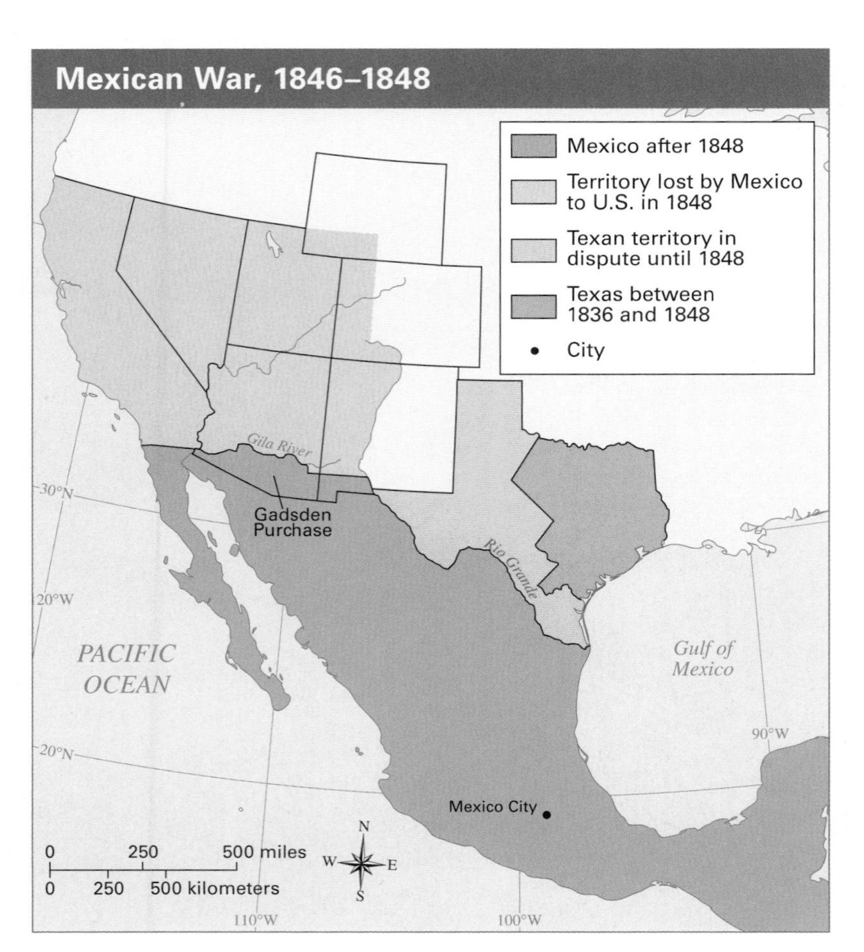

After the war with Mexico, American farmers, ranchers, and miners poured into the new lands. Their arrival changed the lives of people in the Southwest. These newcomers often took land that had previous claims on it. Mexicans and American Indians were offered the poorest jobs. In the years to come, these new settlers would fight many wars against Apaches and other American Indians before finally forcing them onto reservations.

Summary

In this chapter, you read about how the United States spread across North America between 1783 and 1853. You used a map to study key U.S. acquisitions made during this time through purchase, agreement, and war.

Many Americans believed that it was their manifest destiny to spread their way of life all the way to the Pacific Ocean. As the nation gained each new territory, more settlers pushed westward. Their desire for land led to deadly conflicts with American Indians and with Mexico.

Although ranchers, miners, and farmers created new settlements and opportunities, their westward movement also forced American Indians from their homelands and onto reservations. Sometimes, the new settlers took land from former Mexican citizens.

How did the arrival of these new settlers affect the lives of American Indians in the West? How were American Indians treated? What happened to their way of life? Read on to find out.

In the belief that it was their manifest destiny, settlers and miners overcame obstacles to settle the new lands of the West. Here, settlers struggle up a road in the Rocky Mountains.

Reading Further 16

The Cherokee Trail of Tears

The Cherokees had fought other tribes to hold their land. But American settlers were harder to defeat. In the 1830s, the Cherokees were forced to leave the land they loved. They made a harsh journey called the Trail of Tears to their new home. What events led to this move?

In the spring of 1838, 7,000 American soldiers arrived. They had come to round up the Cherokees in New Echota, Georgia and in other parts of the Southeast—and to force them from their homes.

Some soldiers mistreated the Cherokees. Other soldiers felt badly for them. The general in charge thought that he saw tears in the eyes of some troops. The Cherokees had been warned for two years that this day was coming. Still, many tribal members were unprepared. They begged for more time to collect their things, but the soldiers refused.

The scene was heartbreaking. Families picked through their belongings and made agonizing choices. What could they carry with them? What must they leave behind? For many, the move meant leaving the family pet or cherished personal treasures.

A crowd of Americans waited for the Cherokees to depart. It was clear that they would take whatever the tribe left behind. In desperation, a few Cherokees tried to sell items they could not carry. But there was little time to bargain. The soldiers forced the Cherokees to begin a long and brutal march. It would lead to a strange new place, hundreds of miles away.

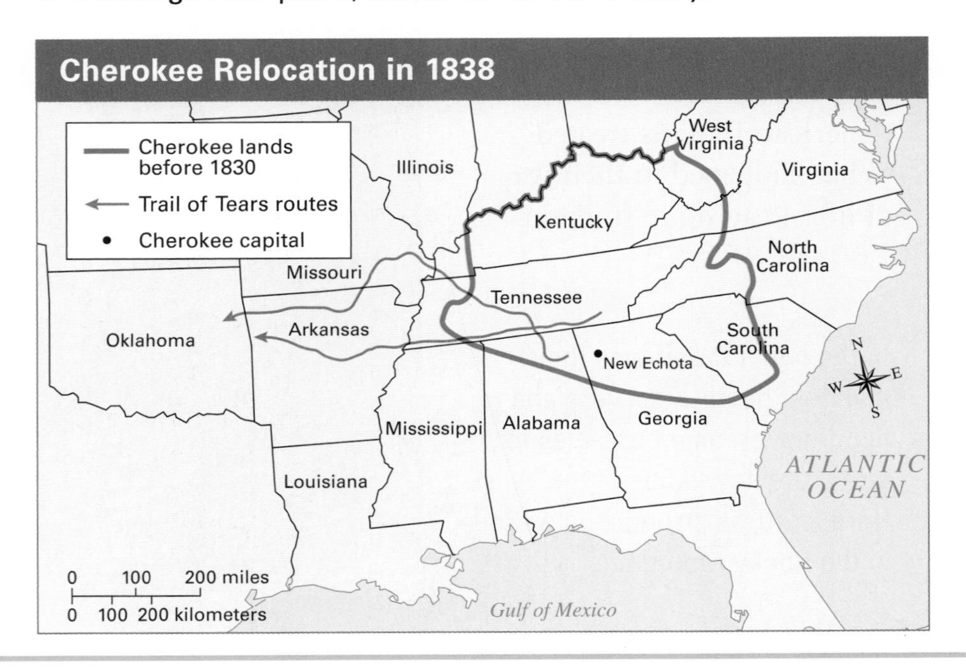

In this painting, *Trail of Tears* by Robert Lindneaux, thousands of Cherokees begin the long march away from their homeland.

Americans Want Land

The events of 1838 had been building for years. The Cherokees were among the last tribes to leave their homes in the Southeast. Others, such as the Choctaws, Creeks, Chickasaws, and Seminoles, had already moved on or been forced out.

The mighty Cherokees had held their homeland for a long time. Their lands once stretched across the Southeast. They had defeated many tribes who wanted their land. These tribes included the Creeks, the Shawnees, and even the powerful Iroquois. But the Cherokees had survived and thrived.

Then, in the late 1700s and early 1800s, white American settlers had begun a steady advance to the west. They had moved beyond their land along the Atlantic Coast. The settlers wanted more land. They saw the forests used by the Cherokees and other tribes for hunting. American farmers could clear and use this land, the settlers had said. Only the American Indians stood in the way of progress.

The U.S. government began working to push the American Indians off their land—to force them west, beyond the Mississippi River. There, the Americans said, the tribes would not be in the way of U.S. settlement.

The United States used several methods to get the American Indians to leave. The government bought their land and gave them new western homes. It harassed them and took their land illegally. It waged war against them.

In all of these ways, American Indians steadily lost their lands east of the Mississippi. The Cherokees were among the last to remain in their eastern homes.

Major Ridge, above, was a Cherokee chief. He signed the treaty agreeing that the Cherokees would leave their land. His people called him a traitor for this action.

Cherokees Try to Live Among Americans

The Cherokees had wanted to keep their lands. But they had chosen not to fight the new settlers. They knew that the Creeks and the Seminoles had suffered serious losses when they had battled the Americans.

Instead, the Cherokees tried to fit in with the settlers. Some Cherokees lived on American-style farms. They sent their children to American-style schools. A Cherokee named Sequoyah created a written form of the Cherokee language. Soon, thousands of Cherokees had learned to read and write.

Still, white settlers did not accept the Cherokees. Settlers fought the Cherokee people and took their land. In 1829, gold was found on Cherokee land in Georgia. Hundreds of gold-seekers rushed to the area. Now there was a greater demand for the U.S. government to remove the Cherokees.

U.S. President Andrew Jackson agreed that the Cherokees must go. He wanted them to leave on their own. He offered to trade their land in the East for land in the West. When they refused, Jackson got angry. He did not stop Georgia's government from sending soldiers to attack the Cherokees. In 1831, the U.S. Supreme Court ruled that Georgia's actions were illegal. But President Jackson did not enforce the ruling.

A small group of Cherokees feared that they would lose their land. They signed a treaty with the U.S. government saying that all the Cherokees would leave their homes by 1838. The tribe would move to new homes in present-day Oklahoma.

Many Cherokee tribe members were furious about the group's actions. They said that the group had had no right to speak for the whole tribe. The treaty should not stand. But the U.S. government disagreed. A few thousand Cherokees gave up and left. Some 16,000 refused to go. And so, in May 1838, the American troops arrived to force the Cherokees out.

The Terrible Journey

The journey west was grueling. A few Cherokees traveled by water. Most of them, however, traveled hundreds of miles on foot. The children and the elderly moved slowly. The trip would last for months.

Along the way, the Cherokees suffered terribly. They had little food and water. Heat, cold, snow, and rain caused great misery. And disease spread quickly in the crowded camps.

The young and the old died first. But soon, even strong men and women began to fall. About 4,000 of the 16,000 Cherokees who began the trip did not survive it. Graves littered the roadside. One survivor wrote, "Children cry and many men cry, and all look sad when friends die, but they say nothing and just put heads down and keep on go towards West." The Cherokees' path became known as the Trail of Tears.

At the journey's end, the Cherokees faced another ordeal. The tribe was still divided over the treaty that had led to their removal. Many leaders that had signed the treaty were killed.

Despite these hardships, the Cherokees survived. They formed a new tribal government in Oklahoma. They settled into new homes. And they kept alive their proud traditions.

Meanwhile, the United States would continue to expand and grow. Settlers quickly filled the land that the Cherokees and the other tribes of the East, such as the Creeks, Choctaws, Chickasaws, and Seminoles, had left behind. Still, Americans kept pressing to the west. The Cherokees would not be the last tribe to come into conflict with the restless, determined people of the young country.

In this painting by Cherokee artist John Guthrie, the owl is a messenger of death above tribe members on the Trail of Tears. Heat, cold, starvation, and disease killed 4,000 Cherokees on the brutal march.

Shadow of the Owl by John Guthrie

The Granger Collection, New York

What do you think this man is doing?

What kind of animal is pulling the wagon?

What do you think this fire is being used for?

What might these American Indians think about the newcomers?

The Diverse Peoples of the West

17

What drew new settlers to the western part of the United States in the 1800s?

17.1 Introduction

In Chapter 16, you learned how the United States expanded west across North America. In this chapter, you will learn about four groups of people who moved to the West during the mid-1800s. You will also read about two groups who were already living there at this time.

People moved to the West for different reasons. Thousands of **pioneers,** or early settlers, were attracted by cheap land. One group wanted to start a new religious community. Other groups were drawn by the discovery of gold in California.

Many new settlers did not care how their actions affected the people who already lived in the West. In this chapter, you will read about what happened to people from Mexico, called **Mexicanos** (MEH-hee-KAH-nohs). You will also read about an American Indian group called the **Nez Percés** (nehz pers).

Look at this drawing of a wagon wheel. This illustrated spoke diagram is a way to organize information. The diagram shows six groups of people who lived in the West. The pictures in the chapter will show you which group is represented by the image in each segment. The hub, or center, of the wheel reminds you that all six groups lived in the same region. The segments illustrate that each group had its own experiences. As you read this chapter, think about how you can use the diagram to record information about the six groups. Which groups were helped as the United States expanded westward? Which groups were harmed?

People in the West in the 1800s

17.2 The West in the Mid-1800s

After the American Revolution, people from Europe continued to arrive in U.S. cities along the East Coast. Many Europeans then headed west in search of land. Some settlers traveled over-land in wagons along the Wilderness Road. From Virginia, this route led settlers across the Appalachian Mountains. They went through the Cumberland Gap in present-day Tennessee. They made their homes in the Ohio and the Mississippi river valleys. Other settlers moved west along water routes. They used canals built in the early 1800s or took steamboats along the rivers.

By the mid-1800s, writers were publishing stories that invited Americans to move farther west. Western land was cheap. Even families with little money could own ranches or farms.

Then, in 1848, news spread that gold had been found in California. Fortune seekers from around the world raced to the West Coast. Many came from the eastern United States.

Magazines told of adventure and cheap land in the West. This issue of *Harper's Weekly* shows a buffalo hunt, but does not mention that white settlers were killing off some American Indians' main source of food, clothing, and shelter.

The Granger Collection, New York

To reach California, some Americans sailed around South America. Others went by boat to the east coast of Panama, in Central America. There, they crossed to the west coast and boarded ships to California.

Most Americans went by land. To get as far west as California, these travelers had to cross hot deserts and climb over steep mountains. In 1849, more than 5,000 people had died along the way, mostly from disease.

Many Spanish-speaking people already lived in the western areas that were once controlled by Spain and then Mexico. Most newcomers had little respect for these people or for their property. Sometimes, the new settlers took land away from families who had lived in the West for 100 years or more.

The U.S. government signed treaties with American Indian tribes to gain tribal lands. Settlers often broke these agreements. And sometimes, without any treaty, the newcomers just took land from American Indians. In these ways, the tribes that had lived in the West for hundreds of years lost their homelands.

Vaqueros took care of cattle on California ranchos. English-speaking cowboys learned important skills from these Mexicanos.

17.3 Mexicanos

One group of people who lived in the West in the mid-1800s was the Spanish-speaking Mexicanos.

In the 1830s, the Mexican government granted huge plots of land called **ranchos** to many wealthy Mexicanos living in California. Most ranchos were devoted to raising cattle. Mexicano ranchers traded cattle hides and tallow, or fat, for other goods.

Skilled *vaqueros* (vah-KAYR-ohs), or cowboys, looked after the cattle. These vaqueros used special clothing and tools. Soon, English-speaking newcomers learned to use these as well. One tool was a rope called *la reata* (lah ree-AH-tah). New settlers called it a lariat. To protect their legs from thorny bushes, vaqueros wore leather coverings called *chaparrerjos* (chah-pah-RAY-hose). English speakers called them chaps. Vaqueros also wore wide-brimmed hats called *sombreros* (sohm-BRAYR-ohs) to protect their heads from the sun.

Mexicanos grew their own food. They grew fruits and other plants that had first come from Spain. These included olives, oranges, figs, and grapes. Mexicanos also grew North American crops such as corn, squash, and beans.

rancho an area of land, usually for raising cattle, granted by Mexico to Spanish and Mexican citizens who lived in North America

Mexicanos loved to make a rich beef stew called *carne asada* (KAHR-nay ah-SAH-dah). And they enjoyed a flat corn bread called *tortillas* (tor-TEE-uhs).

Mexicanos adapted well to the hot, dry climate of the West and the Southwest. They built houses out of thick clay bricks called *adobe.* Adobe stays cooler in hot weather than other materials. To irrigate, or water, their land, Mexicanos dug ditches and shared the water collected in them.

Mexicanos told stories about current events in songs called *corridos* (koh-REE-dohs). They made music with European instruments such as guitars, violins, and trumpets.

The Mexicanos of the West were citizens of Mexico until 1848. At the end of the Mexican War, they became U.S. citizens. Soon, they were outnumbered by gold-seekers and new settlers. The newcomers often saw Mexicanos as foreigners rather than as fellow Americans. Many white settlers had little respect for them and ignored Mexicanos' rights as landowners.

The U.S. government did not protect Mexicanos' property. Many new settlers claimed rancho land for themselves. They burned Mexicanos' crops and shot their cattle. The new culture of the West and the Southwest included many things learned from Mexicanos. But the rancho way of life soon disappeared.

17.4 Forty-Niners

forty-niner a gold-seeker in the California gold rush of 1849

In January 1848, gold was discovered near California's Sierra Nevada. By 1849, news of the discovery had spread across the United States and to Europe and Asia. Suddenly, **forty-niners** were leaving their families, farms, and jobs behind to race to the goldfields. The gold rush was on!

Forty-niners hoped to get rich quickly. Some of them were former slaves or slaves who had run away. These African Americans were seeking freedom as well as gold. The luckiest ones sent money home to buy freedom for relatives.

Miners found much of the gold in rivers. Sometimes, they used knives and spoons to scrape gold from river rocks. Miners also learned to pan for gold. First, they used a pan to scoop up dirt from the riverbed. Then, they swished the pan around in the river. Lighter materials washed away, leaving the heavy gold in the pan.

To get more gold, miners used a cradle, a wooden box on rockers. First, they shoveled the riverbed dirt into the cradle. Then, they poured water over it and rocked the cradle to wash away the lighter material.

Two forty-niners, one African American and one white, shovel gravel into a sluice. The water running through the sluice will separate the gold from the dirt.

Many miners ended up working in groups. They put several boxes together to make a long, narrow box called a sluice (SLOOS). Men on both sides shoveled dirt into the sluice while water ran steadily through it. The water washed away the lighter particles, and the gold remained.

Miners had a hard and lonely life. They lived in leaky tents and shacks far from their families. In the early days of the gold rush, there were few women in the mining towns and camps.

Storekeepers made more money than most miners. Shops sold food, tools, and supplies at high prices. But many miners could eat cheaply by making their own sourdough bread.

There was no government in the goldfields. Miners elected their own officials and made their own rules to protect their belongings and **claims**. Arguments over claim boundaries were often settled with guns. A man who stole a miner's horse or gold was likely to be hanged.

claim a piece of land worked by a miner seeking valuable minerals

In time, gold became harder to find. The gold rush did make some people millionaires. But most forty-niners went home no richer than before. Some stayed in California and started businesses and farms.

immigrant a person who comes from his or her homeland to settle in another country

transcontinental extending across a continent

17.5 Chinese Immigrants

News of California gold reached China about 1851. Within a year, 25,000 Chinese **immigrants** sailed to California, looking for the "Golden Mountain."

Most of these Chinese hoped to earn money for their families and then return home. Many people in China were too poor to afford food or farmland. Local wars and crop failures made life even harder.

But by the time Chinese immigrants arrived in California, most of the gold that was easy to mine was gone. So the newcomers worked together in mines that earlier miners had given up on. The Chinese miners developed new ways of finding gold by using various tools and machines that they designed.

Chinese workers dug tunnels in the Sierra Nevada for the Central Pacific Railroad Company. They earned less, worked more hours, and did more dangerous jobs than other workers.

American miners were jealous. They convinced the state government to place a tax on foreign miners. American miners also used threats and violence to push the Chinese away from the mines.

Many Chinese found work helping to build the first **transcontinental** railroad. The Central Pacific Railroad Company was laying track east from Sacramento, California. The Union Pacific Railroad Company was building west from Nebraska. In time, nearly all the Central Pacific's workers were Chinese, who were skilled at laying track. One crew boss reported that Chinese workers always laid more track than other crews.

Yet, Chinese railroad workers earned less than other workers. The Chinese also had to work longer hours and do riskier jobs. Sometimes they had to carve tunnels through solid rock. Using wicker baskets fastened to ropes, they lowered themselves down the sides of cliffs. Then they drilled holes in the rock and set gunpowder and fuses in the holes. This was very dangerous work.

The basket ropes could break, or the gun powder could explode too soon. Both types of accidents killed workers. And in winter, many workers froze.

The transcontinental railroad was completed in 1869. The Chinese then had to find new ways to earn money. Some opened stores. Others worked as farmers and fishermen. But many white Americans still saw the Chinese as foreigners because the Chinese looked different, had different customs, and spoke a different language. Some Americans accused Chinese workers of taking jobs away from them for less pay. Some Chinese workers were forced to leave their towns. Some were even killed.

In 1882, Congress responded to this anger toward the Chinese, by passing the Chinese Exclusion Act. Exclusion means keeping someone out. The law stopped most Chinese immigrants from entering the United States. Many years passed before Chinese citizens were allowed to enter the United States as freely as they had before.

17.6 Mormons

Most people in the United States went west to get rich. The **Mormons,** however, were looking for religious freedom.

Mormon a person who is a member of the Church of Jesus Christ of Latter-day Saints

In New York in 1830, a man named Joseph Smith founded the Church of Christ, the Mormon religion which would later be called The Church of Jesus Christ of Latter-day Saints. An inspiring preacher, Smith attracted thousands of followers. Many of them joined Smith in heading west.

The Mormons settled in Ohio and Missouri. But other Americans attacked them in their new communities. They objected to Mormon beliefs and the way that Mormons lived apart from their neighbors.

The Mormons were forced to move their settlements from Ohio and Missouri to an Illinois town they called Nauvoo (na-VOO). Non-Mormons in Illinois feared that the Mormons were becoming too powerful. Some Mormon men were accused of having more than one wife, a practice called polygamy. Joseph Smith and his brother were arrested. On June 27, 1844, a mob broke into the jail and killed both of them.

In 1846, the Mormons left Illinois. They fled to Nebraska. Their new leader, Brigham Young, said that they could only be safe if they moved farther west.

The European Mormons above were too poor to buy wagons. Instead, they used handcarts to carry their belongings across the deserts and mountains.

Brigham Young organized thousands of people for the journey and led the first group west in 1847. Along the way, the Mormons built cabins, dug wells, and planted crops for later followers. When they reached Great Salt Lake in Utah, Young said, "This is the right place."

Great Salt Lake is located on a dry, empty plain. The Mormons irrigated their new land by digging ditches and building dams in mountain streams. The group also planted crops and built a well-planned city.

More Mormon groups followed by wagon train. Each morning, a member of the Church awakened the travelers with the sound of a bugle. After doing chores, the Mormons began another long day on the trail. They left messages in animal skulls for other Mormons to find.

missionary a representative sent by a religious organization to try to persuade other people to adopt that religion

Meanwhile, Mormon **missionaries** gained new followers in Europe. These European Mormons who then came to the United States were too poor to buy wagons for their journey west. Instead, they pushed and pulled their belongings in handcarts across the deserts and mountains.

The Mormons settled the territory of Utah. They organized their own political party and made their own laws. They would not be forced from their homes again.

17.7 Oregon Pioneers

In the 1840s, news of Oregon Country spread to the East in several ways. Fur traders told of thick forests and good farmland. Religious leaders sent letters urging settlers to move there. Newspapers and books described a good life of farming, fishing, and trading.

In 1843, a thousand people in Missouri organized a wagon train headed for Oregon. The pioneers loaded the canvas-covered wagons with supplies for their journey. For food, they packed flour, salt, sugar, coffee, and dried fruit. They took cookware, clothing, rifles, tools, spare parts, and medicines. Then they set out on their 2,000-mile journey along the Oregon Trail.

Every day was filled with hard work. Men drove wagons, herded cattle, found campsites, and guarded the wagon train at night. Women set up camp, cooked, and washed clothes. They put the heavy **yokes** on the oxen that pulled the wagons.

yoke a wooden frame that fastens around an animal's neck and is then attached to a wagon or other vehicle

Women also cared for the sick. Travelers caught diseases from living close together. They also suffered from hunger, the heat and the cold, and poisoning from bad water. Many pioneers died along the trail.

On the prairies, the pioneers found plenty of grass for their animals to eat. The wagon trains tried to follow rivers from which they could get water. But crossing rivers with the wagons was difficult and dangerous. Hundreds of people drowned trying to cross rivers. Traveling over steep mountains and hot, dry deserts brought new challenges.

Women played a key role on the trip across the Great Plains to Oregon. They set up tents, cooked, washed clothes, and tended to the children.

The Oregon Trail passed through American Indian lands. Some tribes were friendly. They traded horses with the pioneers or showed the pioneers where to safely cross rivers. Tribes rarely attacked the wagon trains. But American Indians on the plains depended on buffalo for their food. Pioneers were hunting buffalo, and their cattle were eating the buffalo's grass. American Indians living on the plains worried that the buffalo would be killed or frightened away.

For the pioneers who survived the trip, all the hardships were worth the chance for a new life. Each year, more wagon trains came. By 1845, thousands of Americans had traveled the Oregon Trail.

Chief Joseph was a leader of the Nez Percés.

17.8 Nez Percés

The Nez Percés were American Indians who lived in northeastern Oregon, central Idaho, and southeastern Washington. There, they roamed peacefully with herds of prized horses. The tribes ate salmon, wild berries, and root plants. The Nez Percés treasured their relationship with nature.

In the 1840s, white settlers began farming on Nez Percé land. The U.S. government made treaties promising the Nez Percés certain lands, while buying other land for settlers.

Chief Joseph was the leader of the Nez Percé tribe in Oregon's Wallowa Valley. By the 1870s, settlers and gold miners wanted this land. They persuaded the government to force the Nez Percés onto a reservation. Chief Joseph refused to go. The government threatened to send soldiers to force him and his people.

To avoid war, some Nez Percés started toward the reservation. But then angry young warriors killed some white settlers who had mistreated American Indians. Chief Joseph feared that the U.S. soldiers would now attack his tribe. He decided to lead his people to safety in Canada.

Soldiers chased Chief Joseph and several hundred of his followers for more than 1,000 miles. The Nez Percés hid in mountains and canyons, or deep, narrow valleys. Several times, they fought off the soldiers.

At last, the Nez Percés reached the Bear Paw Mountains in Montana, about 40 miles from Canada. They hoped to cross the border the next day. But the soldiers found them. For five days, the Nez Percés fought bravely. Many died. They were cold, hungry, and exhausted. Finally, Chief Joseph surrendered.

"I am tired of fighting," Chief Joseph stated. "Our chiefs are killed. The old men are all dead. It is cold and we have no blankets. The little children are freezing to death. My people, some of them, have run away to the hills, and have no blankets, no food.... I want to have time to look for my children, and see how many of them I can find. Maybe I shall find them among the dead. Hear me, my chiefs! I am tired. My heart is sick and sad. From where the sun now stands I will fight no more forever."

U.S army leaders had promised that the Nez Percés could return to their home country. Instead, the soldiers took the Nez Percés to a reservation in far-off Oklahoma. At least half of the tribe died from disease on the way there and once in their new home.

Eventually, some of the Nez Percés were allowed to return to reservations in Idaho and Washington. But Chief Joseph and his people never lived in their beloved valley again.

Summary

In this chapter, you learned about four groups who moved to the West in the 1800s. You also read about two groups who already lived there.

Most people came to the West in search of land and wealth. These groups included the forty-niners, Chinese immigrants, and Oregon pioneers. The Mormons moved west for religious freedom. All groups faced hardships. Their arrival was also hard on those already in the West, such as Mexicanos and the Nez Percés. Thousands of these people lost their homes, and many lost their lives.

During the 1800s, settlers moved from the eastern part of the United States, through the central plains, to the Pacific coast. This movement brought new resources and chances for many Americans. Read on to learn about one family who settled on the prairie. What hardships did family members face? How did their journey end? And how did we find out about them?

Reading Further 17

Laura Ingalls Wilder on the Prairie

Many people settled west of the Appalachian Mountains in the mid-1800s. As this land grew more crowded, some pioneers chose to move west again. Among them was the family of Laura Ingalls Wilder. She recorded her childhood memories in a series of books. What do her stories tell us about the hopes, dreams, and challenges of these settlers?

Laura Ingalls Wilder Home Association

Laura Ingalls stands next to her older sister Mary (center) and her younger sister Carrie (left) in this photograph from about 1880.

Laura Ingalls Wilder is a beloved American writer. She wrote a series of books based mostly on her own life as a child in a pioneer family. One of these books is called *Little House on the Prairie*. It tells of a family's move to a new home in Kansas, which the author calls Indian country. This is how the story begins:

> "A long time ago, when all the grandfathers and grandmothers of today were little boys and little girls or very small babies, or perhaps not even born, Pa and Ma and Mary and Laura and Baby Carrie left their little house in the Big Woods of Wisconsin. They drove away and left it lonely and empty in the clearing among the big trees, and they never saw that little house again. They were going to the Indian country.
>
> Pa said there were too many people in the Big Woods now. Quite often Laura heard the ringing thud of an ax which was not Pa's ax, or the echo of a shot that did not come from his gun. The path that went by the little house had become a road. Almost every day Laura and Mary stopped their playing and stared in surprise at a wagon slowly creaking by on that road.
>
> Wild animals would not stay in a country where there were so many people. Pa did not like to stay, either. . . .
>
> In the long winter evenings he talked to Ma about the Western country. In the West the land was level, and there were no trees. The grass grew thick and high. There the wild animals wandered and fed as though they were in a pasture that stretched much farther than a man could see, and there were no settlers."

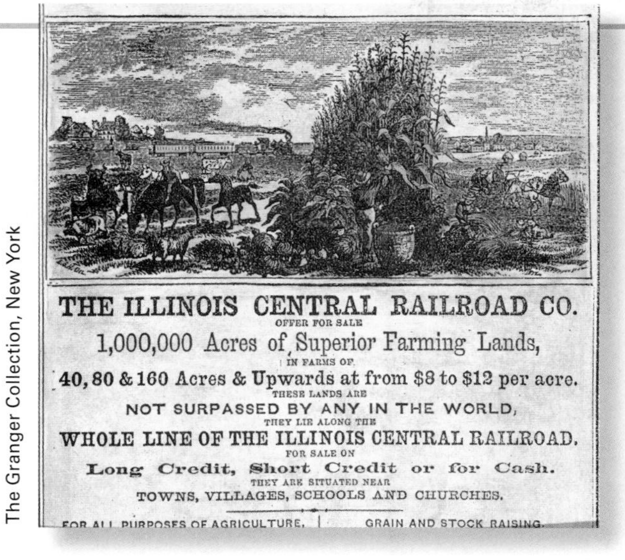

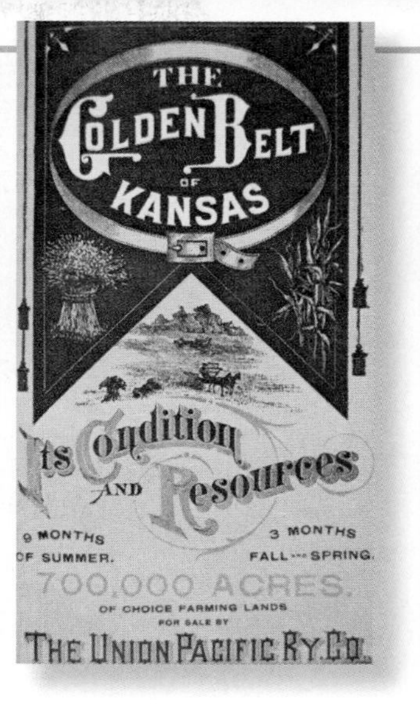

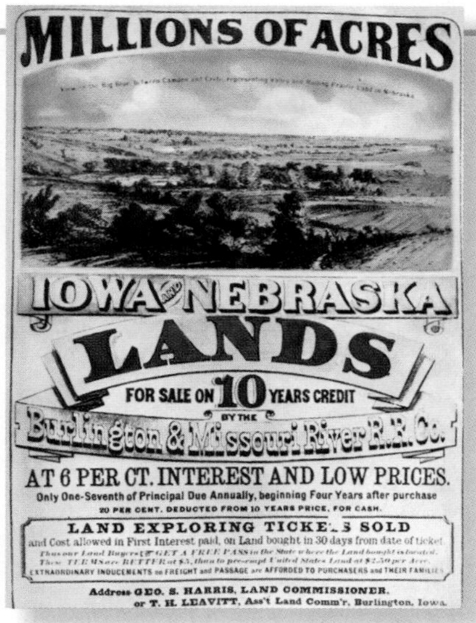

The Granger Collection, New York

These three railroad posters advertise cheap land for sale in the West.

Seeking Land

As a young boy, Laura's father had moved west from New York with his parents. As a man, he relocated his family often, in search of a good farm. The trip to the grasslands of the Great Plains was one such move.

Other people also headed for the wide-open prairie. Many, like the Ingalls, wanted land. And there was lots of it available. In fact, the U.S. government was practically giving land away. Under an 1862 law called the Homestead Act, a settler could pay a small fee and receive a 160-acre piece of land. If the settler lived on the land and farmed it for five years, that land then belonged to him or her. People who got land under this law were called homesteaders.

Why was land so important? At that time, many people made their living by farming. A farm of 160 acres was not large by western standards. It would not make a person rich. But it did give many people a start in life.

Settlers could buy low-priced land from railroad companies. The government gave railroad companies huge parcels of land to encourage them to build railroads in the West. The railroads then sold these lands at low prices.

The promise of land drew many Americans. It also appealed to immigrants from Europe. The Homestead Act made land available even to people who were not yet U.S. citizens. Many Europeans first came to the United States for the chance to get a farm at little cost. In some areas, people born outside the United States made up a large share of the population. For example, nearly half the people living in North Dakota in 1890 were born outside the United States.

One hardship that threatened homesteaders was fast-moving prairie fires.

Hardships on the Prairie

But once on a piece of land, the life of a homesteader was by no means easy. In fact, it was both difficult and dangerous. Laura Ingalls Wilder wrote vividly about these challenges.

To begin with, new settlers had to build everything from scratch. In *Little House on the Prairie,* Laura tells of her Pa's labors. The family lived in a tent while he worked on their home. Wood was scarce on the Kansas prairie. Pa had to cut and haul trees from a creek bottom to their home site. Next, he had to chop and split logs to build the house. Then, Pa had to dig a well by hand so they could have fresh water.

In addition to the hard work, there were many dangers. One was the wild animals. Laura's family had run-ins with packs of wolves and with panthers and other animals. These wild animals were capable of killing other animals, children, and even unwary adults.

Laura's family also tried to keep up good relations with the American Indians in the area. But this was not always easy. Now and then, the Ingalls were troubled by unwelcome visits from American Indians, who took the family's food and other belongings. But the Ingalls knew that their arrival on the prairie had brought hardship for the local tribes. They also knew that their safety depended on getting along with these tribes.

The weather could also be a hazard. Severe cold, tornadoes, lack of rain, dust storms—at different times, each of these could be a danger to homesteaders. Fast-moving prairie fires threatened to burn them out. Hailstorms ruined crops.

Illness was another threat. In Laura's first year on the prairie, her family nearly died from a fever. Later, when Laura had grown up and married, her husband lost the full use of his legs from a serious illness.

Sometimes it is hard to see just what it was that kept Laura and her fellow homesteaders going. In her book *The First Four Years,* an adult Laura, along with her husband, struggles to build a life in what is now South Dakota. Disaster after disaster strikes the young family. Finally, fire destroys their home. After four years, they have little to show for their work. They are deep in debt. They are not even sure they will be able to gain ownership of their homestead. Yet, even in the face of these troubles, Laura and her husband, Manly, are upbeat.

The Granger Collection, New York

Laura Ingalls Wilder poses with her husband, Manly.

> "Was farming a success?
>
> 'Well, it all depends on how you look at it,' Manly said when Laura asked him the question.
>
> They had had a lot of bad luck, but anyone was liable to have bad luck even if he weren't a farmer. There had been so many dry seasons now that surely next year would be a good crop year....
>
> It would be a fight to win out in this business of farming, but strangely she felt her spirit rising for the struggle.
>
> The incurable optimism of the farmer who throws his seed on the ground every spring, betting it and his time against the elements, seemed inextricably to blend with the creed of her pioneer forefathers that 'it is better farther on'—only instead of farther on in space, it was farther on in time, over the horizon of the years ahead instead of the far horizon of the west."

Many homesteaders shared such views. They did not expect easy success. They were ready to work hard to make their futures. All they wanted was a chance. And thousands found that chance on the prairie.

What role do you think these people played on the plantation?

Why do you think this man is riding a mule?

What is this man doing?

Where do you think this wagon is going?

The Causes of the Civil War

18

What factors helped drive apart the North and the South in the mid-1800s?

18.1 Introduction

In Chapter 17, you read about people who lived in the West. In this chapter, you will learn some ways in which Americans disagreed about how to settle the West. In 1861, these conflicting ideas helped cause the bloody **Civil War** between the Northern and the Southern states.

By the mid-1800s, the United States had two distinct regions. The **North** included states in New England, in the Middle Atlantic region, and around the Great Lakes. Northerners busily built cities, factories, and railroads. Most northern workers were free, not enslaved. The **South** included states south of the Ohio River and latitude 36°30' north. This region had few factories or large cities. Most people lived on farms. On plantations, African American slaves planted and harvested crops.

The Southern way of life depended on slave labor. As the United States expanded westward, Northerners and Southerners bitterly disagreed about whether slavery should be allowed in new territories and states.

Look at the drawing of the brother and sister at the right. The sister has a habit her brother does not like. She plays her music loudly and refuses to turn it down. The brother likes quiet. Think of the conflict between the North and the South as a dispute between a brother and a sister. Remember, this kind of comparison is a metaphor.

As you read, think about the brother and sister. Does the brother have the right to make his sister change her habit? What will happen if she refuses?

The Civil War: Like a Family Dispute

The Colt factory, shown here, produced weapons. It was one of many factories in the North that needed workers.

18.2 Differences Grow Between the North and the South

By the mid-1800s, people in the North and the South had developed very different ways of life.

In the North, new industries began to appear. Busy factories made all kinds of products, including new inventions such as the sewing machine. The factories needed workers. Cities grew as people came to find jobs.

Canals and railroads made it possible for farmers, ranchers, and business owners to move goods over long distances. Factory owners in the eastern part of the nation made tools for farmers living a thousand miles to the west. They shipped these tools by railroads. Farmers in western areas sent grain and other crops to feed the people in eastern cities.

All this activity attracted new immigrants from places such as Ireland and Germany. Workers in the North earned wages for their labor. They were free to choose their own jobs. Therefore, these workers were called "free labor."

Unlike the North, the South had few large cities with factories. Its way of life was based on farming and slave labor. Many Southerners worked their own farms. But owners of plantations used slave labor.

By the mid-1800s, the most important plantation crop was cotton. The South's warm weather and rich soil had always been good for growing cotton. But until Eli Whitney invented the cotton gin in 1793, cotton growers did not earn much money. They had to separate the seeds from the cotton by hand. This took a long time and many workers. Whitney's machine did this task quickly. After its invention, cotton became a valuable cash crop. By 1860, southern plantations grew three-fourths of the world's cotton.

As cotton plantations spread, the South began to depend more than ever on having many slaves. Most Northerners did not own slaves. They did not want to see slavery spread to new territories in the West. But white Southerners insisted on their rights to own slaves and to take their slaves with them wherever they settled.

The North and the South had other disagreements, as well. But slavery was one of the key issues that divided them.

Many cotton plantation owners became rich. They used slave labor to plant and harvest the crop.

Union the United States as one country; during the Civil War, the government and the armies of the states that chose to remain a part of the United States

slave state a state in which it was legal to own slaves

free state a state in which it was not legal to own slaves

18.3 The Missouri Compromise

In 1819, disputes over slavery threatened to cause trouble between the North and the South. That year, the territory of Missouri asked to join the **Union** as a slave state. Settlers had been moving into Missouri and other western lands since 1803, when President Thomas Jefferson had made the Louisiana Purchase. Many of these settlers were Southern slave owners looking for new places to grow cotton.

In 1819, there were 11 **slave states** and 11 **free states** in the nation. Northerners did not want to let another slave state into the Union. They did not want the slave states to have more power in Congress than they did.

A fierce debate raged in Congress. For a time, it seemed the Union might fall apart. Then Senator Henry Clay of Kentucky offered a compromise. He proposed that Missouri join the Union as a slave state. At the same time, Maine would join as a free state. This would keep the number of free states and slave states equal. Clay also suggested drawing a line across the map of the western United States at latitude 36°30' north. Except in Missouri, no slavery would be allowed in new states north of that line. Clay's ideas became known as the Missouri Compromise.

For 30 years, this compromise calmed the anger between the North and the South. But the conflict was not settled. Many Northerners still wanted to end slavery. And white Southerners still feared that Northerners would try to change their way of life.

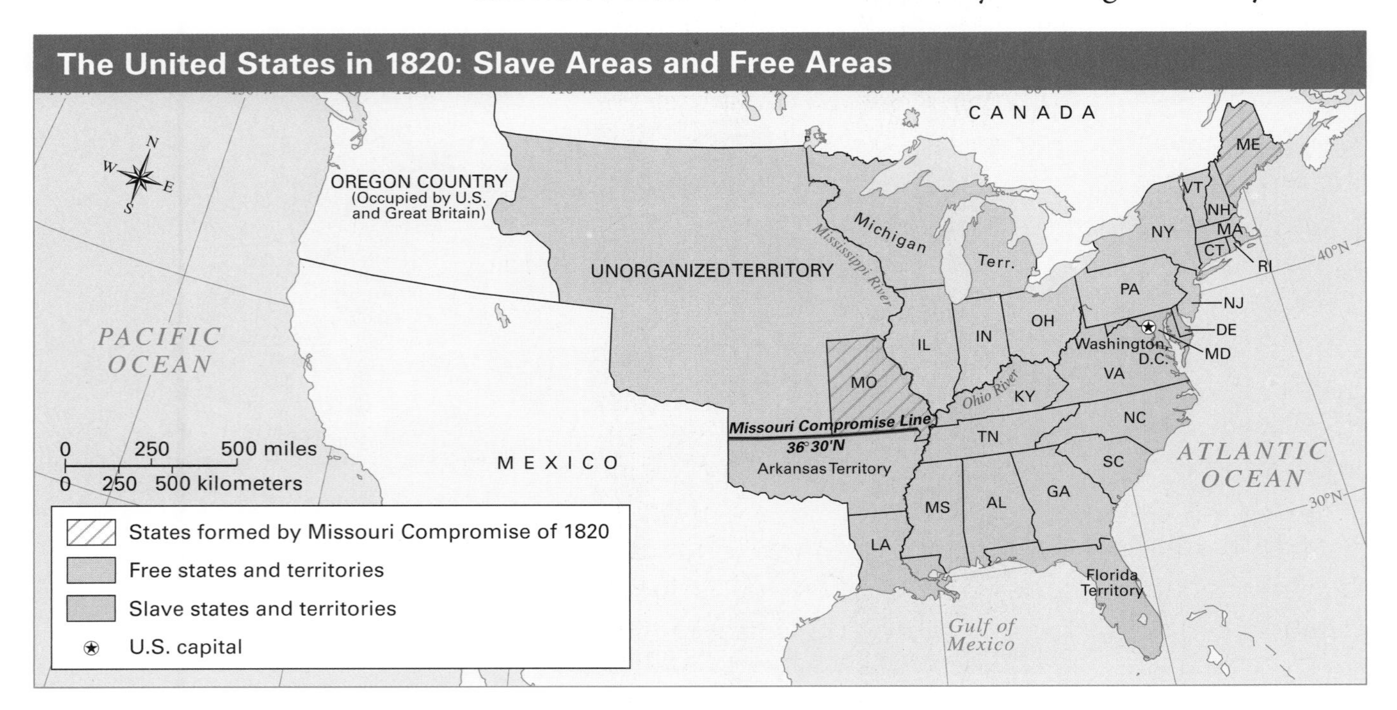

The Underground Railroad helped runaway slaves make the hard journey to freedom.

18.4 Abolitionists and the Underground Railroad

By the 1830s, a growing number of Northerners were speaking out against slavery. Those who took action were called **abolitionists**.

One leading abolitionist was William Lloyd Garrison. He began a newspaper, *The Liberator,* to gain support for ending slavery. Frederick Douglass was another abolitionist leader. He was a former slave who had escaped to New York. Douglass gave powerful speeches against slavery. In 1845, he wrote a book about his terrible hardships as a slave. Both of these men convinced many Northerners that slavery had to end.

To help slaves escape to freedom, abolitionists organized a system called the **Underground Railroad**. It was not under the ground, nor was it a railroad. The members, called "conductors," provided safe houses, called "stations," for escaping slaves. In these locations, runaway slaves could hide and rest. Conductors gave the slaves food and clothing. Then they guided them to the next station.

Many slaves traveled like this all the way to safety in Canada. If they stayed in the United States, even in the free states, slave hunters could find and capture them.

One of the bravest conductors was a former slave named Harriet Tubman. She herself escaped to the North. Then she risked her life by going back 19 times to the South to guide hundreds of other slaves to freedom.

Most Northerners were neither abolitionists nor part of the Underground Railroad. But the actions of those who were abolitionists angered white Southerners. More and more, the North and the South saw each other as enemies.

abolitionist a person who wanted to end, or abolish, slavery

Underground Railroad a system in which abolitionists secretly helped escaping slaves reach freedom

18.5 The Compromise of 1850

In the late 1840s, the North and the South struggled over new western territory. After the Mexican War, the United States had gained a huge amount of land in the West and in the Southwest. This included California. In 1849, California asked to enter the Union as a free state.

Southerners were angered. Now there would be more Congressmen from free states than from slave states. Also, much of California was south of the 36°30' north latitude line. Under the Missouri Compromise, slavery should have been allowed there. Some Southerners began to talk about pulling their states out of the Union in protest.

The Granger Collection, New York

Henry Clay offered the Compromise of 1850 to try to please both the North and South on the issue of slavery.

Once again, Henry Clay offered a compromise. It was called the Compromise of 1850 and included several laws which Congress passed. To please the North, Congress admitted California as a free state. It also stopped the sale of slaves in the nation's capital, Washington, D.C. To please the South, Congress allowed people in New Mexico and in Utah to vote on whether to allow slavery in their territories. Congress also passed the Fugitive Slave Law. This law said that officials in the North would help capture fugitive, or runaway, slaves.

The Fugitive Slave Law surprised and angered many Northerners. In Illinois, a rising political leader named Abraham Lincoln was troubled by this law. Some states reacted by passing laws that forbade officials from helping slave hunters. Abolitionists broke into jails to free captured runaways. And the Underground Railroad was busier than ever.

The Compromise of 1850 left many people upset. Southerners accused the North of wanting to destroy their way of life by stopping slavery. Northerners accused the South of wanting to spread the terrible system of slavery. Later on, Lincoln would warn that the nation could not go on forever "half-slave and half-free."

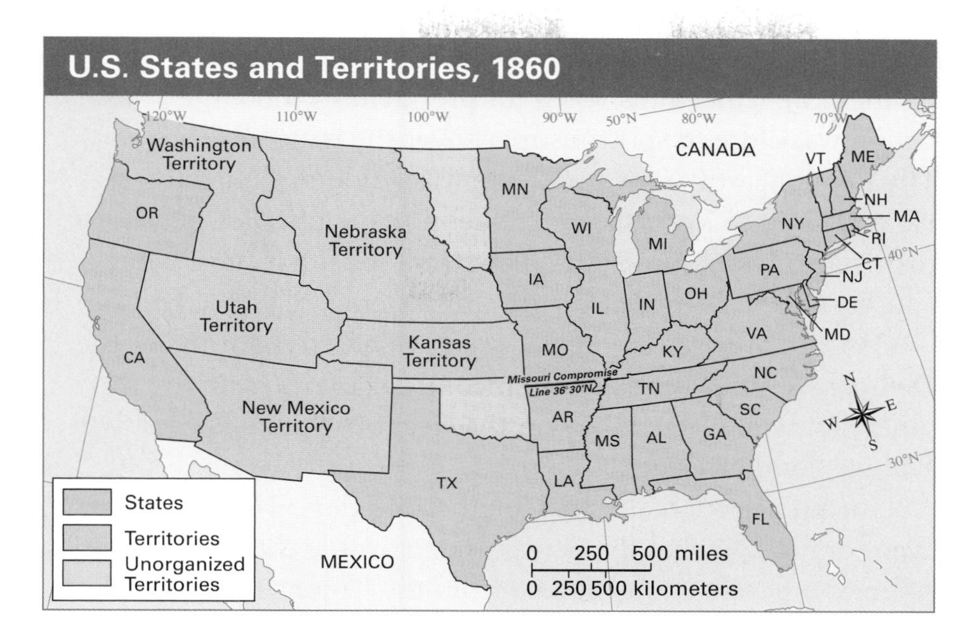

18.6 "Bleeding Kansas"

Tensions between the North and the South grew worse as the territories of Kansas and Nebraska prepared to become states. Both areas were north of latitude 36°30'. Under the Missouri Compromise, both would be free states. But, in 1854, Congress passed the Kansas-Nebraska Act. It said people in the two territories could elect representatives to write state constitutions. In them, the states could either permit or forbid slavery.

This law turned Kansas, the more southern territory, into a battleground. Proslavery settlers and antislavery settlers both raced to Kansas to vote in the election. The proslavery settlers threatened voters who opposed slavery. Americans were now killing each other over slavery.

On election day, the proslavery settlers won by a huge margin. But those who were against slavery did not accept the results. They claimed that men from Missouri had crossed into Kansas to vote illegally for slavery. They ignored the election. Instead, they set up their own government in the town of Topeka.

In 1856, a proslavery mob entered Lawrence, Kansas, to arrest antislavery leaders. The mob burned a hotel and destroyed much of the town. This attack enraged an abolitionist named John Brown. Armed with swords, Brown and a small band of men attacked and killed five settlers at Pottawatomie Creek.

The fighting in Kansas continued throughout the summer. Abolitionists called the conflict "Bleeding Kansas." By the time federal troops restored order, many people had died. For many Northerners and Southerners alike, "Bleeding Kansas" showed that the time for compromise was coming to an end.

secede to officially withdraw from a government or country

Confederacy the nation formed by the 11 states (in order of secession—South Carolina, Mississippi, Florida, Alabama, Georgia, Louisiana, Texas, Virginia, Arkansas, North Carolina, Tennessee) that left the Union

18.7 The Election of Abraham Lincoln

By the time Americans voted for president in 1860, the Union was close to splitting apart over the issue of slavery. The Republican Party's candidate was Abraham Lincoln. He promised to leave slavery alone in the South. But he was firmly against its spread into new territories. For most white Southerners, this made Lincoln their enemy.

Conflict over slavery helped split the other major party, the Democrats. The vote against Lincoln was divided among three other candidates. Lincoln won the election. But he did not win a single Southern state.

Lincoln's election alarmed Southern leaders. They did not even wait to see what the new president would do. One by one, seven Southern states **seceded** from the Union. To protect their right to own slaves, they joined together as the Confederate States of America, or the **Confederacy**. Early in 1861, the Confederacy chose its own president. He was Jefferson Davis of Mississippi.

The new nation moved quickly to take over federal forts and other property in the South. Still, President Lincoln and many other Americans hoped that the Union could be saved without going to war.

But on April 12, 1861, Confederates attacked Fort Sumter. This was a federal fortress in the harbor of Charleston, South Carolina. For 34 hours, Southern cannons shelled the fort. Finally, the Union commander surrendered. The Civil War had begun.

In the South, church bells rang out in celebration. Soon, four more states joined the Confederacy. Most Southerners believed that the United States would allow the Southern states to go without much of a fight. Few imagined how long, bloody, and terrible the Civil War would be.

The Granger Collection, New York

Abraham Lincoln opposed the spread of slavery into new territories. When he was elected president, the South seceded from the Union.

The Granger Collection, New York

On April 12, 1861, Confederate soldiers attacked Fort Sumter and the Civil War began.

Summary

In this chapter, you learned about some key events that led to the Civil War. You used a metaphor to compare a dispute between a brother and sister with the conflicts between the North and the South.

The North and the South were fiercely divided over the spread of slavery. Most people in the North did not have slaves and wanted to keep slavery out of new western lands. White Southerners insisted on their right to own slaves and to bring them into the West.

Twice, Congress tried to keep the peace through compromises. In the end, this failed because of disagreements over the passage of the Fugitive Slave Law, the fighting in Kansas, and Abraham Lincoln's election as president.

After Lincoln's election, 11 Southern states formed a new country, the Confederacy. Its attack on Fort Sumter ended hopes that the Union could be restored peacefully. The Civil War had begun.

What other events increased tensions over slavery during the years before the war? How did one woman draw support from around the world for her antislavery views? How did people in the South respond? Read on to find out.

Reading Further 18

Harriet Beecher Stowe's Book

Harriet Beecher Stowe poured her heart into writing *Uncle Tom's Cabin*. This tale about the horrors of slavery moved many people in the North. At the same time, it angered many in the South. How did this novel help drive the nation apart—and toward the Civil War?

Harriet Beecher Stowe first published chapters of her novel *Uncle Tom's Cabin* in 1851. In one of its best-known scenes, Eliza, a black slave, has learned that her young son has been sold. She decides to run away with him. She flees toward the free state of Ohio. But right on her trail is the slave trader Haley and his helpers, Andy and Sam.

> "A thousand lives seemed to be concentrated in that one moment to Eliza. Her room opened by a side door to the river. She caught her child, and sprang down the steps towards it. The trader caught a full glimpse of her, just as she was disappearing down the bank; and throwing himself from his horse, and calling loudly on Sam and Andy, he was after her like a hound after a deer.

In the 1850s, artists often made black people in book illustrations look like white people. That is the case in this illustration of Eliza's escape.

> In that dizzy moment, her feet to her scarce seemed to touch the ground, and a moment brought her to the water's edge. Right on behind they came; and, nerved with strength such as God gives only to the desperate, with one wild cry and flying leap, she vaulted sheer over the . . . current by the shore, on to the raft of ice beyond. . . .
>
> "The huge green fragment of ice on which she alighted pitched and creaked as her weight came on it, but she stayed there not a moment. With wild cries and desperate energy she leaped to another and still another cake;—stumbling—leaping—slipping—springing upwards again! Her shoes are gone—her stockings cut from her feet while blood marked every step; but she saw nothing, felt nothing, til dimly, as in a dream, she saw the Ohio side . . . ."

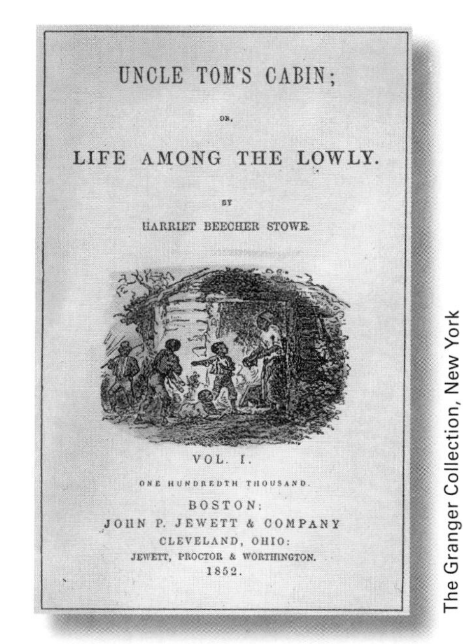
UNCLE TOM'S CABIN;

OR,

LIFE AMONG THE LOWLY.

BY

HARRIET BEECHER STOWE.

VOL. I.

ONE HUNDREDTH THOUSAND.

BOSTON:
JOHN P. JEWETT & COMPANY
CLEVELAND, OHIO:
JEWETT, PROCTOR & WORTHINGTON.
1852.

The Granger Collection, New York

Harriet Beecher Stowe published *Uncle Tom's Cabin* in book form in 1852.

Stowe's Inspirations

Stowe had been raised in Connecticut, far from the South. Her father was an abolitionist. Stowe and her family often talked about the evils of slavery.

But discussing slavery did not prepare Stowe for what she later saw in Cincinnati, Ohio, by the Ohio River. The river separated the free state of Ohio from the slave state of Kentucky. While living in Ohio, Stowe came face-to-face with the cruelties of slavery. She met people active in the Underground Railroad and the runaway slaves that they helped. She was horrified by their stories. Stowe also heard a friend's true account of a young mother's dash to freedom across the frozen river. From this story came the idea for Eliza's escape.

Stowe believed that if people knew more about slavery, they would turn against it. She wanted to write a book that would force readers to see the brutality of the system.

While in Ohio, Stowe heard about the cruelties of slavery, such as slave auctions. She included scenes like the one below in her novel.

Personal tragedy helped Stowe feel the pain suffered by slaves. In 1849, her son died of a disease called cholera. Stowe was grief-stricken. "It was at his dying bed and at his grave that I learned what a poor slave mother may feel when her child is torn away from her," she later wrote. ". . . I felt I could never be consoled for it unless this crushing of my own heart might enable me to work out some great good to others."

Not long after Stowe's loss, Congress began to debate the Compromise of 1850. Like many Northerners, Stowe was angered by the Fugitive Slave Law. Fueled by her grief and anger, Stowe wrote *Uncle Tom's Cabin*. In 1851, she began to publish her story, a chapter at a time, in a weekly newspaper. But before long, in response to public demand, Stowe published the whole story in book form. It came off the presses in March 1852.

Uncle Tom's Cabin was widely read around the world in English and other languages such as Spanish (above). Some Southerners wrote books showing a more positive view of slavery (below).

The Debate Grows More Intense

Uncle Tom's Cabin was widely read. Americans bought 300,000 copies in the first year. The novel was also popular in Europe and in Asia. It appeared in more than 60 languages. Stowe became famous. She was welcomed as a hero in Great Britain in 1853.

The story had a great impact on its readers. In the North, abolitionists were excited. They felt the power of the story. William Lloyd Garrison was a leader in the abolitionist movement. He wrote that the book would "awaken the strongest compassion for the oppressed." He was right.

The debate over slavery was growing in the 1850s. However, many people remained indifferent. That changed after they read *Uncle Tom's Cabin*. Northern readers cried at the suffering of the slaves Eliza and Uncle Tom. Many felt anger and shame over the actions of cruel plantation owner Simon Legree. Feelings against slavery grew.

Some Southerners criticized Stowe's work. They charged that the characters were either too good or too evil, and therefore, not realistic. They claimed that the severe mistreatment of slaves that Stowe described was not true. Since Stowe had never been in the South, they asked, how could she know the truth?

A few Southerners wrote books that challenged Stowe's picture of slavery. They argued that enslaved Africans were better off as slaves than as free people. They wrote that Southern slaves had a better life than white factory workers in the North. Although these books were not as popular as *Uncle Tom's Cabin,* they sharpened the debate about slavery.

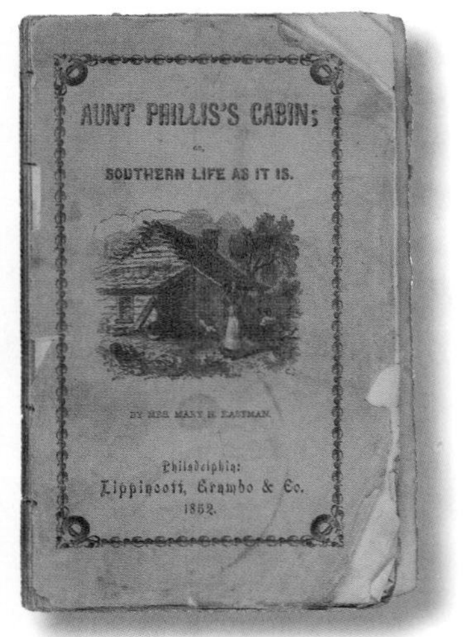

Aunt Phillis's Cabin, Cover, Special Collections, University of Virginia Library

Harriet Beecher Stowe was strongly against slavery. She wrote *Uncle Tom's Cabin* to persuade readers to share her point of view.

Ten years after Stowe published *Uncle Tom's Cabin,* she visited the White House. Abraham Lincoln was president. The Civil War had been raging for a year. It is said that when Lincoln met Stowe, he remarked, "So you're the little woman who wrote the book that started this great war."

In fact, the Civil War had many causes. But this comment helps highlight the impact of Stowe's novel. While Stowe's novel did not cause the war, it did expand the number of Americans who took part in the debate over slavery. Not every Northerner who read the book became an abolitionist. But many began to view slavery in a more negative light.

Meanwhile, many white Southerners felt that the North was growing more hostile to the South. They saw world opinion turning against their way of life. The North and the South had always been able to find ways to compromise. But now, the chance for compromise was slipping away. White Southerners were finding it harder to see a future for themselves as part of the United States.

In the years after Stowe published *Uncle Tom's Cabin,* other events further divided the North and the South. The election of Lincoln in 1860 finally convinced white Southerners that they must go their own way. Soon, soldiers from the North and the South were fighting. The Civil War had begun.

For which side do you think these soldiers are fighting?

For which side do you think these soldiers are fighting?

What kind of weapon is being pulled by this carriage?

The Civil War

What factors contributed to the outcome of the Civil War?

19

19.1 Introduction

In Chapter 18, you learned about the causes of the Civil War. In this chapter, you will learn about the war itself.

More Americans died in the Civil War than in any other war in our nation's history. What was it like to take part in this terrible conflict? To find out, you will visit one of the war's key battlefields.

In July of 1863, about 160,000 Union and Confederate soldiers fought at **Gettysburg** in Pennsylvania. This battle was one of the turning points in the Civil War. As you visit this famous battlefield, you will discover how the two armies fought the war. Who were the men in these armies? What weapons did they use? What kinds of food did they eat? Experience the horrors of combat. Find out about the medical treatment the troops received. Learn what was happening on the home front in both the North and the South.

Look at the Union and the Confederate soldiers to the right. Use the figures to organize information about the Civil War as you read this chapter. Think about what you learn that will help you answer this question: What was life like for soldiers in the Civil War?

Gettysburg: Two Soldiers' Experiences

Each army in the war adopted special uniforms to prevent confusion on the battlefield. To the left, you see a Union soldier. To the right stands a Confederate soldier.

19.2 The Union and the Confederate Armies

In 1861, neither the North nor the South was prepared to fight a war. Both sides needed to build strong armies.

Men signed up to fight for different reasons. Some men hoped to find wealth, adventure, or glory. Others were moved by more patriotic reasons.

In the North, President Abraham Lincoln asked men to fight to preserve the Union. He meant that he wanted to keep the United States as one country. Later on, in January 1863, Lincoln freed slaves in the Confederate states not yet under Union control. This order was called the **Emancipation Proclamation**. It made many Northerners feel that they fought for freedom as well as for the Union.

White Southerners also fought for freedom. They wanted to be free from northern control. And they wanted states to be free to leave the Union. Jefferson Davis, the president of the Confederacy, also called on Southerners to defend their homeland and way of life.

But all these reasons did not draw enough men into the fight. Before the war's end, both sides used an unpopular system—the **draft**—to fill their armies. In the end, millions of men fought in this conflict. And 600,000 of them died.

Much of the Union army was made up of poor farmers. As many as one-fourth of the Union soldiers were immigrants from Europe. By the end of the war there were also about 180,000 African Americans in the Union army and navy. The Confederate troops were mostly farmers and poor white men.

At first, Civil War soldiers chose their own uniforms. But this variety in clothing was confusing on the battlefield. Troops often shot at the wrong men. Soon, both armies adopted official uniforms. Union soldiers wore dark blue jackets, blue pants, and blue caps. Confederate soldiers wore long tan-gray shirts, pants, and jackets.

Early in the war, soldiers went into battle with little training. Gradually, training began to improve. Soldiers performed hundreds of hours of drills. They learned how to march, to change directions on command, and to obey orders quickly.

Both sides also needed good leaders to command their troops. Many of the nation's skilled generals were Southerners. They chose to fight for the Confederacy. The most famous was Robert E. Lee of Virginia. Out of loyalty to his home state, Lee turned down an offer to command the Union armies. Instead, he eventually took control of the Confederate armies. In the North, President Lincoln spent the early years of the war appointing one general after another. He needed someone who could lead the Union armies to victory.

When the fighting began, soldiers on both sides thought that the war would be short and that little blood would be shed. They were wrong.

Emancipation Proclamation President Abraham Lincoln's order to free (emancipate) slaves in states that were still fighting the Union, and to allow African Americans into the Union army and navy

draft the selection of people to serve in an army whether or not they wish to serve

In this painting by eyewitness Edwin Forbes, Union forces defend themselves against attacking Confederates at the Battle of Gettysburg. After the battle, thousands lay dead and wounded.

19.3 Key Battles in the North

During the first two years of the war, the Confederacy won many battles in the East. It kept the Union army from capturing the Confederate capital at Richmond, Virginia.

Then, on September 17, 1862, forces clashed in Sharpsburg, Maryland. Called the Battle of Antietam, it was the first battle on northern soil. It was the bloodiest one-day battle in U.S. military history. It left more than 23,000 men dead. Although neither side defeated the other, it was considered a Union victory because General Lee and his Confederate forces finally retreated. This was a turning point in the war. It led to Lincoln issuing his Emancipation Proclamation.

In 1863, Lee decided that a Confederate victory in the North might convince the Union to ask for peace. He invaded Pennsylvania with most of his army. A large Union army followed at a distance.

On July 1, a group of Confederate soldiers entered the town of Gettysburg. There, they found Union soldiers. Fighting soon broke out.

General George G. Meade led the Union army. He lined up most of his troops on a strip of high ground near Gettysburg. For two days, they beat back fierce Confederate attacks.

On the third day, Lee decided on a brave gamble. He sent General George Pickett and about 15,000 troops to attack the middle of General Meade's defensive line. There, the Union army was strongest. Yelling and waving flags, Pickett's men crossed 400 yards of open fields. They charged up the strip of high ground. But Union bullets and cannonballs tore into them.

Soon, dead bodies covered the ground. A few Confederates reached the top of the ridge. But Union soldiers drove them back. Pickett's Charge had failed.

The Battle of Gettysburg was another major turning point of the war. Lee lost almost one-third of his army. He was forced to return to Virginia. The Confederacy never again invaded the North.

19.4 Military Tactics and Technology

Civil War armies suffered huge losses in battles like Gettysburg. That was partly because of their military tactics. It was also a result of new **technology**.

technology the use of scientific or mechanical knowledge to achieve a practical purpose, such as creating machines and weapons for use in war

In earlier wars, generals had often won battles by attacking enemies head-on with larger armies. Both sides used this tactic during the Civil War. But defenders used several other tactics to fight off large forces. Defending troops tried to find high ground. From there, they could fire down on their attackers. Defenders also dug trenches, or deep ditches. Or they built dirt walls. They took cover in the trenches or behind the walls as they fired at the enemy. If attackers had to cross open ground, they would suffer many casualties.

New weapons helped defenders. As the war went on, more troops used rifles in place of muskets. Rifles were more accurate over longer distances. Now, defenders could shoot attackers before they got close. They could also fire deadly artillery—large, heavy guns like cannons—at attackers. As a result, many bloody battles were no longer decided by troop numbers. In fact, battles often had no clear winner.

Other new technologies also made the Civil War deadly. Railroads helped armies move quickly, especially in the North. The South began using the telegraph to send messages over long distances. Union spies watched enemy movements from hot-air balloons. And, for the first time, ships with iron plating fought each other at sea.

Rifles like the one below were more accurate than muskets from greater distances. Pointed bullets (below) punched through their targets more effectively than did round musket balls.

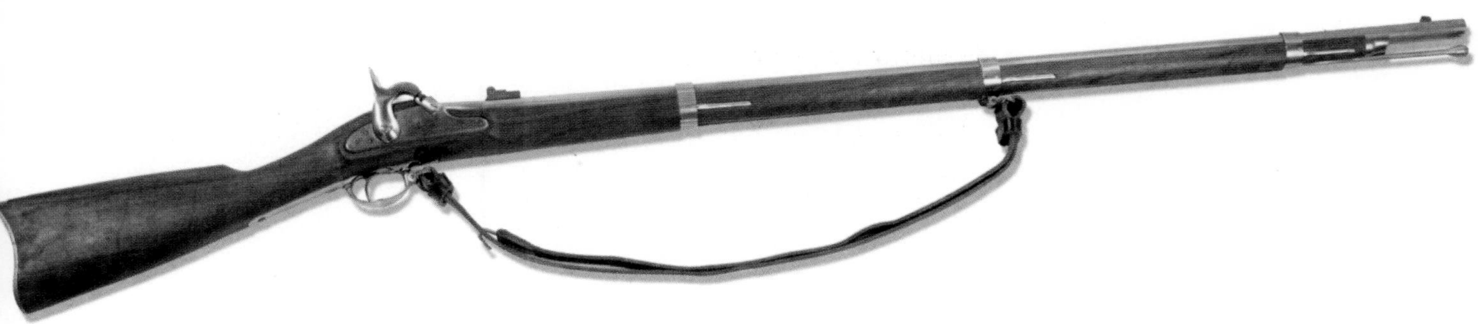

19.5 Combat Conditions

Civil War combat was both frightening and dangerous. Attacks on enemy positions usually started with artillery fire. These big guns filled the air with deafening noise and clouds of stinging, black smoke. Often, troops could not see each other or their enemies. But they could hear the shouts of their commanders and the screams of the wounded.

Commanders then ordered troops to advance. Soldiers walked or ran in rows, elbow to elbow, each row only 13 inches behind the row ahead. Drums beat a pace of 110 steps per minute. Bullets and artillery shells tore into the attackers, causing terrible injuries. Troops fell over the fallen bodies of their fellow soldiers.

Nearing enemy lines, the attacking troops placed bayonets on their rifles. Then they charged toward their opponents, who were firing at them from cover. The soldiers, used to short-range muskets, sometimes waited too long to fire. Their newer rifles had a longer range. When the two sides drew close, men fought face-to-face. They were just a few feet apart when they fired their guns. They often had time for only one shot. Then they used their bayonets and the butts of their rifles to spear or club the enemy.

When battles finally ended, thousands of soldiers on both sides lay dead. Wounded men cried out in thirst and pain. Many of them died before they could get help.

Shells from artillery guns like those shown here could shatter the lines of attacking troops.

19.6 Medical Care

Medical care during the Civil War was poor. More than 200,000 soldiers died from wounds received in battle. More than twice that number died from disease.

Doctors did not have the skills to heal many of the injured and sick troops. They knew little about what caused infections. Surgeons rarely washed their hands or their medical tools. They often operated in dirty tents. As a result, infections spread from one patient to another. And surgeons ran out of medicines, such as anesthetics. These are drugs that make patients unconscious during operations. Without anesthetics, many soldiers suffered great pain during lifesaving operations.

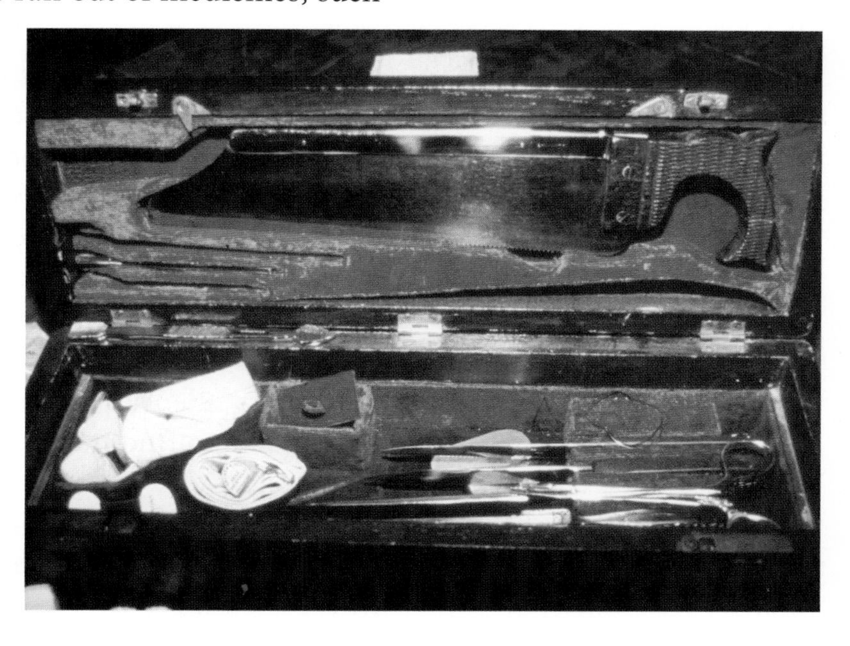

Doctors did their best to save the lives of wounded soldiers with simple tools like these.

Civil War surgeons had only simple tools. They used bone saws to remove wounded arms and legs before infections could kill the injured men. They used bullet probes to remove bullets. With razor-sharp knives called scalpels, they cut through flesh. They applied tight bandages, called tourniquets (TERN-ih-kehts), to stop bleeding. They set patients' limbs in splints to keep broken bones from moving. Doctors made their own pills in special pill molds.

At times, especially in the South, doctors did not have any basic tools and drugs. Instead, they used tree branches for splints, treated burns with cucumbers, and prescribed a tea made from geranium—a flowering plant—for troops with diarrhea.

Diseases spread quickly in both armies' crowded, filthy camps. No one knew about germs. Soldiers drank dirty water. They threw garbage on the ground, attracting rats and flies. Sometimes armies camped near germ-infested swamps.

Often, doctors had incorrect medical information. At times, they gave soldiers medicines that turned out to be harmful.

Thousands of women in both the North and the South tried to ease the suffering of sick and wounded soldiers. Clara Barton, who started the American Red Cross, was one of the many women whose courage and kindness won the soldiers' respect.

19.7 Food and Drink

Poor food caused some of the armies' health problems. It certainly made troops on both sides miserable.

Soldiers had to carry food that would not spoil quickly. Usually, this included beef and pork that was pickled, or preserved in salt water. Pickled meat lasted for a long time. But it was very salty. To try to improve the taste, the men soaked it in water for several hours. Then they fried it in grease before eating it. In place of fresh vegetables, soldiers ate dried cakes of beans, onions, turnips, carrots, and beets. Often these cakes had roots, stalks, and leaves, as well as vegetables, in them.

The Union armies fed soldiers dry biscuits, called hardtack, that were made of flour and water. Hardtack tasted like thick, unsalted, hard crackers. Troops often found worms and weevils, a type of beetle, in the hardtack. Union soldiers also carried coffee beans for making their favorite hot drink. Confederates often boiled a root called chicory to make a coffee-like drink.

Soldiers on both sides searched for fresh food and water in the countryside. When Confederate armies ran short of supplies, soldiers had to find their own food to keep from starving. Both Union and Confederate soldiers hunted for game, picked berries, and took fruit from orchards. They also stole cows, pigs, and chickens from nearby farms. When they could, they raided each other's supplies.

Soldiers on both sides had to put up with food that was often of poor quality.

The Granger Collection, New York

The Granger Collection, New York

General William Sherman and his troops marched through the South, destroying much of the property that lay in their path. This destruction caused terrible shortages on the Southern home front.

19.8 Conditions on the Home Front

Soldiers were not the only ones who suffered. There were troubles on the home front as well.

In the North, many people were angry about the draft. Draft laws allowed rich men to hire others to take their places in the army. Such men could also escape the draft by paying the government $300.

Outraged crowds took part in violent riots against the draft. In 1863, white protesters destroyed the draft offices in New York City. They also burned other buildings. And they attacked innocent African Americans. The rioters did not want to be forced to go to war to free slaves. And they blamed African Americans for taking jobs from white workers. More than 100 people died in the New York riots.

Southerners on the home front faced greater troubles because most of the fighting took place in the South. As the war went on, the South suffered shortages of food and other goods. Many Southerners also lost property when Union armies marched through Southern lands. Sometimes, Union soldiers stole valuable items, such as books, silver, and jewelry. Sometimes, they burned houses, killed farm animals, and set crops on fire.

Despite the many hardships, the war did create some new opportunities for women in both the North and the South. With so many men in the army, women took on more jobs. Many worked as teachers, nurses, and secretaries. Others worked in factories, making equipment for the armies. But men and women alike hoped for the day when the fighting would end. Then families could be together again.

On April 9, 1865, General Robert E. Lee surrendered to General Ulysses S. Grant at Appomattox Court House, Virginia.

19.9 From Gettysburg to Appomattox

At the time of the Battle of Gettysburg, in July 1863, the Union army won another key victory farther west. Troops under General Ulysses S. Grant captured Vicksburg in Mississippi. This was a Confederate fort by the Mississippi River. Its capture gave the Union control of the river. This split the Confederacy in half. It also made General Grant a hero in the North.

In 1864, President Lincoln gave Grant command of all the Union forces. Grant planned to end the war by attacking the South from two directions. He ordered General William Sherman to march through Georgia to the Atlantic Ocean. At the same time, Grant led an army into Virginia. His men were to defeat General Robert E. Lee. Then they would capture the Confederacy's capital, Richmond.

The North had more men and equipment than the South. Grant kept attacking, no matter how many men he lost. The high death toll earned Grant the nickname "butcher." But soon many Confederate soldiers gave up hope. They left their army and went home.

On April 3, 1865, the Union army marched into Richmond. Six days later, on April 9, Lee surrendered to Grant at Appomattox Court House in Virginia.

Grant was generous. He let Confederate troops keep their horses. He had his men share their food with the starving Southerners. By the end of May, the rest of the Confederates had surrendered, too. After four bloody years, the Civil War was over and the Union was preserved.

Summary

In this chapter, you learned about the Civil War. You used images of both a Union and a Confederate soldier to organize information about life for these troops.

You read that soldiers on both sides chose to fight for different reasons. Some hoped for wealth or glory. Others had patriotic ideas.

Most of the fighting took place in the South. But two battles fought on northern soil were turning points in the war. The Battle of Antietam in 1862 was the bloodiest clash in U.S. military history. In 1863, General Lee tried to win in the North, at Gettysburg, Pennsylvania.

By visiting the battlefield at Gettysburg, you learned about many aspects of the war. You learned about soldiers' weapons and food. You learned about military tactics and technology. You read about the poor medical care available at the time. You also learned about hardships suffered on the home front. Finally, you learned how the Union won the war.

The North's victory made the United States one country again. It also brought an end to slavery. But the people of the South still faced many hardships. Former slaves had to build new lives as free people. Southern whites had to come to terms with a new social and political structure. Read on to find out about the South's struggles after the war.

The Civil War

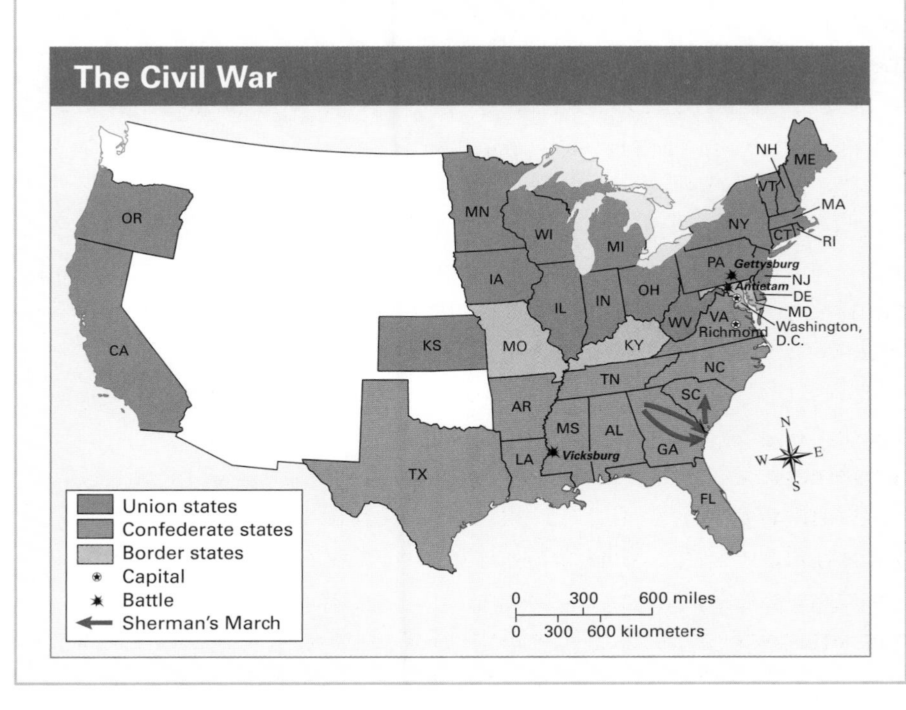

Reading Further 19

Life After Slavery in the South

The end of the Civil War brought an end to slavery. But many hard adjustments lay ahead for white Southerners and their former slaves. Both groups had to figure out how to survive under a new social and economic system. How did the people of the South meet these challenges?

Five days after the war ended, President Lincoln was shot and killed. He had planned to bring the nation together quickly and fairly. After his death, the national government would treat the South more harshly.

The Civil War left much of the South in ruins. Fighting had destroyed houses and farms. Union armies had burned cities and killed or wounded many people.

In addition, the end of the system of slavery became official when the Thirteenth Amendment to the United States Constitution went into effect in 1865. This was one of a series of laws and government actions that Congress ordered as it worked to reunite the country.

These ruins in Columbia, South Carolina, are one example of the damage the South suffered during the Civil War.

The Granger Collection, New York

The end of slavery struck another serious blow to the Southern economy. That economy had been largely built on farming. And much of that farming depended on the work of slaves. Moreover, many white landowners had spent much of their wealth on buying slaves. Now the slaves were free. The slaveholders had lost their investment.

Social life in the South had placed whites and African Americans into strict roles. Whites owned the land. African Americans did the work. **Reconstruction** overturned this way of life. Former slaves became citizens with the same basic rights as other Americans. For a while, life improved for former slaves. But white Southerners resisted these changes. They tried to keep African Americans in their old roles.

Reconstruction the process by which Congress tried to rebuild the South and reunite it with the Union after the Civil War

A New Way of Life

What might former slaves have thought at the end of the war? They were free at last. They did not have to suffer cruel treatment. They could go where they wished. There was even a rumor that the government would give each of them 40 acres and a mule. They could work for themselves and their families.

During Reconstruction, Congress set up the Freedmen's Bureau to help those in need in the South. Mostly, it helped former slaves. The bureau started thousands of schools that helped freed slaves learn to read and write. They also gained other skills that could help them earn a living.

At this time, federal soldiers protected black voters from whites who did not want them to gain political power. Freedmen, or former slaves, could vote in elections and helped build new governments that would protect their rights. In some places, African Americans cast votes to elect friendly candidates to the House of Representatives, the Senate, and the courts.

But making their own way in the South proved difficult for former slaves. They did not get free land. And many whites kept freedmen from building a better life.

During Reconstruction, federal troops in the South helped freed slaves to vote.

The Granger Collection, New York

Sharecroppers, like this Virginia family, worked hard, lived in poor conditions, and earned little.

The Granger Collection, New York

sharecropping a system of farming in which the worker is paid with a share of the crop he or she raises

A New Farming System

Some white Southerners wanted to make the new situation work. Plantation owners had always depended on slaves to work their fields. But now slavery was a thing of the past. The men and women that planters had once treated as property were free.

One Mississippi planter decided to try something new. He would hire the former slaves and again benefit from their labor. Only this time, he would have to pay for their work. He made an offer to the freedmen.

For three years, the freed slaves would work the planter's land. In return for this work, they would get a share of the crop. Then, after three years, the planter would divide the fields. The former slaves would rent sections of the land. They would be their own bosses and raise their own crops. They would pay for the land, seed, and tools by giving the landowner a share of their crops. They would keep what was left of their crops. Many former slaves agreed to this system. It became known as **sharecropping**.

But in some ways, life for sharecroppers did not change all that much. Again, African Americans worked the land for a white landowner. As before, they used his tools and animals and planted his seeds. They lived in shabby houses that slaves had lived in a few years earlier.

Sharecroppers kept a part of the crop they grew. Usually, this was not enough to live on. Often, the white landowner did not give them a fair price for their crop. And the landowner charged the freedmen very high rates for the use of his farming tools and equipment and for other supplies. In many cases, sharecroppers ended the year owing money to the landowner.

Southerners Clash

The sharecropping system spread across the South. A few former slaves were able to prosper. But many fell into a cycle of poverty and debt to white landowners.

Still, many whites were angry that former slaves were renting land. In Mississippi, white landowners worked to put into effect a new law. The law made it illegal for white planters to sell or rent land to former slaves.

But African Americans did not give up. Some fought against unfair sharecropping agreements and laws. They formed groups to help educate and support each other.

White Southerners feared such groups. Often, white mobs attacked gatherings of African Americans. They threatened black leaders. In fact, some white Southerners formed their own special groups to terrorize freedmen. One example was the Ku Klux Klan. At night, members in white robes attacked and even killed African Americans.

By 1877, Reconstruction was over. All the federal troops had left the South. White Southerners began to use fear to keep African Americans from voting. The Ku Klux Klan and other terror groups could now act freely. They became strong all across the South. And Southern states passed laws to separate blacks from whites and to limit the rights of African Americans. These became known as Jim Crow laws.

Many former slaves saw their dream of freedom fade. Some African Americans left the South. One group, known as the Exodusters, moved to Kansas. There, they started farms and built communities. A few freedmen moved back to Africa.

Many former slaves stayed in the South. Slavery had ended. But true freedom would remain, for some time, out of reach.

Many white Southerners clashed with freedmen once Reconstruction had ended.

The Granger Collection, New York

Why do you think these people are protesting?

In what city do you think this demonstration is taking place?

Industrialization and the Modern United States

20

How has life in the United States changed since the Civil War?

20.1 Introduction

In Chapter 19, you read about the Civil War. In this chapter, you will learn about changes in the United States since that time.

At the start of the 19th century, most Americans lived in the countryside. They worked the land, much as their grandparents had. But over time, people developed new inventions. And they found new ways of making products. These changes led people to leave their farms behind for life in the cities. There, they found work in factories and offices.

Changes came faster in the 20th century. Telephones, cars, and airplanes became common. Most homes had radios and then televisions. By the late 1900s, computers and other inventions had created faster ways to communicate. People around the world could share news instantly.

The 20th century was also a time of widespread wars that killed millions of people. These United States took part in these wars.

This century also saw economic and social changes. These helped shape the United States. After the economy collapsed in 1929, the government began to take a more active role in economic decisions. Social change would take place over a longer period of time. But starting in the 1950s, black Americans began pushing for changes in laws to bring equal rights to all Americans.

As the 21st century began, the nation was different from what it had been two hundred years earlier. As you read this chapter, use the timeline at right to organize the changes you read about.

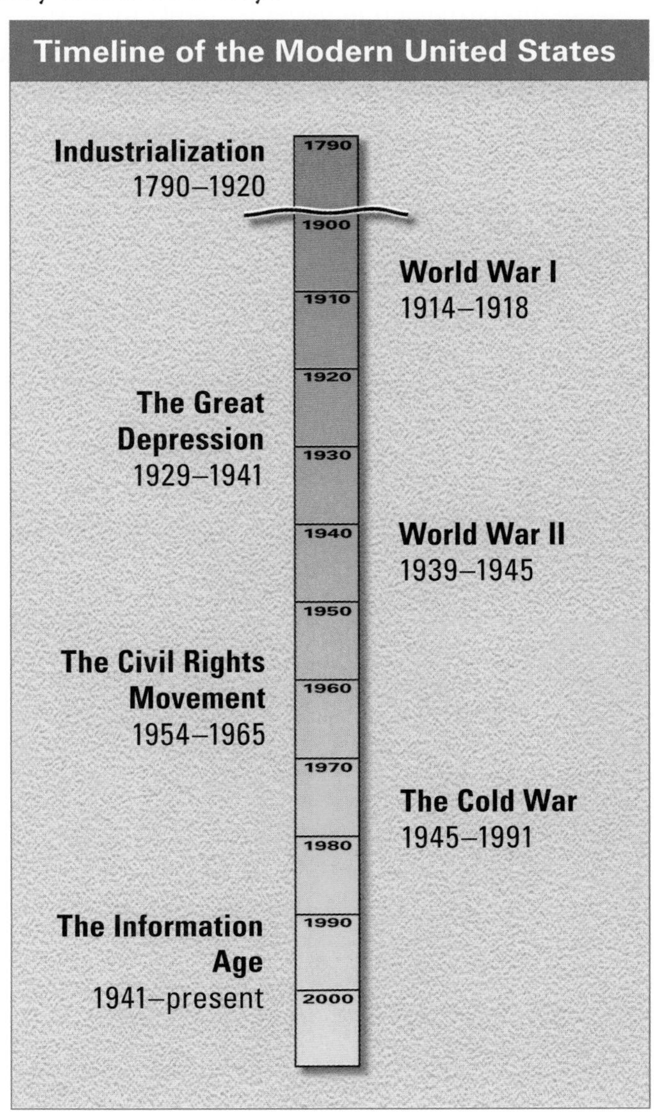

20.2 Industrialization

industrialization the process by which new inventions create industries that use factories to make products and that cause people to move from farms to cities for jobs

After the Civil War, **industrialization** changed the way Americans lived and worked. These changes had begun in the late 1700s. They came more quickly after the Civil War. Before this time, most people lived on farms or in small towns. They rarely traveled far from home. When they did, they were likely to go on foot or ride a horse.

By the mid-1800s, this slow pace of life was changing. Canals, steamboats, and railroads transported people and goods more quickly over longer distances. Many Americans moved to cities and took jobs in factories and offices.

After the Civil War, changes came even faster. The first transcontinental railroad was completed in 1869. Now, people and goods could travel across the entire United States in a week. Factories using new machines and processes could produce and ship huge quantities of items. These items had low prices that many people could afford. Americans who had once grown their own food and made their own clothes could now buy these goods in stores. More workers spent long days in factories.

Huge building projects were part of industrialization. New York City's Brooklyn Bridge, shown here, was one project of the era.

Industrialization continued into the 20th century. Soon, most homes had inventions such as telephones and electric lights. Cars replaced horses and carriages. New building materials, along with the invention of elevators, helped builders in cities create tall buildings called skyscrapers. Everything seemed to be getting bigger and faster.

20.3 World War I

World War I also called the Great War, a conflict fought from 1914 to 1918 by troops from 32 countries

In the summer of 1914, a war broke out in Europe. Today, we call it **World War I**. Competition and mistrust among European countries were its main causes.

For years, various nations had built up their armies and navies. As tensions grew, friendly nations promised to fight together if war broke out. One such group of nations was called the Central powers. It included Germany and Austria-Hungary. Another group was called the Allied forces, or the Allies. It included Russia, France, Italy, Japan, and Great Britain. In 1914, Russia and Austria-Hungary had a dispute. Soon, this conflict drew in other nations. In all, 32 countries, including the United States, became involved.

New inventions gave the armies dangerous weapons, including machine guns, tanks, and poison gas. These weapons enabled troops to kill one another by the thousands. Soldiers on both sides fought from trenches. During weeks and months of bloody battles, armies sometimes moved their trenches just a few yards. When the war ended after four years, more than 10 million soldiers were dead. So were 13 million civilians, many from starvation and disease.

In 1917, the United States entered the war on the side of the Allies. American troops helped defeat Germany and the other nations of the Central powers. After the war, France and Great Britain forced a treaty that punished Germany. The treaty took land from Germany and made the German people pay huge sums of money for the damage done in the war. This treaty created great hardships for the Germans. In time, it would help lead to another costly war.

During World War I, men spent months fighting from muddy trenches. Conditions were miserable, and millions died in the bloody battles.

Great Depression the worst economic slump in history, which began in the United States in 1929 and spread to other parts of the world, lasting until 1939

drought a long period with unusually low rainfall, which hurts growing and living conditions

20.4 The Great Depression

After World War I, the U.S. economy grew steadily. During the 1920s, many Americans put their money into stocks. Stocks are shares in the ownership of companies. When companies do well, the value of stocks goes up. If people sell their stocks at that time, they make money. Stocks are bought and sold on the stock market.

But in 1929, the good times came to an end. The nation entered a period of great hardship known as the **Great Depression**. On October 29, 1929, the stock market crashed. Stocks prices began to drop sharply. People tried to sell their stocks before prices got too low. But all the selling made prices drop even faster. And when people tried to withdraw their savings from banks, the banks did not have enough money. They had loaned it out and could not get it back. As a result, many Americans lost their savings. Soon, banks all over the country were closing.

The economic disaster continued throughout the 1930s. People could not afford to buy goods. This forced many businesses to close, causing workers to lose their jobs. Then the unemployed workers lost their homes. Many families had to live in tents and shacks.

To make matters worse, much of the farmland in the southern Great Plains was ruined by a long **drought**. Little grew. With no crops to sell, farmers lost their farms. More than 2 million people had to leave their land.

To help Americans during this hard time, the national government hired many workers. These workers built roads and bridges. They planted trees. They constructed dams to make electricity. Today, the government still plays a larger role in the economy than it did in the 1920s. And some programs that began in the Great Depression continue today—such as Social Security, which gives income to older and disabled people.

During the Great Depression, many families lost their jobs, homes, and savings.

20.5 World War II

In 1939, war again broke out in Europe. This new conflict, **World War II,** eventually drew in 61 countries. It also changed the role of the United States in the world.

World War II began when Germany's leader, Adolf Hitler, invaded Poland. Hitler had been in power since 1933. He told the German people that the treaty ending World War I was unfair under the terms of that treaty. He wanted Germany not only to take back the land it had lost, but to gain new territory, as well. Hitler also preached hatred against certain people. Among them were the Jewish people.

By mid-1941, Germany and its ally Italy controlled much of Europe and North Africa. Great Britain was under attack, and the Germans were preparing to invade the Soviet Union. The Soviet Union, or USSR, was formed in 1922. It was made up of Russia and the lands it controlled.

At the same time, another German ally, Japan, was invading lands in Asia and islands in the Pacific Ocean. In December 1941, Japan launched a surprise attack on American ships and planes in Pearl Harbor, Hawaii. The attack brought the United States into the war on the side of Great Britain.

By 1945, Hitler was defeated. Japan surrendered after the United States dropped a terrible new weapon, the atomic bomb, on two Japanese cities.

World War II was the most deadly war in history. More than 50 million people died. Among them were 6 million Jews murdered by Hitler's followers. Much of Europe was left in ruins.

After the war, the United States and the Soviet Union became the world's superpowers, or most powerful nations. Since that time, the United States has remained involved in events taking place around the world.

World War II a conflict fought from 1939 to 1945 by troops from 61 countries; the most costly war in history in the number of people killed and the amount of property destroyed

During World War II, the United States had to fight on two fronts—in Europe and in Asia. Here, U.S. soldiers raise the American flag on Iwo Jima, Japan, after a terrible battle against Japan's troops.

Cold War the struggle between democratic nations, led by the United States, and communist nations, led by the Soviet Union, that lasted from 1945 until 1991

nuclear weapons a weapon that releases huge amounts of energy contained in the nuclei (centers) of atoms

20.6 The Cold War

After 1945, a new kind of conflict began between the United States and the Soviet Union. Each supported its own allies around the world as those countries fought hot wars, or conflicts with weapons. But because the two superpowers never fought each other directly, their clash was called the **Cold War**.

The Cold War was a struggle between two types of government and two ways of life. The United States favored economic freedom and a democratic form of government. The Soviet Union favored a system called communism. Under the Soviet Union's form of communism, the government controlled the economy and gave its people little freedom.

Each side wanted other countries to follow its example. The Soviet Union supported communists who tried to take power in the governments of other countries. The United States worked to stop the spread of communism.

Many people died in wars between communists and noncommunists around the world. One such conflict was in Vietnam, in Southeast Asia. In these wars, the United States and the Soviet Union supported opposite sides with money, weapons, and soldiers.

Each superpower feared an attack from the other. To protect themselves, they built up their supplies of **nuclear weapons**. This competition was called the arms race. The two countries soon had more than enough powerful weapons to destroy the world.

There was also competition to reach space first. In the late 1950s, both countries launched satellites, and then rockets, into orbit around Earth. And both sent manned spacecrafts into space.

The final step in the Cold War took place in 1991. At that time, the lands under the control of the Soviet Union declared their independence. But the effects of the Cold War are still felt today. Several countries now have nuclear weapons. There is a danger that someday these will be used. Former Soviet countries still struggle to maintain stable governments and economies.

This cartoon shows the Cold War race between the United States (left) and the Soviet Union (right) to produce more nuclear weapons.

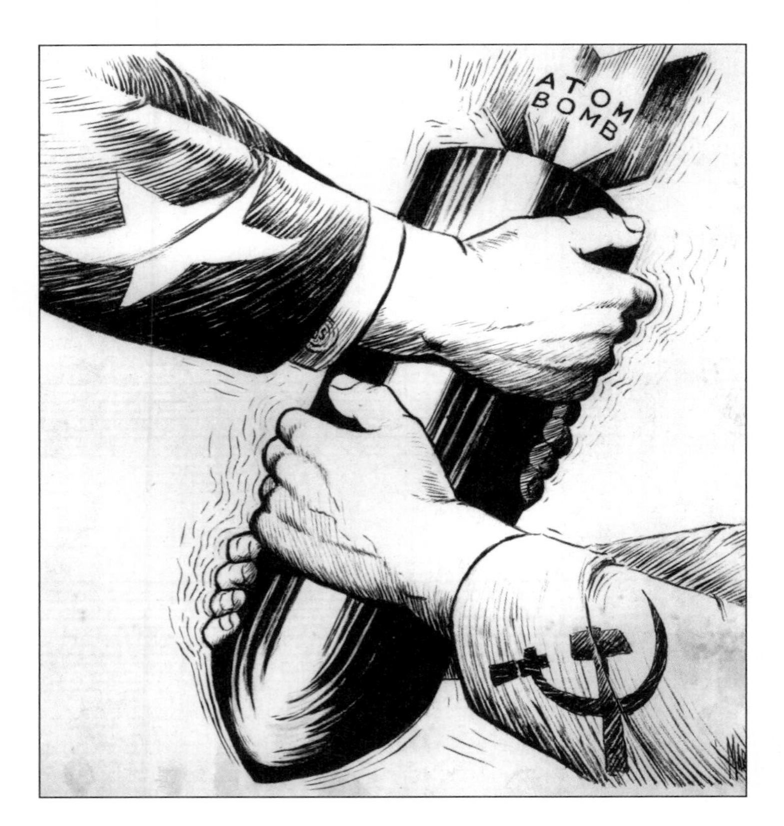

20.7 The Civil Rights Movement

The Civil War ended slavery in the nation. But blacks still faced discrimination, or unfair treatment. In the 1950s and 1960s, people worked to bring about change. This struggle for equal rights was called the **civil rights movement**.

The movement began as a fight against **segregation** in the South. Since the late 1800s, laws and customs in Southern states had separated white and black people. Whites had their own schools, restaurants, hotels, and parks. Blacks couldn't use the water fountains or swimming pools provided for whites. Blacks had to sit in the back of buses and theaters. The facilities for blacks were not as nice as those for whites.

In the 1950s, civil rights leaders planned protests against segregation. African Americans marched in the streets. They tried to get served in white-only restaurants. They refused to sit in the back seats on buses.

Often, blacks and whites working for civil rights were attacked by whites who wanted segregation. Some civil rights workers were killed.

Martin Luther King Jr. was an important civil rights leader. King believed in non-violent protest. His courage and speeches touched millions of people. In 1963, King led more than 200,000 people in a march on Washington, D.C. There, he thrilled many Americans by describing his dream of a day when all people would be treated with equal respect. In the spring of 1968, King was shot and killed while helping black workers in Memphis, Tennessee.

The civil rights movement resulted in laws that protect the rights of all Americans. It also led the way for other groups, such as Mexican Americans and women, to fight against unfair treatment.

In 2008, a new milestone in equality was reached. Barack Obama, a black American, was elected the 44th president of the country.

civil rights movement an organized effort, beginning in the 1950s, to achieve equal rights for black Americans

segregation the separation of people, especially by race; in the years after the Civil War, until the 1960s, a practice enforced in the South by laws and customs

Barack Obama was elected the 44th president and the first black president of the United States on November 4, 2008.

Information Age the period from the start of commercial television (1941) to the present day, in which there is widespread electronic access to information through technology such as computers

20.8 The Information Age

Since World War II, inventions such as the television and the computer have changed the way people communicate and share information. This period is called the **Information Age**.

In the 1950s, television replaced radio as the most popular form of entertainment in people's homes. It also became a major source of information. By the 1990s, more Americans got their news from TV than from newspapers.

Computers caused greater changes. At first, they were huge machines that filled entire rooms and worked slowly. By the 1960s, the machines were more accurate and quicker, allowing many businesses to use computers to do jobs that workers had previously done.

Over time, engineers kept designing computers that were smaller, faster, and more powerful. After the first personal computer was made in 1975, companies began to sell computers that could fit on a desk. People could now use computers to access information both at work and at home. Tiny computers also made their way into other products, such as videocassette recorders (VCRs).

In the 1990s, the Information Age saw the development of the Internet and the World Wide Web. The Internet allowed computers to communicate and share information. The Web brought pictures and sounds to the Internet and made using it easier. People could send messages around the world in seconds. They could get information from millions of sources. This technology created many new jobs in which people use computers to work with information.

Advances occur each year. Today, portable laptop computers are common. Many people own tiny handheld computers that play music and videos. And eight out of ten Americans have cell phones. These can also take photographs and connect to the Internet. Wireless access to the World Wide Web is found in many places. Satellites that orbit Earth allow people to use portable navigation systems in their cars. Who knows what new technology there will be in the years to come?

These students are using a portable laptop computer with wireless Internet access in their school.

Space travel such as this shuttle launch has led to many discoveries that have advanced the Information Age.

Summary

In this chapter, you learned about periods of change in the United States since the end of the Civil War. You used a timeline to organize these periods, from industrialization through the Information Age.

Starting in the late 1700s, inventions and new processes changed the way products were made. This affected where Americans lived and worked.

With new machines, wars became more deadly. In the first half of the 20th century, two widespread wars were fought. The Cold War followed. During this time, the United States and the Soviet Union made weapons that could destroy the world.

Between the two world wars, the Great Depression caused severe hardship for millions of Americans. In response, the U.S. government expanded its focus and took a more active role in the nation's economy.

In the 1950s, two other key changes began to alter American life. The civil rights movement brought more equal rights to black Americans. The Information Age brought instant ways to communicate, enabling people everywhere to get and use large amounts of data. New advances in technology made each year will continue to change American life.

Reading Further 20

Challenges and Hope for Immigrants

Since the Civil War, millions of immigrants have steadily arrived in the United States. Life for these newcomers is not easy. The nation demands much from its people. There are many challenges. Yet, for people such as Trong and Thanh, the rewards are great. What does this country offer people seeking a better life?

For people around the world, the United States stands for many things. Some people see it as a land of freedom. Americans have rights and duties as citizens of a democracy, such as choosing their leaders in elections. Other people view the nation as a land of opportunity. Newcomers can find jobs and get an education. Hard workers can earn a living and sometimes even achieve wealth. Children in an immigrant family have prospects for a good life. These are some of the reasons why so many people have been drawn to this country.

For Trong and Thanh, however, the United States was a place of safety. They escaped with their five children from a government that threatened them. They fled as bombs fell around them. It was 1975. The long Vietnam War was ending. Trong and Thanh had fought for the losing side and were now in danger.

U.S. military helicopters, such as the one shown below, helped many Vietnamese people escape at the end of the Vietnam War. The refugees took only what they could carry as they fled to a new land.

Trong recalled his thoughts as a U.S. helicopter flew him and his family to safety. "I had mixed emotions. I felt that we were going to heaven—the United States. But I already missed my country."

Trong, Thanh, and their children slowly built new lives in the United States. In the process, they helped to change their community—and to make their new country a stronger and richer place.

Working with Americans

Trong and Thanh grew up in Vietnam. But they had a long and strong connection with the United States.

In World War II, Trong's father volunteered to fight with a Vietnamese force that performed secret missions for the United States and its British allies. Recall that the United States and Great Britain fought against Japan in this war. The Japanese had sent their armies into Vietnam and other parts of Southeast Asia. Trong's father worked to help the Allies successfully defeat them.

In 2005, Americans and Vietnamese immigrants who had fought together gathered at a Vietnam War memorial in California to honor those who died in battle.

Years later, Trong himself served with U.S. soldiers in the Vietnam War. This war pitted Vietnamese who favored communism against Vietnamese who did not. The United States fought on the side of the non-communists. The war started in 1946. It would last for more than 30 years.

In this war, Trong did a number of jobs. He was a soldier. Later, he worked as a translator for the Americans. But the war ended badly for the United States—and for Trong. By 1973, the United States had decided to pull its soldiers out of the country. It signed a peace treaty with the communists. But the fighting in Vietnam continued. By 1975, the communists had won. Their forces controlled the country. Trong and other Vietnamese who had helped the United States were in danger. They had to flee.

The U.S. government knew that people like Trong were in trouble. Although there are rules limiting who can move to this country, U.S. leaders allowed Trong and about 135,000 other Vietnamese to move to the United States. Many others would come in the years that followed.

These children are studying English in a Vietnamese-English program at an elementary school in Austin, Texas.

Starting a New Life

At first, Trong and Thanh needed a lot of help. Most of their belongings were left behind when a helicopter took them away from Vietnam. "The evacuation will be very fast, like lightning," Trong told his family. "We don't want people left behind because of suitcases." When they reached the United States, they needed clothes, food, and a place to stay. For these things, they relied for a time on the help of American sponsors.

But Trong and Thanh were proud. They found it hard to depend on the help of others. Within a year of coming to the United States, they struck out on their own.

Life was difficult. They settled in a high-crime neighborhood. Both Trong and Thanh had to work to support their family. It was hard to care for their children. But the couple did the best they could. "We had Vietnamese pride and did not want to take public aid," recalled Trong. "We wanted the American community and authorities to respect us."

This respect did not come easily. "You come here and take our jobs," a co-worker once told Thanh. "Go back wherever you came from." And the children faced teasing at school. Learning English was another challenge for Thanh and the children.

The family also had to adjust to a new way of life. For example, in Vietnam, people did not need to lock their doors. Trong and Thanh soon discovered that they needed locks in their neighborhood. They made other adjustments too.

Still, Trong and Thanh kept trying. They helped themselves by helping others. Trong took a job with a group that helped immigrants. He organized the people in his community. There were many **refugees** from Vietnam and other nations in Southeast Asia. Trong showed these people how to build new lives in the United States. He helped them find solutions to their problems. For example, Trong helped residents work together to combat the crime in the neighborhood. Slowly, conditions began to improve for everyone.

refugee someone who flees from his or her home to another place or country to find safety

Trong also helped neighbors start businesses. These businesses provided jobs and income to immigrants, which made the community stronger. Soon, the former slum was thriving. People came from other neighborhoods to visit the shops and restaurants. Trong and Thanh opened a restaurant that served food from Vietnam. "The first year of the restaurant business was miserable," Trong reported. "But with time, the business grew."

The children were growing up in a new culture. They worked in the restaurant but also liked American clothes and music. They had dreams. One might go to college. One might become a doctor. Anything was possible in their new country.

Trong and Thanh watched their children adapt to different ways. They had all worked hard to become American citizens. It was sometimes difficult to leave parts of their old culture behind. But they would keep some of their traditions. And they looked forward to a bright future in their new homeland.

A large community of Vietnamese Americans lives in California. Many of them enjoy shopping at Saigon Plaza (shown below.)

Being a Good Citizen

Vote!

Introduction to Citizenship

In the Declaration of Independence, Thomas Jefferson wrote that all people are born with certain rights. These include the rights to life, liberty, and the pursuit of happiness.

Jefferson and the other great thinkers who founded our country wanted to protect these rights. They did not want a few powerful people to violate or take away the rights of Americans.

These men created a system of government that they described in a new constitution. And American citizens accepted this government.

A citizen is someone who lives under and owes loyalty to a government. In return for this loyalty, citizens are entitled to certain rights and privileges. And the government provides them with law and order, security, and services.

Who is an American citizen? Anyone born on United States soil is a citizen. The child of an American citizen is also a citizen, even if born outside the United States. People from other countries can also become American citizens. They must go through a process called naturalization. This includes studying English, learning about the history of the United States, passing a test, and taking an oath of allegiance.

Citizens understand the need for a national government. It creates laws, makes treaties with other nations, and collects taxes. It uses tax money to pay for the nation's armed forces, roads and bridges, and other citizen needs.

But Americans believe in a limited government. Our government is of, by, and for the people. This means that U.S. citizens have the power to decide what the government will and will not do. The government protects our rights and provides necessary services. But we hold the power. We elect the people who lead us. And they have power only as long as we allow it.

Our Rights

Americans are born with the right to life, liberty, and the pursuit of happiness. We also enjoy other rights. Our Constitution guarantees these rights, and our laws protect them.

The ten amendments in the Bill of Rights list many of our basic rights. The First Amendment declares that we have the right of free speech. We are free to share our ideas in public—including criticism of our government. People living in some countries do not have this right. They can go to jail for speaking out against their government.

The First Amendment also tells us that we are free to worship in any way we want. The U.S. government cannot support one religion or make people take part in it. Countries in some parts of the world are ruled by religious leaders and their laws reflect certain religious beliefs and practices.

The Fourth Amendment protects Americans from being searched or seized by the government in an unfair way. In some

countries, the police can arrest people or search their homes for no clear reason. But in the United States, that is not allowed.

The Fifth Amendment limits the government's power to take away our property. This is an example of an economic right. The founders of our nation believed that the right to own and enjoy property was vital. Without this right, they believed, freedom would be meaningless.

We have many rights beyond those listed in the Bill of Rights. For example, we have political rights—that is, rights for taking part in government affairs. A key political right of U.S. citizens is the right to vote. Another is running for and holding office.

Our rights do have limits. We cannot use our rights in ways that take away other people's rights. For example, we have freedom of speech, but we cannot say untrue things that might hurt another person. And we cannot falsely yell "fire" in a crowded place and cause a panic. We must exercise our rights in a responsible way. We must respect other people's rights.

Our Responsibilities

With our rights come responsibilities. These are ways in which good citizens behave in order to ensure the well-being of our country. Some are things we must do, such as obeying laws, paying taxes, and serving on a jury. Others are voluntary actions, such as voting and serving in the armed forces.

Citizens must obey the law. Laws protect everyone's rights. When we break the law, we threaten other people's life, liberty, and pursuit of happiness.

Citizens support the government by paying taxes. The government uses this money to do its many jobs. Our taxes pay for the soldiers who protect us. Taxes pay for roads that let us travel with ease. State and local taxes pay for police and fire departments and for our schools, libraries, and parks. Paying taxes is a big part of being a responsible citizen.

Citizens must also serve on juries. We all have a right to a fair trial. Juries help make sure that anyone can get such a trial.

Citizens hold the power of government. One way they use that power is by electing people to serve in government. Citizens can help select the U.S. president and members of

Congress. They can vote for their governor and members of their state government. They can also choose the mayor and other officials of their city or town. Those who are elected serve as representatives of the voters. For this system to work well, citizens need to vote. If they do not vote, they give up their power. Therefore, voting is both a right and a responsibility.

Citizens should make informed decisions. They need to find out about candidates and issues on which they will vote. In the past, citizens could get information by listening to candidates speak, talking with friends, and reading newspapers. Today, voters can also learn by watching television and doing research on the Internet. Then they must use reading and thinking skills to understand the information they have gathered.

Citizens can also shape the actions of government in other ways. They can contact public officials, sign petitions, take part in peaceful demonstrations, and work on or give money to political campaigns or parties.

Some Americans choose to join the nation's armed forces. They act as good citizens by serving in the military and protecting the country.

Students and Citizenship

Young citizens exercise some rights and responsibilities only when they reach a certain age. Usually, you must be 18 in order to have the political right to vote or run for office. You must also be 18 to gain the full economic right to own property.

To keep you safe and help you learn, your school may limit some student rights. For example, schools have wide power to search students. They do this in order to keep drugs and weapons out of schools.

Still, the rights guaranteed in the Constitution apply to people of all ages—including students. Standards may vary in different settings. But students enjoy such basic rights as freedom of speech and freedom of religion, just like other Americans. As you get older, you will be able to enjoy more rights and responsibilities of citizenship.

Students have important responsibilities to fulfill as good citizens. One of these is to work hard in school. Remember, citizens are responsible for being informed voters. They must be able to sort through and examine a great deal of information. They must be able to weigh the benefits and drawbacks of different ideas. These are skills that you develop in school. They help you to become a good citizen.

Students must also obey the laws and rules that apply to them. Laws are enforced by the government. Other rules apply at home, at school, and in the community.

Someday soon you may get a job and receive a paycheck. You may already earn some money. Even as a young person, you may be responsible for filling out a tax return. This is a responsibility of citizenship that people of all ages share.

You may not be old enough to exercise all of your rights and responsibilities. But there are many ways to become involved in civic life. You can take part in efforts to make your home, your school, or your community a better place.

The students at Evergreen High School in Washington offer an example of good citizenship. These students were getting ready for a state academic competition. But they saw that their education had not prepared them to answer many questions about their state government. They decided to write to their representative in the state government.

The students gave their representative an outline of a proposed law. It would require Washington schools to teach students about the state's government. She agreed to help them.

The students designed an action plan. To build support for their law, they met with officials in the state government. They got the officials to back their law. They also spoke to committees in the state legislature that were considering the proposal.

These efforts paid off. The Washington legislature passed the proposed law. Thanks to the work of this group, Washington's students will now receive important lessons about their government. They will be better prepared to be good citizens.

The success of these students proves that by working together, young people can achieve a lot. Individuals can also accomplish a lot. For example, you can start a recycling program at your home or at school. Or you can organize a cleanup for your community. You can volunteer to visit patients in a hospital or you can work on a political campaign.

The key is to get involved. Take an active part in your community. Help make it a better place. You will be doing your job as a good citizen.

In Congress, July 4, 1776
The unanimous Declaration of the thirteen united States of America

Preamble (Introduction)
The Preamble explains why the Declaration was written. The Declaration is a statement to the world that explains why the colonies believe they should be independent.

When in the Course of human events it becomes necessary for one people to dissolve the political bonds which have connected them with another and to assume among the powers of the earth, the separate and equal station to which the Laws of Nature and of Nature's God entitle them, a decent respect to the opinions of mankind requires that they should declare the causes which impel them to the separation.

Statement of Human Rights
This section boldly states that all people have rights that no government can take away. Three of these rights are life, liberty, and the pursuit of happiness. If a government does not respect these rights, the people have the right to change the government. By his actions, the King has failed to respect the colonists' rights.

We hold these truths to be self-evident, that all men are created equal, that they are endowed by their Creator with certain unalienable Rights, that among these are Life, Liberty and the pursuit of Happiness. —That to secure these rights, Governments are instituted among Men, deriving their just powers from the consent of the governed, —That whenever any Form of Government becomes destructive of these ends, it is the Right of the People to alter or to abolish it, and to institute new Government, laying its foundation on such principles and organizing its powers in such form, as to them shall seem most likely to effect their Safety and Happiness. Prudence, indeed, will dictate that Governments long established should not be changed for light and transient causes; and accordingly all experience hath shewn that mankind are more disposed to suffer, while evils are sufferable than to right themselves by abolishing the forms to which they are accustomed. But when a long train of abuses and usurpations, pursuing invariably the same Object evinces a design to reduce them under absolute Despotism, it is their right, it is their duty, to throw off such Government, and to provide new Guards for their future security. —Such has been the patient sufferance of these Colonies; and such is now the necessity which constrains them to alter their former Systems of Government. The history of the present King of Great Britain is a history of repeated injuries and usurpations, all having in direct object the establishment of an absolute Tyranny over these States. To prove this, let Facts be submitted to a candid world.

Statement of Charges Against the King
This section lists more than 20 ways that the King has violated the colonists' rights. By interfering with laws, the King has taken away the colonists' right to govern themselves. Some of his laws have prevented the colonists from pursuing happiness in their own way. And by sending soldiers to fight the colonists, he has even threatened their right to life.

He has refused his Assent to Laws, the most wholesome and necessary for the public good.

He has forbidden his Governors to pass Laws of immediate and pressing importance, unless suspended in their operation till his Assent should be obtained; and when so suspended, he has utterly neglected to attend to them.

He has refused to pass other Laws for the accommodation of large districts of people, unless those people would relinquish the right of Representation in the Legislature, a right inestimable to them and formidable to tyrants only.

He has called together legislative bodies at places unusual, uncomfortable, and distant from the depository of their Public Records, for the sole purpose of fatiguing them into compliance with his measures.

He has dissolved Representative Houses repeatedly, for opposing with manly firmness his invasions on the rights of the people.

He has refused for a long time, after such dissolutions, to cause others to be elected, whereby the Legislative Powers, incapable of Annihilation, have returned to the People at large for their exercise; the State remaining in the mean time exposed to all the dangers of invasion from without, and convulsions within.

He has endeavoured to prevent the population of these States; for that purpose obstructing the Laws for Naturalization of Foreigners; refusing to pass others to encourage their migrations hither, and raising the conditions of new Appropriations of Lands.

He has obstructed the Administration of Justice by refusing his Assent to Laws for establishing Judiciary Powers.

He has made Judges dependent on his Will alone for the tenure of their offices, and the amount and payment of their salaries.

He has erected a multitude of New Offices, and sent hither swarms of Officers to harass our people and eat out their substance.

He has kept among us, in times of peace, Standing Armies without the Consent of our legislatures.

He has affected to render the Military independent of and superior to the Civil Power.

He has combined with others to subject us to a jurisdiction foreign to our constitution, and unacknowledged by our laws; giving his Assent to their Acts of pretended Legislation:

For quartering large bodies of armed troops among us:

For protecting them, by a mock Trial from punishment for any Murders which they should commit on the Inhabitants of these States:

For cutting off our Trade with all parts of the world:

For imposing Taxes on us without our Consent:
For depriving us in many cases, of the benefit of Trial by Jury:

For transporting us beyond Seas to be tried for pretended offences:

For abolishing the free System of English Laws in a neighbouring Province, establishing therein an Arbitrary government, and enlarging its Boundaries so as to render it at once an example and fit instrument for introducing the same absolute rule into these Colonies:

For taking away our Charters, abolishing our most valuable Laws and altering fundamentally the Forms of our Governments:

For suspending our own Legislatures, and declaring themselves invested with power to legislate for us in all cases whatsoever.
He has abdicated Government here, by declaring us out of his Protection and waging War against us.

He has plundered our seas, ravaged our Coasts burnt our towns, and destroyed the lives of our people.

He is at this time transporting large Armies of foreign Mercenaries to compleat the works of death, desolation, and tyranny, already begun with circumstances of Cruelty & Perfidy scarcely paralleled in the most barbarous ages, and totally unworthy the Head of a civilized nation.

He has constrained our fellow Citizens taken Captive on the high Seas to bear Arms against their Country, to become the executioners of their friends and Brethren, or to fall themselves by their Hands.

He has excited domestic insurrections amongst us, and has endeavoured to bring on the inhabitants of our frontiers, the merciless Indian Savages whose known rule of warfare, is an undistinguished destruction of all ages, sexes and conditions.

The Government's Failure to Answer the Colonists' Complaints
This section states that the colonists have tried many times to solve their problems with Great Britain peacefully. Both the King and the British government have failed to answer their complaints. For this reason, the colonists have no choice except to break away from Great Britain.

In every stage of these Oppressions We have Petitioned for Redress in the most humble terms: Our repeated Petitions have been answered only by repeated injury. A Prince, whose character is thus marked by every act which may define a Tyrant, is unfit to be the ruler of a free people.

Nor have We been wanting in attentions to our British brethren. We have warned them from time to time of attempts by their legislature to extend an unwarrantable jurisdiction over us. We have reminded them of the circumstances of our emigration and settlement here. We have appealed to their native justice and magnanimity, and we have conjured them by the ties of our common kindred to disavow these usurpations, which would inevitably interrupt our connections and correspondence. They too have been deaf to the voice of justice and of consanguinity. We must, therefore, acquiesce in the necessity, which denounces our

Separation, and hold them, as we hold the rest of mankind, Enemies in War, in Peace Friends.

We, therefore, the Representatives of the United States of America, in General Congress, Assembled, appealing to the Supreme Judge of the world for the rectitude of our intentions, do, in the Name, and by Authority of the good People of these Colonies, solemnly publish and declare, That these United Colonies are, and of Right ought to be Free and Independent States, that they are Absolved from all Allegiance to the British Crown, and that all political connection between them and the State of Great Britain, is and ought to be totally dissolved; and that as Free and Independent States, they have full Power to levy War, conclude Peace contract Alliances, establish Commerce, and to do all other Acts and Things which Independent States may of right do. —And for the support of this Declaration, with a firm reliance on the protection of Divine Providence, we mutually pledge to each other our Lives, our Fortunes and our sacred Honor.

John Hancock

Statement of Independence
This section declares the colonies' independence. The writers of the Declaration emphasize that they are acting as the representatives of the people. As the Preamble stated, it is the people who have the right to form a new government. The colonies are now a separate country that has all the powers and rights of other nations.

New Hampshire: Josiah Bartlett, William Whipple, Matthew Thornton

Massachusetts: John Hancock, Samuel Adams, John Adams, Robert Treat Paine, Elbridge Gerry

Rhode Island: Stephen Hopkins, William Ellery

Connecticut: Roger Sherman, Samuel Huntington, William Williams, Oliver Wolcott

New York: William Floyd, Philip Livingston, Francis Lewis, Lewis Morris

New Jersey: Richard Stockton, John Witherspoon, Francis Hopkinson, John Hart, Abraham Clark

Pennsylvania: Robert Morris, Benjamin Rush, Benjamin Franklin, John Morton, George Clymer, James Smith, George Taylor, James Wilson, George Ross

Delaware: Caesar Rodney, George Read, Thomas McKean

Maryland: Samuel Chase, William Paca, Thomas Stone, Charles Carroll of Carrollton

Virginia: George Wythe, Richard Henry Lee, Thomas Jefferson, Benjamin Harrison, Thomas Nelson, Jr., Francis Lightfoot Lee, Carter Braxton

North Carolina: William Hooper, Joseph Hewes, John Penn

South Carolina: Edward Rutledge, Thomas Heyward, Jr., Thomas Lynch, Jr., Arthur Middleton

Georgia: Button Gwinnett, Lyman Hall, George Walton

Preamble
The Preamble says that the Constitution receives its authority from the people of the United States. The people agree to form a government to protect their rights and provide for safety and order.

We the people of the United States, in Order to form a more perfect Union, establish Justice, insure domestic Tranquility, provide for the common defence, promote the general Welfare, and secure the Blessings of Liberty to ourselves and our Posterity, do ordain and establish this Constitution for the United States of America.

Article I: The Legislative Branch
The government's lawmaking branch is Congress, made up of a Senate and a House of Representatives. The comments below point out some of the specific powers of this branch.

Article I

Section 1. All legislative Powers herein granted shall be vested in a Congress of the United States, which shall consist of a Senate and House of Representatives.

Section 2. The House of Representatives shall be composed of Members chosen every second Year by the People of the several States, and the Electors in each State shall have the Qualifications requisite for Electors of the most numerous Branch of the State Legislature.

No Person shall be a Representative who shall not have attained to the Age of twenty five Years, and been seven Years a Citizen of the United States, and who shall not, when elected, be an Inhabitant of that State in which he shall be chosen.

Representation in the House: In the House, the number of representatives for each state depends on the number of people who live in the state.

[Representatives and direct Taxes shall be apportioned among the several States which may be included within this Union, according to their respective Numbers, which shall be determined by adding to the whole Number of free Persons, including those bound to Service for a Term of Years, and excluding Indians not taxed, three fifths of all other Persons.][1] The actual Enumeration shall be made within three Years after the first Meeting of the Congress of the United States, and within every subsequent Term of ten Years, in such Manner as they shall by Law direct. The number of Representatives shall not exceed one for every thirty Thousand, but each State shall have at Least one Representative; and until such enumeration shall be made, the State of New Hampshire shall be entitled to choose three, Massachusetts eight, Rhode-Island and Providence Plantations one, Connecticut five, New-York six, New Jersey four, Pennsylvania eight, Delaware one, Maryland six, Virginia ten, North Carolina five, South Carolina five, and Georgia three.

When vacancies happen in the Representation from any State, the Executive Authority thereof shall issue Writs of Election to fill such Vacancies.

Checks and balances: Impeachment. Only the House has the power to impeach federal officials.

The House of Representatives shall choose their Speaker and other Officers; and shall have the sole Power of Impeachment.

1. Changed by Section 2 of the Fourteenth Amendment

Section 3. The Senate of the United States shall be composed of two Senators from each State, [chosen by the Legislature thereof,][2] for six Years; and each Senator shall have one Vote.

Representation in the Senate: Each state is represented by two Senators.

Immediately after they shall be assembled in Consequence of the first Election, they shall be divided as equally as may be into three Classes. The Seats of the Senators of the first Class shall be vacated at the Expiration of the second Year, of the second Class at the Expiration of the fourth Year, and of the third Class at the Expiration of the sixth Year, so that one third may be chosen every second Year; [and if Vacancies happen by Resignation, or otherwise, during the Recess of the Legislature of any State, the Executive thereof may make temporary Appointments until the next Meeting of the Legislature, which shall then fill such Vacancies.][3]

No Person shall be a Senator who shall not have attained to the Age of thirty Years, and been nine Years a Citizen of the United States, and who shall not, when elected, be an Inhabitant of that State for which he shall be chosen.

The Vice President of the United States shall be President of the Senate, but shall have no Vote, unless they be equally divided.

The Senate shall choose their other Officers, and also a President pro tempore, in the Absence of the Vice President, or when he shall exercise the Office of President of the United States.

The Senate shall have the sole Power to try all Impeachments. When sitting for that Purpose, they shall be on Oath or Affirmation. When the President of the United States is tried, the Chief Justice shall preside: And no Person shall be convicted without the Concurrence of two thirds of the Members present.

Checks and balances: Impeachment. Only the Senate has the power to put impeached officials on trial.

Judgment in Cases of Impeachment shall not extend further than to removal from Office, and disqualification to hold and enjoy any Office of honor, Trust or Profit under the United States: but the Party convicted shall nevertheless be liable and subject to Indictment, Trial, Judgment and Punishment, according to Law.

Section 4. The Times, Places and Manner of holding Elections for Senators and Representatives, shall be prescribed in each State by the Legislature thereof; but the Congress may at any time by Law make or alter such Regulations, except as to the Places of choosing Senators.

2. Changed by the Seventeenth Amendment
3. Changed by the Seventeenth Amendment

The Congress shall assemble at least once in every Year, and such Meeting shall be [on the first Monday in December,][4] unless they shall by Law appoint a different Day.

Section 5. Each House shall be the Judge of the Elections, Returns and Qualifications of its own Members, and a Majority of each shall constitute a Quorum to do Business, but a smaller Number may adjourn from day to day, and may be authorized to compel the Attendance of absent Members, in such Manner, and under such Penalties as each House may provide.

Each House may determine the Rules of its Proceedings, punish its Members for disorderly Behaviour, and, with the Concurrence of two thirds, expel a Member.

Each House shall keep a Journal of its Proceedings, and from time to time publish the same, excepting such Parts as may in their Judgment require Secrecy; and the Yeas and Nays of the Members of either House on any question shall, at the Desire of one fifth of those Present, be entered on the Journal.

Neither House, during the Session of Congress, shall, without the Consent of the other, adjourn for more than three days, nor to any other Place than that in which the two Houses shall be sitting.

Section 6. The Senators and Representatives shall receive a Compensation for their Services, to be ascertained by law, and paid out of the Treasury of the United States. They shall in all Cases, except Treason, Felony and Breach of the Peace, be privileged from Arrest during their Attendance at the Session of their respective Houses, and in going to and returning from the same; and for any Speech or Debate in either House, they shall not be questioned in any other Place.

No Senator or Representative shall, during the Time for which he was elected, be appointed to any civil Office under the Authority of the United States, which shall have been created, or the Emoluments whereof shall have been encreased during such time; and no Person holding any Office under the United States, shall be a Member of either House during his Continuance in Office.

Proposing laws: Either house of Congress can propose and vote on new laws. Only the House can propose new taxes.

Section 7. All Bills for raising Revenue shall originate in the House of Representatives; but the Senate may propose or concur with Amendments as on other Bills.

4. Changed by Section 2 of the Twentieth Amendment

Every Bill which shall have passed the House of Representatives and the Senate, shall, before it becomes a Law, be presented to the President of the United States; If he approve he shall sign it, but if not he shall return it, with his Objections to that House in which it shall have originated, who shall enter the Objections at large on their Journal, and proceed to reconsider it. If after such Reconsideration two thirds of that House shall agree to pass the Bill, it shall be sent, together with the Objections, to the other House, by which it shall likewise be reconsidered, and if approved by two thirds of that House, it shall become a Law. But in all such Cases the Votes of both Houses shall be determined by Yeas and Nays, and the Names of the Persons voting for and against the Bill shall be entered on the Journal of each House respectively. If any Bill shall not be returned by the President within ten Days (Sundays excepted) after it shall have been presented to him, the Same shall be a Law, in like Manner as if he had signed it, unless the Congress by their Adjournment prevent its Return, in which Case it shall not be a Law.

Checks and balances: Overriding the President's veto. Bills passed by Congress become laws when the President signs them. If the President vetoes (rejects) a bill, Congress can overrule the President's veto by a two-thirds vote of both houses.

Every Order, Resolution, or Vote to which the Concurrence of the Senate and House of Representatives may be necessary (except on a question of Adjournment) shall be pre-sented to the President of the United States, and before the Same shall take Effect, shall be approved by him, or being disapproved by him, shall be repassed by two thirds of the Senate and House of Representatives, according to the Rules and Limitations prescribed in the Case of a Bill.

Section 8. The Congress shall have Power To lay and collect Taxes, Duties, Imposts and Excises, to pay the Debts and provide for the common Defence and general Welfare of the United States; but all Duties, Imposts and Excises shall be uniform throughout the United States

Creating and collecting taxes: Congress has the power to create and collect taxes.

To borrow Money on the credit of the United States;

To regulate Commerce with foreign Nations, and among the several States, and with the Indian Tribes;

To establish an uniform Rule of Naturalization, and uniform Laws on the subject of Bankruptcies throughout the United States;

To coin Money, regulate the Value thereof, and of foreign Coin, and fix the Standard of Weights and Measures;

Creating a system of money: Congress has the power to create a national currency (system of money).

To provide for the Punishment of counterfeiting the Securities and current Coin of the United States;

To establish Post Offices and post Roads;

To promote the Progress of Science and useful Arts, by securing for limited Times to Authors and Inventors the exclusive Right to their respective Writings and Discoveries;

Creating federal courts: Congress has the power to create new federal courts.

To constitute Tribunals inferior to the supreme Court;

To define and punish Piracies and Felonies committed on the high Seas, and Offenses against the Law of Nations;

Declaring war: Only Congress can declare war on another country.

To declare War, grant Letters of Marque and Reprisal, and make Rules concerning Captures on land and Water;

Creating and paying for armed forces: Congress has the power to create an army and navy, and to raise the money to pay for them.

To raise and support Armies, but no Appropriation of Money to that Use shall be for a longer Term than two Years;

To provide and maintain a Navy;

To make Rules for the Government and Regulation of the land and naval Forces;

To provide for calling forth the Militia to execute the Laws of the Union, suppress Insurrections and repel Invasions;

To provide for organizing, arming, and disciplining, the Militia, and for governing such Part of them as may be employed in the Service of the United States, reserving to the States respectively, the Appointment of the Officers, and the Authority of training the Militia according to the discipline prescribed by Congress;

To exercise exclusive Legislation in all Cases whatsoever, over such District (not exceeding ten Miles square) as may, by Cession of particular States, and the Acceptance of Congress, become the Seat of the Government of the United States, and to exercise like Authority over all Places purchased by the Consent of the Legislature of the State in which the Same shall be, for the Erection of Forts, Magazines, Arsenals, dock-Yards and other needful Buildings;—And

Making other laws: Congress has the power to make all laws that are needed to carry out the government's powers under the Constitution.

To make all Laws which shall be necessary and proper for carrying into Execution the foregoing Powers, and all other Powers vested by this Constitution in the Government of the United States, or in any Department or Officer thereof.

Section 9. The Migration or Importation of such Persons as any of the States now existing shall think proper to admit, shall not be prohibited by the Congress prior to the Year one thousand eight hundred and eight, but a Tax or duty may be imposed on such Importation, not exceeding ten dollars for each Person.

The Privilege of the Writ of Habeas Corpus shall not be suspended, unless when in Cases of Rebellion or Invasion the public Safety may require it.

No Bill of Attainder or ex post facto Law shall be passed.

No Capitation, or other direct, Tax shall be laid, unless in Proportion to the Census or Enumeration herein before directed to be taken.[5]

No Tax or Duty shall be laid on Articles exported from any State.

No Preference shall be given by any Regulation of Commerce or Revenue to the Ports of one State over those of another: nor shall Vessels bound to, or from, one State, be obliged to enter, clear, or pay Duties in another.

No Money shall be drawn from the Treasury, but in Consequence of Appropriations made by Law; and a regular Statement and Account of the Receipts and Expenditures of all public Money shall be published from time to time.

No Title of Nobility shall be granted by the United States: And no Person holding any Office of Profit or Trust under them, shall, without the Consent of the Congress, accept of any present, Emolument, Office, or Title, of any kind whatever, from any King, Prince, or foreign State.

Section 10. No State shall enter into any Treaty, Alliance, or Confederation; grant Letters of Marque and Reprisal; coin Money; emit Bills of Credit; make any Thing but gold and silver Coin a Tender in Payment of Debts; pass any Bill of Attainder, ex post facto Law, or Law impairing the Obligation of Contracts, or grant any Title of Nobility;

No State shall, without the Consent of the Congress, lay any Imposts or Duties on Imports or Exports, except what may be absolutely necessary for executing it's inspection Laws: and the net Produce of all Duties and Imposts, laid by any State on Imports or Exports, shall be for the Use of the Treasury of the United States; and all such Laws shall be subject to the Revision and Controul of the Congress.

5. See Sixteenth Amendment

No State shall, without the Consent of Congress, lay any Duty of Tonnage, keep Troops, or Ships of War in time of Peace, enter into any Agreement or Compact with another State, or with a foreign Power, or engage in War, unless actually invaded, or in such imminent Danger as will not admit of delay.

Article II: The Executive Branch
The head of the Executive Branch is the President. The comments below point out some of the specific powers of this branch.

Article II

Section 1. The executive Power shall be vested in a President of the United States of America. He shall hold his Office during the Term of four Years, and, together with the Vice President, chosen for the same Term, be elected, as follows

Each State shall appoint, in such Manner as the Legislature thereof may direct, a Number of Electors, equal to the whole Number of Senators and Representatives to which the State may be entitled in the Congress: but no Senator or Representative, or Person holding an Office of Trust or Profit under the United States, shall be appointed an Elector.

[The Electors shall meet in their respective States, and vote by Ballot for two Persons, of whom one at least shall not be an Inhabitant of the same State with themselves. And they shall make a List of all the Persons voted for, and of the Number of Votes for each; which List they shall sign and certify, and transmit sealed to the Seat of the Government of the United States, directed to the President of the Senate. The President of the Senate shall, in the Presence of the Senate and House of Representatives, open all the Certificates, and the Votes shall then be counted. The Person having the greatest Number of Votes shall be the President, if such Number be a Majority of the whole Number of Electors appointed; and if there be more than one who have such Majority, and have an equal Number of Votes, then the House of Representatives shall immediately choose by Ballot one of them for President; and if no Person have a Majority, then from the five highest on the List the said House shall in like Manner choose the President. But in choosing the President, the Votes shall be taken by States, the Representation from each State having one Vote; A quorum for this Purpose shall consist of a Member or Members from two thirds of the States, and a Majority of all the States shall be necessary to a Choice. In every Case, after the Choice of the President, the Person having the greatest Number of Votes of the Electors shall be the Vice President. But if there should remain two or more who have equal Votes, the Senate shall choose from them by Ballot the Vice President.][6]

The Congress may determine the Time of choosing the Electors, and the Day on which they shall give their Votes; which Day shall be the same throughout the United States.

6. Changed by the Twelfth Amendment

No Person except a natural born Citizen, or a Citizen of the United States, at the time of the Adoption of this Constitution, shall be eligible to the Office of President; neither shall any person be eligible to that Office who shall not have attained to the Age of thirty five Years, and been fourteen Years a Resident within the United States.

[In Case of the Removal of the President from Office, or of his Death, Resignation, or Inability to discharge the Powers and Duties of the said Office, the Same shall devolve on the Vice President, and the Congress may be Law provide for the Case of Removal, Death, Resignation or Inability, both of the President and Vice President, declaring what Officer shall then act as President, and such Officer shall act accordingly, until the Disability be removed, or a President shall be elected.][7]

The President shall, at stated Times, receive for his Services, a Compensation, which shall neither be increased nor diminished during the Period for which he shall have been elected, and he shall not receive within that Period any other Emolument from the United States, or any of them.

Before he enter on the Execution of his Office, he shall take the following Oath or Affirmation:—"I do solemnly swear (or affirm) that I will faithfully execute the Office of President of the United States, and will to the best of my Ability, preserve, protect and defend the Constitution of the United States."

Section 2. The President shall be Commander in Chief of the Army and Navy of the United States, and of the Militia of the several States, when called into the actual Service of the United States; he may require the Opinion, in writing, of the principal Officer in each of the executive Departments, upon any Subject relating to the Duties of their respective Offices, and he shall have Power to grant Reprieves and Pardons for Offenses against the United States, except in Cases of Impeachment.

Commanding the armed forces: The President is Commander-in-Chief of the armed forces of the United States.

Granting pardons: The President can grant pardons for federal crimes, except in cases of impeachment.

He shall have Power, by and with the Advice and Consent of the Senate, to make Treaties, provided two thirds of the Senators present concur; and he shall nominate, and by and with the Advice and Consent of the Senate, shall appoint Ambassadors, other public Ministers and Consuls, Judges of the supreme Court, and all other Officers of the United States, whose Appointments are not herein otherwise provided for, and which shall be established by Law: but the Congress may by law vest the Appointment of such inferior Officers, as they think proper, in the President alone, in the Courts of Law, or in the Heads of Departments.

Checks and balances: Treaties and appointments. The President can sign treaties with other countries. But the Senate must approve treaties by a two-thirds vote. The President can name certain officials and federal judges, but the Senate must approve the President's choices.

7. Changed by the Twenty-Fifth Amendment

The President shall have Power to fill up all Vacancies that may happen during the Recess of the Senate, by granting Commissions which shall expire at the End of their next Session.

Powers of leadership: The President can propose ideas for new laws and reports to Congress on the State of the Union. In emergencies, the President can call Congress into special session.

Section 3. He shall from time to time give to the Congress Information of the State of the Union, and recommend to their Consideration such Measures as he shall judge necessary and expedient; he may, on extraordinary Occasions, convene both Houses, or either of them and in Case of Disagreement between them with Respect to the Time of Adjournment, he may adjourn them to such Time as he shall think proper; he shall receive Ambassadors and other public Ministers; he shall take Care that the Laws be faithfully executed, and shall Commission all the Officers of the United States.

Checks and balances: Impeachment. Presidents and other federal officials can be removed from office if they misuse their powers.

Section 4. The President, Vice President and all civil Officers of the United States, shall be removed from Office on Impeachment for, and Conviction of, Treason, Bribery, or other high Crimes and Misdemeanors.

Article III: The Judicial Branch
The judicial branch consists of the Supreme Court and other federal courts. The comments below point out some of the specific powers of this branch.

Article III

Section 1. The judicial Power of the United States, shall be vested in one supreme Court, and in such inferior Courts as the Congress may from time to time ordain and establish. The Judges, both of the supreme and inferior Courts, shall hold their Officer during good Behaviour, and shall at stated Times, receive for their Services, a Compensation, which shall not be diminished during their Continuance in Office.

Checks and balances: Interpreting the Constitution. The judicial branch has the power to decide whether laws and treaties are constitutional.

Resolving disputes: Federal courts have the power to settle disputes involving the federal government, different states, or citizens of different states.

Section 2. The judicial Power shall extend to all Cases, in Law and Equity, arising under this Constitution, the Laws of the United States, and Treaties made, or which shall be made, under their Authority, —to all Cases affecting Ambassadors, other public Ministers and Consuls; —to all Cases of admiralty and maritime Jurisdiction, —to Controversies to which the United States shall be a Party; —to Controversies between two or more States, —[between a State and Citizens of another State;][8] between Citizens of different States, —between Citizens of the same State claiming Lands under Grants of different States, [and between a State or the Citizens thereof, and foreign States, Citizens or Subjects.][9]

In all Cases affecting Ambassadors, other public Ministers and Consuls, and those in which a State shall be Party, the supreme Court shall have original Jurisdiction. In all the other Cases before mentioned, the supreme Court shall have appellate Jurisdiction, both as to Law and Fact, with such Exceptions, and under such Regulations as the Congress shall make.

8. Changed by the Eleventh Amendment
9. Changed by the Eleventh Amendment

The Trial of all Crimes, except in Cases of Impeachment; shall be by Jury, and such Trial shall be held in the State where the said Crimes shall have been committed but when not committed within any State, the Trial shall be at such Place or Places as the Congress may by Law have directed.

Section 3. Treason against the United States, shall consist only in levying War against them, or in adhering to their Enemies, giving them Aid and Comfort. No Person shall be convicted of Treason unless on the Testimony of two Witnesses to the same overt Act, or on Confession in open Court.

The Congress shall have Power to declare the Punishment of Treason, but no Attainder of Treason shall work Corruption of Blood, or Forfeiture except during the Life of the Person attainted.

Article IV

Article IV: Relations Between the States
This article says that each state must honor the laws and authority of other states, as well as the rights of their citizens. The article also describes how new states can be added to the Union.

Section 1. Full Faith and Credit shall be given in each State to the public Acts, Records, and judicial Proceedings of every other State; And the Congress may by general Laws prescribe the Manner in which such Acts, Records and Proceedings shall be proved, and the Effect thereof.

Section 2. The Citizens of each State shall be entitled to all Privileges and Immunities of Citizens in the several States.

A Person charged in any State with Treason, Felony, or other Crime, who shall flee from Justice, and be found in another State, shall on Demand of the executive Authority of the State from which he fled, be delivered up, to be removed to the State having Jurisdiction of the Crime.

[No Person held to Service or Labour in one State, under the Laws thereof, escaping into another, shall, in Consequence of any Law or Regulation therein, be discharged from such Service or Labour, but shall be delivered up on Claim of the party to whom such Service or Labour may be due.][10]

Section 3. New States may be admitted by the Congress into this Union; but no new State shall be formed or erected within the Jurisdiction of any other State; nor any State be formed by the Junction of two or more States, or Parts of States, without the Consent of the Legislatures of the States concerned as well as of the Congress.

The Congress shall have rower to dispose of and make all needful Rules

10. Changed by the Thirteenth Amendment

and Regulations respecting the Territory or other Property belonging to the United States; and nothing in this Constitution shall be construed as to Prejudice any Claims of the United States, or of any particular State.

Section 4. The United States shall guarantee to every State in this Union a Republican Form of Government, and shall protect each of them against Invasion; and on Application of the Legislature, or of the Executive (when the Legislature cannot be convened) against domestic Violence.

Article V: Amending the Constitution
This article describes how the Constitution can be amended, or changed. Amendments must be ratified (approved) by three-fourths of the states.

Article V

The Congress, whenever two thirds of both houses shall deem it necessary, shall propose Amendments to this Constitution, or, on the Application of the Legislatures of two thirds of the several States, shall call a Convention for proposing Amendments, which in either Case, shall be valid to all Intents and Purposes, as Part of this Constitution, when ratified by the Legislatures of three fourths of the several States, or by Conventions in three fourths thereof, as the one or the other Mode of Ratification may be proposed by the Congress; Provided that no Amendment which may be made prior to the Year One thousand eight hundred and eight shall in any Manner affect the first and fourth Clauses in the Ninth Section of the first Article; and that no State, without its Consent, shall be deprived of it's equal Suffrage in the Senate.

Article VI: The Constitution as the Supreme Law of the Land
This article makes the Constitution the supreme (highest) law of the nation. No federal or state law can contradict the Constitution.

Article VI

All Debts contracted and Engagements entered into, before the Adoption of this Constitution, shall be as valid against the United States under this Constitution, as under the Confederation.

This Constitution, and the Laws of the United States which shall be made in Pursuance thereof; and all Treaties made, or which shall be made, under the Authority of the United States, shall be the supreme Law of the Land; and the Judges in every State shall be bound thereby, any Thing in the Constitution or Laws of any State to the Contrary notwithstanding.

The Senators and Representatives before mentioned, and the Members of the several State Legislatures, and all executive and judicial Officers, both of the United States and of the several States, shall be bound by Oath or Affirmation, to support this Constitution; but no religious Test shall ever be required as a Qualification to any Office or public Trust under the United States.

Article VII

The Ratification of the Conventions of nine States, shall be sufficient for the Establishment of this Constitution between the States so ratifying the Same.

Done in Convention by the Unanimous Consent of the States present the Seventeenth Day of September in the Year of our Lord one thousand seven hundred and Eighty seven and of the Independence of the United States of America the Twelfth In Witness whereof We have hereunto subscribed our Names,

G. Washington — President and deputy from Virginia

New Hampshire: John Langdon, Nicholas Gilman

Massachusetts: Nathaniel Gorham, Rufus King

Connecticut: Wm. Saml. Johnson, Roger Sherman

New York: Alexander Hamilton

New Jersey: Wil. Livingston, David Brearley, Wm. Paterson, Jona. Dayton

Pennsylvania: B. Franklin, Thomas Mifflin, Robt. Morris, Geo. Clymer, Thos. FitzSimons, Jared Ingersoll, James Wilson, Gouv. Morris

Delaware: Geo. Read, Gunning Bedford, Jr., John Dickenson, Richard Bassett, Jaco. Broom

Maryland: James McHenry, Dan. of St. Thos. Jenifer, Danl. Carroll

Virginia: John Blair, James Madison, Jr.

North Carolina: Wm. Blount, Richd. Dobbs Spaight, Hu. Williamson

South Carolina: J. Rutledge, Pierce Butler, Charles Cotesworth Pinckney, Charles Pinckney

Georgia: William Few, Abr. Baldwin

Attest William Jackson Secretary

Article VII: Ratifying the Constitution

This article says that the Constitution must be ratified (approved) by 9 of the original 13 states.

Original Ten Amendments: The Bill of Rights
Passed by Congress September 25, 1789
Ratified December 15, 1791

Congress cannot make laws that violate Americans' basic freedoms, including freedom of speech, religion, and the press. Citizens have the right to gather peacefully and to ask the government to correct wrongs.

Amendment 1

Basic freedoms

Congress shall make no law respecting an establishment of religion, or prohibiting the free exercise thereof; or abridging the freedom of speech, or of the press, or the right of the people peaceably to assemble, and to petition the Government for a redress of grievances.

Citizens have the right to own and carry weapons.

Amendment 2

Right to bear arms

A well regulated Militia, being necessary to the security of a free State, the right of the people to keep and bear Arms, shall not be infringed.

In peacetime, the government cannot force citizens to let soldiers stay in their homes.

Amendment 3

Quartering of soldiers

No Soldier shall, in time of peace be quartered in any house, without the consent of the Owner, nor in time of war, but in a manner to be prescribed by law.

Government officials cannot search citizens or their property, or seize their belongings, without good reason. Normally, searches and seizures require a warrant approved by a judge.

Amendment 4

Search and arrest

The right of the people to be secure in their persons, houses, papers, and effects, against unreasonable searches and seizures, shall not be violated, and no Warrants shall issue, but upon probable cause, supported by Oath or affirmation, and particularly describing the place to be searched, and the persons or things to be seized.

Citizens who are accused of crimes have certain basic rights. They cannot be tried twice for the same crime, or be forced to testify against themselves. They cannot be jailed or lose their property except through proper legal actions.

Amendment 5

Rights in criminal cases

No person shall be held to answer for a capital, or otherwise infamous crime, unless on a presentment or indictment of a Grand Jury, except in cases arising in the land or naval forces, or in the Militia, when in actual service in time of War or public danger; nor shall any person be subject for the same offence to be twice put in jeopardy of life or limb, nor shall be compelled in any criminal case to be a witness against himself, nor be deprived of life, liberty, or property, without due process of law; nor shall private property be taken for public use, without just compensation.

Amendment 6

Right to a fair trial

In all criminal prosecutions, the accused shall enjoy the right to a speedy and public trial, by an impartial jury of the State and district wherein the crime shall have been committed; which district shall have been previously ascertained by law, and to be informed of the nature and cause of the accusation; to be confronted with the witnesses against him; to have compulsory process for obtaining witnesses in his favor, and to have the assistance of counsel for his defence.

Citizens who are accused of crimes have the right to a trial by jury that is fair and public. They have the right to question witnesses, and they have the right to a lawyer.

Amendment 7

Rights in civil cases

In Suits at common law, where the value in controversy shall exceed twenty dollars, the right of trial by jury shall be preserved, and no fact tried by a jury shall be otherwise re-examined in any Court of the United States, than according to the rules of the common law.

Citizens have the right to demand a jury trial to settle disputes over things of value.

Amendment 8

Bail, fines, punishment

Excessive bail shall not be required, nor excessive fines imposed, nor cruel and unusual punishments inflicted.

Bail and fines that are set by a court must be reasonable. Punishments for crimes cannot be cruel or unusual.

Amendment 9

Rights retained by the People

The enumeration in the Constitution of certain rights shall not be construed to deny or disparage others retained by the people.

The government must respect all the rights of Americans, including rights that are not listed in the Constitution.

Amendment 10

States' rights

The powers not delegated to the United States by the Constitution, nor prohibited by it to the States, are reserved to the States respectively, or to the people.

The states, and the people, keep any powers that the Constitution does not specifically give to the federal government.

Later Amendments

Amendment 11

Lawsuits against states

The Judicial power of the United States shall not be construed to extend to any suit in law or equity, commenced or prosecuted against one of the United States by Citizens of another State, or by Citizens or Subjects of any Foreign State.
Ratified February 7, 1795.

People cannot sue a state in federal court if they are citizens of a different state, or of a foreign country.

The Vice President will be elected separately from the President. In the original Constitution, the candidate who finished second in the voting for President automatically became Vice President. Under that system, the President and Vice President were likely to be political enemies. The 12th Amendment allows the same political party to win the elections for both President and Vice President.

Amendment 12

Presidential elections

The Electors shall meet in their respective states, and vote by ballot for President and Vice-President, one of whom, at least, shall not be an inhabitant of the same state with themselves; they shall name in their ballots the person voted for as President, and in distinct ballots the person voted for as Vice-President, and they shall make distinct lists of all persons voted for as President, and of all persons voted for as Vice-President, and of the number of votes for each, which lists they shall sign and certify, and transmit sealed to the seat of the government of the United States, directed to the President of the Senate;—The President of the Senate shall, in the presence of the Senate and House of Representatives, open all the certificates and the votes shall then be counted;—The person having the greatest number of votes for President, shall be the President, if such number be a majority of the whole number of Electors appointed; and if no person have such majority, then from the persons having the highest numbers not exceeding three on the list of those voted for as President, the House of Representatives shall choose immediately, by ballot, the President. But in choosing the President, the votes shall be taken by states, the representation from each state having one vote; a quorum for this purpose shall consist of a member or members from two-thirds of the states, and a majority of all the states shall be necessary to a choice. [And if the House of Representatives shall not choose a President whenever the right of choice shall devolve upon them, before the fourth day of March next following, then the Vice-President shall act as President, as in the case of the death or other constitutional disability of the President.]* The person having the greatest number of votes as Vice-President, shall be the Vice-President, if such number be a majority of the whole number of Electors appointed, and if no person have a majority, then from the two highest numbers on the list, the Senate shall choose the Vice-President; a quorum for the purpose shall consist of two-thirds of the whole number of Senators, and a majority of the whole number shall be necessary to a choice. But no person constitutionally ineligible to the office of President shall be eligible to that of Vice-President of the United States. Ratified June 15, 1804. Superseded by Section 3 of the Twentieth Amendment

No person in the United States can be kept as a slave. No person can be forced to work for someone else, except as a legal punishment for a crime.

Amendment 13

End of slavery

Section 1. Neither slavery nor involuntary servitude, except as a punishment for crime whereof the party shall have been duly convicted, shall exist within the United States, or any place subject to their jurisdiction.

Section 2. Congress shall have power to enforce these article by appropriate legislation.

Ratified December 6, 1865.

Amendment 14

Civil rights

Section 1. All persons born or naturalized in the United States and subject to the jurisdiction thereof, are citizens of the United States and of the State wherein they reside. No State shall make or enforce any law which shall abridge the privileges or immunities of citizens of the United States; nor shall any State deprive any person of life, liberty, or property, without due process of law; nor deny to any person within its jurisdiction the equal protection of the laws.

Section 2. Representatives shall be apportioned among the several States according to their respective numbers, counting the whole number of persons in each State, excluding Indians not taxed. But when the right to vote at any election for the choice of electors for President and Vice President of the United States, Representatives in Congress, the Executive and Judicial officers of a State, or the members of the Legislature thereof, is denied to any of the male inhabitants of such State, being twenty-one years of age, and citizens of the United States, or in any way abridged, except for participation in rebellion, or other crime, the basis of representation therein shall be reduced in the proportion which the number of such male citizens shall bear to the whole number of male citizens twenty-one years of age in such State.

Section 3. No person shall be a Senator or Representative in Congress, or elector of Pre-sident and Vice President, or hold any office, civil or military, under the United States, or under any State, who, having previously taken an oath, as a member of Congress, or as an officer of the United States, or as a member of any State legislature, or as an executive or judicial officer of any State, to support the Constitution of the United States, shall have engaged in insurrection or rebellion against the same, or given aid or comfort to the enemies thereof. But Congress may by a vote of two-thirds of each House, remove such disability.

Section 4. The validity of the public debt of the United States, authorized by law, including debts incurred for payment of pensions and bounties for services in suppressing insurrection or rebellion, shall not be questioned. But neither the United States nor any State shall assume or pay any debt or obligation incurred in aid of insurrection or rebellion against the United States, or any claim for the loss or emancipation of any slave; but all such debts, obligations and claims shall be held illegal and void.

Section 5. The Congress shall have power to enforce, by appropriate legislation, the provisions of this article.
Ratified July 9, 1868

All Americans, including former slaves, have the right to be treated as citizens. For example, states must respect the constitutional rights of all citizens. States must give all their citizens equal protection in their laws. In addition, they cannot deny the right of eligible men to vote in federal elections. If they do, they will lose some of their representatives in Congress.

The 14th Amendment also deals with other questions that arose because of the Civil War. For instance, it prevents people from being elected to office who have rebelled against the United States. It also says that the federal government is not responsible for Confederate debts.

States cannot deny anyone the right to vote simply because of the person's race or color, or because the person used to be a slave.

Amendment 15

Voting rights

Section 1. The right of citizens of the United States to vote shall not be denied or abridged by the United States or by any State on account of race, color, or previous condition of servitude.

Section 2. The Congress shall have power to enforce this article by appropriate legislation.
Ratified February 3, 1870.

Congress has the power to collect taxes from individual citizens based on their income (wealth).

Amendment 16

Income taxes

The Congress shall have power to lay and collect taxes on incomes, from whatever source derived, without apportionment among the several States, and without regard to any census or enumeration.
Ratified February 3, 1913.

Members of the Senate will be elected directly by voters. Previously, Senators were elected by state legislatures.

Amendment 17

Senatorial elections

The Senate of the United States shall be composed of two senators from each State, elected by the people thereof, for six years; and each Senator shall have one vote. The electors in each State shall have the qualifications requisite for electors of the most numerous branch of the State legislature.

When vacancies happen in the representation of any State in the Senate, the executive authority of such State shall issue writs of election to fill such vacancies: Provided, That the legislature of any State may empower the executive thereof to make temporary appointments until the people fill the vacancies by election as the legislature may direct.

This amendment shall not be so construed as to affect the election or term of any Senator chosen before it becomes valid as part of the Constitution.
Ratified April 8, 1913.

This amendment outlawed the making and selling of liquor (alcohol) in the United States. The 21st Amendment removed this amendment from the Constitution.

Amendment 18

Prohibition of liquor

Section 1. After one year from the ratification of this article, the manufacture, sale, or transportation of intoxicating liquors within, the importation thereof into, or the exportation thereof from the United States and all territory subject to the jurisdiction thereof for beverage purposes is hereby prohibited.

Section 2. The Congress and the several States shall have concurrent power to enforce this article by appropriate legislation.

Section 3. This article shall be inoperative unless it shall have been ratified as an amendment to the Constitution by the legislatures of the several States, as provided in the Constitution, within seven years from the date of the submission hereof to the States by the Congress.
Ratified January 16, 1919. Repealed by the Twenty-First, December 5, 1933

Amendment 19

Women's suffrage

The right of citizens of the United States to vote shall not be denied or abridged by the United States or by any States on account of sex.

Congress shall have power to enforce this article by appropriate legislation.
Ratified August 18, 1920.

Neither the federal government nor the states can deny people the right to vote because of their sex. This amendment guaranteed the right of women to vote.

Amendment 20

Terms of office

Section 1. The terms of the President and Vice President shall end at noon the 20th day of January, and the terms of Senators and Representatives at noon on the 3d day of January, of the years in which such terms would have ended if this article had not been ratified; and the terms of their successors shall then begin.

Section 2. The Congress shall assemble at least once in every year, and such meeting shall begin at noon on the 3d day of January, unless they shall by law appoint a different day.

Section 3. If, at the time fixed for the beginning of the term of the President, the President elect shall have died, the Vice President elect shall become President. If a President shall not have been chosen before the time fixed for the beginning of his term, or if the President elect shall have failed to qualify, then the Vice President elect shall act as President until a President shall have qualified; and the Congress may by law provide for the case wherein neither a President elect nor a Vice President elect shall have qualified, declaring who shall then act as President, or the manner in which one who is to act shall be selected, and such person shall act accordingly until a President or Vice President shall have qualified.

Section 4. The Congress may by law provide for the case of the death of any of the persons from whom the House of Representatives may choose a President whenever the right of choice shall have devolved upon them, and for the case of the death of any of the persons from whom the Senate may choose a Vice President whenever the right of choice shall have devolved upon them.

Section 5. Sections 1 and 2 shall take effect on the 15th day of October following the ratification of this article.

This amendment changes the dates when elected federal officials began serving their terms. It also deals with special situations, such as the death of a President-elect before the start of the President's term in office.

Section 6. This article shall be inoperative unless it shall have been ratified as an amendment to the Constitution by the legislatures of three-fourths of the several States within seven years from the date of its submission.
Ratified January 23, 1933.

The 18th Amendment is repealed (removed from the Constitution).

Amendment 21

Repeal of Prohibition

Section 1. The eighteenth article of amendment to the Constitution of the United States is hereby repealed.

Section 2. The transportation or importation into any State, Territory, or possession of the United States for delivery or use therein of intoxicating liquors, in violation of the laws thereof, is hereby prohibited.

Section 3. The article shall be inoperative unless it shall have been ratified as an amendment to the Constitution by conventions in the several States, as provided in the Constitution, within seven years from the date of the submission hereof to the States by the Congress.
Ratified December 5, 1933.

Presidents cannot serve more than two full terms in office.

Amendment 22

Term Limits for the Presidency

Section 1. No person shall be elected to the office of the President more than twice, and no person who has held the office of President, or acted as President, for more than two years of a term to which some other person was elected President shall be elected to the office of the President more than once. But this Article shall not apply to any person holding the office of President when this Article was proposed by the Congress, and shall not prevent any person who may be holding the office of President, or acting as President, during the term within which this Article becomes operative from holding the office of President or acting as President during the remainder of such term.

Section 2. This article shall be inoperative unless it shall have been ratified as an amendment to the Constitution by the legislatures of three-fourths of the several States within seven years from the date of its submission to the States by the Congress.
Ratified February 27, 1951.

Amendment 23

Washington, D.C., suffrage

Section 1. The District constituting the seat of government of the United States shall appoint in such manner as the Congress may direct:

A number of electors of President and Vice President equal to the whole number of Senators and Representatives in Congress to which the District would be entitled if it were a state, but in no event more than the least populous State; they shall be in addition to those appointed by the States, but they shall be considered, for the purposes of the election of President and Vice President, to be electors appointed by a State; and they shall meet in the District and perform such duties as provided by the twelfth article of amendment.

Section 2. The Congress shall have power to enforce this article by appropriate legislation.
Ratified March 29, 1961.

This amendment gives the District of Columbia the right to participate in electing the President and Vice-President. The District of Columbia is the nation's capital and is not part of any state.

Amendment 24

Abolition of poll taxes

Section 1. The right of citizens of the United States to vote in any primary or other election for President or Vice President, for electors for President or Vice President, or for Senator or Representative in Congress, shall not be denied or abridged by the United States or any State by reason of failure to pay any poll tax or other tax.

Section 2. The Congress shall have power to enforce this article by appropriate legislation.
Ratified January 23, 1964.

No state can deny someone the right to vote because the person failed to pay a special voting tax. Before this amendment, some states used a tax to prevent African Americans from voting.

Amendment 25

Presidential succession

Section 1. In case of the removal of the President from office or of his death or resignation, the Vice President shall become President.

Section 2. Whenever there is a vacancy in the office of the Vice President, the President shall nominate a Vice President who shall take office upon confirmation by a majority vote of both Houses of Congress.

Section 3. Whenever the President transmits to the President pro tempore of the Senate and the Speaker of the House of Representatives his written declaration that he is unable to discharge the powers and duties of his office, and until he transmits to them a written declaration to the contrary, such powers and duties shall be discharged by the Vice President as Acting President.

This amendment deals with situations in which the President dies or is unable to carry out his duties. It spells out when the Vice President should act for the President or take over as President. It also says how a new Vice President should be elected if the Vice President dies or leaves office between elections.

Section 4. Whenever the Vice President and a majority of either the principal officers of the executive departments or of such other body as Congress may by law provide, transmit to the President pro tempore of the Senate and the Speaker of the House of Representatives their written declaration that the President is unable to discharge the powers and duties of his office, the Vice President shall immediately assume the powers and duties of the office as Acting President.

Thereafter, when the President transmits to the President pro tempore of the Senate and the Speaker of the House of Representatives his written declaration that no inability exists, he shall resume the powers and duties of his office unless the Vice President and a majority of either the principal officers of the executive department or of such other body as Congress may by law provide, transmit within four days to the President pro tempore of the Senate and the Speaker of the House of Representatives their written declaration that the President is unable to discharge the powers and duties of his office. Thereupon Congress shall decide the issue, assembling within forty-eight hours for that purpose if not in session. If the Congress, within twenty-one days after receipt of the latter written declaration, or, if Congress is not in session, within twenty-one days after Congress is required to assemble, determines by two-thirds vote of both Houses that the President is unable to discharge the powers and duties of his office, the Vice President shall continue to discharge the same as Acting President; otherwise, the President shall resume the powers and duties of his office.
Ratified February 10, 1967.

The federal government and the states cannot deny citizens who are 18 years and older the right to vote.

Amendment 26

18-year-old suffrage

Section 1. The right of citizens of the United States, who are eighteen years of age or older, to vote shall not be denied or abridged by the United States or by any State on account of age.

Section 2. The Congress shall have power to enforce this article by appropriate legislation.
Ratified June 30, 1971.

Congress cannot change the pay of Senators and Representatives who are serving in that session of Congress. Changes in pay will take effect only after the next election for the House of Representatives.

Amendment 27

Congressional pay raises

No law, varying the compensation for the services of the Senators and Representatives, shall take effect, until an election of Representatives shall have intervened.
Ratified May 7, 1992

The Pledge of Allegiance

I pledge allegiance to the Flag
of the United States of America,
and to the Republic
for which it stands,
one Nation under God, indivisible,
with liberty and justice for all.

The Star-Spangled Banner

September 20, 1814
By Francis Scott Key

Oh, say can you see, by the dawn's early light,
What so proudly we hailed at the twilight's last gleaming?
Whose broad stripes and bright stars, through the perilous fight,
O'er the ramparts we watched, were so gallantly streaming?
And the rockets' red glare, the bombs bursting in air,
Gave proof through the night that our flag was still there.
O say, does that star-spangled banner yet wave
O'er the land of the free and the home of the brave?

On the shore, dimly seen through the mists of the deep,
Where the foe's haughty host in dread silence reposes,
What is that which the breeze, o'er the towering steep,
As it fitfully blows, now conceals, now discloses?
Now it catches the gleam of the morning's first beam,
In full glory reflected now shines on the stream:
'Tis the star-spangled banner! O long may it wave
O'er the land of the free and the home of the brave.

And where is that band who so vauntingly swore
That the havoc of war and the battle's confusion
A home and a country should leave us no more?
Their blood has wiped out their foul footstep's pollution.
No refuge could save the hireling and slave
From the terror of flight, or the gloom of the grave:
And the star-spangled banner in triumph doth wave
O'er the land of the free and the home of the brave.

Oh! thus be it ever, when freemen shall stand
Between their loved homes and the war's desolation!
Blest with victory and peace, may the heaven-rescued land
Praise the Power that hath made and preserved us a nation.
Then conquer we must, for our cause it is just,
And this be our motto: "In God is our trust."
And the star-spangled banner forever shall wave
O'er the land of the free and the home of the brave!

160°W
120°W
80°W
40°W
0°
80°N
60°N
40°N
20°N
0°
20°S
40°S
60°S
80°S
Equator
NORTH AMERICA
SOUTH AMERICA
PACIFIC OCEAN
ATLANTIC OCEAN
ATLANTIC OCEAN
ARC
0 1,500 3,000 miles
0 1,500 3,000 kilometers

0°
40°E
80°E
120°E
160°E
RCTIC OCEAN
EUROPE
ASIA
AFRICA
PACIFIC
OCEAN
INDIAN
OCEAN
AUSTRALIA
N
NW
NE
W
E
SW
SE
S
ANTARCTICA

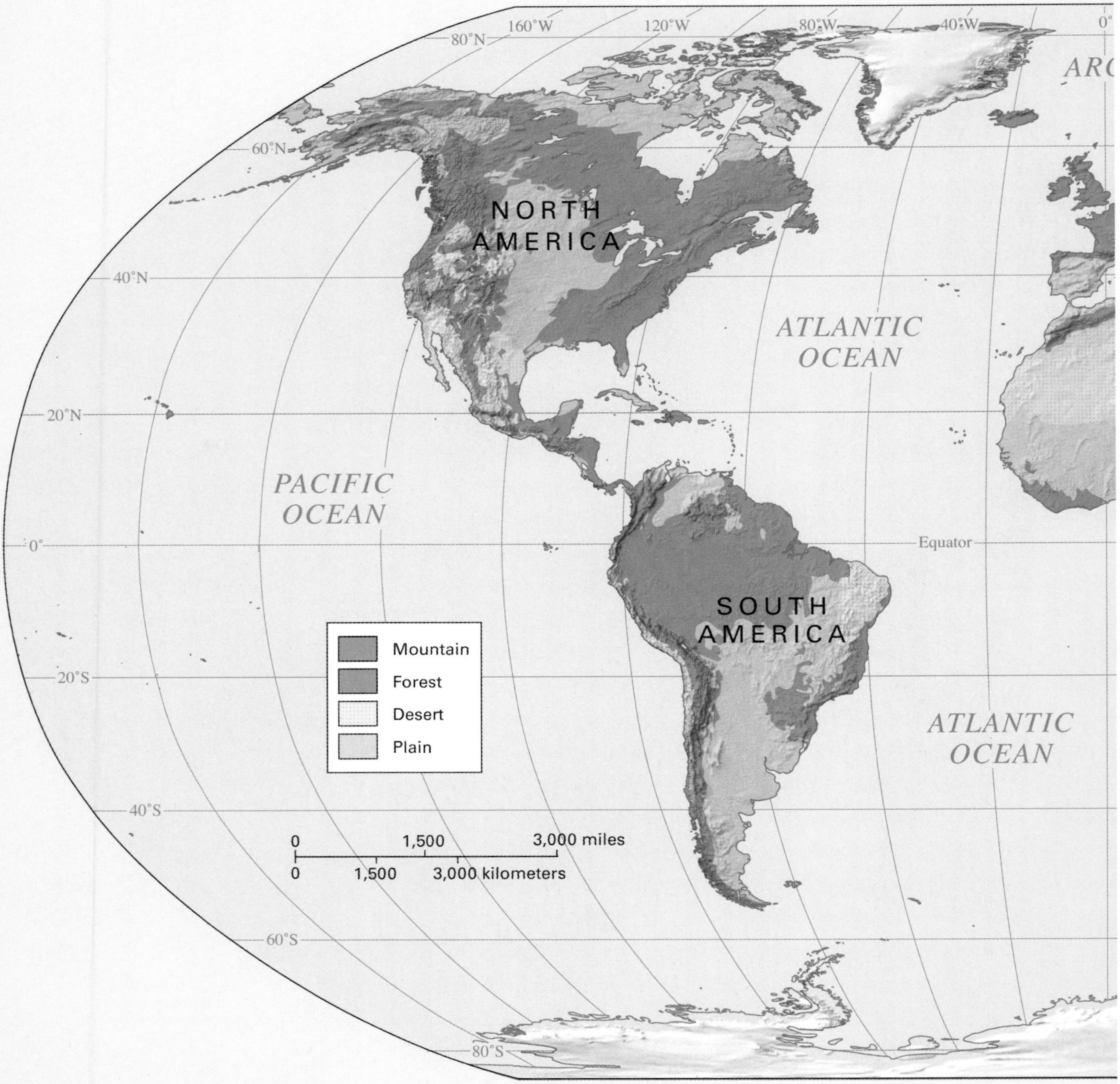

World Physical Map

160°W
120°W
80°W
40°W
0°
80°N
60°N
40°N
20°N
0°
20°S
40°S
60°S
80°S

ARC

NORTH AMERICA

ATLANTIC OCEAN

PACIFIC OCEAN

Equator

SOUTH AMERICA

Mountain
Forest
Desert
Plain

ATLANTIC OCEAN

0 1,500 3,000 miles
0 1,500 3,000 kilometers

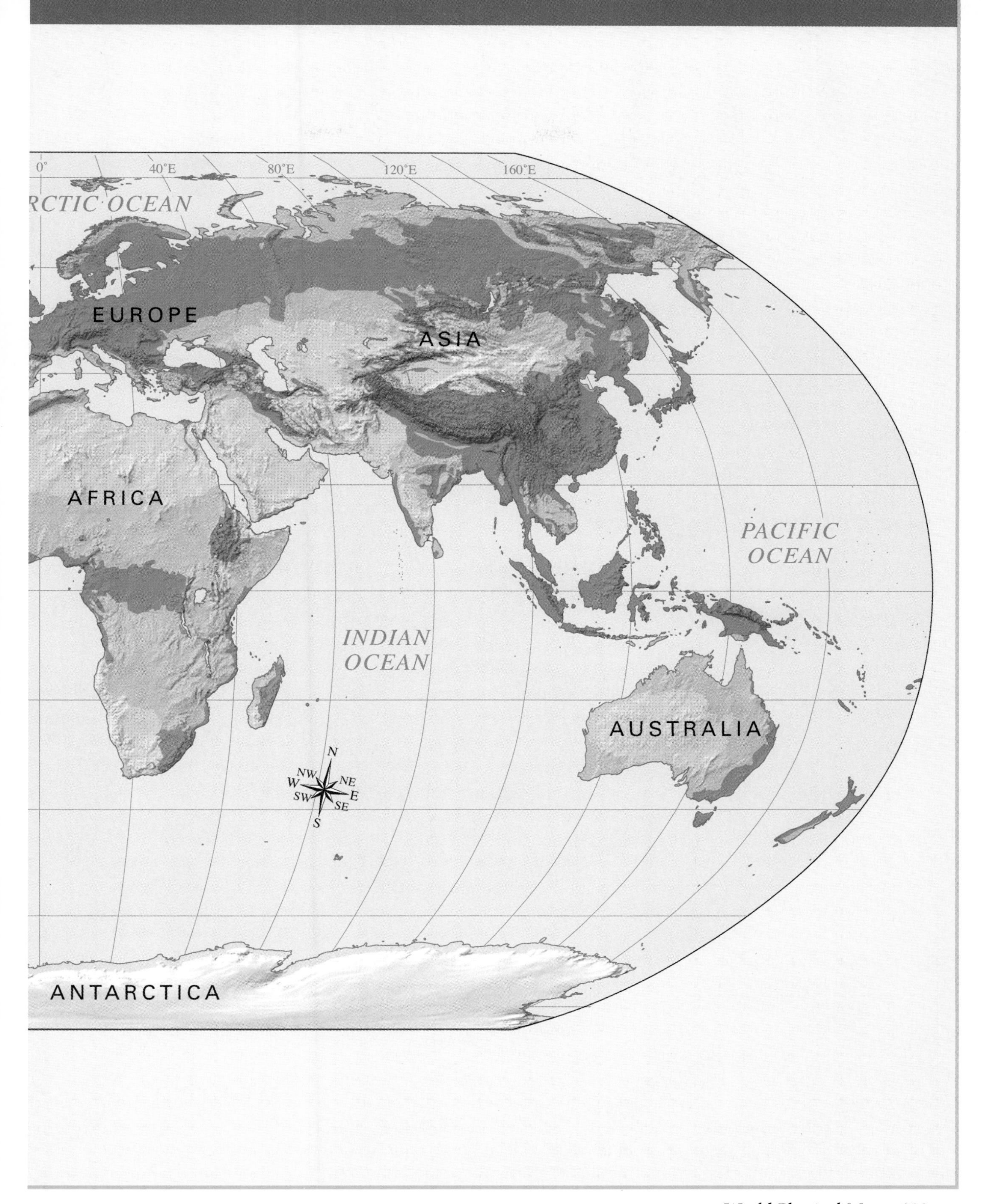
0°
40°E
80°E
120°E
160°E
RCTIC OCEAN
EUROPE
ASIA
AFRICA
PACIFIC
OCEAN
INDIAN
OCEAN
AUSTRALIA
N
NW
NE
W
E
SW
SE
S
ANTARCTICA

United States Political Map
CANADA
Washington
Olympia
45°N
Helena
Montana
North
Dakota
Bismarck
Salem
Oregon
Boise
Idaho
South
Dakota
Pierre
Wyoming
40°N
125°W
Cheyenne
Nebraska
Salt Lake
City
Carson City
Sacramento
Nevada
Denver
Utah
Colorado
California
Kansas
35°N
Santa Fe
Oklahoma
City
Arizona
New Mexico
Phoenix
PACIFIC
OCEAN
120°W
ARCTIC OCEAN
70°N
Texas
Alaska
Austin
Hawaii
160°W
Kauai
PACIFIC
OCEAN
Oahu
Niihau
Molokai
Honolulu
Maui
Lanai
Kahoolawe
60°N
170°W
Juneau
PACIFIC
OCEAN
150°W
140°W
20°N
MEXICO
0
400 miles
0
400 kilometers
160°W
0
150 miles
0
150 kilometers
Hawaii

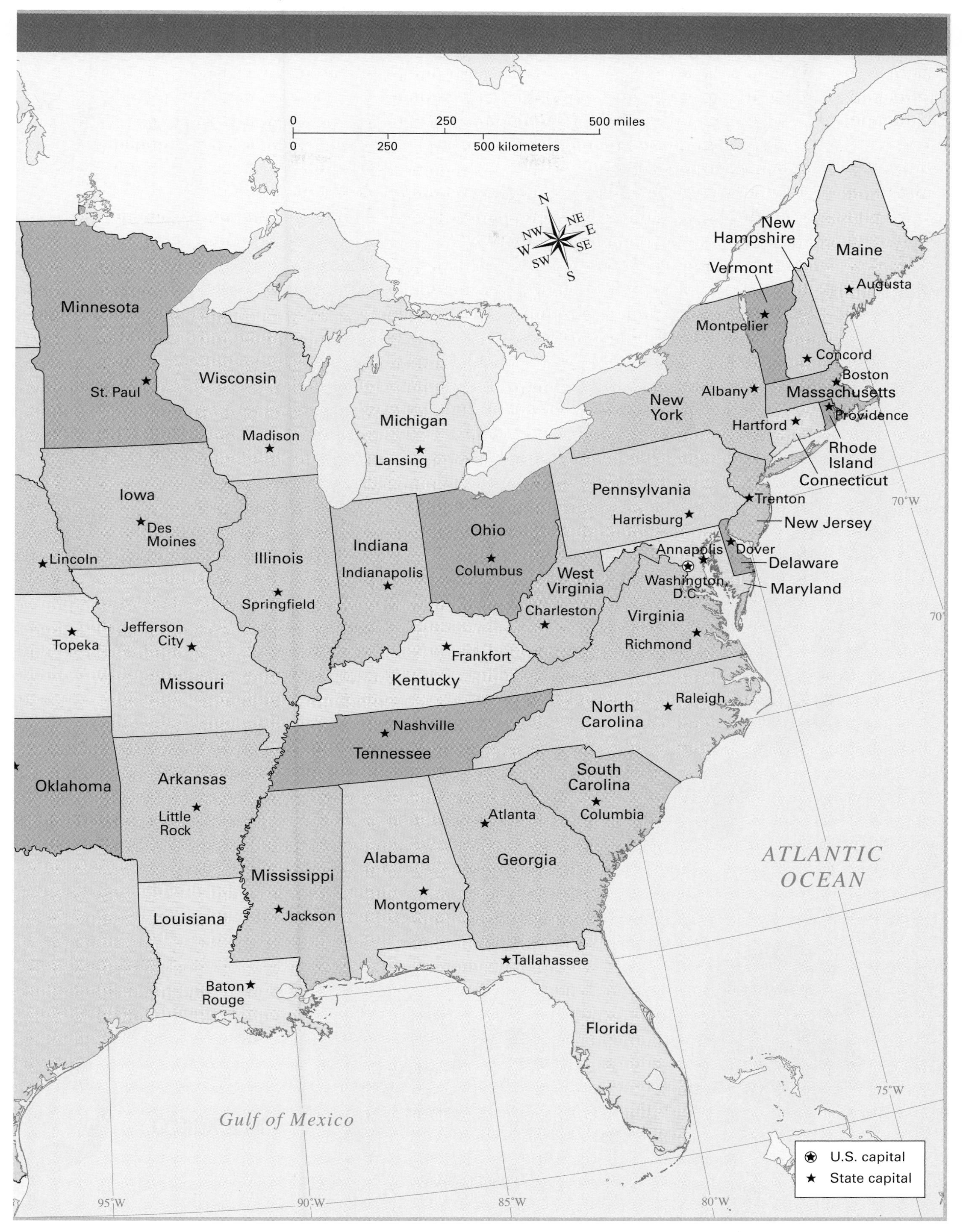
0
250
500 miles
0
250
500 kilometers
N
NE
E
SE
S
SW
W
NW
Minnesota
St. Paul
Wisconsin
Madison
Michigan
Lansing
Iowa
Des Moines
Lincoln
Illinois
Springfield
Indiana
Indianapolis
Ohio
Columbus
Pennsylvania
Harrisburg
New York
Albany
Vermont
Montpelier
New Hampshire
Concord
Maine
Augusta
Massachusetts
Boston
Providence
Rhode Island
Hartford
Connecticut
Trenton
New Jersey
Dover
Delaware
Annapolis
Maryland
Washington, D.C.
West Virginia
Charleston
Virginia
Richmond
Kentucky
Frankfort
Topeka
Jefferson City
Missouri
Tennessee
Nashville
North Carolina
Raleigh
South Carolina
Columbia
Oklahoma
Arkansas
Little Rock
Mississippi
Jackson
Alabama
Montgomery
Georgia
Atlanta
Louisiana
Baton Rouge
Tallahassee
Florida
ATLANTIC OCEAN
Gulf of Mexico
70°W
70°
75°W
95°W
90°W
85°W
80°W
U.S. capital
State capital

United States Physical Map

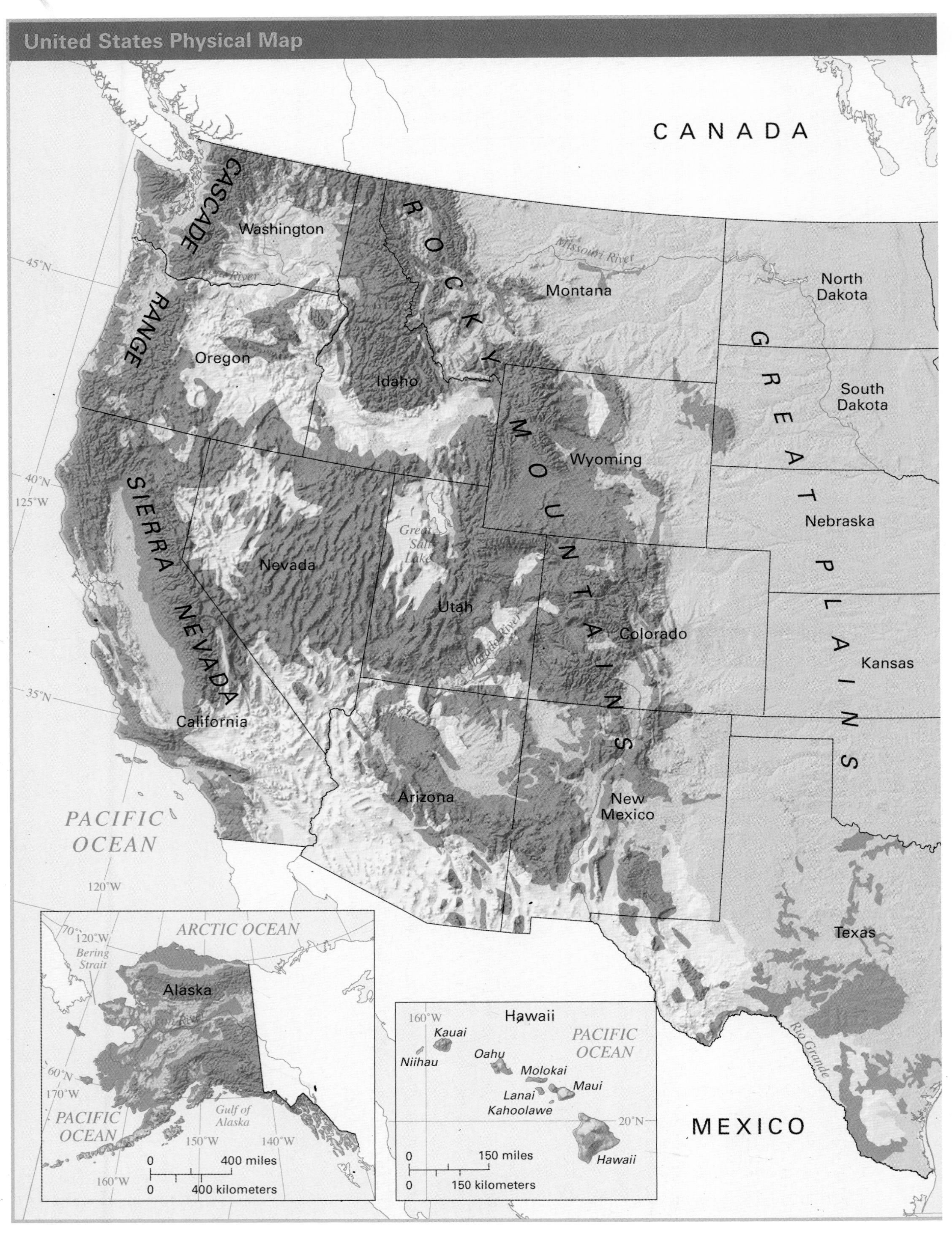

0
250
500 miles
0
250
500 kilometers
N
NE
E
SE
S
SW
W
NW
Lake Superior
Lake Michigan
Lake Huron
Lake Ontario
Lake Erie
St. Lawrence River
Mississippi River
Missouri River
Ohio River
Mississippi River
Minnesota
Wisconsin
Michigan
Iowa
Illinois
Indiana
Ohio
Pennsylvania
New York
Vermont
Maine
New Hampshire
Massachusetts
Rhode Island
Connecticut
New Jersey
Delaware
Maryland
West Virginia
Virginia
Kentucky
Missouri
Tennessee
North Carolina
South Carolina
Arkansas
Oklahoma
Mississippi
Alabama
Georgia
Louisiana
Florida
APPALACHIAN MOUNTAINS
ATLANTIC OCEAN
Gulf of Mexico
70°W
75°W
80°W
85°W
90°W
95°W
Mountain
Forest
Desert
Plain

A

abolitionist A person who wanted to end, or abolish, slavery.

acquisition Something that is gained, or acquired. The United States made a number of land acquisitions between 1783 and 1853 to reach the West Coast.

act A law created or passed by a government. For example, the Stamp Act was a law that was passed by the British Parliament.

adapt To adjust, or change, ideas and ways of living to fit a new situation, such as a new environment.

adaptation A change or adjustment in a way of life that allows people to survive in a particular environment.

Age of Exploration The period of time, beginning in the late 1400s, in which European explorers sought new routes to Asia and discovered the Americas.

ally One person or nation united with another for a common purpose.

amendment A change to the Constitution.

the Americas The land masses of North America, Central America, and South America.

annex To add or incorporate (a new territory) into a country.

appeal To request that a case or a decision be reviewed by a higher court.

apprentice A person who learns an occupation by getting experience under a skilled worker.

archaeologist A scientist who studies artifacts to learn about past cultures.

artifact An object made by a group of humans, such as tools and clothes. Artifacts help us understand the ways of life of the people who made them.

Articles of Confederation The document that set up the first government of the United States. The government had limited powers.

assembly A body of lawmakers.

astrolabe An early scientific tool used to observe and calculate the position of the sun and other stars.

B

bill A draft of an idea for a law that is considered by lawmakers.

Bill of Rights The first 10 amendments to the Constitution that protect the rights and freedoms of American citizens.

boundary The geographic line between two places, such as two countries.

boycott To protest by refusing to use or buy a good or service.

C

cabinet A group of advisors to the president, including the heads of important departments in the executive branch.

cede To give up territory, usually as the result of a treaty.

capitol The main government building, in which lawmakers meet.

cash crop A crop that is grown in large quantities for sale

checks and balances The system under which each branch of government limits, or checks, the powers of the other branches.

civil Non-criminal cases involving disputes among individuals about property, money, or other personal matters.

civil rights movement An organized effort, beginning in the 1950s, to achieve equal rights for black Americans.

Civil War The bitter conflict fought from 1861 to 1865 between the states that remained in the Union and the states that seceded and formed the Confederacy.

claim A piece of land worked by a miner seeking valuable minerals.

climate Aspects of weather, such as temperature, rainfall, and wind, that are measured over time in an area.

Cold War The struggle between democratic nations, led by the United States, and communist nations, led by the Soviet Union, that lasted from 1945 until 1991.

colonist A person who settles in a colony.

colony A community ruled by another country, not by its own people.

compass A tool or instrument for finding directions by first locating north.

compromise An agreement in which each side gives up some of what it wants.

Confederacy The nation formed by the 11 states (in order of secession–South Carolina, Mississippi, Florida, Alabama, Georgia, Louisiana, Texas, Virginia, Arkansas, North Carolina, Tennessee) that left the Union.

conquistador a Spanish explorer who came to the Americas in the 1500s and claimed large areas of land for Spain. *Conquistador* means "conqueror" in Spanish. The conquistadors often conquered native peoples and ruled over them in the name of Spain.

constitution A document that describes how a government will work.

Constitutional Convention The meeting called by the states in 1787 to improve the Articles of Confederation that instead wrote a new constitution.

contagious disease A sickness that can pass quickly from one person to another as germs are spread by touch or through the air. For example, influenza ("the flu") is a contagious disease.

craftsman A person who works at a job that requires manual or artistic skill.

cultural region An area of the world where people develop similar ways of life, or cultures. For example, American Indians in North America lived in several cultural regions. The groups within each region had similar cultures.

culture Way of living of a group of people. A group's culture includes such things as its language, beliefs, tools, types of homes, and ways of working and playing.

D

Declaration of Independence The document that announced that the American colonies were breaking away from Great Britain and explained why.

delegate A person who represents others at a convention or conference.

democratic Relating to a form of government in which people have the power to rule themselves, often through elected representatives.

dilemma A situation in which a person is forced to make a decision even though he or she does not like any of the choices.

draft The selection of people to serve in an army whether or not they wish to serve.

drought A long period with unusually low rainfall, which hurts growing and living conditions.

due process Proper legal procedures, such as a fair trial.

E

East Indies Southeast Asia, including India, Indonesia, and Malaysia.

economy The way that a particular region or country uses resources to produce and sell or trade goods and services to meet people's needs and wants.

Emancipation Proclamation President Abraham Lincoln's order to free (emancipate) slaves in states that were still fighting the Union, and to allow African Americans into the Union army and navy.

enlist To agree to serve in an army or a navy.

environment The natural surroundings of a place, including land, water, air, plants, and animals. For example, grasslands and deserts are two types of environments.

equality The state of having the same rights and privileges as others.

executive branch The branch that carries out, or executes, laws.

expedition A group of people sent to explore unknown places.

explorer A person who travels in search of new geographical information. For example, the Europeans who sailed unknown seas in the 1500s looking for new routes to Asia were explorers.

F

First Continental Congress A meeting of delegates from 12 colonies, held to present complaints to King George III, to set up a boycott of British goods, and to arrange a second meeting if needed.

forty-niner A goldseeker in the California gold rush of 1849.

free state A state in which it was not legal to own slaves.

G

Gettysburg The site of an 1863 Civil War battle won by the North that was a turning point in the war.

geographic term A word that names a landform or body of water. Examples of geographic terms include *bay, sea, peninsula,* and *island.*

geography The study of our physical surroundings and how humans interact with them. Often, *geography* is used to mean the physical surroundings themselves, such as "the geography of the United States." People who study geography are called *geographers.*

globe A sphere that is a model of Earth and most accurately represents it.

gorge A narrow, deep valley with steep sides.

government The organization that makes the laws in a country, state, or community and has the power to enforce them.

grant To give something to someone of lower rank as a favor or privilege.

Great Depression The worst economic slump in history, which began in the United States in 1929, and spread to other parts of the world, lasting until 1941.

griot A western African storyteller who recites the history of a tribe or family.

H

home front Areas away from the fighting in a country at war.

I

immigrant A person who comes from his or her homeland to settle in another country.

impeach To accuse or charge a government official, such as the president, with a crime or misconduct.

import To bring into a country, especially for sale.

indentured servant A person who works for a period of time to pay off money owed for a debt, such as passage from Europe or other debts.

independence Separation from, or freedom from control by, another country or government.

industrialization The process by which new inventions create industries that use factories to make products and that cause people to move from farms to cities for jobs.

industry A group of businesses that produce certain goods or services.

Information Age The period from the start of television (1941) to the present day, in which there is widespread electronic access to information through technology such as computers.

isthmus A narrow strip of land connecting two larger land areas.

J

Jamestown The first successful English colony in North America, it was founded in 1607 in present-day Virginia.

judicial branch The branch that interprets laws and settles disagreements about them; "judicial" comes from the word *judge*.

jury A group of citizens who are chosen to decide the outcome of a trial.

K

kiva A circular area, sometimes underground, where tribe members talk, work, or perform religious ceremonies.

L

landform a physical feature of Earth's surface such as a mountain or a plain.

latitude An imaginary line called a parallel that circles Earth from west to east. Parallels of latitude measure in degrees how far north or south of the equator a place on Earth is located.

legislative branch The branch that makes laws: to legislate is to make laws.

longitude An imaginary line called a meridian that runs from the North Pole to the South Pole. A meridian of longitude measures in degrees how far east or west of the prime meridian a place on Earth is located.

Loyalist A person in the American colonies who opposed independence and wanted the colonies to remain under the control of the king and Great Britain.

M

manifest destiny An American belief in the 1800s that it was the natural right of the United States to expand westward to the Pacific Ocean.

marsh Wet, low-lying land that is poorly drained.

massacre The murder of several or many people who cannot defend themselves.

mercenary A soldier hired to fight for a foreign army.

Mexicano A person born in Mexico

mesa A flat-topped hill with steep sides.

Middle Passage The voyage of slave ships across the Atlantic Ocean, from West Africa to the West Indies and the American continents.

migrate To move from one region of the world to another region.

migration Movement of people from one country or area of the world to a new home in another country or area.

militia A body of mostly untrained part-time soldiers who did required military service and were available for full-time paid duty when needed.

Minuteman A Patriot volunteer who was paid and trained to be ready to fight at a minute's notice.

missionary A representative sent by a religious organization to try to persuade other people to adopt that religion.

monarchy A form of government in which a ruler holds power for life.

Mormon A person who is a member of the Church of Jesus Christ of Latter-day Saints.

N

nation-state An independent country whose people mostly share a common identity.

natural resource Something from nature that is useful to people, such as soil, water, and minerals.

New World The name that Europeans used to refer to the Americas.

neutral Not taking sides. In the American colonies, many people remained neutral and did not support either side (Loyalist or Patriot) in the fight for independence from Great Britain.

Nez Percé A member of an American Indian group that lived in areas of present-day states including northeastern Oregon, central Idaho, and southeastern Washington.

nomadic Moving from place to place, often with changes in the seasons, to follow sources of food. For example, some

American Indian groups were nomadic, while others stayed in the same place year-round.

North The region of the United States in the mid-1800s that included states in New England, in the Middle Atlantic section, and around the Great Lakes. This region had many cities, factories, and railroads. Most of its workers were free.

Northwest Passage The supposed route across the northern part of North America that Europeans were looking for but never found. The explorers had hoped to find a northwest passage from the Atlantic Ocean to the Pacific Ocean so that they could get from Europe to Asia more quickly.

nuclear weapon A weapon that releases huge amounts of energy contained in the nuclei (centers) of atoms.

O

origin story A tale that a group of people tells about where they came from and how the Earth came to be.

overseer A person who was in charge of the work of slaves and could punish them for disobeying him.

P

Parliament The lawmaking part of the British government, similar to the Congress in the United States.

Patriot A person in the American colonies who wanted the colonies to become independent from Great Britain.

physical feature A part of Earth's surface that is a landmass or a body of water. Physical features of the United States include the Rocky Mountains, the Mississippi River, and the Great Plains.

pictograph A picture that represents an important event or idea.

pioneer One of the first people to settle in a territory.

plantation A large farm on which crops are grown by free workers or slaves who live on the land.

Plymouth A town started in 1620 by early English settlers called Pilgrims. Plymouth is located in present-day Massachusetts.

politics The activities of governments and the people who work in them.

prejudice Having a negative judgment or opinion of something or someone that is not based on facts.

proclamation An official public announcement.

protest To object in a public way to something that one believes is wrong or unfair.

R

rancho An area of land, usually for raising cattle, granted by Mexico to Spanish and Mexican citizens who lived in North America.

ratify To approve; to make a written document official by signing it.

Reconstruction The process by which Congress tried to rebuild the South and reunite it with the Union after the Civil War.

refugee Someone who flees from his or her home to another place or country to find safety.

repeal To cancel, or undo, a law.

republic A form of government in which citizens elect representatives who are responsible to the people.

reservation An area of land set aside by the United States government for American Indians to live on.

resolution A statement that expresses the wishes or decisions of a group.

revolution The overthrow of one government and its replacement with another.

Roanoke The name of the island where the first English settlement was started in North America in 1587. Roanoke is located near the coast of present-day North Carolina.

royal colony A colony that is controlled directly by a king or queen, who usually appoints a royal governor.

rule of law A set of public laws that apply to all people equally, with no one getting special treatment.

S

secede To officially withdraw from a government or a country.

Second Continental Congress The meeting of delegates from the American colonies that began in Philadelphia in 1775. The Congress approved the Declaration of Independence and acted as the colonies' government during the American Revolution.

segregation The separation of people, especially by race; in the years after the Civil War, until the 1960s, a practice enforced in the South by laws and customs.

settlement A small community that is started in a new place.

sharecropping A system of farming in which the worker is paid with a share of the crop he or she raises.

slave auction A public sale in which slaves were sold to the highest bidders.

slave state A state in which it was legal to own slaves.

slave trade The exchange of captured people for goods.

South The region of the United States in the mid-1800s that included states south of the Ohio River and latitude 36°30' north. This region had few factories or large cities. Most people lived on farms. African slaves worked on plantations.

spiritual A type of religious song that developed among enslaved Africans and that expressed deep emotion.

strategy An overall plan for winning a war, such as how and where to use an army or navy.

T

tactic A planned action, such as a way of moving or using troops, aimed at reaching a certain goal.

taxation without representation Forcing people to pay taxes when they have had no say in making the law that created the tax. American colonists were angry about paying taxes that were passed by the British Parliament, where they had no representatives to present their views.

technology The use of scientific or mechanical knowledge to achieve a practical purpose, such as creating machines and weapons for use in war.

territory A large region of land.

trade A craft or an occupation that requires manual, artistic, or mechanical skill.

traitor A person guilty of betraying or acting against his or her own country.

transcontinental Extending across a continent.

treason The crime of acting to overthrow your ruler or betray your country.

treaty A formal agreement between two or more nations.

triangular trade The exchange of slaves and goods among Europe, the Americas, and West Africa, using shipping routes across the Atlantic Ocean.

turning point An event that leads to a dramatic change.

tyrant A ruler who uses his or her power harshly.

U

Underground Railroad A system in which abolitionists secretly helped escaping slaves reach freedom.

Union The United States as one country; during the Civil War, the government and the armies of the states that chose to remain a part of the United States.

V

veto To reject a bill and prevent it from becoming a law, a power that belongs only to the president.

volunteer Person who performs a service for free.

W

West Indies Islands that lie between southeastern North America and northern South America, and separate the Caribbean Sea from the Atlantic Ocean.

Williamsburg The capital town of the British colony of Virginia, where the colony's government met.

World War I Also called the Great War, a conflict fought from 1914 to 1918 by troops from 32 countries.

World War II A conflict fought from 1939 to 1945 by troops from 61 countries; the most costly war in history in the number of people killed and the amount of property destroyed.

Y

yoke A wooden frame that fastens around an animal's neck and is then attached to a wagon or other vehicle.

A

B

T

U

V

W

Y

Photographs

Cover and title page

RF/Getty Images

Table of Contents

i: RF/Getty Images **iv T:** Brand X/SuperStock; **iv M:** Library of Congress **iv B:** National Museum of American Art, Washington D.C./Art Resource, NY. *Comanche Village,Women Dressing Robes and Drying Meat* by George Catlin
v T: Jonathan Blair/National Geographic Image Collection **v M:** North Wind Picture Archives
v B: Virginia Museum of Fine Arts
vi T: Library of Congress **vi M:** The Granger Collection, NY **vi B:** Colonial Williamsburg Foundation
vii T: North Wind Picture Archives
vii M: Library of Congress **vii B:** Historical Society of Pennsylvania
viii T: Yale University Art Gallery
viii M: The Granger Collection, NY
viii B: The Granger Collection, NY
ix T: The Granger Collection, NY
ix M: The Granger Collection, NY
ix B: Library of Congress
x T: Library of Congress **x B:** AP Wideworld

Chapter 1

2: Brand X/SuperStock **6:** James Brunker/Alamy **10:** RF **11:** NASA/Corbis **14:** North Wind Picture Archives **15:** SuperStock

Chapter 2

16: Library of Congress **18:** Greg Vaughn/Alamy **20 L:** Lowell Georgia/Corbis **20 R:** Tom Bean
21 L: Bilderbuch-Design Pics/Corbis **21 R:** AlaskaStock **22:** Library of Congress **23:** Marilyn Angel Wynn-Nativestock Pictures/Corbis **24:** National Museum of the American Indian-Smithsonian Institution **25:** National Museum of the American Indian/Smithsonian Institution **26:** National Museum of the American Indian/Smithsonian Institution **26 BL:** National Museum of the American Indian/Smithsonian Institution **26 BR:** National Museum of the American Indian/Smithsonian Institution
27: John Anderson Collection/Nebraska Historical Society

Chapter 3

28: National Museum of American Art, Washington D.C./Art Resource, NY. *Comanche Village,Women Dressing Robes and Drying Meat* by George Catlin (including details from painting)
30: Smithsonian Institution **31:** R. Berenholtz **32:** Kim Todd **33:** James Steinberg/ Photo Researchers **34:** Library of Congress **35:** Easttcott-Momatiuk/Woodfin Camp & Associates **36:** Jeff Greenberg/The Image Works **38:** New Bedford Whaling Museum **39:** Museum of History and Industry/Corbis **40:** Miles Ertman/Masterfile **41:** The Granger Collection, NY **42:** Lee Snider-Photo Images/Corbis **43:** Library of Congress

Chapter 4

44: Jonathan Blair/National Geographic Image Collection
44 BL: Jonathan Blair/National Geographic Image Collection
44 BM: Jonathan Blair/National Geographic Image Collection
44 BR: Jonathan Blair/National Geographic Image Collection
46: Pritt J. Vesilind/National Geographic Image Collection **47 L:** British Museum/Art Resource, NY
47 R: IPhoto Franca Principe and Sabina Bernacchini-IMSS Florence
48: Scala/Ministero per i Beni e le Attività culturali/Art Resource, NY **49:** The Pierpont Morgan Library/Art Resource, NY **50 BL:** RF **50 BR:** Scott Camazine/Photo Researchers, Inc. **51:** B. Strode/Woodfin Camp & Associates **52:** North Wind Picture Archives **53:** North Wind Picture Archives **54:** *St. Bartholomew's Day Massacre, 24th August 1572* (oil on panel), Dubois, Francois (1529-1584)/Musee Cantonal des Beaux-Arts de Lausanne, Switzerland, Photo Â© Held Collection/The Bridgeman Art Library **55:** Erich Lessing /Art Resource, NY **55 B:** Rijksmuseum, Amsterdam

Chapter 5

56: North Wind Picture Archives
59: The Granger Collection, New York **60 B:** Stock Montage
61 B: Giraudon /Art Resource, NY **62 B:** American Museum oF Natural History, New York **63 T:** Réunion des Musées Nationaux/Art Resource, NY **64 T:** The Granger Collection, New York
65 B: Library of Congress **66 B:** North Wind Picture Archives
69: Bildarchiv Preussischer Kulturbesitz/Art Resource, NY **70:** Private Collection, The Stapleton Collection/The Bridgeman Art Library

Chapter 6

72: Virginia Museum of Fine Arts
74: North Wind Picture Archives
75: The Granger Collection, NY
76: National Portrait Gallery, Smithsonian Institution/Art Resource, NY **77:** The Pilgrim Society **78:** The Granger Collection, NY **80:** North Wind Picture Archives **82:** North Wind Picture Archives **83:** Aurora/Getty Images
83: Freedom Trail Foundation

Chapter 7

84: Library of Congress **87:** Bettmann/Corbis **88:** Stock Montage **89:** Library of Congress **90:** West, Benjamin (1738-1820)/ Bridgeman Art Library **91:** *The Founding of Maryland 1861* by Emmanuel Leutze/The Maryland Historical Society **92:** Library of Congress **93:** Library of Congress **94:** North Wind Picture Archives **95:** North Wind Picture Archives **96:** The Granger Collection, NY

Chapter 8

98: The Granger Collection, NY **100 B:** Bettmann/Corbis **101:** North Wind Picture Archives **102:** Library of Congress **104:** Library of Congress **105:** Library of Congress **106:** Library of Congress **107:** The Granger Collection, NY **108:** James Davis; Eye Ubiquitous/Corbis **109:** Alex Dorgan-Ross/AP Photo **110:** Bettmann/Corbis **111:** North Wind Picture Archives

Chapter 9

112: Colonial Williamsburg Foundation **114:** Colonial Williamsburg Foundation **115:** Colonial Williamsburg Foundation **116:** Colonial Williamsburg Foundation **117:** Colonial Williamsburg Foundation **118:** Colonial Williamsburg Foundation **119:** Colonial Williamsburg Foundation **120:** Colonial Williamsburg Foundation **121:** The Granger Collection, NY **122:** Colonial Williamsburg Foundation **123:** Arco Images GmbH/Alamy **124:** Colonial Williamsburg Foundation **126:** Colonial Williamsburg Foundation **128:** North Wind Picture Archives/ Alamy **129:** North Wind Picture Archive **130:** Library of Congress **131:** The Granger Collection, NY

Chapter 10

132: North Wind Picture Archives **134:** Library of Congress **136:** The Granger Collection, NY **137:** Library of Congress **138:** Library of Congress **139:** Library of Congress **140:** Northwind Picture Archives **141:** Library of Congress **142:** The Granger Collection,NY **143:** Bridgeman Art Library **144:** The Granger Collection, NY **145:** The Granger Collection, NY

Chapter 11

146: Library of Congress **148:** The Granger Collection, NY **149:** Massachusetts Historical Society **150:** The Granger Collection, NY **151:** The Granger Collection, NY **152:** The Granger Collection, NY **153:** *Mrs James Warren* (Mercy Otis) about 1763; by John Singleton Copley/Museum of Fine Arts, Boston **154:** Samuel Adam,about 1772; by John Singleton Copley/ Museum of Fine Arts, Boston **155:** The Granger Collection, NY **156:** U.S. Senate Collection **157:** Virginia Historical Society **158:** The Granger Collection, NY **159:** St. John's Church Foundation

Chapter 12

160: Historical Society of Pennsylvania, *The Congress Voting Independence* by Robert Edge Pine and/or Edward Savage (Accession #1904) **160 L:** Library of Congress **160 M:** Library of Congress **160 R:** Library of Congress **162:** *A View of The South Part of Lexington* by Amos Doolittle/Connecticut Historical Society **163:** Library of Congress **164:** Bettmann/ Corbis **165:** Bettmann/Corbis **166:** Library of Congress **167:** George Washington (1732-99) Appointed Commander in Chief, published 1876 (colour litho), Currier, N. (1813-88) and Ives, J.M. (1824-95)/ Private Collection, Peter Newark American Pictures/The Bridgeman Art Library **168:** Yale University Art Gallery **169 R:** The Granger Collection, NY **169 L:** Library of Congress **170:** The Granger Collection, NY **171:** Colonial Williamsburg Foundation

Chapter 13

172 T: Yale University Art Gallery **172 BL:** Library of Congress **172 BR:** Library of Congress **174:** The Granger Collection, NY **175:** The Granger Collection, NY **176:** The Granger Collection, NY **177:** Bettmann/Corbis **178:** The Metropolitan Museum of Art **179:** The Granger Collection, NY **182:** North Wind Pictures **183:** The Granger Collection, NY **184:** Superstock **185:** North Wind Picture Archives

Chapter 14

186: The Granger Collection, NY **188:** North Wind Picture Archives **189:** The Granger Collection, NY **190:** Reuters/Jason Reed/ Landov **191:** Peter Gridley-FPG/ Getty Images **192:** Peter Gridley-FPG/Getty Images **193:** Peter Gridley-FPG/Getty Images **195:** The Granger Collection, NY **196:** Visions of America-Joe Sohm/ Getty Images **197:** British Museum/ Art Resource **198:** Bettmann/ Corbis **199:** North Wind Picture Archives

Chapter 15

200: The Granger Collection, NY **202:** Library of Congress **203:** Evan Vucci /AP Worldwide **204:** The Granger Collection, NY **205 T:** North Wind Picture Archives **205 B:** Spencer Grant/Stock Boston **206:** RF/Masterfile **207:** Jim

Pickerell/Stock Boston **208:** Bob Daemmrich/The Image Works **210:** Bettmann/CorbisS **211:** Bettmann/Corbis **212 T:** Wally McNamee/Corbis **212 B:** Bettmann/Corbis **213:** Bob Daemmrich/The Image Works

Chapter 16

214: The Granger Collection, NY **216:** Library of Congress **217:** Library of Congress **218:** Courtesy of The Montana Historical Society **219:** Library of Congress **220:** The Bridgeman Art Library **221:** Dan Mieduch **222:** The Granger Collection, NY **223:** Library of Congress **227:** Bridgeman Art Library **228:** MPI/Hulton Archive/Getty Images **229:** John Guthrie/Guthrie Studios

Chapter 17

230 T: The Granger Collection, NY **231 TM:** The Granger Collection, NY **230 BML:** The Granger Collection, NY **230 B:** The Granger Collection, NY **230 BR:** The Granger Collection, NY **232:** The Granger Collection, NY **233:** The Bancroft Library/University of California, Berkeley **235:** California State Library **236:** Library of Congress **238:** Handcart Pioneer, by C.C.A.Christensen © by Intellectual Reserve, Inc., Courtesy of the Museum of Church and Art, Used by Permission **239:** Library of Congress **240:** Denver Public History Collection,Western History Collection **242:** Laura Ingalls Wilder Home Association **243 L:** The Granger Collection, NY **243 M:** The Bridgeman Art Library **243 R:** Bettmann/Corbis **244:** North Wind Picture Archives/Alamy **245:** The Granger Collection, NY

Chapter 18

246 T: Library of Congress **246 BL:** Library of Congress **246 BML:** Library of Congress **246 BMR:** Library of Congress **246 BR:** Library of Congress **248:** Library of Congress **249:** Library of Congress **251:** Library of Congress **252:** The Granger Collection, NY **254:** The Granger Collection, NY **255:** The Granger Collection, NY **256:** The Bridgeman Art Library **257 T:** The Granger Collection, NY **257 B:** The Granger Collection, NY **258 T:** MPI/Getty Images) **258 B:** *Aunt Phillis's Cabin,* Cover, Special Collections, University of Virginia Library **259:** Bettmann/Corbis

Chapter 19

260 T: Library of Congress **260 BL:** Library of Congress **260 BM:** Library of Congress **260 BR:** Library of Congress **262 L:** Bettmann/Corbis **262 R:** The Museum of The Confederacy **264:** The Granger Collection, NY **265 T:** Sanchez-Vetter Collection/Cheryl Fenton Photography **265 B:** Van Meir Collection/Cheryl Fenton Photography **266:** The Granger Collection, NY **267:** National Museum of Civil War Medicine, Frederick, MD **268:** The Granger Collection, NY **269:** The Granger Collection, NY **270:** Tom Lovell/National Geographic Society Image Collection **272:** The Granger Collection, NY **273:** The Granger Collection, NY **274:** The Granger Collection, NY **275:** The Granger Collection, NY

Chapter 20

276 T: AP Wideworld Photo **276 BL:** AP Wideworld Photo **276 BR:** AP Wideworld Photo **278:** *Brooklyn Bridge,* ca 1883. Photoengraving by Shugg Brothers/Museum of The City of New York, 34.401, Bequest of Mrs.J.Insley **279:** Bettmann/Corbis **280:** Library of Congress **281:** Library of Congress **282:** Library of Congress **283:** Jim Bourg/Reuters **284:** Jose Luis Pelaez, Inc.-Blend Images/Corbis **285:** Bettmann/Corbis **286:** Bettmann/Corbis 287: David McNew/Getty Images **288:** Bob Daemmrich **289:** Kayte M. Deioma/PhotoEdit

Being a Good Citizen

290-291 Background: Tetra Images/RF/Corbis **290-291:** Kim Kulish/Corbis **290 TR:** RF/SuperStock **290 B:** Kim Kulish/Corbis **292:** Beathan/Corbis **293:** Carlos Barria/Reuters/Corbis **294-295:** Craig Lassig/epa/Corbis **296:** Tetra Images/RF/Corbis **297:** James Leyse/Corbis **299 L:** Richard Hutchings/Corbis **299 R:** Robert Michael/RF/Corbis

Art

17: Len Ebert **68:** Len Ebert **73:** Gary Undercuffler **113:** Len Ebert **133:** Carol Heyer **161:** Len Ebert **194:** QYA Design Studio **201:** Gary Undercuffler **211:** QYA Design Studio **231:** Susan Jaekel **247:** Susan Jaekel

Artists represented by Ann Remen-Willis, Artist Representative and Art Manager:
Len Ebert
Carol Heyer
Susan Jaekel
Gary Undercuffler